BRITISH AND AMERICAN PLAYWRIGHTS
1750–1920

General editors: Martin Banham and Peter Thomson

William Hooker Gillette

OTHER VOLUMES IN THIS SERIES

Already published:

W.S. GILBERT edited by George Rowell
HENRY ARTHUR JONES edited by Russell Jackson
DAVID GARRICK AND GEORGE COLMAN THE ELDER
   edited by E.R. Wood
TOM ROBERTSON edited by William Tydeman

Further volumes will include:

THOMAS MORTON AND GEORGE COLMAN THE
   YOUNGER edited by Barry Sutcliffe
J.R. PLANCHÉ edited by Don Roy
A.W. PINERO edited by Martin Banham
DION BOUCICAULT edited by Peter Thomson
CHARLES READE edited by M. Hammet
TOM TAYLOR edited by Martin Banham
ARTHUR MURPHY AND SAMUEL FOOTE edited by George
   Taylor
H.J. BYRON edited by J.T.L. Davis
AUGUSTIN DALY edited by Don Wilmeth and Rosemary Cullen

Plays by
William Hooker Gillette

ALL THE COMFORTS OF HOME
SECRET SERVICE
SHERLOCK HOLMES

Edited with an Introduction and Notes by
Rosemary Cullen and Don B. Wilmeth

CAMBRIDGE UNIVERSITY PRESS

Cambridge

London   New York   New Rochelle

Melbourne   Sydney

Published by the Press Syndicate of the University of Cambridge
The Pitt Building, Trumpington Street, Cambridge CB2 1RP
32 East 57th Street, New York, NY 10022, USA
296 Beaconsfield Parade, Middle Park, Melbourne 3206, Australia

First published 1983

Printed in Great Britain at the University Press, Cambridge

Library of Congress catalogue card number: 82–14692

British Library Cataloguing in Publication Data
Gillette, William Hooker
Plays by William Hooker Gillette. – (British and
American playwrights 1750–1920)
I. Title   II. Wilmeth, Don B.
III. Cullen, Rosemary   IV. Series
812′.4   PS1744.G2
ISBN 0 521 24089 1 hard covers
ISBN 0 521 28431 7 paperback
WD

GENERAL EDITORS' PREFACE

It is the primary aim of this series to make available to the British and American theatre plays which were effective in their own time, and which are good enough to be effective still.

Each volume assembles a number of plays, normally by a single author, scrupulously edited but sparingly annotated. Textual variations are recorded where individual editors have found them either essential or interesting. Introductions give an account of the theatrical context, and locate playwrights and plays within it. Biographical and chronological tables, brief bibliographies, and the complete listing of known plays provide information useful in itself, and which also offers guidance and incentive to further exploration.

Many of the plays published in this series have appeared in modern anthologies. Such representation is scarcely distinguishable from anonymity. We have relished the tendency of individual editors to make claims for the dramatists of whom they write. These are not plays best forgotten. They are plays best remembered. If the series is a contribution to theatre history, that is well and good. If it is a contribution to the continuing life of the theatre, that is well and better.

We have been lucky. The Cambridge University Press has supported the venture beyond our legitimate expectations. Acknowledgement is not, in this case, perfunctory. Sarah Stanton's contribution to the series has been substantial, and it has enhanced our work.

Martin Banham
Peter Thomson

CONTENTS

ILLUSTRATIONS

ACKNOWLEDGEMENTS

In the preparation of this volume of plays by William Gillette the editors have been grateful for the assistance of a large number of individuals, including Dorothy L. Swerdlove, curator of the Billy Rose Theatre Collection at Lincoln Center, Louis Rachow, curator and librarian of the Walter Hampden—Edwin Booth Theatre Collection and Library at The Players in New York, and W.H. Crain, curator of the Hoblitzelle Theatre Arts Library at the University of Texas. Jeanne T. Newlin, curator, and Martha R. Mahard, assistant curator, of the Harvard Theatre Collection, were extremely helpful in locating appropriate illustrations for this collection; we are grateful to the Harvard Theatre Collection for allowing us to reproduce these photographs. We are especially appreciative of the assistance and kindness given us by Roberta K.R. Bradford and Joseph S. Van Why, director, of the Stowe—Day Foundation in Hartford, Connecticut, where we spent a number of productive hours and gathered much of the material used in the preparation of this volume. We are grateful to Stowe—Day for allowing us to publish the manuscript versions of Gillette's *Secret Service* and to make use of the variants of *Sherlock Holmes* in their superb Gillette collection. The New York Public Library (Billy Rose Collection) has permitted us to use the manuscript version of *Sherlock Holmes* in its possession. Mr Joseph K. Hooker has responded generously to our requests, as have Mr and Mrs Douglas Whyte, heirs of Hall Cowen, William Gillette's brother-in-law and heir to a large number of his manuscripts, notes, and other personal records, now at Stowe—Day. A great number of sources would not have been available to us without the services of interlibrary loan and the assistance of Brown University's librarian in charge of this important office, Elizabeth Coogan. A word of thanks to Prof. Brenda Murphy, St Lawrence University, for her useful suggestions, and to Prof. Stephen Archer, University of Missouri, for sharing with us his bibliographical work on Gillette. Finally, Martin Banham, in particular, and Peter Thomson, general editors, and Sarah Stanton, representing Cambridge University Press, have responded to our numerous queries with enthusiasm and precision.

I William Hooker Gillette

INTRODUCTION

William Hooker Gillette was born on 24 July 1853 into a prominent Hartford, Connecticut, family. His father, Francis Gillette (1807–79), an early abolitionist and a proponent of the temperance movement, served for a year as a United States Senator and later led the Free Soil Party in Connecticut. William Gillette's mother, Elizabeth Daggett (Hooker) Gillette (1813–93), was a descendant of one of the founders of the city of Hartford and of the families that first settled Massachusetts and Connecticut. Of William Gillette's three brothers and two sisters, only his sister Elizabeth, married to George Henry Warner, and his brother Edward remained alive when he reached adulthood. The family lived in the Nook Farm section of Hartford, the home of Harriet Beecher Stowe, Charles Dudley Warner, Richard Burton, Mark Twain, and other noted writers and intellectuals of the mid nineteenth century. William Gillette grew up in an atmosphere of learning, but not in one that was particularly hospitable to his theatrical leanings.

As a boy, Gillette published a magazine called *Hail Columbia* and entertained his friends and family with a miniature theatre of his own making. He wrote the plays, worked the marionettes, and supplied the music by imitating musical instruments. Later, he organized his own acting company and performed in his home for the local church Ladies' Benevolent Society. In high school, he wrote and appeared in a one-act farce called *Bullywingle the Beloved*, about a man who fancies himself pursued by many women. All these ventures were quite successful, gaining for Gillette a reputation as a clever, inventive boy and a 'born actor'.

Gillette was also active in his school years in speaking contests. He delivered an oration from *Julius Caesar* and an address entitled 'Opposition' as part of his high school graduation exercises. Influenced by his father's ideas on public speaking, Gillette delivered his addresses with hesitations, stumblings, and frequent changes of pace. He attempted to deliver a speech as if it were being given for the first time, and although his delivery was out of the ordinary, he succeeded in impressing his audiences. This is the first instance of his use of a technique that he was later to develop into his theory of the 'illusion of the first time in acting'.

Rather than attending college, as might have been expected of a young man of his background, Gillette spent the next year or so touring around the towns of Connecticut, giving impersonations of famous actors of the day, among them Edwin Booth, E.A. Sothern, and Joseph Jefferson. He also included imitations of some of the statesmen of the period, drawn from his father's memories of his days in the Senate. The lecture platform, while respectable and therefore comparatively acceptable to his proper New England family, proved insufficient to hold his interest for long, and in 1873 he left home to seek a career on the stage.

His first appearances were in 1875 as an unpaid walk-on in Ben DeBar's company in St Louis, Missouri, and in New Orleans, Louisiana, in O.D. Byron's *Across the Continent*. When his money ran out, and DeBar declined to pay him for his services, Gillette was forced to return home to Hartford. Soon, however, through the intervention of Mark Twain, a family friend, he obtained a small role in the stage adaptation of Twain's *The Gilded Age*, entitled *Colonel Sellers*. Twain regarded Gillette's stage ambitions as a joke and was later astounded to see his young friend develop into a much admired actor.

Gillette joined John T. Raymond's company and appeared in *Colonel Sellers* on tour and at the Park Theatre in New York. On 11 and 12 January 1875 he returned to Hartford with the company for two performances. In 1875 and 1876 he appeared in a wide variety of roles with the Boston Museum company and enjoyed his first real success as Prince Florian in Gilbert's *Broken Hearts*. He took the part without rehearsal when Harry Murdock fell ill; later he was allowed to retain the part in the play's revival.

It has frequently been recorded that during the time William Gillette spent in New York with the company of *Colonel Sellers*, and when he was in Boston with Raymond's company, he attended classes at Harvard, the Massachusetts Institute of Technology, Yale University, and the College of the City of New York. It appears that none of this is true, but there is evidence that he did spend one year at Boston University's Monroe School of Oratory. This seems likely, because of his early interest in public speaking, and in view of the fact that he resumed his lecture-platform tours between seasons with Raymond's company.

In 1877, Gillette again headed west and joined Ben Macauley's stock company in Cincinnati, Ohio, and Louisville, Kentucky. He played small parts in a wide range of new plays and old favorites. Later he joined the Kate Claxton Company, touring in a number of similar plays. During this period, Gillette, playing only the smallest of roles, learned the essentials of his craft and gained an appreciation of the technique of the theatre that would serve him well throughout his career.

While with Macauley's company, Gillette began to write plays in earnest. He worked on an early version of *The Professor* and completed a one-act play which had a disastrous single performance at the Queen's Theatre in Toronto. The company, under the impression that the play was a 'nigger act', a term then used for the outline of an improvised skit, totally ignored the playwright's lines, and, singing and dancing, cavorted madly about the miserable Gillette. Gillette returned to New York with his play the next day. In 1879, while living at home during his father's final illness, Gillette completed a five-act script called *The Twins of Siam*, based on the lives of Eng and Chang, the original Siamese twins.

Gillette was determined to see *The Professor* produced, and for two years he bedeviled every manager he could find in the hope of interesting someone in backing a production. In desperation, he produced the play himself, trying it out in Columbus, Ohio, New Haven, Hartford, and Philadelphia. Critical opinion was mixed at best, and caused Gillette to begin revising at once. A year later, once more with the assistance of Mark Twain, he succeeded in persuading Charles Frohman to finance a production. It was the beginning of a long and profitable association for the two men.

The Professor opened in New York at the Madison Square Theatre and ran for 151 performances, a very creditable showing for its day. Subtitled 'A Character Study', the play is about a professor of astronomy, who, to please his aunt, proposes marriage to a variety of young ladies, finally succeeding in winning Daisy Brown. The story line is minimal; the actions of the characters make little sense, but the play owed its success to its elaborate and realistic production and to Gillette's own humorous portrayal of the absurd professor. These two characteristics were to become the hallmarks of a Gillette play.

During 1882, Gillette toured the country with *The Professor*. It was at this time that he met and married Helen Nickles (1860–88) of Detroit, Michigan. Very little seems to be known about Mrs Gillette. A warm and attractive person, she accompanied her husband on all his tours.

While searching for a producer for *The Professor*, Gillette worked on an adaptation of Frances Hodgson Burnett's *Esmeralda* for the stage. It became the second Gillette play to be produced by Charles Frohman, opening at the Madison Square Theatre on 29 October 1881; it ran until 7 October 1882 and then toured the country. The play was constructed around the familiar story of a young girl whose domineering mother removes her from the orbit of the poor young man in whom she is interested. Eventually, the young man turns out to be rich, and Esmeralda and her father defy the mother's wishes. According to Arthur H. Quinn, 'Gillette laid out the play, Mrs Burnett wrote the dialogue and then Gillette revised it, so that the drama may be looked upon in a real sense as a collaboration.'[1]

The play was very well received in America and, along with *The Professor*, contributed to the early success of the Madison Square Theatre. *Esmeralda* was Gillette's first play to be presented in England, opening at the St James's Theatre on 20 October 1883, under the title *Young Folks' Ways*. John E. Owens played Esmeralda's timid father, and Madge Robertson Kendal and William Kendal were in the cast. The London critics were nearly unanimous in disliking the play, one critic going so far as to wonder what the Kendals were doing in such an ill-conceived enterprise.

Gillette's next venture was a tour during 1883 and 1884 of Bronson Howard's *The Young Mrs Winthrop*, playing the part of Douglas Winthrop. During this time, he worked on an adaptation and translation of Gottfried Von Moser's play *Der Bibliothekar*, which he first called *The Tutor* and then renamed *Digby's Secretary*. With the permission of the German author, Gillette mounted a production at the New York Comedy Theatre in 1884. At the same time, A.M. Palmer planned a rival production at the Madison Square Theatre of another translation, called *The Private Secretary*, by the Englishman Charles Hawtrey. Gillette opened his play on 29 September 1884, fifteen minutes before the Madison Square version was to open, thus establishing precedence. Gillette won the legal battle that ensued, primarily because his was the authorized translation. A compromise was reached in which the best parts of both versions were combined under the title *The Private Secretary*. Gillette played in this version for several seasons under A.M. Palmer's management.

The play is about a young man, Douglas Cattermole, who, to avoid his debts, impersonates the newly hired private secretary of a country squire. The young man and his friend, a nephew of the squire, persuade the hapless secretary, the Rev. Robert Spaulding, to stay in town away from the country house, but, naturally, he ignores the advice. Eventually, after innumerable complications, the young man's debts are discharged and he marries Edith Marsland, his friend's sister. Gillette played the part of the foolish Rev. Robert Spaulding, a role considerably enlarged in his version of the play. A sequence involving spiritualism was introduced, in which Spaulding acted as a medium, reflecting the popularity of séances. The play was enormously successful; Gillette appeared in it nearly 1,500 times in the next three years, 'close to the point of insanity'.[2] This experience may well have spurred Gillette to develop further his technique of the 'illusion of the first time in acting' in order to retain some freshness in the part.

During his tour with *The Private Secretary*, Gillette worked on a very different sort of play, the first of the group of plays for which he is now chiefly remembered. The play was *Held by the Enemy*, a drama of the American Civil War. The central conflict involved two officers of the Union, Colonel Brant and Brigadier Surgeon Fielding, and the Confederate Lieutenant Hayne, all of whom are in love with Hayne's cousin and fiancée, Eunice McCreery. When Hayne is captured by Brant as a spy in Union-occupied Richmond, Fielding, in an attempt to rid himself of his rival, accuses Brant of stating falsely that he took an incriminating document from Hayne. Rather than allow an innocent man to suffer, Hayne admits that he is a spy, is convicted, and shortly after is wounded in trying to escape during a bombard-ment. The McCreery family obtains permission to remove Hayne's body from a military hospital and bring it through the lines. Fielding attempts to stop them by claiming that Hayne is not really dead; Brant objects to an examination of the body in order to spare Eunice's feelings. Just as the commanding general is about to order the examination, Eunice promises to marry Fielding if he will go along with her deception. Finally, Hayne is saved, both he and Fielding are persuaded to relinquish their claims on Eunice, and she and Brant are reunited. The play includes a charm-ing and humorous subplot involving a romance between Eunice's sister Susan and Thomas Henry Beene (or Blane), a war correspondent for *Leslie's Weekly*.

Held by the Enemy opened on 22 February 1886 at the Criterion Theatre in Brooklyn, New York, but went largely unnoticed until it reopened, after extensive revisions, under Charles Frohman's management at the Madison Square Theatre on 16 August 1886. Critics were inclined to think that the play was full of improbable situations and stock characters. They pointed to the unlikeliness of a man's feigning death in a military hospital under such public circumstances. The technical effects and staging, as usual in a Gillette play, won praise. The approbation of the public kept it running in New York for 640 performances.

Held by the Enemy was one of the first significant plays to use the Civil War as a background, and the spectacular effects occasioned by the bombardment heightened the intensity of the personal conflicts on the stage. This play, Gillette's first attempt to write a serious drama on American themes, included a number of elements that were to become trademarks of his best style. The realistic settings for the McCreerys' house, the court martial scene, the military hospital, and the particularly effective episode in Act III, during which one wall of Hayne's prison is demolished on stage by the explosion of a shell, testify to Gillette's belief that visual effects were all-important and could serve to divert the audience's attention from any improbabilities of plot. In this play he introduced to the stage a number of techniques that were revolutionary in his day. He dressed his soldiers in muddy and ragged costumes, as if they had actually just come off the battlefield, instead of in the parade dress common on the stage at the time; he invented a device to simulate the sound of approaching hoofbeats, and his stage effects included the very realistic sounds of cannon and gunfire.

Several of Gillette's characters are early versions of types that would reappear throughout his best works. The immense calm and resolution of Colonel Brant and Lieutenant Hayne, outdoing each other in feats of self-renunciation and nobility, prefigure the actions of Dumont/Thorne in *Secret Service*. The character of Thomas Beene, the reporter, is a variant of the glib, quick-witted character who would later appear as Lewis Dumont in *Secret Service*, Alfred in *All the Comforts of Home*, Augustus Billings in *Too Much Johnson*, and Sherlock Holmes. Perhaps the most effective elements of the play were its fast-moving action, particularly in Act III when Beene witnesses the efforts of the military to direct the battle at Torrey's Bridge, and the prolonged suspense of the court martial scene, the episode in the military hospital, and the final confrontation of Brant and Fielding. Gillette was to employ these two elements in later years to produce the most memorable scenes of *Secret Service* and *Sherlock Holmes*.

After its New York run, *Held by the Enemy* played at the Boston Museum from 27 December 1886 until 5 March 1887. Charles Frohman took the play to London, where it opened at the Princess's Theatre on 2 April 1887, with Gillette repeating his portrayal of Thomas Henry Beene. In the summer of 1887, Gillette toured the western United States with the play.

Gillette's next project was an adaptation of Rider Haggard's popular novel *She*. It opened at Niblo's Garden in New York in a lavish production by I.B. Rich and Alfred Hayman on 29 November 1887. Initial critical reception was poor; the play was criticized for its excessive length, lack of characterization, and incoherent structure. With the rewriting assistance of David Belasco, a revised version was substituted toward the end of the play's New York run. Subsequently, *She* was favorably received by audiences both in New York and in cities on its tour, enjoying a comfortable and profitable run.

Gillette's next work was an original play, *A Legal Wreck*, which he also issued in novel form to coincide with the New York opening. The play is about a young orphan, brought up by a retired sea captain, and includes a narrator who directs much of the action, played with considerable success in the New York production by Sidney Drew. *A Legal Wreck* opened at the Madison Square Theatre on 14 August 1888. It met with some critical success and was popular with audiences. Much of the criticism pointed out that the point of view of the play was uncertain, that the audience could not be sure whether the play was meant to be serious or comic. This ambiguity in moral tone and perspective, only moderately successful in *A Legal Wreck*, was used to good effect in Gillette's later plays *Secret Service* and *Sherlock Holmes*.

Shortly after the opening of *A Legal Wreck*, Gillette suffered a personal tragedy with the sudden death of his wife Helen at the age of twenty-eight, from a ruptured appendix. Gillette retired from the stage, living in virtual seclusion either in his rural home in Tryon, North Carolina, or with his relatives in Hartford. He never remarried, though throughout his life his name was linked to many of the pretty young actresses he cast in his plays. Gillette, who often during this period did not enjoy good health, turned more and more to playwriting as a source of income and as a means of remaining active professionally. In 1889 he dramatized Mrs Humphrey Ward's novel *Robert Elsmere*, which opened at the Union Square Theatre on 29 April 1889.

His next play was a rather literal translation and adaptation of Carl Lauf's *Ein Toller Einfall*, which he called *All the Comforts of Home*. In its barest outline, this play is a descendant of Ben Jonson's *The Alchemist*. A young man is left in charge of his uncle's house during his absence. With his assistant, he conceives the notion of making money by letting out rooms to an assortment of lodgers. Among them are an opera singer, a retired grocer, the grocer's wife, and their daughter – with whom the young man promptly falls in love. Various complications arise before the lodgers are ejected, the uncle returns home, and the lovers are united. The play is a farce, with fast-moving action and endless twists of plot.

All the Comforts opened on 3 March 1890 at the Boston Museum, with Henry Miller as the young Alfred Hastings and Maude Adams as Evangeline Bender, the grocer's daughter. Critics dismissed the play as a not particularly original farce, but were familiar enough with Gillette's knack for appealing to the popular taste to admit that the play would probably be a success. One reviewer noted: 'If this sort of thing is to be done at all – against which in passing we protest – it could not be done better than by the Museum Company. It is to be – shall we say feared? – that the play will so catch the popular taste with its bait of laughter, as to hold the stage indefinitely.'[3] Maude Adams, appearing in one of her earliest successes, made such an impression as Evangeline that her co-star Henry Miller was prompted to suggest that Gillette add a love scene for her.

All the Comforts of Home opened in New York at Proctor's 23rd Street Theatre on 8 September 1890. The *New York Times* reviewer remarked that 'As it is very good, as farce goes, and is uncommonly well acted, it is safe to assume that it will be successful here . . . it lacks the originality and timely fun of some of the pieces constructed from native material by Mr [Edward] Harrigan and Mr Charles Hoyt, although Gillette does not, of course, go to the limits of wild frivolity that Harrigan and [Tony] Hart reach'.[4] The play ran until 18 October 1890, and the following year Charles Frohman took it to London, where it opened on 24 January 1891 at the Globe Theatre.

All the Comforts of Home is a rather slight play, but it worked very well on the stage, and a number of adaptations were made of it over the years. A comparison of Gillette's play with another version written a few years later by Maurice Hageman, called *A Crazy Idea* (published in Chicago by The Dramatic Publishing Company *c.* 1897), shows that Gillette's talent lay in constructing effective visual scenes from his material. In Hageman's version of a scene in which the retired grocer's wife listens in on her husband's conversation with the opera singer, she simply listens in at one of the doors. Gillette, however, places Mrs Bender behind a transom over one of the doors, thereby creating a more arresting visual image, and one that allows greater comic possibilities when the husband's previous dalliance with the opera singer is revealed.

Another curious difference between the two plays lies in the relationship between the nephew and his henchman. In Gillette's version the servant, Tom, is an enthusiastic, dim-witted yokel, devoted to Alfred's interests. It is a fairly standard way of treating such a relationship. In Hageman's version, Tom becomes Daniel Webster White, 'a colored gem'man of many accomplishments'. The relationship of the two is very nearly the reverse of that in Gillette's play. Daniel delivers numerous witty asides, all of which disparage his employer's schemes and mental attainments. Daniel is by far the cleverer of the two, and it is he who directs most of the enterprises that the conspirators embark on. Daniel is such a strong personality that he stands far above the rest of the characters in Hageman's otherwise lacklustre play. He might have made a welcome addition to Gillette's play; on the other hand, it might be argued that the presence of such a cynical observer would have unbalanced the finely tuned working of Gillette's amusing little play.

In 1919, a musical version, *Fifty-Fifty*, based on Gillette's play by Margaret Michael and William Lennox with music by Leon DeCosta, was produced at the Comedy Theatre in New York on 27 October. It is a pared down, vulgarized version of Gillette's play. The opera singer Fifi Oritanski has become 'Fluffy La Grange' and has acquired a contingent of six girls, ostensibly singers in her company. There is little doubt left about the real profession of these ladies. The language in the play has been updated and coarsened, and the song lyrics are banal and bear no relation to the action of the play. The musical is a far cry from Gillette's play.

In 1942, a revised version of *All the Comforts of Home*, by Helen Jerome, was produced on 25 May at the Longacre Theatre in New York. It was not a success, and the play ran for only eight performances. The play was a shortened version of Gillette's original, in two acts and four scenes, and the language was modernized, although the sense of the lines remained essentially the same. The asides were removed altogether. The end of Act I is slightly different from Gillette's version: Alfred, Emily, and Pettibone all remain on the stage together. Most of the other changes are minor, and the play is basically the same.

Gillette's next play was a farce, *Mr Wilkinson's Widows*, an adaptation of a French farce, *Feu Toupinal* by Alexandre Bisson. The play, which opened at Proctor's 23rd Street Theatre in New York on 30 March 1891, dealt with the complications ensuing when two widows discover that they had been married to the same man on the same day. The farce included a number of improbabilities and mysteries that are never resolved; Gillette ends his play with the central problem still existing.

In 1892 Gillette adapted another play by Bisson, *La Famille Pont-Biquet*, calling it *Settled Out of Court*. It opened on 8 August 1892 at the Fifth Avenue Theatre and in September travelled to Boston, where it played at the Columbia Theatre. The next year Gillette experienced his first real failure with the production of *Ninety Days*, a costly production, which, for a time, ruined Gillette financially. The play opened in New York at the Broadway Theatre on 6 February 1893. The plot, if it can be so called, involved the adventures of an American baseball team travelling around the world, but was really only an excuse to mount the elaborate sets and technical effects that Gillette loved. The reviews were, for the most part, negative. Although the production was praised, it was pointed out that '*Ninety Days* is a compound of almost every phase of the drama except its legitimate elements.'[5] For once, audiences did not respond to Gillette's stagecraft, and the play closed within a month.

Ninety Days was a low point for Gillette financially and professionally, but it also marked the end of the depression and ill health that had plagued him since his wife's death in 1888. His mother's death, on 16 December 1893, did not drive him back into seclusion, and the following year he returned to the stage for the first time since 1887.

The play was *Too Much Johnson*, Gillette's adaptation of a French farce, *La Plantation Thomassin* by Maurice Ordonneau. It concerned the adventures of Augustus Billings, played by Gillette, who has been deceiving his wife with a number of ladies, using the name of Johnson and giving the excuse that he has been off visiting his plantation in Cuba. There is, of course, a real Johnson and a real plantation, and a confusion of identities and purposes sets in when Billings, his wife, his mother-in-law, his latest conquest (and her husband), and the fiancée of the real Johnson, all meet on a cruise ship bound for Cuba. Billings lies and tricks his way out of every predicament, and ultimately makes his escape, with Mrs Billings and her mother none the wiser.

Augustus Billings was an excellent part for Gillette, for in it he could display the smooth talking and the fast thinking that he had used so admirably as Beene in *Held by the Enemy*. The play was none too successful in its try-outs in Waltham, Holyoke, and Springfield, Massachusetts, and even Gillette was not confident of its success. His long-time producer, Charles Frohman, however, reassured the playwright, who was half convinced that the play should be closed. 'Nonsense', said Frohman. 'I have booked it for New York and for a long tour afterward.' 'Why?', asked Gillette in astonishment. 'I saw your performance', was the reply.[6]

Too Much Johnson played for a short time in Brooklyn, and opened in New York at the Standard Theatre on 26 November 1894. It was a great popular success, and Gillette was able to recoup some of the losses sustained during the production of *Ninety Days*. Critical opinion was not entirely favorable: French-style farces were going out of fashion. Gillette's performance was praised, and as Frohman had predicted, the production in New York was followed by an extensive road tour.

In 1898 the play was performed in London with Gillette repeating his role as Augustus Billings. The play proved enormously popular with London audiences, but the critics were not so enthusiastic. They perceived resemblances between the character of Captain Thorne in *Secret Service* that Gillette had recently played in London, and concluded that he lacked versatility as an actor. While there is a certain truth to this judgement, it must also be said that Gillette knew what he did well and had the sense to stick to it.

In 1964 *Too Much Johnson* was revived briefly in New York at the Phoenix Theatre. Walter Kerr, reviewing the production for the *Herald Tribune*, thought that the play had not aged well, but noted that 'at least once in the evening [I] saw a gesture that seemed effortlessly in charge of itself . . . Ah, [I] thought, I'll bet that's the way William Gillette did it. No fuss. No feathers. Finesse.'[7] The play, in an adaptation by Burt Shevelove, opened on 15 January 1964, and ran for 23 performances.

Gillette's next project proved to be one of his greatest and most enduring hits. It was another play using the American Civil War as a background, and was entitled *Secret Service*. The play told the story of a Union spy, Lewis Dumont, who, as Captain Thorne, infiltrates the Confederate Army in Richmond, Virginia, where he falls in love with Edith Varney, the daughter of a Confederate general. Thorne's object is to pass a message to the Union Army by means of the telegraph. He is nearly discovered when his brother, a captured Union soldier, is placed in the same room with him. The brother gives Thorne a secret message, then shoots himself to divert suspicion from Thorne. In the most exciting and memorable scene in the play, Thorne takes possession of the telegraph office and attempts to send his message, while being observed by Edith Varney and her Southern suitor, Benton Arrelsford, of the Confederate War Office, who is convinced that Thorne is a spy. He is stopped and his identity is questioned by Arrelsford and the Southern General Randolph, but Edith Varney rescues him by producing the commission as a telegraph officer which she had obtained for Thorne in order to keep him in Richmond and away from the fighting. Thorne begins to send the message, but ultimately refuses to do so because he does not want to profit from Edith's attempt to save his life; he tries to escape but is captured at the Varney home, where he has come to visit his dead brother. Thorne is sentenced to be shot, but the sentence is commuted by General Randolph because the message had not actually been sent and no harm has been done. Thorne is made a prisoner of war, and it is understood that he and Edith Varney will be reunited at the end of the war.

In a subplot that is remarkably well integrated into the main action, next-door neighbor Caroline Mitford and young Wilfred Varney discover their love for each other. Caroline's attempt to send a love message to Wilfred at the front causes considerable confusion at the telegraph office, when it is suspected that the message is actually Thorne's signal to the Union Army.

The play owes a great deal to Gillette's earlier play *Held by the Enemy*. It focuses on the effects of the war on a Southern family (and significantly not on the issues involved), it is concerned with the difficult choices the characters must make between love and patriotism, and it shows men on opposing sides of the conflict attempting to win the love of the same woman. The charming Caroline Mitford is a more fully-developed version of Susan McCreery in *Held by the Enemy*, and the quiet dignity of Mrs Varney recalls that of the elder McCreery. The high point of both plays comes in a suspenseful scene in which the spy is always in danger of exposure. Gillette said that he wrote *Secret Service* around its famous telegraph scene; it is almost as if he rewrote *Held by the Enemy* around it.

The play opened in Philadelphia on 13 May 1895 at the Broad Street Theatre, with Maurice Barrymore in the role of Captain Thorne. There are differing opinions as to the play's initial critical reception; whatever the truth of the matter, it is clear that Gillette, always ready to discard ineffective material, did some rewriting before the play was brought to New York. The most important alteration was the substitution of Gillette for Barrymore as Captain Thorne. Barrymore, a romantic matinée idol, was not at all well-suited to the understated part of the cool and quick-witted Captain. It was the perfect role for Gillette, and in it he scored his greatest success to date.

Secret Service opened in New York at the Garrick Theatre on 5 October 1896. For once, the play's critical reception matched the audience's enthusiasm. Gillette's natural style of acting was praised, and Odette Tyler, as Caroline Mitford, was, as Arthur Hornblow wrote in his review of the play in *Leslie's Weekly*, 'the life of the lighter portions of the play'.[8] The play itself was praised for its realism: the first act begins at eight o'clock, and each succeeding act begins an hour later; there are no asides or curtain speeches, so that the audience follows the development of the play as it unfolds. The costuming is in keeping with the reality of a society at war and under siege: no crisp, immaculate uniforms or elaborate evening dresses are to be seen. Throughout the latter half of the play the sounds of an artillery bombardment can be heard behind the actors' voices.

Secret Service ran in New York until 6 March 1897. Immediately afterwards it moved to Boston, opening on 8 March at the Boston Museum and running until 24 April. Charles Frohman took the play to London, where it opened on 15 May at the Adelphi Theatre with Gillette leading a cast that included the young Ethel Barrymore in a small role.

The play created a sensation in London; it was wildly popular with audiences, and the critics, on the whole, approved of the play. The reviewer for the *Illustrated Sporting and Dramatic News* remarked that 'the author of this showily-devised and incisively-written melodrama is fortunately able, as actor, to do the fullest justice to the character of his unconventionally conceived hero, whose coolness and resource, together with his nonchalance at moments of extreme personal peril, are indicated with reserved force of the most useful kind. Mr Gillette is, moreover, no less happy in the support which he brings with him from New York. Every part in the play, and there are many, is rendered with smoothness, spirit, and discretion, while the exciting whirl of warfare is conveyed with a verisimilitude which is very rare indeed and owes much to the quiet and even balance of the work all around.'[9] Fault was found with the probability of some of the events but the fast action, the suspense, and Gillette's performance ensured the play's success. George Bernard Shaw, in his review of the play, pointed out the extent to which Gillette's showmanship could distract an audience from the moral questions that could be raised by the play: '*Secret Service* . . . has a capital situation, in Mr Gillette's best style, at the end of the second act. But this, like all the other situations, takes a huge deal of leading up to, and leads to nothing itself, being so speedily forgotten that before half an hour has elapsed the heroine quite forgets that it has involved, apparently, an act of fratricide on the part of the hero. The hero, by the way, is a spy . . . he first spied on the South, and then, at the critical moment, betrays the North for purely personal reasons. Altogether an unredeemed rascal. But Mr Gillette plays him with so manly an air that the audience does not stop to ask what it is applauding; and everybody seems delighted.'[10] It was Gillette's handling of this tension between love and duty that created a large part of the suspense and contributed greatly to the success of the play.

Gillette played *Secret Service* in London until 4 August 1897. He became enormously popular with London audiences and was constantly in demand at social gatherings. All the excitement took its toll on Gillette, never a very robust man, or one given to socializing. He left *Secret Service* in London in ill health, but recovered in time to reopen the play in New York on 1 September 1897 at the Empire Theatre. *Secret Service* was so popular in London that an English company was formed, with William Terriss in the role of Captain Thorne. This company was compared unfavorably with Gillette's, although the appeal of the play kept it running. The play was closed on 16 December 1897 when Terriss was murdered at the stage door by a deranged fellow actor.

Secret Service toured the United States during 1898 and 1899, including dates in Gillette's home town of Hartford and in San Francisco. On 2 October 1897, it became Charles Frohman's first production to open at the Renaissance Théâtre in Paris, with the famed French actor Lucien Guitry as Thorne. Gillette revived the play frequently; throughout his career he played it 1,791 times. It was most recently revived in 1976 by the Phoenix Theatre Company at The Playhouse in New York and later televised by the Public Broadcasting System.

Secret Service was used as the basis for a parody, entitled *Secret Servants*, by

Henry E. Joel (pseudonym of Edgar McPhail Smith). This work, written around the turn of the century, is subtitled 'a romance of the Cuban war' and is a musical version of Gillette's play, in which the characters speak in rhymed couplets. It is perfect nonsense and illustrates that Gillette's works are fragile constructions that do not stand up well to adaptation by others.

Secret Service is Gillette's most significant literary work, and the one for which he should be remembered as a playwright. In it he brought together all the elements that had made his earlier plays successful. He was insistent upon technical realism in his productions and knew the value of fast-moving action in maintaining an audience's interest. He created suspense not only by inventing situations in which the audience was kept constantly waiting for something to happen, but by creating characters whose motivations and actions were always open to change and to question. He gave his play a strong center in the character of Captain Thorne, and in his performance contrasted his coolness effectively with the more exuberant playing of the other characters. It seems now no coincidence that it was in 1898 that Gillette was made a member of the National Institute of Arts and Letters.

While Gillette was touring with *Secret Service*, he was working on another adaptation of a French farce. Based on *Jalouse* by Alexandre Bisson and Adolphe Leclerq, the play, entitled *Because She Loved Him So*, opened on 28 October 1898 in New Haven at the Hyperion Theatre, and on 16 January 1899 moved to the Madison Square Theatre in New York. The play, well received by audiences, is a humorous study of the effects of jealousy on a young couple. According to A.H. Quinn, 'the adaptation was made with Gillette's usual skill, for he succeeded in preserving the light touch of the original while omitting the unnecessary indelicacy'.[11]

The success of *Secret Service* had improved Gillette's finances immeasurably, and he was now well on his way to becoming one of the wealthiest theatrical figures of his day. In addition to his home in Tryon, North Carolina, he now owned a boat called the *Aunt Polly*, a steam launch that he used to cruise the New England coast.

In 1898, while touring with *Secret Service*, Gillette was approached by Charles Frohman with the idea of dramatizing Sir Arthur Conan Doyle's immensely popular Sherlock Holmes stories. Gillette was much taken by the idea and wrote to Doyle asking permission. Doyle agreed, and Gillette set to work, first examining a five-act version that Doyle himself had written. With his sure instinct for what would play well on the stage, Gillette saw that this treatment was unworkable and discarded it.

He fashioned a play based very loosely on three Holmes stories: 'A Scandal in Bohemia', 'The Final Problem', and 'A Study in Scarlet'. With a fine disregard for the sensibilities of Holmes purists, Gillette cabled to Doyle, 'May I marry Holmes?' Doyle replied that 'you may marry or murder or do what you like with him'. There is a story that the manuscript of *Sherlock Holmes* was destroyed in a San Francisco hotel fire, and that Gillette was forced to write the play all over again. It appears, however, that this is a romantic exaggeration, since a charred typescript of all but the first act is held by the Stowe—Day Foundation in Hartford. Gillette, presumably, was only compelled to reconstruct the first act.

In 1899, with his text for *Sherlock Holmes* substantially complete, Gillette travelled to England to consult with Doyle. He was invited to Doyle's home, Undershaw, for lunch. John Dickson Carr, in his biography of Doyle, describes the meeting:

> ... out of [the London train] in a long grey cape, stepped the living image of Sherlock Holmes. Not even Sidney Paget had done it so well in a drawing. The clear-cut features, the deep-set eyes, looked out under a deerstalker cap; even Gillette's age, the middle forties, was right. Conan Doyle ... contemplated him open-mouthed. The actor, in his turn face to face with the image of an oversized Dr Watson, stared back.[12]

Gillette returned to the United States, confident that *Sherlock Holmes* would be a success.

After a three-performance try-out at the Star Theatre in Buffalo, New York, beginning on 24 October 1899, the play opened in New York on 6 November at the Garrick Theatre. For the occasion, Gillette delivered a curtain speech in which he remarked:

> About a year ago it seemed to me that the drama was insufficiently supplied with scoundrels. In former attempts at dramatic work I had endeavored to keep them out, but in this new light which broke upon me I saw that it was a serious mistake. Not only is it extremely unlikely and unlifelike that the twenty or so persons comprising the characters in a play could be found without at least twelve or fifteen bad people among them, but the exclusion of the criminal elements is a grave financial error as well. The public likes them and will pay liberally to see them. The dramatist, as we all know, is not a student of the drama, he is a student of the public. He must learn what it likes and dislikes. As I have indicated it likes villains — and it certainly ought to have them. If I ever write another play — which I quite agree with you in hoping I won't — I fully intend to make all the people desperate and annoying characters.[13]

These remarks, while intended to be taken lightly, serve to illustrate Gillette's convictions about his role as a playwright and demonstrate the reasons for his success. He knew that *Sherlock Holmes* was not a great or even a good play, taken on its own merits. He was, however, fully aware of the great public appetite for Sherlock Holmes in any form, and recognized that it could be a role that coincided perfectly with his own theatrical gifts. He realized that part of the appeal of his works was in the innovations he introduced: here, in *Sherlock Holmes*, the use of villains as major characters, the lighting-effects, the use of dramatic pauses, and the effect of ending a scene quietly.

The critics were in perfect accord. *Sherlock Holmes* was 'buncombe and claptrap' but it was superb theatre.[14] Alan Dale, in the *New York Journal and Advertiser*, wrote that 'until past eleven o'clock you were plunged through a thick

II Gillette as Sherlock Holmes. Caricature by 'Spy' (Leslie Ward), published in *Vanity Fair*, 1907

detective atmosphere to creepy music, "dark" stages, and all the necessaries of rampant melodrama . . . it was the very creme de la creme of Sherlock Holmes . . . through all the hair-breadth and gaspy incidents he posed. And you kept your eyes upon him . . . no such type has ever flitted across our vision before'.[15] A.H. Quinn gave the play short shrift, maintaining, with some truth, that 'it was only the superb acting of Gillette which carried the play into favor here and abroad'.[16]

The plot of the play concerns Holmes' efforts to acquire a packet of incriminating letters for a royal client, and, in so doing, to capture the criminal mastermind Professor Moriarty. To accomplish these aims, Holmes resorts to a number of stratagems that work very effectively on the stage. To make Alice Faulkner reveal where she has hidden the letters, Holmes creates a diversion by starting a fire; Alice's involuntary glance reveals the hiding place. In the second act, while confronting Professor Moriarty, Holmes neatly removes the cartridges from the villain's gun, thus frustrating Moriarty's attempt to shoot him. In the most famous and thrilling scene of the play, Holmes goes to the Stepney Gas Chamber to recover the letters. Moriarty and his henchmen again attempt to murder Holmes, but he escapes with Alice Faulkner by knocking out the lantern and misdirecting the villains with the light from his cigar. In the final act, Holmes captures Moriarty, who is disguised as a cabman, by slapping handcuffs on his wrists as he bends to strap up Holmes' luggage. Finally, Alice voluntarily relinquishes the letters, and the play ends, 'her head against his breast and her face turned to front or near it, for final spotlight which holds the two faces for a moment, then slowly fades out'.[17]

Besides the impact of Gillette's performance, the play owed its success to its suspenseful action and to the innovative technical elements that Gillette employed. He was among the first to underscore the concept of the 'fourth wall' by the position of the lantern in the Stepney Gas Chamber. His use of lighting was revolutionary in its day; he made use of the 'fade out' to end his scenes, and began each act by bringing the lights up slowly in a darkened theatre. When the play toured in England after its run in London, it was advertised as 'with the Lyceum lighting effects', so renowned had they become. He created a sensation by ending the acts quietly, rather than at a moment of high tension. His last line in Act II: 'Billy! You're a good boy!' shocked the audience with its offhand quality.

Sherlock Holmes ran in New York for 236 performances, after which the play toured the United States until the summer of 1901. On 2 September 1901 it opened in try-out at the Shakespeare Theatre in Liverpool, and made its London debut on 9 September at the Lyceum Theatre. The play was an even greater success in England than it had been in America, although the critics were predictably unimpressed with the quality of the play. Gillette's performance was praised for the 'calm self command and yet lightning alertness' that he displayed as Sherlock Holmes.[18] Gillette contributed a footnote to theatre history when he hired for the part of Billy in the London production of the play a thirteen-year-old orphan named Charlie Chaplin. The play ran in London until 11 April 1902, and then went on a six-week tour of England and Scotland. Gillette returned to the United States considerably exhausted on 19 June, but touring companies kept the play going in England and throughout the world for several years.

Gillette revived *Sherlock Holmes* many times in the next thirty-five years. Versions of it appeared in 1906, 1910, 1915, and 1923. In 1905 he returned with the play to London, and in 1916 he appeared in his only motion picture, a seven-reel silent version of *Holmes* for Essanay, with Edward Fielding as Dr Watson and Ernest Maupain as Professor Moriarty. Unhappily, this screen version has been lost.

In 1929, at the behest of producer George C. Tyler, Gillette began a farewell tour of *Sherlock Holmes*. When first proposed, the trip was to last only six weeks; eventually, Tyler outlined a route that lasted well into 1930. Gillette, then aged seventy-four, worried that the stress of the role would be too much for him, but he bore up well. The first performance of the tour took place on 15 November 1929 in Springfield, Massachusetts, and the tour ended at Princeton University in New Jersey on 12 May 1930. Later in the year, Gillette appeared on radio for the first time in a half-hour version of Doyle's Sherlock Holmes tale 'The Adventure of the Speckled Band'. It took place on 20 October, as one of a series of radio dramas based on the Holmes stories, called, rather ludicrously, 'The George Washington Coffee Sherlock Holmes Series' on NBC's WEAF Radio in New York. During the breaks, Dr Watson was called upon to attest that he always refreshed himself with George Washington Coffee while detecting with Holmes.

Gillette appeared on the stage as Sherlock Holmes for the last time in 1932, in the 'second half' of the farewell tour. It began in Boston on 28 December 1931 and ended in Wilmington, Delaware, on 19 March 1932. Gillette's last performance in *Sherlock Holmes* was in a 'tabloid version' for WABC's Radio Theatre in New York on 18 November 1935.

Over the years, Gillette had become totally identified with the character of Holmes. The artist Frederic Dorr Steele, illustrator of the Arthur Conan Doyle stories, said in answer to the question, 'Which came first, Gillette's play or Steele's pictures?': 'The play first saw the calcium in 1899, but *The Return of Sherlock Holmes*, with my pictures, was not published until four years later. Everybody agreed that Mr Gillette was the ideal Sherlock Holmes, and it was inevitable that I should copy him . . . But while the actor was seen by thousands, the magazines and books were seen by millions; so after a score of years had gone by, few could remember which "did it first" '.[19] Thus, audiences who saw the play for the first time in its 1929–32 revival were struck by Gillette's exact correspondence to all their notions about how Sherlock Holmes should look and act.

Gillette played the role over 1,300 times between 1899 and 1935. As was his custom, he made numerous changes to the play as he went along. As Vincent Starrett notes in his introduction to the 1935 edition of Sherlock Holmes: 'as made by Mr Gillette, between seasons or between revivals, the changes were intended to lend speed or effectiveness to the drama as seen and heard by a theater audience. Long speeches were made into short ones, and some were dropped entirely; references that had no bearing on the swift and chronological development of the

narrative were eliminated.'[20] The most significant changes took place at the end of
the play. The ultimate result, in all cases, is that the famous ending with the spotlight on Alice and Holmes, is retained. The dialogue leading up to it underwent
many changes. Essentially, the direction that they took is that, as Gillette grew
older and as Holmes' romance with Alice grew less credible, it fell to Alice's part to
become more persuasive and insistent, with the result that the scene grew longer. In
one of the middle versions, Holmes and Alice entered into a five-year engagement,
but prudence intervened, and in the 1929−32 version it was deleted, because
Gillette deemed it better that 'it left it at least doubtful whether S[herlock] was
going to be so foolish as to marry Alice Faulkner'.[21]

In these late endings, Alice is allowed the last word:

> ALICE: (*interrupting*) But listen please! − I want you to − oh, I want to
> tell you! − All that is nothing − *nothing* − because whatever life
> you have left is my life too − all my life − all the life I want!
> (HOLMES *looks down in her eyes for an instant − then puts his
> arms around her and draws her close to him, her head against his
> breast and her face turned to front or near it, for final spotlight
> which holds the two faces for a moment, then slowly fades out.*)[22]

In a revised version published by Samuel French in 1976, the ending is drastically
changed, and reads:

> HOLMES: Your powers of observation are somewhat remarkable, Miss
> Faulkner − and your deduction is quite correct! I suppose − indeed
> I know − that I love you. (HOLMES *sits on edge of desk.*) I love
> you. (ALICE *starts to move toward* HOLMES *but he stops her.*) But,
> I know as well what I am − and what you are − I know that no such
> person as I seared − (ALICE *turns away from him opening her hand
> bag to take out the famous 'Sherlock Holmes' meershaum [sic] pipe
> to give him as a present.*) drugged, poisoned, should ever dream of
> being a part of your sweet life. There is every reason why I should
> say good-bye and farewell! (ALICE *turns to him offering him the
> pipe.*) There is every reason − (HOLMES *takes the pipe, looks at it
> in ecstasy, then grabs* ALICE *and kisses her on the mouth.*)[23]

Presumably, this was done because the play no longer had to conform to the
requirements of an aging William Gillette. It is, however, very much in contrast to
the author's convictions about the way the role should be played.

The impact of Gillette's portrayal of Sherlock Holmes was deep and lasting. In a
letter written to Gillette on the occasion of the farewell tour, Sir Arthur Conan
Doyle wrote: 'my only complaint [is] that you make the poor hero of the anaemic
printed page a very limp object as compared with the glamour of your own personality which you infuse into his stage presentment'.[24] This tribute exactly
corresponded to Gillette's own ideas on the use of the actor's personality; in an
article in *Vanity Fair* some years earlier he had called it 'the most singularly important factor known to man for infusing the Life-Illusion into modern stage

creations'.[25] This use of personality, along with the technique he called the 'illusion of the first time in acting', led a critic, Clayton Hamilton, to say in 1930: 'I believe that many of these younger people will be astonished to discover that William Gillette is not an old-fashioned actor, but is just as modern in his methods as the players in the finest play of recent seasons . . . The reason is that Mr Gillette, at the climax of his career in the now distant eighteen nineties, was thirty years ahead of his time.'[26] A later assessment by Walter Kerr, on the occasion of a revival of *Sherlock Holmes* in 1974 lends the perspective of time to the matter:

> There is a legend about actor—playwright Gillette, and there was a time of day about him. Legend has it that he invariably instructed his fellow actors to pull out all the stops, to 'do it up brown', whereupon he strolled into their midst and underplayed them, seeming the sanest, the most controlled, the most 'natural' of the group. The ploy would obviously have worked marvelously when he was doing Holmes, making a coil of quietness in the melodramatic maelstrom.
>
> And there was a reason why some such tactic might have been perfectly feasible in 1899 and for a fairish time thereafter. Gillette wrote just as the theater was turning over, gradually surrendering its taste for opulent melodrama in favor of a more plausible restraint. But both options still existed, could stand side by side on stage — in the slightly earlier *Secret Service* as well as in *Holmes*.[27]

Sherlock Holmes stands as William Gillette's greatest creation as an actor and as a theatrical personality, although as a play it is overshadowed by the earlier *Secret Service*.

Innumerable other dramatized versions of Sherlock Holmes' adventures exist, one or two based on Gillette's version of the Doyle stories. In 1972, the play, in a 'new adaptation' by Dennis Rosa, played for 28 performances, beginning on 22 December, at the Cleveland Play House in Cleveland, Ohio. Two years later, the same version was performed for 42 performances by the Trinity Square Repertory Company in Providence, Rhode Island, beginning on 16 April 1974. The best-known revival of Gillette's play in recent years was the Royal Shakespeare Theatre's production in 1974 of the 1899 version of the play, with John Wood as Sherlock Holmes and Philip Locke as Professor Moriarty. It opened on 1 January 1974 in London for 179 performances, before going on tour. Later, the production was brought to New York, where it opened on 12 November 1974 for 219 performances.

A remarkably silly motion picture, *The Adventures of Sherlock Holmes' Smarter Brother, based on the play 'Sherlock Holmes' by William Gillette,* was produced in 1975 by 20th Century Fox. It concerned the adventures of Holmes's brother, Sigerson (who does not appear anywhere in the Holmes canon), and the only relation it bears to Gillette's play is that it includes Professor Moriarty and the recovery of a packet of incriminating documents. The popular musical play *Baker Street*, by Jerome Coopersmith, with music and lyrics by Marian Grudeff and

Raymond Jessel, is based loosely on the Doyle story, 'A Scandal in Bohemia', which Gillette used as the basis for the Alice Faulkner part of *Sherlock Holmes*, but it is not based on the Gillette play.

While Gillette was appearing in *Sherlock Holmes* in New York, London, and on tour, he busied himself with a number of projects. For several years he had been interested in appearing in his own production of *Hamlet*. He kept notebooks, designed scenery and effects, and worked on a version of the text, cutting a good deal of the dialogue and substituting elaborate stage directions. His *Hamlet* was never produced. Perhaps fortunately, since a more un-Shakespearean actor than Gillette can hardly be imagined, Charles Frohman succeeded in distracting him from it with the offer of the title role in J.M. Barrie's *The Admirable Crichton*.

The play opened at the Lyceum Theatre in New York on 17 November 1903, and ran for twenty-six weeks; the following season it toured the country for thirty weeks. The play was a success, although Gillette never particularly cared for the part. During this time, he was working on a one-act sketch called *Moving Day*, and in August 1904 he began work on his next full-length play, which he entitled *Clarice*.

In March 1905 he appeared as Sherlock Holmes again, this time in a one-act sketch called *The Painful* [or *Frightful*, or *Harrowing*] *Predicament of Sherlock Holmes*, at a benefit for the Metropolitan Opera House. On 14 April the sketch was given again at the Criterion Theatre in a benefit for the Actors' Society of America. Ethel Barrymore appeared with Gillette in the playlet about a woman who comes to see Holmes and talks so much that he cannot get in a word. Gillette did not utter one word in the piece, in a neat joke on his ability to focus the audience's attention on himself no matter what he did on stage.

In the summer of 1904, Gillette, who as a result of the time spent in England over the past few years with *Secret Service* and *Sherlock Holmes* had acquired many friends abroad, made the first of what came to be his annual trips to Europe, visiting Wales and the Alps. On 4 September 1905 he opened in *Clarice* in Liverpool, and the following week took the piece to London, opening on 13 September at the Duke of York's Theatre. It was not a great success, having only a short run. Gillette attempted to stimulate business by adding *The Painful Predicament of Sherlock Holmes* as a curtain-raiser, but soon decided to finish the season with a revival of *Sherlock Holmes*.

During the fall, Gillette revised *Clarice* and on 25 December 1905 it opened in its new form in Boston, where it was a popular, though not a critical, success. The play toured several towns in New England simultaneously with its engagement in Boston. It opened in New York on 16 October 1906 at the Garrick Theatre. The play is about an elderly man, Doctor Carrington, who is in love with his ward, Clarice. Tricked by another suitor into believing that he is dying of tuberculosis, Carrington sends Clarice away. Later, discovering that it is a plot, the doctor feigns suicide, the truth is uncovered, and Carrington and Clarice are reunited. The play is a romantic melodrama, in which Gillette forsook his interest in action for emphasis

on character. The plot was flimsy and full of unbelievable situations, which the
critics readily pointed out. Max Beerbohm, in a generally unfavorable review, did
remark on Gillette's talent for holding the audience's attention without a word of
dialogue:

> I feel that his favourite portion of 'Clarice' is that in which he, solitary on
> the stage, takes from his pocket the flower that the heroine has given him,
> and looks at it for a long time, eloquently, and then puts it back in his
> pocket, and then walks slowly to the window, and thinks, and takes the
> flower out of his pocket, and looks at it for a very long time, very
> eloquently, and then restores it to his pocket, and then walks slowly to
> his writing-table, and seats himself, and thinks very deeply, and then takes
> the flower out of his pocket, and after a while, begins to pick it to pieces,
> petal by petal. How long this scene lasted I do not know. I did not time it
> by my watch. I was wrapt in contemplation of (that which my heart told
> me was) Mr Gillette's own innocent pleasure in being able to hold the
> attention of the audience — his own innocent pride in his own magnet-
> ism.[28]

Clarice was otherwise notable for bringing to the public attention the young actress
Marie Doro, who very quickly thereafter achieved great popularity.

In 1907 and 1908 Gillette was absorbed in travelling and writing. He visited the
Canary Islands, Scotland, Switzerland, and Italy, and wrote a one-act play called
The Red Owl, about a woman whose brother steals some valuable securities from
her husband while he is asleep. On 15 June 1908 Gillette's one-act play *That Little
Affair of Boyd's*, which he had written in 1904, was produced at the Columbia
Theatre in Washington, DC, and, retitled *Ticey*, moved to the Liberty Theatre in
New York on 18 December. The play, about an actress who disguises herself as a
servant in order to help a stubborn playwright whose works are not suitable for the
theatre, did not prove successful.

Gillette returned to the stage in 1908 as Maurice Brachard in an adaptation of
Henri Bernstein's *Samson*, a popular French melodrama. It opened in early October
at the Criterion Theatre. The part of the tormented millionaire who seeks the
financial ruin of a man he thinks has seduced his wife was foreign to Gillette's
temperament as an actor, and the strain of performing wore down his health. For
two years afterwards, he neither wrote a play nor performed in one. In 1909 he
travelled to Germany, largely for his health.

Two of Gillette's one-act plays were performed in London in 1909. *The Robber*,
a revised version of *The Red Owl*, opened at the Coliseum on 9 August, with
Constance Collier, who had played Gillette's wife in *Samson*. On 6 September
Among Thieves was produced at the Palace Theatre. This play was set in the western United States and was about a man who was in hiding as a result of participat-
ing in a New York robbery.

In 1910 Gillette's last significant play, *Electricity*, was presented in Boston at
the Park Theatre on 26 September, and on 31 October it moved to New York

where it opened at the Lyceum Theatre. Although it was unsuccessful in its day, contemporary examination reveals that the play has weathered better than some of Gillette's more popular plays.

The play is about a rich girl, Emeline Twimbly, who, filled with imperfectly absorbed ideas about social responsibility and feminism, refuses to entertain James Hollender, the wealthy and idle young man who is in love with her. In order to gain her affection, he changes places with Bill Brockaway, a young electrician who has come to install lights in the Twimbly home. In an amusing scene of contrasts, Emeline and a friend, both very elegant young ladies, pay a call on the working-class home of the real electrician and his family. Eventually, Hollender is forced to confess his deception, and is accepted by Emeline when he proposes to go to work in the electrical business with Bill Brockaway.

The humor in the play lies chiefly in Emeline's mixture of social consciousness and naivety, and in the mildly rowdy drunken scenes with Bill Brockaway. Gillette's passion for things mechanical and for technical effects is demonstrated in his use of the installation of electrical wiring in a home as the focus of his play. Curiously, though a charge leveled at him in connection with *All the Comforts of Home*, that he eschewed topicality, cannot be brought here, the play was still not a success in its day.

Later in the season, and continuing into 1911, Gillette revived in repertory five of his most popular plays, *The Private Secretary*, *Held by the Enemy*, *Too Much Johnson*, *Secret Service*, and *Sherlock Holmes*, at the Empire Theatre in New York. In this period, he began to return to the lecture platform, delivering on 10 January 1910 an address to the Theatrical Managers Association, in which he upheld his conviction that it was respectable and right for playwrights and managers to follow the public taste. In 1912, during Theodore Roosevelt's Progressive Republican Party campaign, Gillette spoke on behalf of the party in a number of cities across the country. It seems at first out of character for a distinguished actor and playwright to become so involved in a political campaign at that time, but it must be recalled that as the son of a politically active man who had at one time been a United States Senator Gillette had a long familiarity with politics and campaigning.

In March 1913 Gillette addressed the graduating class of the American Academy of Dramatic Arts, and in November he delivered his famous lecture 'The Illusion of the First Time in Acting' at the fifth joint session of the American Academy of Arts and Letters and the National Institute of Arts and Letters in Chicago. This technique had been implicit in all his performances throughout his career; it laid great stress on the use of the actor's personality, and in giving the appearance that the words and actions of a character have just occurred to him at the moment that they are heard and seen on the stage. As he explained his theory:

> ... unfortunately for the actor he knows or is supposed to know his part. He is fully aware — especially after several performances — of what he is going to say. The Character he is representing, however, does *not* know what he is going to say, but, if he is a human being, various thoughts occur

to him one by one, and he puts such of these thoughts as he decides to,
into such speech as he happens to be able to command at the time. Now it
is a very difficult thing — and even now rather an uncommon thing — for
an actor who knows exactly what he is going to say to behave exactly as
tho he didn't; to let his thought (apparently) occur to him as he goes
along, even tho they are there in his mind already; and (apparently) to
search for and find the words by which to express those thoughts, even
tho these words are at his tongue's very end. That's the terrible thing —
at his tongue's very end! Living and breathing creatures do not carry their
words in that part of their systems: they have to find them and send them
there — with more or less rapidity according to their facility in that respect
— as occasion arises.[29]

Gillette's essay provides a thoughtful rationale for the pauses, the hesitations, the
stumblings, the rapid movements that so fascinated audiences and critics in his most
memorable roles. Gillette gives no precise instructions about how this 'illusion' is to
be maintained; it is far easier to describe how not to do something than how to do
it. He contents himself with recommending that 'the whole must have that
indescribable Life-Spirit or Effect which produces the Illusion of Happening for the
First Time'.[30]

The following year, Gillette began work on his retirement home in Hadlyme,
Connecticut, overlooking the Connecticut River. Called 'Seventh Sister', the house
is really a castle, based on a medieval design. Gillette, with his interest in gadgetry,
invented a number of devices to tailor the castle to his requirements, including a
miniature door for the convenience of his many cats. Seventh Sister 'contained
twenty-four rooms, forty-seven huge doors and forty-nine types of bolts, for which
Gillette drew all the sketches and many of which he himself turned out in his own
workshop'.[31] The house was set in over a hundred acres of woodland, and in 1930
Gillette constructed a miniature railway in his grounds; in his later years he
delighted in taking guests for rides around the estate. Gillette Castle, as it has come
to be known, is now a part of Gillette Castle State Park in Connecticut. His beloved
miniature railroad, despite his fears that it would be sold to 'some blithering sap-
head', was purchased after his death by an amusement park in Southington, Connecticut, and still runs along the shores of Lake Compounce.[32]

While work on Seventh Sister was under way, Gillette visited Europe on his
annual trip in the summer of 1914, and found himself in Paris when war was
declared. Later in the year, he returned to the stage in his own reworking of the
Scott—Stephenson translation of Sardou's play *Diplomacy*, with Marie Doro and
Blanche Bates. It opened at Charles Frohman's Empire Theatre on 20 October
1914. It was well-received by audiences in New York and on its subsequent tour.

In 1915 and 1916 Gillette embarked on the first of what was to be a long series
of 'farewell tours', playing *Sherlock Holmes* to enthusiastic audiences around the
country. On 7 May 1915, a long association came to an end when Charles Frohman
died in the sinking of the *Lusitania*. Gillette, one of the pallbearers at the funeral,

was to have accompanied Frohman on his trip to Europe, but was forced to bow out owing to a contract to play in Philadelphia.[33] Later in 1915, Gillette was elected to membership in the American Academy of Arts and Letters.

In 1917 Gillette was back in New York appearing in Clare Kummer's *A Successful Calamity*. It opened at the Booth Theatre on 5 February 1917, and was followed by a road tour. The play, written by a niece of Gillette, is about a millionaire who tests his family's affection for him by pretending to be bankrupt. Gillette was supported by an excellent cast, including Estelle Winwood and Roland Young, and the play proved a great success.

The next year Gillette performed in his second J.M. Barrie play, *Dear Brutus*. After try-outs in Atlantic City, New Jersey, and Washington, DC, the play opened in New York on 23 December 1918, at the Empire Theatre. Gillette played an artist who, in a fantasy, acquires the daughter he had always wanted. Helen Hayes, as Margaret, was the latest in a long line of young actresses whose careers Gillette fostered. The play was an enormous success and ran for 184 performances. *Dear Brutus* toured the United States in 1919 and 1920, playing in Boston, Philadelphia, Chicago, and other cities.

In 1921 Gillette appeared for the last time in a new play that he had written. *The Dream Maker*, adapted from a short story by Howard E. Merton, opened at the Empire Theatre in New York on 21 November 1921. The play was a melodrama in which Gillette, as Dr Paul Clement, succeeds in outwitting a group of villains who are attempting to blackmail the daughter of a woman he once loved. Alexander Woollcott, in his review of the play for the *New York Times* (22 November 1921), wrote that:

> It is really a Sherlock Holmes grown old who whimsically but effectively thwarts the crooks that roam through the new piece . . . and it is the same William Gillette grown older who plays the part in the same old ringing whispers. Time has changed the look of him, and he fools time by making this new character of his bent, and as gray and as rickety as possible. But time has diminished in no degree the great charm and skill and distinction which used to lend a glamour to certain penny dreadfuls in days gone by and which lend a glamour now to *The Dream Maker*.

Although his performance was well-received, melodramas of this sort had begun to seem dated, and the play ran for only 82 performances. At the final performance Gillette announced his retirement, but in 1922 and 1923 he came out for yet another farewell tour, with revivals of *Dear Brutus*, *Sherlock Holmes*, and *The Private Secretary*.

In the 1920s Gillette spent a good deal of time at Seventh Sister, inventing in his workshop, riding about on his motorcycle (until a serious accident forced him to give it up), amusing himself with his miniature railroad and his large collection of scrapbooks. He kept up his writing in his later years: for over fifteen years he had worked on his 'Vignettes', a collection of sketches, including 'Death and the Child' and 'In a Castle', none of which was ever published. In 1914 he had written *The*

Butterfly on the Wheel, and he completed a one-act comedy, *How Well George Does It*, in 1919. In 1923 his play *Winnie and the Wolves*, based on stories by Bertram Akey, was produced, not very successfully, on 21 May at the Lyric Theatre in Philadelphia. Gillette turned more to prose in the 1920s, and in 1927 his novel, *The Astounding Crime on Torrington Road*, a detective story about an inventor, was published. It was well-received, not least because the author was the well-known actor and playwright William Gillette. His last work, which he never completed, was a two-act play entitled *The Crown Prince of the Incas*.

Gillette's next major effort was the first half of his revival tour of *Sherlock Holmes*; after it closed, in the late spring of 1930, Gillette spent the month of June ꜱcollecting a sheaf of honorary degrees at college graduation exercises. Columbia University awarded him an honorary LL.D. on 3 June; two weeks later, on 16 June, he received an honorary M.A. from Trinity College in his home town of Hartford. The week after that he travelled to Dartmouth College in Hanover, New Hampshire, to accept an honorary LL.D., and on 19 June he was awarded an honorary M.A. by Yale University in New Haven, Connecticut. In 1931 Gillette was honored by the National Institute of Arts and Letters, of which he had been a member since 1898, with a gold medal for his lifetime achievement as a playwright. This prestigious award, given only once every ten years, had gone to Augustus Thomas in 1913, and to Eugene O'Neill in 1922.[34]

After the second half of his *Sherlock Holmes* farewell tour in 1932, Gillette returned to Seventh Sister, where he led a busy life in retirement. The attraction of the theatre was still strong, and in 1936 he was persuaded to return to the stage in a revival of Austin Strong's *Three Wise Fools*. The play, about three old men who interest themselves in a young girl whose mother all three had loved in years past, opened at the Shubert Theatre in Newark, New Jersey, on 13 January 1936. It toured a number of cities in the east and ended its run at the Golden Theatre in New York in March. Critics enthusiastically applauded Gillette's performance; Brooks Atkinson, reviewing the play for the *New York Times* (2 March 1936), wrote:

> For old Findley, the tart financier, is the most profane, sardonic, and ill tempered of the three curmudgeons, and likewise the most sentimental. This sort of thing is ripe for the Gillette talents. The dry, precise voice, the accurate underplaying, the considered accent, and the marvelous suggestion of affection and intellect under the imperturbable mask, the drone of reflection — these are the sort of things that restore the admiration Mr Gillette's acting has always fostered, and they suit Old Findley down to the boards. By seeming to throw away all the best things in the part Mr Gillette has always made them most enchanting.

Gillette, who had lost none of his ability to mesmerize an audience, still held to his notions of underplaying and relying on the force of his personality.

In December 1936 Gillette entered Hartford Hospital for treatment of a lingering cold. He appeared to be on the mend, and returned to Seventh Sister, but in

April he was hospitalized again. William Gillette died on 29 April 1937 in Hartford Hospital. There was no funeral, and he was buried in the Gillette family plot in Riverside Cemetery in Farmington, Connecticut, next to his wife Helen.

William Gillette is remembered today principally for his portrayal of Sherlock Holmes, and this fame has tended to obscure his contributions to the development of the American theatre in his day. He introduced and popularized a cool, understated, realistic style of acting, in marked contrast to the florid and romantic styles that had dominated the theatre up to that time. In his roles he drew heavily on his own personality and was most comfortable in parts that called for an impression of detachment, calmness and mental energy. He was not a particularly versatile actor: classic parts and serious or romantic dramas were outside his scope. He was, however, superb as the quick-witted Captain Thorne and incomparable as Sherlock Holmes. He took his work as an actor very seriously, devoting many hours to perfecting the smallest details of his roles, and through his writings and speeches he was one of the earliest popular actors to elucidate the methods of his craft.

Gillette was endlessly innovative and inventive in stage design and technical effects. His productions were always memorable for new lighting-techniques, complex and elaborate settings, accurate historical costuming, and the realistic sounds of horses, guns, and battles. His passion for detail as well as his sure appreciation of the public taste led him to include these elements in all his plays and often led to popular successes even when critical reception was poor. Commonplace as they seem now, in Gillette's day his use of sound and lighting-effects was revolutionary and added to the effect of realism that he built up in his plays, although the final product was only superficially realistic.

It is clear that *Secret Service*, with its fast-moving action, suspense, and the tension between the demands of love and duty, is his most significant achievement as a playwright, but the flamboyance of his performance in *Sherlock Holmes* made it the play with which he is always identified. Many of his translations and adaptations were slight efforts, but the rapid pace and natural dialogue lent many of them an air of realism which was novel at the time. The addition of Gillette's natural style of acting and dazzling effects transformed many a commonplace situation into an immensely appealing popular entertainment. When Gillette died in 1937, the theatre in which he had begun his career had been totally changed, and Gillette had played no small part in this transformation. Realism in acting, in settings and effects, and in the plays themselves was now the accepted order of the day, and it was toward this end that Gillette had always worked during his lengthy career.

NOTES

1   Arthur Hobson Quinn, *A History of the American Drama from the Civil War to the Present Day* (New York: F.S. Crofts and Co., 1943), p. 215.
2   Montrose J. Moses, 'William Gillette', *Theatre Guild Magazine*, January 1930, p. 34.

3   Clipping in William Gillette files, New York Public Library, Billy Rose
     Theatre Collection, Lincoln Center for the Performing Arts.
4   *New York Times*, 9 September 1890. Quoted in Georg William Schuttler,
     'William Gillette, Actor and Playwright' (unpublished Ph.D. dissertation,
     University of Illinois at Urbana–Champaign, 1975), p. 14.
5   *New York Press*, 7 February 1893. Quoted in Schuttler, 'William Gillette',
     p. 16.
6   Daniel Frohman and Isaac F. Marcosson, *Charles Frohman: Manager and
     Man* (New York: Harper and Brothers, 1916), pp. 156–7.
7   *New York Herald Tribune*, January 1964. Quoted in Doris Cook, *Sherlock
     Holmes and Much More; or Some of the Facts About William Gillette*
     ([Hartford]: The Connecticut Historical Society, 1970), p. 43.
8   *Leslie's Weekly*, 22 October 1896.
9   *Illustrated Sporting and Dramatic News*, 22 May 1897. Quoted in Horst
     Frenz and Louise Wylie Campbell, 'William Gillette on the London Stage',
     Queen's Quarterly, LII (November 1943), p. 447.
10   George Bernard Shaw, *Plays and Players* (London: Oxford University
     Press, [1952?]), p. 240.
11   Quinn, *History of the American Drama*, p. 228.
12   John Dickson Carr, *The Life of Sir Arthur Conan Doyle* (New York:
     Harper and Brothers, *c.* 1949), p. 117.
13   *Sherlock Holmes; Farewell Appearance of William Gillette, 1929–1932*
     ([New York, 1932?], souvenir booklet), p. 17.
14   Clipping in William Gillette file, New York Public Library, Billy Rose
     Theatre Collection, dated 7 November 1899. Quoted in Schuttler, 'William
     Gillette', p. 86.
15   *New York Journal and Advertiser*, 7 November 1899.
16   Quinn, *History of the American Drama*, p. 229.
17   William Gillette, *Sherlock Holmes. A Play Wherein is Set Forth the Strange
     Case of Miss Alice Faulkner by William Gillette*. Based on Sir Arthur
     Conan Doyle's Incomparable Stories. With an introduction by Vincent
     Starrett and preface by William Gillette. Reminiscent notes by Frederic
     Dorr Steele and line drawings by Frederic Dorr Steele (Garden City, New
     York: Doubleday, Doran and Company, 1935), p. 191.
18   Frenz and Wylie, 'Gillette on the London Stage', pp. 453–4.
19   William Gillette, *Sherlock Holmes* (1935), p. xxxvii.
20   *Ibid.*, pp. xv–xvi.
21   William Gillette, MSS.73.392, dated March 1935, Stowe–Day Foundation,
     Hartford, Connecticut.
22   William Gillette, *Sherlock Holmes* (1935), p. 191.
23   William Gillette, *Sherlock Holmes. A Comedy in Two Acts by Arthur
     Conan Doyle and William Gillette* (New York: Samuel French, *c.* 1976),
     pp. 129–30.
24   Sir Arthur Conan Doyle, letter dated 25 October [1929?] in *Letters of
     Salutation and Felicitations Received by William Gillette on the Occasion
     of his Farewell Tours in Sherlock Holmes* [New York?, 1929]. The editors
     have used a copy of a broadside version of these collected letters at the
     Stowe–Day Foundation and a booklet version at the New York Public
     Library, Billy Rose Theatre Collection.
25   *Vanity Fair*, March 1916, in Gillette file, Billy Rose Theatre Collection,
     New York Public Library.

26 Clayton Hamilton, 'The Final Episode of Sherlock Holmes', *Theatre Magazine*, 1 (January 1930), p. 36.
27 Walter Kerr, *Journey to the Center of the Theater* (New York: Alfred A. Knopf, 1979), p. 64.
28 Max Beerbohm, *Around Theatres* (New York: Alfred A. Knopf, 1930), vol. II, p. 504.
29 William Gillette, *The Illusion of the First Time in Acting*. With an introduction by George Arliss (New York: printed for the Dramatic Museum of Columbia University, 1915), pp. 40–1.
30 *Ibid.*, p. 43.
31 Cook, *Holmes and Much More*, p. 70.
32 *Ibid.*, p. 92.
33 'The Call Boy's Chat', *Philadelphia Inquirer*, 2 February 1930. Quoted in H. Dennis Sherk, 'William Gillette: His Life and Works' (unpublished Ph.D. dissertation, Pennsylvania State University, 1961), p. 142.
34 Schuttler, 'William Gillette', pp. 28–9.

BIOGRAPHICAL RECORD

24 July 1853	William Hooker Gillette born in Hartford, Connecticut.
June 1886–October 1867	Produced a magazine called 'Hail Columbia'.
March 1873	Presented a one-act farce of his own called *Bally-wingle the Beloved*.
April 1873	Graduated from high school; delivered oration from *Julius Caesar* and an address entitled 'Opposition'.
Fall 1873–4	Acting apprenticeship in St Louis (Grand Opera House) and New Orleans (DeBar's St Charles Theatre). First speaking roles in support of Lawrence Barrett in St Louis (roles unknown).
Fall 1874	Acted small role of the Foreman of the Jury in *The Gilded Age* on tour with John T. Raymond's company. In January advanced to larger role of Counsel for the Defense.
1875–Summer 1876	Continued apprenticeship with Raymond at the Globe Theatre in Boston. First important role: Guzman in *Faint Heart Ne'er Won Fair Lady*. Attended Boston University's Monroe School of Oratory for one year.
September 1876	Began two-year stint with Macauley's Stock Company in Cincinnati, Ohio, and Louisville, Kentucky.
July 1879	Completed unproduced five-act script *The Twins of Siam*.
Summer 1879	Try-out of first full-length play, *The Professor*, in Columbus, Ohio.
29 October 1881	*Esmeralda* opened in New York at the Madison Square Theatre and ran until the summer of 1882. Seen in London at the St James's Theatre, 20 October 1883, as *Young Folks' Ways*.
1 June 1882	Married Helen Nickles (1860–88) of Detroit, Michigan, in Windsor, Ontario, Canada.
29 September 1884	*Digby's Secretary* opened at the New York Comedy Theatre.
November 1884	Began three-year tour in *The Private Secretary*.
22 February 1886	First performance of Gillette's Civil War play *Held by*

28

	the Enemy at Criterion Theatre, Brooklyn, with Gillette as Blane.
16 August 1886	*Held by the Enemy* at Madison Square Theatre, New York.
2 April 1887	*Held by the Enemy* at the Princess's Theatre, London.
29 November 1887	*She* presented at Niblo's Garden in New York.
14 August 1888	Gillette's original play *A Legal Wreck* (published in novel form as well) opened at the Madison Square Theatre. Published in 1900.
1 September 1888	Helen Gillette died, aged 28. Gillette retired from the stage for five years and turned to writing in lieu of public appearances.
29 April 1889	Dramatization of *Robert Elsmere* presented at Union Square Theatre, New York, and later at Hollis Street Theatre, Boston.
3 March 1890	Premiere of *All the Comforts of Home* at the Boston Museum.
8 September 1890	New York premiere of *Comforts* at Proctor's 23rd Street Theatre, presented by Charles Frohman.
Fall–Winter 1890	In the Saluda Mountains near Tryon, North Carolina, a favorite retreat (first visit to Tryon in 1889).
24 January 1891	*All the Comforts of Home* at Globe Theatre, London.
30 March 1891	Gillette's farce *Mr Wilkinson's Widows* opened in New York at Proctor's after a try-out in Washington, DC (23 March 1891).
Spring 1891	Built lodge in Tryon, later expanded and called 'Thousand Pines'.
July–August 1892	Ocean voyage; brief stay in France.
8 August 1892	*Settled Out of Court* opened at Fifth Avenue Theatre, New York.
January 1893	Wrote *The War of the American Revolution*, nine scenes with historical commentary. Manuscript indicates it was written for the 'Barnum & Bailey people' for a libretto to use with their 'Vast Episodic Drama of the Revolution'.
6 February 1893	Opening of *Ninety Days*, his worst failure to date, at Broadway Theatre, New York; ran barely a month.
26 November 1894	Premiere at Standard Theatre, New York, of *Too Much Johnson* (originally *Sugar Business*). Gillette as Augustus Billings, his first appearance since his wife's death.
13 May 1895	*Secret Service* premiered at Broad Street Theatre,

	Philadelphia, with Maurice Barrymore in dual role of Thorne/Dumont.
5 October 1896	New York opening of *Secret Service* at the Garrick Theatre with Gillette in dual roles. Established his acting style noted for coolness and finesse. Ran until 6 March 1897; revived at the Empire Theatre on 1 September 1897.
15 May 1897	*Secret Service* at the Adelphi Theatre, London, with Gillette as Thorne/Dumont, and Ethel Barrymore in a small role. Play revived frequently thereafter; Gillette during his career played Thorne 1,791 times. Gillette replaced in August after a breakdown; returned to US. London run suspended on 16 December after murder of William Terriss, Gillette's replacement.
2 October 1897	*Secret Service* at Renaissance Théâtre in Paris.
1898	Became member of the National Institute of Arts and Letters.
28 October 1898	*Because She Loved Him So* (also called *Weatherby's Fiancée*) at Hyperion Theatre, New Haven, Connecticut.
18 April 1898	*Too Much Johnson* with Gillette as Billings at Garrick Theatre, London.
16 January 1899	New York premiere of *Because She Loved Him So* (Madison Square Theatre).
Spring 1899	In London to confer with Arthur Conan Doyle on dramatization of *Sherlock Holmes*.
24 October 1899	*Holmes* at Star Theatre, Buffalo, New York.
6 November 1899	New York premiere of *Holmes* (Garrick Theatre). Closed 16 June 1900 (236 performances), followed by US tour until Summer 1901. Gillette played Holmes more than 1,300 times in the course of his career, in many revivals, with box office receipts of over $1,500,000.
September 1901	Try-out of *Holmes* at Shakespeare Theatre, Liverpool, on 2 September; London debut 9 September at Lyceum. Despite mixed reviews, the production was more successful than in US, running until 11 April 1902. Productions toured England, without Gillette, until the mid 1920s.
1902	Enlarged *Aunt Polly*, a houseboat already acquired by 1898 (destroyed by fire in late 1930s).

17 November 1903	Played butler Crichton in James Barrie's *The Admirable Crichton* at Lyceum Theatre, New York.
May–June 1904	Began the first of his annual trips to Europe.
October 1904	Completed *A Private Theatrical* (retitled *A Maid-of-All Work*), a play in four parts. Produced in 1908 as *Ticey; or, That Little Affair of Boyd's*.
24 March 1905	Appeared with Ethel Barrymore in his one-act *The Painful Predicament of Sherlock Holmes* for a benefit at the Metropolitan Opera House.
4 September 1905	*Clarice* opened with try-out in Liverpool.
13 September 1905	*Clarice* opened at the Duke of York's Theatre, London, closing after thirteen performances.
3 October 1905	*The Painful Predicament* presented as a curtain-raiser with youthful Charlie Chaplin as the page-boy Billy; a week later Gillette revived *Sherlock Holmes*.
25 December 1905	*Clarice* in reworked version, opened in Boston.
16 October 1906	*Clarice* opened in New York (Garrick Theatre).
15 June 1908	*Ticey; or, That Little Affair of Boyd's* at Columbia Theatre, Washington, DC; at Liberty Theatre, New York, 18 December.
19 October 1908	Appeared as Maurice Brachard in Henri Bernstein's *Samson* at Criterion Theatre, New York; exhausted by this taxing role, Gillette did not write or act for almost two years.
9 August 1909	One-act play *The Robber* (rearrangement of *The Red Owl*, written in 1907–8) produced at London Coliseum for Constance Collier.
6 September	One-act play *Among Thieves* produced at Palace Theatre, London.
Late 1910	Last significant play, *Electricity*, performed unsuccessfully at the Park Theatre, Boston, 26 September, and at Lyceum, New York, 31 October.
Late 1910–April 1911	Appeared in repertory at Empire Theatre, New York, reviving five of most successful plays.
October 1912	Began career as platform lecturer; spoke for Bull Moose cause during 1912 political campaign.
March 1913	Addressed graduating class of American Academy of Dramatic Arts.
November 1913	Delivered lecture 'The Illusion of the First Time in Acting' (published 1915) at fifth joint session of the American Academy of Arts and Letters and National Institute of Arts and Letters, in Chicago.

1914–19	Designed and built a 'castle' on a hill ('Seventh Sister') near Hadlyme, Connecticut, overlooking the Connecticut River.
Summer 1914	Toured Europe; in Paris when war declared.
20 October 1914	Opened in his modernization of Sardou's *Diplomacy* (*Dora*); toured afterwards and had an extended run in Chicago.
November 1915	Elected to the American Academy of Arts and Letters.
5 February 1917	Opened at the Booth Theatre, New York, in Clare Kummer's *A Successful Calamity*, followed by a tour after a long New York run.
23 December 1918	After brief try-out tour, opened in New York in James Barrie's *Dear Brutus*.
1919	Wrote one-act comedy *How Well George Does It* (published 1936).
Fall 1919–Spring 1920	Tour of *Dear Brutus*.
21 November 1921	*The Dream Maker* opened at Empire Theatre, New York.
1922–3	Another farewell tour.
21 May 1923	Production of play *Winnie and the Wolves* at Lyric Theatre, Philadelphia.
1927	Publication of Gillette novel, *The Astounding Crime on Torrington Road* (Harper and Brothers).
15 November 1929	Beginning of final farewell tour in *Sherlock Holmes* under management of George C. Tyler in Springfield, Massachusetts; tour ended at Princeton University, 12 May 1930.
June 1930	Received honorary degrees at Columbia University, Trinity College, Dartmouth College and Yale University.
20 October 1930	'The Adventure of the Speckled Band', one of a series of radio dramas based on Sherlock Holmes, broadcast on WEAF Radio (NBC) in New York ('The George Washington Coffee Sherlock Holmes Series').
11 November 1931	Received the gold medal of the National Institute of Arts and Letters for work as a dramatic author.
28 December 1931	Began second half of *Sherlock* tour in Boston; tour ended in Wilmington, Delaware, 19 March 1932.
18 November 1935	Final appearance as Holmes in fifteen-minute tabloid version on WABC Radio Theatre in New York.
13 January 1936	Opened in last stage vehicle, Theodore Findley in

	Austin Strong's *Three Wise Fools*, at Shubert Theatre, Newark, New Jersey. Toured until early March.
1932–6	Worked on last play, *The Crown Prince of the Incas*; never completed.
29 April 1937	Died in Hartford following complications from a bad cold from which he had suffered for several months.

A NOTE ON THE TEXTS

The texts for the plays in this volume were assembled from a variety of sources, both manuscript and printed. In all cases, lengthy period stage directions were condensed and clarified. Many directions unnecessary to an understanding of the plays were simply omitted. We have endeavored to strike a balance between a reproduction of the author's style, in concise terms, and the modern director's right to stage the plays according to the requirements and conventions of the contemporary stage. In some instances, particularly in the telegraph scene in *Secret Service* and in the gas chamber scene in *Sherlock Holmes*, we have retained the author's very explicit stage directions because we believe that the physical relationships of the characters in these scenes are vital to an understanding of the play. In contemporary production, the stage directions will of course be adjusted to suit the desires of the director and the arrangement of the stage.

The text of *All the Comforts of Home* is taken from the version first printed in 1897 for H. Roorbach. The stage directions have been considerably abbreviated for this version. The text of *Secret Service* is taken from the one published in 1898 by Samuel French and includes emendations found in the revised version published by A.H. Quinn in his *Representative Plays*, 1917. The text for *Sherlock Holmes* is based on the typescript with manuscript corrections found in the Billy Rose Collection of the New York Public Library's Theatre and Drama Collection at Lincoln Center. This text was used in preference to all others (and there are many) because it seemed to be substantially the text that Gillette used for the majority of his performances of *Sherlock Holmes* throughout his career. The text of 1935, published by Doubleday, Doran, and Co., incorporates many of the changes Gillette made throughout his lifetime, and is the text with which most readers are familiar. The exact nature of the changes Gillette made to *Sherlock Holmes* over the years is discussed at greater length in the Introduction to this volume. The most recently published text, that issued by Samuel French in 1976, is substantially revised for modern production and was not considered here as an example of Gillette's work.

Gillette was prone to inconsistencies in spelling. We have regularized the majority of these where confusion might result. He also devised his own punctuation rules, frequently as a means to suggest a line reading or emphasis for the actor. We have chosen to retain his punctuation in virtually all instances. Gillette's writing style is a clear reflection of American nineteenth-century practice, and though it is sometimes strange to the contemporary eye, we have not altered what we consider significant indicators of Gillette's attempt to write for the stage rather than the page. This is perhaps most obvious in the methods used to suggest dialect, such as the Southern speech in *Secret Service* and various English dialects in *Sherlock Holmes*.

ALL THE COMFORTS OF HOME

A comedy in four acts

First produced at the Boston Museum, 3 March 1890, with the following cast:

ALFRED HASTINGS	John Mason
TOM McDOW	George W. Wilson
THEODORE BENDER	George C. Boniface
JOSEPHINE BENDER	Annie M. Clarke
EVANGELINE BENDER	Miriam O'Leary
MR EGBERT PETTIBONE	Thomas L. Coleman
ROSABELLE PETTIBONE	Lilian Hadley
EMILY PETTIBONE	Evelyn Campbell
CHRISTOPHER DABNEY	Erroll Dunbar
FIFI ORITANSKI	Emma V. Sheridan
AUGUSTUS McSNATH	James Burrows
VICTOR SMYTH	Junius B. Booth
THOMPSON	H.P. Whittemore
GRETCHEN (Fifi's maid)	Miss Blake
BAILIFF	Edward Wade

Subsequently produced in New York at Proctor's 23rd Street Theatre, 8 September 1890, with Henry Miller as ALFRED and Maude Adams as EVANGELINE.

III Composite photograph of the cast of *All the Comforts of Home*. From left to right: Victor, Fifi, Josephine, Theodore Bender, Evangeline, Alfred, Tom, Pettibone and Mrs Pettibone (original cast)

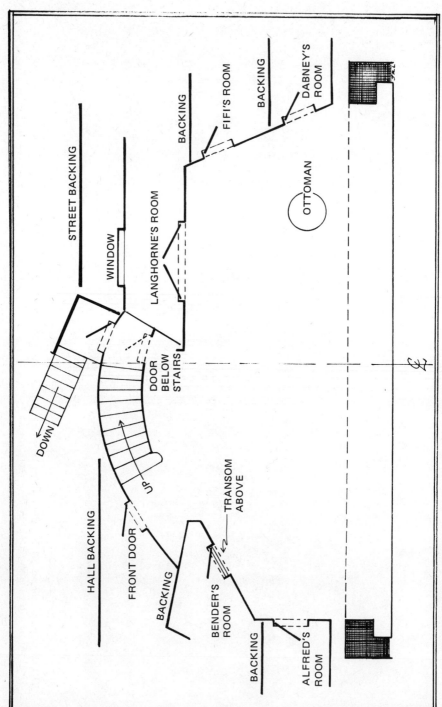

IV *All the Comforts of Home*: floorplan, based on Gillette's original floorplan

38

ACT I

Parlor or drawing room in EGBERT PETTIBONE's *house. A handsome room, luxuriously furnished. Large square or arched opening up R.C., through which is seen a large heavy door up R., to open on stage, and also the lower part of a winding stairway, leading up, and practical, with balustrade, etc. A door up R. faces toward middle of front of stage. This door has a transom above it to open. The door opens on the stage. Door down R. Wide or double doors up L.C., to open up stage. Interior backing showing a window and above this street backing. Door down L. Door up L. or L.3. Doors R. and L. are each backed with handsome interior pieces. A small table up L., either in corner or against wall, to pull out for bus. An ottoman or short lounge L. Shelves for books, ornaments, etc., against wall L., for bus. (*BENDER *upsetting things,* ACT III.) *Handsome table R.C. Upright piano up C., or at R. A large and elegantly mounted mirror up R., either just above door R.3 or up C. This mirror may be a part of some large and elegant piece of furniture. Handsomely framed pictures hang on walls R. and L. and up stage. Chairs, etc., in room back of door up L.C. and furniture of a characteristic nature up above opening up R. Discovered,* EGBERT PETTIBONE, *pacing up and down and around room in a very excited state, with a letter in his hand. Drops into chair; looks at the letter; buries face in hands. Jumps suddenly up and paces again. Repeats chair bus.*

PETTIBONE: I have suspected it all along! Now it is no longer suspicion — it is certainty. I was cautioned against marrying a young wife — at my age. Ah! — kind friends (*eyes up to ceiling*) — kind friends — you were right. (*Letter to light.*) I have a copy of her letter — making the appointment. 'Come this afternoon between one and two o'clock. No one will be here to disturb us!' Oh! I have arranged that! Some one will be here to disturb you Mr — Mr — Victor Smythe!

> (*Enter* EMILY PETTIBONE, *outside door; hat and walking dress on, as if just in from street. She has two or three small parcels and a little satchel such as ladies carry for shopping. She is about to pass the wide door of room when her father's conduct attracts her attention. She comes into the room a little way, watching him, and soon bursts into a merry laugh.* PETTIBONE *turns quickly. Conceals letter.*)

EMILY: How many laps have you made since breakfast? (*Laughs again. Comes down L. of* PETTIBONE.) Do tell me what is the matter this morning.
PETTIBONE: (*Goes to and fro and stops, meeting her.*) Matter? Nothing!
EMILY: (*peremptorily, but goodnaturedly*) You hid a letter — I want to see it!
PETTIBONE: No! No! (*avoiding her*)
EMILY: What! As bad as that! I shall have to report this to my stepmamma.
PETTIBONE: What! Report that I — that I — (*aside*)
EMILY: (*Bursts out laughing again.*) Oh — but you're in a state!
PETTIBONE: (*Recovers.*) Ah— e — hear! It's only business, my child.
EMILY: Business! (*Looks incredulous.*)
PETTIBONE: Listen! You have often expressed a wish to travel — to see the world.
EMILY: Yes; but you needn't go into convulsions about it, papa! I can wait a little!
PETTIBONE: You will not have to wait! We start to-day!

EMILY: Oh! you dear — (*about to embrace him*) good —

PETTIBONE: (*stopping her*) No! We haven't time for that!

EMILY: Goodness! You must be in an awful hurry!

PETTIBONE: Hurry? I am in a — (*Stops in midst of rising rage; aside*) No — no — no! She must not suspect. (*aloud*) Emily, my dear (*Kisses her, but in an excited and mechanical fashion.*), I am suddenly compelled to go to the Continent on business of vast importance. I shall take you and — and your stepmother with me.

EMILY: Oh! That is simply heavenly!

PETTIBONE: You have only half an hour to get ready!

EMILY: Ready now — walk right off with you — only want to throw some things into a trunk.

PETTIBONE: Your trunks are packed.

EMILY: (*surprised now*) Dear me, Popsy, but you are in a hurry! Did Katy —

PETTIBONE: I told her to put in everything she saw. (*Rings bell on table R. violently, dropping it in excitement.*)

EMILY: (*aghast*) Everything she saw — Mercy!

        (*Enter KATY, door up L.C.*)

PETTIBONE: My daughter's trunks — are they packed yet? Are they packed, I say?

KATY: Yes, sir — they are sir.

PETTIBONE: And — Mrs Pettibone — her trunks — our trunks — ?

KATY: They're all ready, sir — but she doesn't understand why —

PETTIBONE: (*suddenly forgetting himself*) Eh! (*eagerly*) What did she say, eh?

KATY: She said it was her opinion, sir, as you was gone completely crazy.

PETTIBONE: She's right! I — e — Go and tell her she's right, do you hear? (*Fumes about.*)

KATY: Yes, sir!

        (*Exit KATY. EMILY, who has been watching PETTIBONE, bursts into laughter.*)

PETTIBONE: Do! And if she wants to know — (PETTIBONE *stops suddenly and looks sheepish.*)

EMILY: (*solemnly, shaking finger at* PETTIBONE) Popsy — there's something at the bottom of all this!

PETTIBONE: No! (*shaking head emphatically*) Nothing at all, only business. (*Turns, shaking head, muttering about business. Paces out into hall. Knock outside. Calling off, to someone*) Is that the cab? Is the cab there, I say?

VOICE: (*outside*) Yes, sir; and the men are here for the luggage.

PETTIBONE: Send them up the other way. The other way, you fool!

VOICE: Yes, sir.

EMILY: (*starting*) Mercy! I must see if Katy has put in everything — and my bird — and, and — oh, dear! (*Runs off through the double doors.*)

PETTIBONE: (*Looks at watch nervously as he paces.*) Now, why doesn't Alfred come! I sent word from the office an hour ago that he must come at once — and it's long after that now. He must stay here in the house — he can't object — far better quarters than the little garret where he's lodging now. And I must let him know that I approve of his suit with Emily — and I must give directions about the house. Confound it! We haven't fifteen minutes — and — all these things to be settled!

> (*Enter* MRS PETTIBONE *from the double doors. She is very deliberate and cool, a contrast to the others.*)

PETTIBONE: (*aside*) Ah — my wife — Now for it! Have you attended to the packing, Madam?

MRS PETTIBONE: (*Sits at table; chilly tone.*) Oh, yes — I have nothing to do but attend to your orders.

PETTIBONE: We are about to start on a — a little trip.

MRS PETTIBONE: (*Looks at* PETTIBONE.) Ah! When do we go, pray?

PETTIBONE: (*watching her narrowly*) We leave — this morning. (*aside, quickly*) She started!

MRS PETTIBONE: (*aside*) Poor Victor! He will be heartbroken.

PETTIBONE: Come, come! It is nearly time. Your things — Your — your — (*Stops as he meets her gaze.*)

MRS PETTIBONE: (*Rises, looks calmly at* PETTIBONE; *walks leisurely to the double doors; turns.*) I suppose it has not occurred to you to tell me where we are going — whether to Asia, Africa, the North Pole, or the Sandwich Islands?

PETTIBONE: I — I — You will know before — before —

MRS PETTIBONE: Before I get there? That would be delightful! (*Exit through double doors.*)

PETTIBONE: (*standing speechless, looking after her*) Oh — you are very composed! Yet I saw you start once — and — and this letter — this letter! (*Grinds teeth.*)

> (*Enter* ALFRED HASTINGS *from outside door, carrying a parcel with cuffs and shirts, etc., showing at the ends; a few books; a pair of foils; a set of boxing-gloves; a pair of riding-boots; a long pipe, and a bootjack.*)

PETTIBONE: What in the name of common-sense kept you all this time? I said at once! At once!

ALFRED: Kind and severe uncle and guardian, you did. But you also ordered me to bring all my belongings, as I was to stay here. These orders of yours clashed. My landlady objected to the removal of my property.

PETTIBONE: Then you left it, of course?

ALFRED: Oh, no; I brought it.

PETTIBONE: Those?

ALFRED: These. (*Puts things on table.*)

PETTIBONE: Is that all?

ALFRED: No; I have quite an assortment of pawn-tickets in my pockets. (*Sits luxuriously at table.*) It's the best way to have property — a fellow can move so easily.

PETTIBONE: (*starting suddenly*) Well, we have no time to talk. (*Becomes more and more excited.*) I am starting on a journey with my family.

ALFRED: (*slight surprise*) Don't say!

PETTIBONE: Yes. You are to stay here and take care of the house. No one is to know where I am going. Not a soul — not a soul.

ALFRED: Well, where is it?

PETTIBONE: I – haven't made up my mind.

ALFRED: Devilish good idea! So long as you don't know, I don't think anybody else is likely to discover.

PETTIBONE: If they do – if he follows us –

ALFRED: (*Watches* PETTIBONE *quietly, then rises.*) Let me feel your pulse.

PETTIBONE: Nonsense! Don't interrupt me – we have only four minutes. Now, as to my daughter Emmy. You love her – don't interrupt – I know it – it's all right – you have my consent.

ALFRED: By Jove! (*as if to seize* PETTIBONE's *hand*)

PETTIBONE: (*pulling away*) No – we haven't time for that! (*Goes to desk nervously. Throws papers about excitedly.*)

ALFRED: (*aside*) Gave his consent – but doesn't know what he's saying. I'll make him put it in writing. (*Scrawls quickly on note-book. Aloud*) Sign this.

PETTIBONE: What is it?

ALFRED: Your consent. You might die – I think you will.

PETTIBONE: Well, well! (*Scrawls his name.*) You are not rich – but I can trust you.

ALFRED: Thanks. So can I.

PETTIBONE: It is said cousins should not marry – that their children are liable to be lunatics. Nonsense! Perfect rubbish!

ALFRED: Nothing in it.

PETTIBONE: Nothing. (*Laughs derisively.*) Ha, ha, ha!

ALFRED: Absurd! Ha, ha!

PETTIBONE: Ridiculous! Ha, ha, ha! Simply ridiculous! Why, look here! My own parents were cousins themselves!

ALFRED: (*Stops laughing; aside*) By Jove! There's something in it after all!

PETTIBONE: Now, listen! I will tell you why I leave town so suddenly. It is because my wife (*Grasps* ALFRED's *sleeve; hisses in his ear.*) is deceiving me! She is false! False!

ALFRED: Now you're wrong, Uncle, believe me!

PETTIBONE: 'Believe me!' Don't I know? Oh! I have overlooked a good many things. Dudes and coxcombs paying all sorts of attention to her – confound them! (*Paces.*) But now I have proof – proof, I tell you! I have seen a fine gentleman lingering near for some time – following us to concerts, theatres, operas, – always getting a seat as near as possible. There have been looks exchanged – there have been letters written –

ALFRED: The deuce!

PETTIBONE: Ah! you begin to see! (*Paces.*)

ALFRED: No, sir; I don't see anything!

PETTIBONE: (*vehemently, glancing off*) Then, look! see something! Her letter! Making an appointment – here! Two o'clock! 'No one to disturb us!' Ugh! Read! Read! (*Paces.* ALFRED *looks at letter, and gives a whistle.* PETTI-BONE *starts.*) Ugh! Don't do that – read – read!

ALFRED: 'My dear Mr Smythe: I will grant you the interview you ask. Come this afternoon between one and two o'clock. My husband is at his business then, and no one will be here to disturb us. You must be very cautious, however, or you will spoil all. Yours ever, Rosabelle Pettibone.' (*Turns it over.*) This is in your handwriting, I observe.

PETTIBONE: Yes — I copied it; and then I sent the original on. He will get it! He will come! His name is Victor Smythe, damn him — and there will be some one here to disturb him!

ALFRED: Of course. You will wait and fight him!

PETTIBONE: Fight? That is what he wants — to put me out of the way! No, sir! I am going to surprise him! He will find you here to receive him!

ALFRED: Jove! You surprise me!

PETTIBONE: And you must give him a reception that he won't forget. (*Doubles fists and pantomimes.*)

ALFRED: I must, eh? (*Smiles.* PETTIBONE *sighs vigorously.* ALFRED *laughs.*) All right. I'll attend to the gentleman.

PETTIBONE: You will?

ALFRED: Certainly! Delighted — dislocate his nose.

PETTIBONE: (*delighted*) That's it!

ALFRED: Knock out an eye.

PETTIBONE: Good! Ha, ha!

ALFRED: Lacerate an ear.

PETTIBONE: Ha, ha! Yes! Ha, ha!

ALFRED: Do him up generally.

PETTIBONE: Do him up! Ha, ha!

ALFRED: Then — to avoid unpleasant results — tell him it was all a terrible mistake — wrong man — apologize — sew up his ear — set his nose — write a prescription — and charge him five pounds.

PETTIBONE: Ha, ha! You're a nephew after my own heart!

ALFRED: No! It's your daughter's heart I'm after.

PETTIBONE: Yes! I see! Ha, ha! (*Both laugh.* PETTIBONE, *suddenly*) What! (*Looks at watch.*) It's time to start! Merciful powers! Suppose the fellow should find me here! (*Calls off.*) Here — Emmy! Rosabelle! Hurry! Hurry! (*Dances back to* ALFRED. *Gets things from pockets.*) Here — money — carry you through this month. I'll send more soon. Take good care of everything — keys. Look out for this one — key to wine-cellar.

> (*Enter* MRS PETTIBONE. *She is in travelling costume. Carries several parcels, and is buttoning her glove.*)

MRS PETTIBONE: Ah, Alfred! I suppose you have not heard that we —

PETTIBONE: Yes, yes! He is to live here and take care of the house. If any one comes, he will receive them! (MRS PETTIBONE *starts slightly.* PETTIBONE *crosses to* ALFRED — *quickly.*) Did you see that?

> (ALFRED *nods.* PETTIBONE *picks up overcoat, hat, still keeping his eye on* MRS PETTIBONE.)

MRS PETTIBONE: (*aside*) If I could only get word to him not to come!

PETTIBONE: Come, come! No more delay! (*Calls.*) Emmy! Emmy! (*Glances excitedly at* MRS PETTIBONE *now and then.*)

EMILY: (*offstage*) Coming, papa! Coming!

MRS PETTIBONE: (*approaching* ALFRED) Your uncle seems to be having some kind of a fit to-day.

ALFRED: (*aside*) A mis-fit, I should say.

EMILY: (*Enters, through double doors, with travelling things, birdcage with bird, followed by* KATY, *also prepared for journey, and leading pug dogs by strings, or carrying them.*) Here I am — and — (*Sees* ALFRED.) O Alfred! Good-bye! (*Holds out her hand to him.*) Did you ever hear of such a sudden start?

ALFRED: (*to* EMILY) Your father has consented.

EMILY: What!

ALFRED: Look at that! (*Shows paper.*)

EMILY: He's crazy! (*Gives* ALFRED *a look.*)

PETTIBONE: (*He and* MRS PETTIBONE *have filled time getting ready.*) Emily! You don't intend to carry the birds! And your dogs, Rosabelle —

EMILY: But how could we leave them, with no one to take care of the darlings?

PETTIBONE: Didn't I say that Alfred is to stay here?

EMILY: Oh! Then you shall take care of my little birdies!

MRS PETTIBONE: (*Takes dogs from* KATY *and hurries to* ALFRED.) And my darlings! I'll trust them to you, Alfred! (*Gives them to him.*)

EMILY: There are the seeds. (*Gets them from* KATY *and puts packages in* ALFRED*'s hands.*) And you know about the fresh water every morning?

PETTIBONE: We must go, I tell you.

> (*Both ladies exclaim, and hurry toward outside door.*)

MRS PETTIBONE: They must have a walk every day — and no meat! And — (*getting sponge and soap from* KATY)

EMILY: (*to* ALFRED) And if their feathers come out —

MRS PETTIBONE: Oh — and the bath-sponge and soap — the dog soap — (*Puts it under* ALFRED*'s arm.*)

EMILY: And green things. Come, mamma!

> (PETTIBONE *calls. All call good-bye, and exit outside door, leaving* ALFRED *loaded with cages, dogs, and any truck that can go with them.*)

ALFRED: Good-bye! Good-bye! (*Follows them to the door, waving dogs, bird-cages, etc.; stumbles about.*) I'll take care of everything! (*Comes back into room.*) I'll give these things a dose of arsenic. Here — they can just go in here for the present. (*Puts dogs, birds, etc., off at upstage left door. Surveys the place.*) This isn't so bad! Uncle Egbert's jealousy may be deuced annoying to him, but I don't mind it in the least. An elegant mansion at my disposal — not to speak of the key to the — (*Smiles.*) Now, if I could only think of some way to raise the money for old Hiflin's note that comes due to-morrow, I'd be perfectly serene. As I can't, I'll be serene anyway. Let's see — he didn't leave me enough to — (*Looks at contents of envelope.*) No — oh, no — bare expenses, I — oh, by Jove! I forgot all about Tom. (*Goes through double doors and opens back window. Speaks off.*) Hello, there! Tom! Come in; you'll find the door open! (*Shuts window and comes back.*) I can give him a lodging now; that'll help the poor chap along a little, anyhow. Heaven knows I'd give him money if I had it; he's had a hard row to hoe. (*Sits luxuriously in easy-chair, half reclining. Smokes. Enter* TOM McDOW *from outside, stopping uncertainly at entrance to room.*) Hello!

TOM: Gee-whiffles! This ain't the place, is it?

ALFRED: Yaas — I've decided to take the house for a few months, although it isn't quite up to what I wanted.

TOM: Holy smoke! You must 'a' struck it rich!

ALFRED: Thomas, this is my uncle's house. He had gone abroad with his entire family. I am to stay here and look out for things. You are to stay and look out for me!

TOM: Yes, sir. What shall I go at first, sir?

ALFRED: Well, the first thing required is to entertain a certain gentleman named Victor Smythe, who is expected to call here between one and two. Thomas, remove my raiments. (TOM *takes* ALFRED's *traps off table, puts them into room down right and returns.* ALFRED *raises himself a little absently, feeling for watch. Pulls out pawn-ticket.*) Ah! My watch is being — 'hem — regilded. (*Reclines again.*) No matter. We can tell the time by Smythe. When he comes it'll be about one o'clock.

TOM: Will we receive him with honor, sir?

ALFRED: Eh? Oh, yes! We will honor him with one of the most scientific thrashings known to art.

TOM: (*Puts himself into pugilistic attitude.*) Thrashings? You don't mean — (*motion or two — absently, looking questioningly at the same time at* ALFRED)

ALFRED: That is the idea. I've given my word to attend to it — and I trust I can count upon you — to —

TOM: Count, Mr Hastings! I'd do anything in the world for you.

ALFRED: Thanks —

TOM: After your kindness to me, sir, and getting me out of that there scrape —

ALFRED: That's all right (*Waves hand to quiet* TOM.)

TOM: And borrowin' the money to do it —

ALFRED: But I know all about it, my boy.

TOM: And promisin' to take me into your office —

ALFRED: (*emphatically*) When I have one, Thomas.

TOM: Quite right, sir. And this note that's a-bothering you, Mr Hastings — if I could only think of some way to fix it — I'd — (*Looks about.*) If this was on'y your house, now, we could sell it, couldn't we?

ALFRED: Yes — or let it — and live on the income in affluence and luxury.

TOM: (*Tries all the chairs by sitting on them one after another.*) This here funnitoor an' fixin's would fetch a tidy little pile — an' here we are only two of us to sit in 'em. It's clear waste, sir, that's what it is!

ALFRED: Wait a minute. (*Looks around.*) It's all right!

TOM: Is it, though?

ALFRED: (*Rises.*) Yes. We'll let these rooms to lodgers! (TOM *glances about quickly.* ALFRED, *excitedly*) It's one of the most desirable places in town. Make 'em pay a month in advance, of course.

TOM: Of course — or two months — or a year, sir!

ALFRED: No — a month will do. Then I can take care of that infernal note, and keep out of the clutches of the law. I want you to go in with me on this —

TOM: I'd do anything in the world for —

ALFRED: Yes — I know. I can't pay you, though — haven't got it. But I'll take you into partnership, by Jove!

TOM: (*doubtfully*) What'll that do to me, sir?

ALFRED: We go in together, don't you see? I run the — er — the business part of it — you take care of the lodgers — we divide the profits.

TOM: Divide the prof —

ALFRED: You get half.

TOM: I gits — half! Do you really mean it, sir? (ALFRED *nods.* TOM, *delighted*) Ha, ha, ha!

ALFRED: (*Laughs and slaps* TOM *on back.*) May make your fortune, my boy.

TOM: It ain't that, sir! I don't care for the money — but — ge-whiffles! I gits half! Ha, ha, ha! That's the first time as such a thing ever occurred to me — I give ye my word, it is. (*Hops about with delight.*) What's to do sir? Oh — just gimme something to do — quick! (TOM *in his restlessness is near outside door.*)

ALFRED: The first thing is to get a sign out announcing lodgings to let; a nicely painted —

TOM: Yes, sir! (*Exit quickly, outside door.*)

ALFRED: Artistic sort of thing that will attract. Hello, the fellow's gone! (*Looks about.*) This is a clever scheme, by Jove! and he put it into my head. He'll be just the one to help me with it too. He'd do anything in the world for me. Never saw a fellow so grateful as he was shen I pulled him through that little scrape he was foolish enough to get into. (*Sits and writes.*) Now, I suppose some sort of a lease or agreement is necessary — or — let me see — 'Rules for Lodgers'. That's it! Rules is what I want. First. 'Rent must be paid strictly in advance.' (*Writes it. Looks about as if trying to think of something else.*) That's the only rule that seems to occur to me. In this case — oh — ah — (*Writes.*) 'Children and dogs' — what is it that children and dogs do? Oh, yes — (*Writes.*) That settles children and dogs. Here's another. (*Writes.*) 'Anything ordered will be charged extra.' That doesn't sound quite right, someway; but it'll have to go.

TOM: (*entering from outside, breathless*) Here it is, sir!

ALFRED: What?

TOM: The sign. (*Shows a nicely painted sign which reads: 'Elegantly furnished apartments to let.' The bottom portion is evidently broken or torn off.*)

ALFRED: In Heaven's name where did you get that?

TOM: Just down the street.

ALFRED: Buy it?

TOM: Not much — took it off a house.

ALFRED: Good gracious, my boy, that's going too far!

TOM: Only four doors past the corner, sir.

ALFRED: But, see here — you'll get us into trouble — it's theft, or burglary, or something of that kind.

TOM: Theft? No, sir. It says 'ere, 'elegantly furnished apartments', sir. They warn't nothing of the kind — they're terrors.

ALFRED: How do you know?

TOM: I see 'em through the winders, sir; the furnishin's is vile. An I says to myself,

I'll take down this lyin', swindlin' sign, an' put it where it'll speak the truth, and nothin' but the truth — an' that's on this here house, sir. An' up she goes — an' I gits half! (*Exit, outside door.*)

ALFRED: But I say — here, Tom! He's certainly taking hold of the business with a vengeance. If he goes on like this, we'll end up with elegantly furnished apartments in the police station.

TOM: (*Enters, breathless.*) It's up, sir — an' they's three parties as stands starin' at it a-ready, with their eyes as big as oyster shells.

ALFRED: But first, as to the rooms. We'll have to settle how much we're going to ask. (*He goes to different doors, followed by* TOM.)

TOM: (*murmuring to himself*) An' I gits half!

ALFRED: It isn't arranged like an ordinary house for lodgings, is it?

TOM: No, sir, I can't say as it is. (*very downcast*)

ALFRED: All the better.

TOM: (*suddenly reviving spirits*) Yes, sir. All the better.

ALFRED: More homelike —

TOM: (*eagerly*) So it is!

ALFRED: (*surveying the room*) Lodgers will have the use of this big drawing-room, with the conservatory and large front windows commanding a view of the park. Nothing like it. All the comforts of home. I say, that's a good thing — don't forget it. Give it to 'em strong, Tom.

TOM: Yes, sir. Give 'em what, sir?

ALFRED: That idea — it sounds well. All the comforts of home.

TOM: Quite right, sir. (*aside*) I'll go an' paint it on to the bottom of that there bill — 'All the comforts of home'.

ALFRED: (*going up and looking through double doors*) Now, Tom, about prices. This room has an alcove adjoining.

TOM: Yes, sir.

ALFRED: Five pound, ten.

TOM: Fi pun, ten.

ALFRED: (*about to write it down in book*) I'll put it down.

TOM: (*Sudden yell; seizes* ALFRED's *right arm.*) No! don't ye do it — oh, it's worth it — it's worth it!

ALFRED: Keep quiet. I'm only going to put it down in this book.

TOM: (*sheepishly — after staring an instant*) Oh! I thought ye was a-goin' to put the price down.

ALFRED: (*Goes to transomed door at right, followed by* TOM.) Here are two very good rooms.

TOM: Very good rooms, very go —

ALFRED: (*Turns quickly;* TOM *stops suddenly.*) Three windows.

TOM: Three an' a 'alf, sir — you didn't count that there thing. (*Points to transom over door.*)

ALFRED: That's nothing.

TOM: Nothing! It's worth ten bob extra at least, sir.

ALFRED: What possible use is the thing?

TOM: Use, sir? Can't the parties as lodges there stand on a chair or table an' git a beautiful prospect of w'ats a-goin' on in this here drorin'-room?

ALFRED: Never thought of that. (*amused*) I'll slap on the ten bob, and call it seven guineas.

TOM: (*partly aside*) An' I gits half, oh!

ALFRED: See here! There are no beds in some of these rooms.

TOM: I'll git 'em, sir.

ALFRED: Where?

TOM: Down the street.

ALFRED: (*Makes a spring, and grabs* TOM *by collar.*) I say — this sort of thing won't do, you know. Bring some down from up-stairs.

TOM: Yes, sir. (*Bounds up stairway.*)

ALFRED: We won't let the rooms up there until these are taken. Now, let me see — I must roost down here where I can keep an eye on the things. I'll take this room (*Indicates door down stage right.*) — it's the smallest of the lot.

TOM: (*calling from above*) Mr Hastings! W'ich o' these here beds'll I fetch down?

ALFRED: I'll go and look at them. (*Exit up the stairs.*)

> (*Timid knock several times. Enter* VICTOR SMYTHE *from outside. He looks into room cautiously.*)

SMYTHE: (*near door*) At last — at last I am here — in the very house where she lives — under the same roof that shelters her! I can scarcely realize it! It (*hand on heart, as if its palpitation hurt him*), it is all like a — a dream — a dream!

> (*Tremendous bang of falling furniture overhead.* SMYTHE *jumps in alarm.*)

TOM: (*upstairs*) Gee-whiffles!

SMYTHE: What was that! Every noise alarms me, for she said I must be very cautious. She must have sent every one out of the way — no one even to answer the door. That was so thoughtful of her. Now, if I can only get her to consent, and to intercede for me with Emily, I shall be the happiest man in the whole universe. And — she has already promised it. I suppose I ought to let her know I am here — she — she must be about somewhere. (*Goes towards stairs and looks about.*) Oh — my heart seems to almost —

> (*Two large feather beds and blankets fall on* SMYTHE *from above. He screams out in alarm as he falls half buried among them.* TOM *rushes down the stairs and falls into* SMYTHE *and the bedding; faces* SMYTHE *just as he is rising from among the bedding, ready to throw bolster.*)

TOM: (*rising*) That was odd, now wasn't it?

SMYTHE: (*rising from under bed*) Yes — it was a little odd. But no matter.

TOM: (*glancing critically at the bedding*) No — there ain't no pertickler harm done, sir.

SMYTHE: I knocked several times — but as no one answered, I just looked in.

TOM: Quite right, sir. I'll attend to you in just a minute. (*Drags bedding down across stage towards door up stage left, upsetting chairs, tables, etc.*)

SMYTHE: (*following*) But I just wanted to see — (*Steps on blanket and is tripped by it.*)

TOM: (*dragging things*) You can see 'em in a minute, sir. We're just a-puttin' the beds in. (*Exit left.*)

SMYTHE: (*Watches* TOM *in astonishment, hand to heart. Wipes brow.*) This is one of the servants. What shall I say to him? How — how can I be cautious? And yet she said 'be cautious, or you will spoil all'.

TOM: (*running in at door left*) Now, sir — ha, ha! I suppose you saw it?

SMYTHE: (*uncertainly*) Oh, yes; I — I saw it.

TOM: (*to himself*) He saw it! He saw that there bill with 'All the Comforts of Home' writ on it. That's w'at fetched 'im.

SMYTHE: I beg your pardon — but I'm afraid I've made a mistake.

TOM: (*quickly, alarmed*) Oh, no, you hain't! (SMYTHE, *startled, backs up toward outside door.*) Won't you look at the rooms?

SMYTHE: (*uncertainly*) Wh — what rooms? (*A bolster falls from above.* SMYTHE, *startled still more, backs away.*)

TOM: (*Runs quickly and calls up stairway.*) Say, you don't want to heave down no more o' them fur a minute — I'm a-waitin' on a customer.

SMYTHE: (*aside*) A — customer! A cus —

TOM: (*to* SMYTHE *quickly*) Now, sir, just have a look at 'em. They're simply entrancin'.

SMYTHE: I — I would like to speak to your employer, if you please.

TOM: Sorry — but ye can't just now, unless you yell up them stairs.

SMYTHE: (*cautiously, mysteriously*) I alluded to the mistress of the house.

TOM: Well, we ain't got as fur as that yet. But the lodgin's —

SMYTHE: How's that! Surely, I have always seen your master in company with a lady.

TOM: Quite likely, sir — an' so have I. But it don't follow as 'e's married to 'er, just from that.

SMYTHE: Not married? Not —

TOM: No, sir — not by no means. But these here lodgin's is —

SMYTHE: Great Heaven! (*hand to brow*) Why, this — this is horrible — and I loved the daughter — I — Great Heaven! Where would I have got to had you not opened my eyes? Here! (*Gives* TOM *money.*) Take this! Let me go! (*Exit, outside door.*)

TOM: (*Stares after* SMYTHE *an instant. Glances at the money in his hand, then throws the bolster off through archway, and meets* ALFRED *as he comes down from upstairs.*) That there individual ain't had enough sleep lately.

ALFRED: Well — have you captured a lodger?

TOM: The man was clean out of his head.

ALFRED: What did he do? (*Comes down into room.*)

TOM: He inquired for the lady of the house.

ALFRED: What!

TOM: Mebbe it was howin' to them beds fallin' on 'im.

ALFRED: Great Heavens, Tom! He has escaped us.

TOM: Eh?

ALFRED: Victor Smythe.

TOM: Gee-whiffles! (*Both rush through double doors. Throw up window and look out.*)

ALFRED: And I promised to receive him!

TOM: I'll go and drag him back, sir!

ALFRED: Here! Stop! Somebody's just going in at the door! (*Both look around.*)

TOM: (*looking out*) It's the same party, sir. He's comin' back for somethin'.

ALFRED: He'll get it, too.

TOM: We won't make no mistake this time.

> (ALFRED *and* TOM *quickly stand each side of outside door, ready to pounce upon* SMYTHE. *Knocking on door, from outside, several times.* ALFRED *and* TOM *signal each other to be ready. Enter* CHRISTOPHER DABNEY, *quietly and carefully. He turns to close door, so that his back is toward* ALFRED *and* TOM. *They suddenly jump upon him ferociously. Both shout or exclaim on climax.*)

ALFRED *and* TOM: Now we've got you! Throttle him! (DABNEY *gives cry of terror; they drag him into room.*)

ALFRED *and* TOM: Now, give it to him! Bang his nose for him!

TOM: (*alone; seeing* DABNEY) Stop! This ain't him at all!

ALFRED: Oh, the deuce! (DABNEY *gasps and gurgles, overcome with terror.*) Beg your pardon, sir — all a mistake!

TOM: Yes — you're the wrong man! It warn't your fault, though!

ALFRED: Very sorry it occurred.

DABNEY: Gi — gi — (*Motions.*) A chair!

ALFRED *and* TOM: Yes, sir! (*They let go of* DABNEY. *He sinks. They catch him again.* TOM *manages to get chair to him from behind table. They seat him in it with some difficulty.*)

DABNEY: Oh — thank you!

TOM: (*absentmindedly*) An' I gits half!

ALFRED: It was too bad; by Jove, it was!

DABNEY: Oh — never mind, sir! I was taken somewhat by surprise — you — the — oh! The fact is, I am a very nervous man. (*Shakes head sadly.*) Dreadfully nervous. Sometime you shall know why —

ALFRED: Yes — some other time. (*to* TOM) A glass of water — quick!

TOM: Yes, sir.

DABNEY: Sometime — (TOM *brings glass of water from table.*)

ALFRED: (*taking it*) Have a little water, sir! (DABNEY *wobbles nervously in chair.*)

TOM: Have another chair!

DABNEY: Thanks — there on my temples. (ALFRED *wets* DABNEY's *temples with the water.*)

TOM: A little on the bald spot, sir? (*Rubs bald spot on* DABNEY's *head, and about to pour water from pitcher on his head.*)

DABNEY: Don't! don't! don't! (TOM *stops.*) For Heaven's sake, don't rub anything there — friction in that locality sets me all on edge!

TOM: Quite right, sir. (*Gets the pitcher and tumbler, and returns to* DABNEY.)

DABNEY: (*to* ALFRED) I seem to feel better now.

ALFRED: Very glad, I assure you.

DABNEY: (*looking at* ALFRED) 'Hem — yes — er. (*Rises.*) Good-morning! (TOM *puts back the chair behind table.*)

ALFRED: How d'ye do?

DABNEY: You have — lodgings to let here?

ALFRED *and* TOM: (*together;* TOM *turning quickly to* DABNEY) Yes! Yes, sir!

ALFRED: Charming lodgings.

TOM: Can't be beat.

ALFRED: (*Pushes* TOM *aside.*) Will you look at them, sir?

TOM: Yes — just take one look, that's all! (ALFRED *motions* TOM *to be quiet.* TOM, *aside*) An' I gits half!

DABNEY: Yes — I — give me your arm, please. I'm still a little —

ALFRED: Certainly.

TOM: Cer — (ALFRED *motions* TOM *off.* DABNEY *takes* ALFRED's *arm. They go left.* TOM *follows eagerly.*)

DABNEY: (*stopping*) I do hope it's quiet and tranquil here?

ALFRED: Perfectly quiet.

TOM: Peaceful as the tomb, sir.

DABNEY: Ugh! (*gasp*) Don't speak of such things!

TOM: (*quickly starting, as if to prevent another fit*) No, sir! No — I take it back, sir!

DABNEY: No — er — children, I hope?

ALFRED: Not one.

DABNEY: No dogs? cats? parrots? pugs? puppies? canaries, and such things?

TOM: Anythin' you want, sir, we'll have it cooked to order!

ALFRED: Nothing of the kind, sir! (*pulling out paper*) You can see by the rules, sir how it is. 'Hem. 'First: rent payable strictly in advance. Second: children and dogs must keep off the grass. Third: anything ordered will be charged extra.'

DABNEY: Ah — those are the rules? Well, I hope they will be enforced about the dogs, anyway. (*They go left;* TOM *opens second door.*)

ALFRED: Every time, sir!

TOM: If I once ketch a dog here, sir, I'll — (DABNEY *goes into upstage left door. Dogs bark and jump at his shins.* DABNEY *yells and jumps about, and falls into chair holding feet in air.* TOM *and* ALFRED *shout, catching dogs, etc.* ALFRED *tries to soothe* DABNEY.)

ALFRED: (*shouting to* TOM) Take 'em up-stairs!

TOM: Quite right, sir! (*Rushes up-stairs with dogs.*)

ALFRED: Don't be alarmed, I beg.

DABNEY: (*on ottoman*) Er — er — I can't — bear a dog!

ALFRED: Neither can I — they are the most repugnant creatures on the face of the earth to me. The question is, how the devil they came here. Are they yours?

DABNEY: (*Rises.*) Mine! Mercy, no!
            (*Enter* TOM.)

ALFRED: Thank Heaven for that! I cannot let lodgings to people who keep dogs!

TOM: No, we can't let no one in these here lodgin's as keeps dogs!

ALFRED: No matter how respectable they otherwise appear. (DABNEY *looks helplessly from one to the other, shaking head to signify his innocence.*) But, as you say they are not yours, suppose you just glance at this room — it's much pleasanter than the other.

TOM: Yes. (*They conduct* DABNEY *to downstage left door.*)

DABNEY: Very well, I will look. But — are you quite sure — (*They come to door of room and open it.* DABNEY *shrinks and lifts feet, fearing more dogs.*)

ALFRED: Oh – quite, sir! Allow me to look in first –

TOM: Allow me. (*Rushes in and out again.*) Not a vestige of one of 'em, sir – an' the ones as was in that there room, I dropped 'em off o' the roof o' the house.

DABNEY: (*Sits on ottoman; face contortion.*) Er – oh – oh – don't – don't!

TOM: There he goes again, sir!

ALFRED: What seems to be wrong with you this time?

DABNEY: Oh – er – the horrible – idea! Dropped off the roof! (*Covers face.*)

TOM: (*to* ALFRED) It seems to give 'im a fit, sir, whichever way you put it.

DABNEY: Is this the apartment? (*Looks at downstage left door.*)

ALFRED: Yes – I'm sure it'll please you.

DABNEY: Um! Quiet, you say?

TOM: Well, I should say! The back yard is cat proof, and we've had the pavin' stones padded, so's to keep 'em from echoin' when any one whispers. (*Both look at him expectantly.*)

DABNEY: What terms do you ask?

TOM: (*quickly*) Er – yes. What terms do we ask?

ALFRED: With breakfast and attendance, six guineas.

TOM: (*aside*) An' I gits half! (*Rubs the plush of a chair absentmindedly.*)

DABNEY: (*Contorts face, shrinks, draws up one leg. Breaking out*) Don't! don't! don't! (*facial contortion*)

TOM: Look out! He's goin' into another o' them spasms.

ALFRED: The price is too high?

DABNEY: (*Motions before he can speak.*) Eh! Eh! Eh! For Heaven's sake don't let him rub that plush – the sound drives me wild! (ALFRED *motions* TOM *away.* TOM *retires a little.*) I'll take the lodgings.

TOM: (*exultantly*) Oh!

DABNEY: A month in advance, I believe you said? (*Pays* ALFRED. TOM *looks on with delight.*) I can move in at once, can't I?

ALFRED *and* TOM: Certainly. O yes!

TOM: Sooner, sir, if you like! (*Looks at bills in* ALFRED'*s hands. Rubs his hands together.* ALFRED *suddenly clutches* TOM. *Both look at* DABNEY, *but he does not notice.*)

ALFRED: (*to* TOM) If you don't keep away, you'll ruin the whole business!

TOM: Quite right, sir! (*Starts to bound up stairway, stumbles, and falls, catching baluster.* DABNEY *and* ALFRED *start in alarm.*)

DABNEY: Oh!

TOM: (*quickly on his feet*) An' I gits half! (*Exit up the stairs.*)

ALFRED: Calm yourself, sir – he's gone.

DABNEY: That person seems to affect my nerves painfully. I – I was born nervous, sir; an inheritance from my mother. My father was a musician, and I was put through a course to follow the same profession, and soon got an appointment to teach in a large conservatory. That was my ruin. Imagine – imagine – if you can – with my nerves – thirty pianos, innumerable violins, several cornets, piccolos, and cellos (ALFRED *sits on arm of chair, disgusted.*), crowded together in a rather small building, until the air seemed to split and bellow and boil with a perfect frenzy of the discords of pandemonium. Then, sir, to put a finishing stroke, I was ambitious enough to write an opera – and it was accepted. I quarrelled with the conductor, the soloists, orchestra, chorus-singers, was insulted by the stage-manager, and finally hissed by the audience. (*Rises, goes over to* ALFRED. *Buries face in hands.* ALFRED *attempts to rise and get away.* DABNEY *puts him back on arm of chair.*) Young man, let me advise you, if you want some cheerful occupation for your leisure hours, forge, counterfeit, burglarize, kill, rob, blow up everything with dynamite, commit suicide; but for Heaven's sake, don't write anything for the theatre! (*He falls into armchair.* ALFRED *rises from arm.*)

ALFRED: No — I've no intention of doing so. (*aside*) An interesting case, this is. I'll make my first attempt at practice on him.

> (*Knock outside;* TOM *rushes down-stairs, and opens outside door.* DABNEY *shrinks on hearing the rush.* ALFRED *soothes him.*)

DABNEY: Oh, dear! What is that rushing and jumping about?

ALFRED: Nothing, sir, I assure you.

> (*Enter* JUDSON LANGHORNE, *from outside door. He is very much of a swell; carries a small cane and gloves; dudish manners, with some impertinence.*)

LANGHORNE: Aw! Mawning! How de do? Lodgings to let heah?

ALFRED: Ah — yes.

LANGHORNE: Yaas. (*Twirls his cane.*) Ha, ha! I read your bill —

ALFRED: That's all right, sir — it was put there to read. 'All the Comforts of Home.'

LANGHORNE: Aw, yes — elegantly furnished lodgings — all the comforts of home. Nice ideah — really — ha, ha!

ALFRED: (*to* TOM) You attend to the gentleman, Thomas.

TOM: Yes, sir. This way, sir! The most excruciatingly elegant apartment as ever you seen in your life lays right here! (TOM *rushes* LANGHORNE *toward double doors.*)

LANGHORNE: Aw, don't say! Haw, haw!

TOM: Yes, I do say! Haw, haw! (*Both exit through double doors.*)

DABNEY: I hardly like the way that young man flourishes about with his cane. (*Shows nervousness.*)

ALFRED: Don't believe he'll continue it long, sir. It would exhaust him too much.

DABNEY: Do you think so?

> (LANGHORNE *and* TOM *enter.*)

LANGHORNE: I rather like the box, deah boy, and I think I'll take it.

TOM: Quite right, dear boy. (*Goes quickly to* ALFRED, *who turns to him, so that* DABNEY *will not hear.*) He's took it, sir!

ALFRED: Here — you attend to this one. See about his luggage. (*Goes to* LANG-HORNE.)

TOM: Yes, sir. (*Goes to* DABNEY. *Coming suddenly to his side and speaking in his ear*) Where shall I git it, sir?

DABNEY: Ugh! (*contortion of features*) Don't, don't — don't scream in my ear like that.

TOM: I was a-askin' about your luggage, sir.

DABNEY: I'll give you directions, and you must be, oh, so careful! (DABNEY *and* TOM *continue talking in pantomime.*)

LANGHORNE: (*kneeling on one knee on ottoman*) Judson Langhorne — yaas, deah boy; ha, ha, ha! I suppose I have the pleasure of addressing the — aw — lord of the — aw — castle. (*Whirls cane. DABNEY shrinks, and dodges slightly.*)

ALFRED: To some extent, sir. I understand you have decided to take the apartment.

LANGHORNE: Yaas — aw — yaas. I'll take it — and I want to go right in, if you don't mind.

ALFRED: Go in just when you please, sir, and stay in as long as you please We're free and easy here.

LANGHORNE: Aw — free and easy — that suits me chawmingly, deah boy!

ALFRED: But the lodgings, I regret to say, are not free — (LANGHORNE *looks at* ALFRED.) — although they may be easy.

LANGHORNE: (*laughing boisterously*) No — of course not! Haw, haw!

ALFRED: And our rule is a month in advance.

LANGHORNE: (*sudden drop*) Aw — yaas.

ALFRED: You grasp the idea, of course?

LANGHORNE: Yaas — I grasp — but — (*bright idea*) Aw — can you change me a fifty-pound note? (*hand in pocket*)

ALFRED: Oh, yes.

LANGHORNE: (*Stops, paralyzed.*) You can!

ALFRED: Certainly — send out, and have the change for you in two minutes.

LANGHORNE: Aw! (*much relieved*) Aw, no! Couldn't think of troubling you so much, deah boy. No hurry at all. (*Goes to his door.*) I'll remain right here; and when you have the change handy, let me know. (*Exit into room and closes doors.*)

ALFRED: Another one! By Jove, the business is flourishing! (DABNEY *is doing gymnastic exercises in explaining things to* TOM. TOM *imitates him, as if trying to get the idea.*) What the deuce is he up to now?

DABNEY: Now, don't forget the soda-powders, dumb-bells, rowing-machine, and sponges.

TOM: Quite right, sir.

    (LANGHORNE *sings a scale unsuccessfully in a loud voice. All listen.*)

DABNEY: (*Rises; starts with shriek.*) Ah — stop it! Stop it! I can't stand it! (*Dances about.*)

ALFRED: Oh, the devil! (*Goes up to* LANGHORNE's *door.*)

TOM: Gee-whiffles!

    (DABNEY *sits again.* LANGHORNE *begins to sing, 'Down in a Coal Mine'.*)

DABNEY: Horrors! What's that he's singing?

TOM: 'Down in a Coal Mine.' (DABNEY *stops his ears.*)

ALFRED: Hang the coal mine! Go and tell him there's a strike. Stop his howling, someway.

TOM: Yes, sir. I'd do anything in the world for you, sir. (*Exits into* LANGHORNE's *room, closing door. Sings as he goes. Inside room, singing suddenly stops.*)

DABNEY: Has — has he stopped? (*fingers out of ears cautiously*)

ALFRED: Yes, sir; it's all right now. (*Noise of banging furniture is heard in* LANG-
HORNE's *room.* ALFRED *and* DABNEY *start and turn. Enter* TOM, *with
bloody face, limping.*)

TOM: Oh, I'd do anything in the world for you, sir!

ALFRED: What did the fellow do?

TOM: Gee-whiffles! Can't ye see?

ALFRED: Let me have a word with him.

TOM: (*stopping* ALFRED) No, sir! Don't ye do it! I've just had a word with 'im —
an' it ain't encouragin'. (*Wipes blood from face.*)

DABNEY: The fellow is terrible! I shall not stay. (*Starts to leave.*)

          (ALFRED *and* TOM *both remonstrate with* DABNEY. *They bring
          him back.*)

ALFRED: But, my dear sir —

TOM: We'll fix 'im for ye.

DABNEY: But his singing — (*contortion of horror*)

ALFRED: Stop a moment! An uncle of mine, who also is nervous, had a new thing
the other day — an audiphone — just what you want. You put it in your ears,
and you can't hear a sound! (*Looks around.*)

TOM: Yes, sir; you couldn't hear the last trump ef it was ter be played!

ALFRED: Here it is. (*Finds a box on the desk, opens it, and hands* DABNEY *two
small articles for the ears.*) There, sir, try it — wonderful!

TOM: Wonderful!

DABNEY: Dear me, I'm so nervous! Is this the way?

ALFRED *and* TOM: Yes! Yes!

          (DABNEY *puts audiphones in his ears, and looks about.*)

ALFRED: How do you like it?

          (DABNEY *looks at* ALFRED *and* TOM, *unconscious of having been
          addressed.*)

TOM: He says, how do you like it?

DABNEY: Eh?

ALFRED *and* TOM: How do you like it?

DABNEY: (*Looks delighted.*) Ha, ha, ha! I cannot hear a sound!

TOM: You're a broken-down old jackass.

DABNEY: (*joyfully*) Thanks — a thousand thanks! Perfectly splendid! I won't go.
I'll stay. (*Crosses to his door.*) Ha, ha, ha! (*Exits into his room.*)

ALFRED: By Jove, that was a lucky thought!

TOM: Yes, sir; but we'll want a lot of 'em if that there feller's goin' to keep up his
singin' 'Down in the Coal Mine'.

          (*Knock outside*)

ALFRED: The door, Tom.

TOM: Yes, sir. (*Bounds off and opens door.*)

ALFRED: I wonder what kind of a creature we'll get now!

          (*Enter* FIFI ORITANSKI, *followed by her maid, and ushered in
          with great ceremony by* TOM, *who backs down near* ALFRED, *and
          stands admiring her.* FIFI *is dressed very stylishly, but is not over-
          dressed, and has the manner of a lady who knows the world pretty*

well. ALFRED *bows, and* TOM *bows in sympathy with* ALFRED, *without knowing it.*)

FIFI: You have apartments — furnished — I believe?

ALFRED: Yes, madam. (*aside*) By Jove, she's pretty!

TOM: (*aside*) Yes, by Jove, she's pretty — ha, ha!

ALFRED: (*to* TOM) Shut up!

TOM: (*Starts.*) I said she was — (*threatening sign from* ALFRED) Quite right, sir. (TOM *goes up stage rather dejectedly, and lingers, watching. To himself, absent-mindedly*) An' I gits half!

FIFI: I am looking for a pretty front room, and a smaller one adjoining for my maid.

ALFRED: (*Goes to upstage left door and opens it.*) Oh, yes, with maid adjoining. Do you think this would suit you at all?

FIFI: (*Crosses and looks into room.*) Oh, charming! Why, it's the cosiest place I've seen anywhere.

TOM: (*unable to repress himself; stepping forward*) Right you are, miss — it's a —

ALFRED: (*quickly, to* TOM) Sh! — (TOM *starts and retires silenced.*) Sh!

TOM: (*aside; sotto voce*) Oh, I'd do anything in the world for you, sir!

(FIFI *has turned, surprised.*)

ALFRED: Don't be alarmed, miss! He's harmless. (TOM *gives* ALFRED *a look, and turns and walks away.*)

FIFI: (*coming into room*) The apartment is lovely. But this room — whose is this?

ALFRED: This is a drawing-room which is for the use of all. We thought it would be a pleasant innovation.

TOM: All the comforts o' — (ALFRED *stops* TOM.)

FIFI: Oh, what a charming idea! But I'm afraid such apartments will be far too expensive for me.

ALFRED: 'Hem! (TOM *comes down a little, listening.*) Oh, no — only — six guineas.

FIFI: Oh!

ALFRED: Er — five pounds.

TOM: (*to* ALFRED, *quickly*) No, sir! No, sir! It was six quid, sir. Six quid!

ALFRED: (*shaking* TOM *off*) Hold your tongue!

TOM: (*aside; sotto voce; sadly*) An' I gits half!

FIFI: My, that isn't high at all!

TOM: (*aside*) No, it ain't!

FIFI: I will take the rooms, if you please.

ALFRED: (*bowing*) Delighted, I assure you.

FIFI: There's my card. (*Takes out pretty case. Hands* ALFRED *card.*)

ALFRED: Ah! Thank you. (*Absently fondles card to breast.*) I — I — 'hem —

FIFI: Well?

ALFRED: Yes — that is — I hope you will like it here.

FIFI: (*graciously*) Ah — how could I help it — such a sweet place — and such a charming landlord!

ALFRED *and* TOM: Ah!

TOM: (*aside, exultantly*) An' I gits half!

FIFI: (*to maid*) Gretchen, have my things brought over here.

GRETCHEN: Yes'm. (*Exits, outside door.*)

FIFI: I suppose I can move right in?

ALFRED *and* TOM: Oh, yes!

FIFI: You see, if I went, you might forget and rent the rooms to somebody else. (*Laughs, and exits into her room.*)

ALFRED *and* TOM: (*eagerly*) Oh, no! (*They recover, and look at each other.*)

ALFRED: By Jove, she's a beauty! Such an air of aristocracy! Wonder what her name — oh! (*Looks at card.*) 'Fifi Oritanski!' Charming name!

TOM: Ain't it divine!

ALFRED: An angel — such grace — and her eyes — did you notice her eyes, Tom?

TOM: I noticed one on 'em, sir.

ALFRED: One of them! What do you mean?

TOM: It was all as I had a call on — seein as I gits half.

ALFRED: Oh — ha, ha — I forgot that! And, by the way (*Takes out bills and offers* TOM *part of them.*), here's your share of what I got from the old duffer in there.

TOM: (*stoutly*) No, sir!

ALFRED: It's your share, I say.

TOM: No, sir! I wouldn't take it on no account. It ain't the money I cares for — it's only the bare idea of gittin' half. No, sir!

ALFRED: Oh, well, I'll settle with you some other time. Come, we must finish up-stairs. (*They start toward the stairs.*) We may let apartments up there yet. (*Both exit up stairs.*)

TOM: Quite right, sir!

> (*Pause. Knock on outside door several times. Enter* THEODORE BENDER, JOSEPHINE BENDER, *and* EVANGELINE BENDER. *They look about for some one.*)

BENDER: This is the place, I suppose.

JOSEPHINE: Why didn't you ring the bell?

BENDER: I couldn't find any bell.

EVANGELINE: (*timidly*) Papa, wasn't the bell on the house next to this?

BENDER: No, no!

JOSEPHINE: (*sinking into chair*) Theodore, it's outrageous! I cannot walk another step.

BENDER: (*coming down to her*) Whose fault is it, I'd like to know? You are never suited. I have said from the first we ought to have spent our few weeks in town at a hotel. There is one at the next corner. (*Sits.*)

> (EVANGELINE *surveys the room demurely.*)

JOSEPHINE: That will do, Theodore. I know perfectly well why you prefer a hotel. (EVANGELINE *sits near them.*) I've noticed how you — Evangeline, you needn't cock up your ears when your father and mother are discussing family affairs. (EVANGELINE *rises and examines pictures on wall.*) I've noticed that you were much more interested in the attractiveness of the waiting-maids than in the comfort of the room.

BENDER: Oh, Josephine, my dear!

JOSEPHINE: In addition to that, the expenses are simply scandalous.

BENDER: Well, well, we need not mind a few pounds more or less. We've feathered our nest pretty well.

JOSEPHINE: Yes; because I keep my thumb on your hardly-earned shillings — and I intend to do so still.

BENDER: (*Sighs.*) I know it.

JOSEPHINE: Is there a living soul in this house?

BENDER: (*Rises.*) Ah, here's some one at last!

DABNEY: (*Enters from his room and walks up and down in great glee, not observing the* BENDERS.) An excellent invention! I can hear absolutely nothing!

JOSEPHINE: (*meeting* DABNEY) Sir, we have come to look at the —
  (DABNEY *stops and looks at her.*)

BENDER: (*coming to* DABNEY) We want to see the apartment, sir.
  (DABNEY *looks blank.*)

JOSEPHINE: Why, he must be hard of hearing!

BENDER *and* JOSEPHINE *and* EVANGELINE: (*together; coming close to*
  DABNEY*; loud voices*) We want to look at the rooms.

DABNEY: Did somebody make a remark?

JOSEPHINE: Rooms! Rooms! Rooms!
  (BENDER *joins in the effort. Motions* EVANGELINE, *who joins in
  also in a sweet, high key.*)

JOSEPHINE *and* BENDER *and* EVANGELINE: Rooms! Rooms! Rooms! (*They
  stop, out of breath.*)

DABNEY: (*after looking at them an instant*) Delightful! Heavenly! Ha, ha! (*Dances
  a little.*)
  (JOSEPHINE, EVANGELINE, *and* BENDER *move away, alarmed.*)

EVANGELINE: Mamma, what's the matter with him?

JOSEPHINE: He's crazy — don't go near him, child. Come! Come!
  (*Enter* TOM *and* ALFRED, *rushing down-stairs.*)

ALFRED: For heaven's sake, get him away; he'll ruin the whole business!

TOM: Quite right, sir! (*Hustles* DABNEY *off into his room, going in with him.*)

ALFRED: (*Bows to the* BENDER *family as if nothing were wrong.*) It was all a
  mistake, madam, I assure you. I am the proprietor of the house.

JOSEPHINE *and* BENDER *and* EVANGELINE: Oh!

ALFRED: That was merely a nervous gentleman who is quite deaf.

BENDER: Yes — we noticed it.

ALFRED: (*aside*) By Jove! What a lovely girl!

JOSEPHINE: Hum! We came to look at the lodgings, sir, which you advertise.

ALFRED: Ah! Yes? (*expectantly*)

JOSEPHINE: But I'm afraid you haven't very quiet people here.

ALFRED: Let me assure you, madam, they are so quiet that it is like a Sunday-
  school.
  (LANGHORNE *suddenly sings in his room 'Home, Sweet Home', in
  loud voice. All start.*)

JOSEPHINE: Mercy! What is that dreadful noise?

ALFRED: (*aside*) Confound the fellow — he will make a beggar of me!
  (FIFI *suddenly starts practicing the scales in her room.*)

BENDER: (*pricking up his ears*) Ah! A woman's voice! (*Starts toward* FIFI's
  door.*)

JOSEPHINE: Theodore!

(BENDER *stops suddenly. Noise of banging and crashing inside* DABNEY's *room. Enter* TOM.)

TOM: (*Calls.*) Help! Help! Help! Oh, Mr Hastings! The man in there has got them audiphones down in his ears, an' he can't git 'em out! He's smashin' everythin' to smithereens!

   (*Noise of banging furniture and crashing glass in* DABNEY's *room. All start, alarmed. Enter* DABNEY, *in agony, dancing about, overturning furniture, and calling for help at the top of his voice.* JOSEPHINE *and* EVANGELINE *scream, and run hither and thither.* BENDER *dodges, alarmed, calling out.* TOM *and* ALFRED *hold* DABNEY.)

DABNEY: Help! Pull 'em out! Help! It'll be the death of me!

CURTAIN

ACT II

Scene is same as Act I. Small changes are made in the position of the furniture, etc., as if a few days had passed, and the house had been used. Enter LANGHORNE *from outside, in haste, as if he had been pursued by some one. He closes door with bang, and stands a moment, breathing hard. Soon he strolls down into room, recovering himself.*

LANGHORNE: What a dooce of a chase the fellow gave me! (*Wipes brow carefully. Twirls mustache.*) Upon my soul, I had no ideah my tailor could run so. He ought to enter for one of the — aw — what do you call — it's at the Agricultural Hall. Lucky thing I threw him off the scent; for if he found out I'm heah — dooce take it — I'd have to move again.

   (*Enter* TOM *from up-stairs, with tray of breakfast things.*)

LANGHORNE: Look heah!

TOM: (*Who was crossing with tray, stops suddenly.*) Same to you, sir.

LANGHORNE: In case any one should honor me with a call during the course of the next few days — I'm — aw — not at home. (*Turns, and goes up to his door. Turns back.*) You'd better remember it too, or I'll cut off your ears.

TOM: Quite right, sir; and when you undertake it, you'll find as the ears has got somethin' to say on the subject.

LANGHORNE: (*bullying*) What — you dare to — (*as if to strike with cane*)

TOM: (*drawing back the breakfast tray threateningly*) Look out, or you'll git a dose of coffee an' eggs what'll refresh ye wonderful! You took me by surprise the other day, when ye flung that there furnitoor about; but ye better lay low now, ef ye know what's good for ye.

LANGHORNE: Such — aw — impertinence — from a servant!

TOM: I'd respectfully inform you as I ain't no servant. No, sir! (*swelling up with dignity*) I'm in on it.

LANGHORNE: In on it?

TOM: (*turning grandly*) Yes — in on it. (*proudly*) I gits 'alf.

   (*Exit* LANGHORNE *into his room. Bell rings violently in* DABNEY's *room.* TOM *suddenly drops from his grand manner.*)

TOM: Comin', sir — comin! (*Starts toward* DABNEY's *room. Bell rings from up-stairs.* TOM *stops and starts toward the stairs.*) There goes that up-stairs lodger, as always wants to know what time it is. (*Calls up-stairs.*) Well, sir!

VOICE: (*above*) Won't somebody tell me what time it is?
        (*Bell rings violently in* DABNEY's *room.*)

TOM: It's a quarter before — (*Breaks.*) Comin', sir — comin!
        (*Bell rings again from up-stairs.*)

VOICE: (*above*) I say, can't somebody tell me what time it is?

TOM: Be there in a minit, sir.

VOICE: Twenty minutes to what?

ALFRED: (*entering from his room, downstage right*) Tom, hold on! (TOM *stops and meets* ALFRED.) Has she been out? (TOM *looks blankly at* ALFRED, *who glances off.*) Have you — have you seen her this morning?

TOM: No, sir, I ain't. Who did you mean?

ALFRED: Why — the little — er (*Motions toward the* BENDER *door.*) — that is — Miss Bender.

TOM: Oh, yes, sir; I seen her.

ALFRED: (*eagerly*) Yes; did she — did she leave any word — any —

TOM: Oh, yes; I'd almost forgot — I — (*Bell rings violently in* DABNEY's *room.*) Oh, Lord! Yes, sir! Coming! (*Starts toward* DABNEY's *door.*)

ALFRED: But wait — I want to know — wait!
        (TOM *stops. Bell rings up-stairs.*)

VOICE: (*above*) Is anybody going to tell me what time it is, or not?

TOM: (*Starts up a little. Bell rings violently in* DABNEY's *room.*) Gee-whiffles! Could you just tell that up-stairs man the time? If I don't give the musical galoot this here breakfast, he'll have one of them terrible spasms. (TOM *rushes off to* DABNEY's *room.*)

ALFRED: (*going up*) Confound the up-stairs man! He's the worst nuisance in the lot. (*Calls up-stairs.*) Did anybody speak up there?

VOICE: (*up-stairs*) Yes, I spoke — Struthers.

ALFRED: Ah, I thought I heard your voice, Mr Struthers. Did you want anything?

VOICE: Want anything? My soul! I've been asking what time it is, at the top of my voice, for the past fifteen minutes. I want to set my watch.

ALFRED: Sorry you had so much trouble. It is now between a quarter-past ten and twenty minutes before two. (ALFRED *comes forward with an air of triumph.*)

VOICE: (*up-stairs; very distinctly*) Thanks. I was five minutes slow.

ALFRED: (*aside*) Well, by Jove! (*Comes down, looking longingly at the* BENDER *door.*) It's useless. I can't do anything but watch for her — and think of her — and dream of her. The sweet little witch, with her roguish eyes! How shy she was at first; but when her charming timidity wore away — when she grew to have confidence in me — (*An ecstatic look; he sinks on a chair. Sighs. Suddenly looks up.*) Great Heavens! What have I been thinking of all this time! (*Rises.*) Oh, this is outrageous! I didn't suppose the little darling would take everything I said in earnest, until I found I was taking it in earnest myself. I must pull up, confound me! I must let her know in some way of my engagement to Emily.

TOM: (*entering from* DABNEY's *room in a hurry*) Say, since you've been
a-doctorin' that cove in there, he's took on most singular.
ALFRED: I'll look in on him again, by and by.
TOM: Ef I was you, I wouldn't. Every time you look in he takes on worse. (*Bell
rings in* DABNEY's *room.*) Yes, sir! Coming! (TOM *starts off.*) He'll git that
bell wore out ef he goes on like this. (*Stops suddenly.*) Gee-whiffles! (*Takes
out note from pocket.*) I'd nearly forgot it again, sir. She told me to give it
into your own hands, and I –
ALFRED: (*Snatches note.*) What! (*Opens it eagerly.*)
TOM: (*aside*) There's one thing sure, an' that is that he's took clean off his feet.
(*Bell rings in* DABNEY's *room.*) Coming, sir – coming. (*Exits.*)
ALFRED: (*Absorbed in note – reads.*) 'Dear Mr Hastings: Mamma and papa are
going out this morning, but I have such a dreadful headache that I cannot go
with them. I hope you will not be alarmed about the headache, as it is one of
the kind that comes on when I would rather have a call from some one I
know than go to the Park!' (*Laughs ecstatically, and kisses the note.*) 'I have
so much to tell you, and I hope you will be glad to see me. Your own
Evangeline.' (*Looks up ecstatically.*) 'Your own Evangeline!' (*Kisses note
again. Sudden revulsion. Starts to his feet.*) By Jove! Gone as far as this
already! (*Walks about.*) Oh, see here, my boy, this sort of thing won't do! It
won't do at all.
> (*Enter* BENDER *from his room, upstage right, carrying pipe and bag
> of tobacco, etc. He looks at* ALFRED *a moment, holding door open
> behind him.*)
JOSEPHINE: (*Speaks from in her room.*) Now, remember what I say!
BENDER: (*speaking back through door*) Yes, my love. (*Closes door quickly, with
muttered blasphemy. Turns.* ALFRED *and* BENDER *face each other.*) Young
man, I am about to give you a piece of advice.
ALFRED: (*Smiles.*) Kind, I'm sure!
BENDER: Before you marry, ask your intended her opinion of the fragrant weed.
She will tell you at that time that she adores it. Proceed at once to write this
statement down in black and white, and make her sign it.
ALFRED: (*laughing*) Is that a necessary formality?
BENDER: It'll save you many unhappy hours. (*Glances nervously at his door.*) You
may now witness the result of my failure to procure such a document. (*Holds
up pipe, etc.*) I am driven from home. Dressing gown and slippers must be
abandoned in order to find a place outside for a soothing whiff.
ALFRED: Not outside. Right here, Mr Bender.
BENDER: (*pleased*) You allow it?
ALFRED: Certainly. 'All the Comforts of Home', you know.
BENDER: Yes; but that isn't a comfort of home according to my experience.
(*Lights pipe with great satisfaction. Chuckles. Smokes.*) I'd like to compli-
ment you, Mr Hastings.
ALFRED: How so?
BENDER: You've got a way with you, sir, that affects my wife in a most extra-
ordinary manner. (*puffing*)
ALFRED: You surprise me!

BENDER: Really! Makes her almost amiable. (*Starts suddenly and looks at his door.*)

ALFRED: (*laughing*) Oh, I'm sure she is always that.

BENDER: (*drily*) Are you? (*Puffs.*)

JOSEPHINE: (*opening door*) Theodore!

BENDER: Yes, my angel! What did you wish?

JOSEPHINE: Oh, I only want to keep track of you, that's all. (*Closes door.*)

BENDER: (*Motionless, face impassive, he exchanges a glance with* ALFRED. ALFRED *amused.*) That's all. Possibly you think it's a pleasure to be under police supervision.

ALFRED: (*laughingly*) But I'm afraid you give Mrs Bender some reason for this distrust.

BENDER: (*Pleased; takes pipe out of mouth; eyes twinkle. He glances around.*) Well, I must confess that I have always been — 'hem — an admirer — a devoted admirer — of the fair sex. (*Rises and walks nearer to* ALFRED.) And I cannot say entirely without success. Ha, ha, ha! (*Laughs and digs* ALFRED *in the ribs. Both laugh.*)

ALFRED: Ha, ha! I begin to see.

BENDER: Of course in our little town there isn't much latitude.

ALFRED: No; rather limited, I suppose.

BENDER: Yes, decidedly. (*Glances toward his room.*) Decidedly limited. But here in London I did hope to have a little romance or two.

ALFRED: And Mrs B., I presume, is keeping the latitude down pretty low here?

BENDER: Down to nothing, sir.

TOM: (*Enters from* DABNEY's *room and crossing toward stairs.*) Now he's a-callin' fur camomile tea and a bottle of chloroform. (*As he is going, bell rings up-stairs. Shouts up-stairs from door.*) Quarter past eleving! (TOM *rushes off outside door.*)

BENDER: I say, what female voice did I hear a short time ago?

ALFRED: Oh, that was Miss Oritanski.

BENDER: Ah — er! Miss Oritanski lives in the house, then?

ALFRED: Oh, yes; her apartments are there — opposite yours. (*amused at* BENDER's *eager interest*)

BENDER: Indeed! Such charming neighbors — and I didn't know it! I — ha, ha! (*Looks longingly at* FIFI's *door.*)

JOSEPHINE: (*coming to door*) Theodore, are you there?

BENDER: (*Starts visibly.*) Eh — oh — yes, yes; I'm here! (*Grinds his teeth and mutters.* JOSEPHINE *closes door.*)

TOM: (*entering from outside door*) Doctor, that there nervous galoot ordered a drink o' chloroform, an' them drug-shop chaps won't let me have it unless I gits an order.

ALFRED: I'll go and write you a prescription — one that'll make him sleep for a month.

TOM: Yes, sir. Wish you would, sir.

ALFRED: Make yourself perfectly comfortable, Mr Bender. (*Exits into hall, followed by* TOM.)

BENDER: (*following a little way*) Thanks, my boy, I'm perfectly comfortable, so

long as Mrs Bender doesn't come out. (FIFI's *door opens.*) Ah, I really believe
— Miss Oritanski is — ha, ha! (*Glances nervously toward his room.* FIFI
enters.) Upon my soul, she's pretty as a picture! (*Chuckles; delighted and
anxious.*)

FIFI: (*aside*) Dear me, what can I do? My dressmaker will not send the other
costume unless I pay her bill to-day, and the management has refused to
advance me another penny. (*Sits on ottoman.*)

BENDER: (*aside*) Wonder if I could venture to address her? (*Glances around
toward his wife's door.*) I'll chance it, anyhow. (*Takes a hasty survey of himself in a large mirror. He comes down with a slight embarrassment, and a trifle
of anxiety.*) Ah — ha — ha — Miss Oritanski, I believe! (FIFI *looks quickly
around at* BENDER.) I hope you won't take offence at my seeming presump-
tion, but as I'm to some extent a neighbor of yours, I thought you might
allow me to introduce myself.

FIFI: Certainly — what name?

BENDER: E — Bender — Theodore — Theodore Bender. And entirely and most
devotedly at your service.

FIFI: (*politely, but with a slight frigidity*) Very much pleased, I'm sure.

BENDER: (*Approaches her; gives a glance toward his door.*) I — 'hem — I am a
retired — e — business man — from one of the provincial towns, and am
spending a few weeks in London for pleasure, and — e — recreation —
recreation. (*Smiles, glancing at his door.*)

FIFI: (*aside; the dawn of a sudden idea shown by her eyes*) Retired! Then he's rich.
(*Rises and bows. Aloud*) You cannot imagine how pleased I am at having such
an agreeable neighbor. (*Sits again.*)

BENDER: (*aside; chuckles*) She likes me! (*Lingers, occasionally looking nervously
at his door.*) Are you here — for — e — recreation?

FIFI: Oh, dear, no! I'm not so fortunate as that. I have an engagement.

BENDER: (*not understanding*) Oh — engagement?

FIFI: Yes. I am singing at the Opera Comique.

BENDER: Opera Comique! (FIFI *nods demurely. To himself*) An actress!
(*Chuckles.*) The dream of my life has been to meet one, and here it is actually
fulfilled. The dream of my life fulfilled — and (*sudden change*) — the dream
of my wife in the next room.

FIFI: Won't you sit down, Mr Bender.

BENDER: Ah, thank you. (*He is about to accept the invitation, and starts toward
FIFI as if to sit. He stops suddenly, and looks nervously at his wife's door.*)
Ahem — I — I believe I'd rather stand. (*with a longing look at the seat by
FIFI's side*) My doctor has ordered me to — e — take all the exercise I can.

FIFI: And won't he let you sit down? Dear me! How dreadfully you must suffer.

BENDER: Yes — I suffer (*Glances toward his door.*) — more than I can tell. (*aside*)
Ah! if we were only somewhere else! (*a thought*) I wonder if I could? (*Goes
to his door; pauses.*) I'll try it. Confound it, I'd try anything. (*He quietly
turns key in door. Look of joy.*) Ha, ha! I've locked her in!

FIFI: Mr Bender!

BENDER: (*Starts.*) Eh — oh, yes! (*Goes toward* FIFI *with great relief evident in his
manner.*) I was just — e — locking my door.

FIFI: I saw you were.

BENDER: So many valuables in there — it's safer you know.

FIFI: Yes. (*nodding demurely*) Safer to keep them there.

BENDER: Yes, ha, ha! (*Laughs in an uncertain manner.* FIFI *bursts into a merry laugh.* BENDER *laughs with her, then suddenly stops.*) 'Hem — e — perhaps we'd better not laugh quite so audibly.

FIFI: Perhaps not — the valuables might hear.

BENDER: Ahem — yes, they might. (*He is about to sit by* FIFI'*s side, on ottoman.*)

FIFI: (*Rises.*) What! disobeying the doctor's orders, Mr Bender? (*Sits.*)

BENDER: Oh — d — e — hang the doctor's orders! (*Sits on ottoman.*) Er — Miss Oritanski — I've been smoking here. If I'd known you were coming out —

FIFI: Don't speak of it, Mr Bender. I like it.

BENDER: (*rapturously; aside*) She likes it. (*aloud*) So you're singing at the Opera Comique? (FIFI *nods.*) What — e — what part?

FIFI: In the new piece tomorrow, I'm Prince Vladimir.

BENDER: Prince Vladimir! (*Draws a sigh of delight.*) How perfectly — e — sweet you must look in the part of a prince.

FIFI: I'm going to try one of the costumes on this morning. Would you like to see it?

BENDER: Like to — I — (*Sudden stop, and looks at his door.* FIFI *laughs lightly, amused.*) It would delight me beyond words.

FIFI: There's only one obstacle.

BENDER: (*Looks at his door.*) I know it.

FIFI: (*laughingly*) Oh, I don't mean the valuables.

BENDER: What, another!

FIFI: Ah, Mr Bender! I am afraid you don't know dressmakers.

BENDER: Well, I've met — 'hem — a few.

FIFI: But not mine. Oh, she's a tyrant! Now, what do you think she has done to-day?

BENDER: (*blinking in expectation of a horrible revelation*) What has she done to-day?

FIFI: Refused to send my most important costume because there is a trifle due on the bill. Of course I shall send to the management and have it attended to, but the delay — and the insult! (*Rises and walks indignantly.*) The humiliation!

BENDER: (*Rises and follows her.*) Outrageous! (*Thinks.*) My dear young lady — would you consider it intrusive — if I — I asked the favor of — e — arranging this little matter?

FIFI: (*turning; feigned surprise*) You!

BENDER: Ah — don't misconstrue me! It has been the dream of my life — to — do something for Art.

FIFI: Oh, how good you are! I feel that you are a friend. (*Impulsively holds out her hands.* BENDER *eagerly kisses her hand;* FIFI *retreats quickly a step or two.* BENDER *glances at his door and gives* FIFI *an uncertain smile.*) Ah, I am afraid I have been too frank with you!

BENDER: No, no, not at all! Not at all!

FIFI: And yet — it seems to me that I could trust you.

BENDER: You could — you could!

FIFI: But (*Speaks doubtfully.*) I'm dreadfully afraid it would hardly be right.

BENDER: Yes, but —

FIFI: Well, I will put your friendship to the test. Wait just a moment, and I'll get the bill. (*Exits quickly into her room.*)

BENDER: (*delighted; chuckles*) Ha, ha! We're getting along charmingly. Charmingly! Ah (*walking*), I haven't forgotten all I knew. No! (*Shaking head in merriment and chuckling to himself. Comes before his wife's door and stops; stands looking at it.*) And Josephine locked in too, ha, ha, ha! That wasn't bad, now — that wasn't half bad.

FIFI: (*entering with a bill*) Here it is, Mr Bender.

BENDER: Give it to me.

FIFI: (*playfully holding it away*) My, how imperious you are! (*Imitates him.*) 'Give it to me.'

BENDER: Ah — but I beg — (*Tries to get the bill.*)

FIFI: You are in a hurry because you want to get rid of me.

JOSEPHINE: (*rattling her door*) Theodore! Theodore!

BENDER: Here, quick! Yes, my love!

FIFI: There, take it! (*Hurriedly puts bill into BENDER's hand. Skips to her door.*) Ta-ta! (*Throws a kiss to BENDER and exits into her room.*)

JOSEPHINE: Theodore! what does this mean?

BENDER: (*hastening to door*) What is it, my angel?

JOSEPHINE: Open this door.

BENDER: Why, is it locked? (*Unlocks and opens door.*) How did that occur?

JOSEPHINE: (*Enters, dressed for the street, and bringing BENDER's hat and cane. Putting them on table, she strides on, looking about in silence, with evident suspicion.*) Did you lock that door?

BENDER: I, my love!

JOSEPHINE: It's perfectly evident that you did.

BENDER: (*looking at his pipe*) Ah — ahem — you — I was smoking — and —

JOSEPHINE: Well?

BENDER: I thought the smoke might get in, you know. Ahem — (*slight start, realizing he has made a blunder*) Of course it must have been in a fit of abstraction, my dear.

JOSEPHINE: Um! It was a fit of something, I've no doubt. (*aside*) I wonder if anything has been going on?

BENDER: (*aside*) She'll be over it before long. (*Glances aside at the bill. Starts.*) Ha, eighty-six pounds!

JOSEPHINE: (*turning*) I am ready to go now, Theodore.

BENDER: (*aside*) Jerusalem! I haven't a fiver to my name. She takes care of the money. Now, how the devil —

JOSEPHINE: What is the matter with you this morning?

BENDER: Eh? Me? Oh — nothing. Come, my dear. (*Starts toward outside door.*)

JOSEPHINE: (*following; aside*) I shall watch that man very closely.

BENDER: Isn't Evangeline coming?

JOSEPHINE: You know very well she has a headache.

BENDER: I thought it might be better.

JOSEPHINE: She says it's worse – and – (*aside*) Now, I think of it, I'd better just lock the door. One can never be too careful with young girls. (*Locks door and puts key into her pocket.*)

BENDER: Good Lord, I've got to get this money somehow!

JOSEPHINE: (*going to table to get hat and cane*) There's your hat. There's your cane. (*She jams his hat upon his head.*) Come!

BENDER: Yes, my angel! (*Turns at outside door and glances toward* FIFI's *door.*)
    (*Enter* TOM *from the stairs and* ALFRED *from outside, meeting* JOSEPHINE *and* BENDER. TOM *has a cup of tea and a package; he crosses to* DABNEY's *door and exits.*)

JOSEPHINE: (*sweetly*) Ah, Mr Hastings, good-morning!

ALFRED: (*Bows politely and crosses around in front of table, and up to* JOSEPHINE.) Good-morning, my dear Mrs Bender. Off for a little constitutional?

JOSEPHINE: (*very pleasantly*) Yes; isn't it a lovely day? (*very sweetly*) Come, Theodore.
    (BENDER *gets in a look at* ALFRED. *Eyes up.*)

ALFRED: A very charming time to you!

BENDER: (*to* ALFRED, *at door*) Oh, don't, my boy! (JOSEPHINE *laughs. She and* BENDER *exit outside door.*)

ALFRED: (*coming down*) They're safely gone. Now to Evangeline! (*Goes to door and knocks cautiously.*) The little darling!

EVANGELINE: Who is it?

ALFRED: How is your headache, Miss Bender?

EVANGELINE: Oh, is it you? (*Tries to open door.*)

ALFRED: Yes; who else should it be?

EVANGELINE: Why, I can't get out.

ALFRED: Is the door locked?

EVANGELINE: Yes; isn't the key there?

ALFRED: No; but I'll soon have one. (*Feels quickly in pockets. Glances about. Runs to table and looks.*)

TOM: (*entering from* DABNEY's *room and going across quickly toward stairs*) Now he wants a mustard plaster, and a pail o' hot water for his feet.

ALFRED: Tom!

TOM: (*startled*) Gee-whiffles! I didn't see you, sir.

ALFRED: Haven't you any keys about you? I must open that door.

TOM: (*pulling out bunch of keys*) Quite right, sir. (*Tosses them to* ALFRED.) I ain't never seen nothin' that one o' them wouldn't open. (*Hurries to outside door.*)

ALFRED: Ah – thanks.

TOM: Don't mention it. (*aside*) An' I gits 'alf! (*Starts off; bell rings up-stairs. Yells up-stairs.*) 'Alf-past eleving! (*Exit.*)

VOICE: (*up-stairs*) I want to know what – oh –
    (*Enter* LANGHORNE *from his room, crossing toward outside door.*)

ALFRED: Ah, Mr Langhorne, going out for a stroll?

LANGHORNE: Yah – yah, my deah boy. (*Exit.*)

(ALFRED *quickly tries keys to* EVANGELINE's *door and soon opens it. He leaves the key in the lock. Enter* EVANGELINE, *demurely.*)

EVANGELINE: Wasn't it dreadful of mamma to lock me in?

ALFRED: Simply diabolical. But do you happen to remember, little dear, what it is that laughs at locks? (*Takes* EVANGELINE's *hand in his.*)

EVANGELINE: That laughs at locks?

ALFRED: Yes.

EVANGELINE: (*looking down; shakes head*) No – I – I haven't any idea.

ALFRED: Shall I tell you?

EVANGELINE: (*Looks at him.*) Perhaps you'd better not.

ALFRED: Yes – but perhaps I'd better. (*She looks up.*) It is love.

EVANGELINE: (*Looks at ground.*) Oh – (*Looks at him.*) I thought love laughed at locksmiths, Mr Hastings.

ALFRED: (*Laughs.*) It laughs at anything, Evangeline, that tries to keep us apart. (*pause*)

EVANGELINE: (*Gets away, slightly embarrassed. She turns suddenly and goes to* ALFRED.) Alfred – oh! (*Covers mouth with hand in embarrassment.*)

ALFRED: (*quickly*) That's right – that's right!

EVANGELINE: Listen. Mamma locked me in. It shows that she's suspicious, and will come back any moment to look after me.

ALFRED: How very unfeeling on her part!

EVANGELINE: Oh, but that's the way mothers are, you know; so very suspicious and watchful.

ALFRED: So it is – and I can't say I blame them very much for it either; that is, I don't blame your mother. Why, if you belonged to me – (*Pauses, looking into her eyes.*)

EVANGELINE: (*timidly*) If – if – I belonged to you?

ALFRED: (*with feeling*) If you were mine, little dear, my own, you know, and nobody's else, I'd be watchful too. Why, I'd be simply wretched every moment you were out of my sight.

EVANGELINE: Would you?

ALFRED: Indeed, I would!

EVANGELINE: How do you know?

ALFRED: (*low and earnest voice*) Because – because I am now (*slight pause*). So you see, it wouldn't be right for me to find fault with your mother for being watchful, would it?

EVANGELINE: (*suddenly starting away*) No – and she is – dreadfully (*Looks about anxiously.*) – and we must be very careful. You stand there in that door (*pointing towards doorway to stairs and outside and going herself to her door.* ALFRED *moves toward outside door.*), and I will stay close by this door. Then we can talk; and when you hear any one coming, I can run in, and you must be sure to lock the door just the way it was.

ALFRED: Ah – but –

EVANGELINE: Please! please! please! Any one coming? (*They take up positions as* EVANGELINE *suggested.*)

ALFRED: But, Evangeline — can't I come a little nearer?

EVANGELINE: Oh, this is quite near! See (*Reaches out hand.*), you can reach my hand from there.

ALFRED: (*quickly catching her hand, and holding it*) So I can!

EVANGELINE: Oh — I didn't mean for you to do it!

ALFRED: (*nearer to her*) My little darling! Have you thought of me once — since yesterday?

EVANGELINE: (*after pause*) Hundreds and hundreds of times.

ALFRED: You have! (*Holds her in his arms.*)

EVANGELINE: (*with some embarrassment*) Yes. Have you — thought of — of me any?

ALFRED: Thought of you! Will you believe me if I tell you how much?

EVANGELINE: Oh, yes! I could never doubt your word — that is, if it is not too much, you know.

ALFRED: I'm afraid it is — if I should really tell you how much I've thought of you.

EVANGELINE: Then perhaps you'd better not. But you might just tell me how many times; perhaps I would believe that.

ALFRED: How many times? (*She nods demurely.*) How many times I've thought of you? (*She nods.*) Only once.

EVANGELINE: Once! (ALFRED *nods.*) Since yesterday.

ALFRED: Only once — since yesterday; for I've thought of nothing else, my little darling — and no one else — and so that one thought has lasted me the whole time.

EVANGELINE: (*Reconciled, she allows him to draw her close again.*) O Alfred! I cannot bear to think we are to leave London in only a few weeks.

ALFRED: What matter, my little love — I shall follow you wherever you go.

EVANGELINE: Will you? I — I don't know how it is, but even on the second day we came here, it seemed as if we had known each other for hundreds and hundreds of years. You were so good — so kind — and so, of course — I liked you very much — you see.

ALFRED: Liked me? Ah — but don't you — just a little more than like — just a little?

EVANGELINE: (*embarrassed, in a low voice*) I like you — very much — of course —

ALFRED: How much? Enough to make it love — just a little love?

EVANGELINE: (*pause*) I'm afraid so.

ALFRED: (*holding her*) You dear! (*Holds* EVANGELINE's *hand. Suddenly, she buries her face on his bosom in confusion.* ALFRED, *aside*) Merciful heavens! What have I been saying?

        (*Enter* TOM *from outside.*)

TOM: All the Comforts of Home! (*Perceives them.*) Beg parding! (*Exit upstairs.* ALFRED *and* EVANGELINE *start away from each other quickly.*)

EVANGELINE: Did he see that I — that you — that we — ?

ALFRED: No — I don't think he saw it. But I have a better idea than the one you had a while ago. There's Langhorne's room — no one in it. Window commands view of street — we can chat there, and see the moment any one comes near the house. (*Holds out his hand.*)

EVANGELINE: That is a good place. (*Takes his hand, and they both skip quickly into* LANGHORNE's *room and stand near the window, so that they are in sight. They converse.*)

> (*Enter* BENDER *suddenly from outside, breathing as if he had come in a violent hurry.*)

BENDER: I've escaped! That is to say, by some unfortunate accident I lost my wife in the crowd. (*Looks at* FIFI's *door.*) That money! There's only one way — I must raise it on Josephine's diamonds. She scarcely ever wears them — and I'll write Bleecker for the money, and get them out again before she notices it. (*Goes down to his door.*) But the devil of it is, what Evangeline will say. If I could only get her out of the room on some pretext or other! (*Listens at door.*) She seems to be asleep. My soul — that would be fortunate! (*He opens door very cautiously and looks in.*) Why, she isn't there! (*Looks about.*) All the better — all the better! (*Exit into room.*)

> (*Bell rings in* DABNEY's *room. Pause. Bell rings again. Enter* BENDER *from his room with a jewel case which he tries to conceal under his coat.*)

BENDER: There, ha! ha! Burglarizing my own room! But where the deuce can Evangeline be? I'll lock the door — for I'll be back immediately. (*Locks door, taking key out.*) How careless, to leave the house open like this! Some one might have got in as easy as not, and stolen these diamonds, and then what in the devil's name would I have done? (*Goes toward stairs, putting key in his pocket.*)

VOICE: (*upstairs*) Is anybody there?

BENDER: (*starting, frightened*) Ough! Oh, Lord! (*Recovers; speaks up-stairs.*) Yes; what do you want?

VOICE: (*up-stairs*) I want to know what time it is?

BENDER: The devil take him!

VOICE: (*up-stairs*) I want to set my watch.

BENDER: (*calling up-stairs*) Well, set it back three-quarters of an hour. (*Exit, outside door.*)

> (*Bell rings long and continuously in* DABNEY's *room.*)

ALFRED: (*coming down into room, followed by* EVANGELINE) Good heavens! What a fiendish disturbance that fellow in there makes!

EVANGELINE: What did you give him such an unearthly bell for?

ALFRED: The only one I could find. By Jove — a good idea! Do you know how they go to work to muffle a bell?

EVANGELINE: Why, yes; just tie a piece of flannel around the tongue.

ALFRED: I will proceed to muffle Dabney's bell. (*Squeezes her hand.*) Be back in a minute, darling. (*Exit into* DABNEY's *room.*)

EVANGELINE: (*stopping near her door*) He loves me! He loves me! And I — I love him too! Yet there is something he is keeping from me — I can see that! Oh, I would be very happy — if I were sure — (*meditates sadly; suddenly happy again. Going to her door*) But if he loves me — what else could I want? (*Tries to open door. Startled at finding it fastened.*) Locked! (*Tries again.*) Locked; and the key gone! Oh, dear! (*Frightened; she looks about.*) If mamma should come! Alfred — Mr Hastings, I mean! What shall I do? (*She darts about and suddenly turns into* LANGHORNE*'s room and shuts door.*)

(*Enter* THOMPSON *from outside, with* BAILIFF.)

THOMPSON: (*coming into room followed by* BAILIFF) This is where 'e lives, sir, and there's 'is room. I was in 'ere this morning, and found hout.

BAILIFF: (*crossing over*) Very well, where's my warrants? (*Gets out papers.*)

(*Enter* TOM, *from stairs, crossing behind them hastily with mustard plaster and pail of steaming hot water.* BAILIFF *and* THOMPSON *start toward* LANGHORNE*'s door.* TOM *runs quickly against them with pail of hot water, spilling some of it.*)

TOM: I begs your pardon, gents; but what's wantin'?

THOMPSON: We've come 'ere to attach Mr Langhorne's things.

TOM: Gee-whiffles! Well, I likes that!

BAILIFF: We're werry glad as you likes it, young man. So if you please stand out o' the way.

TOM: (*slight threatening motion with pail of hot water*) Oh, it's that, is it? But supposin' I don't please?

BAILIFF: (*loud voice*) You'd interfere with the law, would ye?

TOM: Oh, no! But afore you gits away with everything I'd just make certain as we had enough o' Langhorne's luggage to settle up our little rent.

BAILIFF: (*loud voice*) Look 'ere. I don't know nothink about your little rent, nor do I care.

(BAILIFF *and* THOMPSON *stand in front of table.*)

TOM: (*loud*) I see you don't; an' it makes me have to do all the carin' myself — so —

ALFRED: (*Enters from* DABNEY*'s room.*) What's all this row about?

BAILIFF: I've a warrant 'ere to attach the property of one Langhorne.

TOM: One Langhorne? That's all there is — ef ye was leavin' us another, I wouldn't care.

ALFRED: (*Goes toward* TOM.) No use, Tom — we've got to submit.

TOM: An' let 'em take everything, sir?

ALFRED: No other way, my boy. (*Trying to persuade* TOM *to move away from door. They remonstrate with each other.*)

(*Enter* JOSEPHINE *from outside, excited and breathless.*)

JOSEPHINE: (*bustling into room*) Where is my husband? Have you seen my husband, I say?

THOMPSON: (*to whom the remark seemed to be addressed*) No; an' I don't want to see 'im, neither. (*He and* BAILIFF *cross over to* TOM.)

JOSEPHINE: (*going excitedly about*) To leave me in that way — in the middle of a crowded street — with teams and omnibuses — and — and — oh! (*Angry exclamation; stamps foot.*)

BAILIFF: Come — I can't wait here!

TOM: (*over* ALFRED*'s shoulder*) There ain's no one asked ye to.

ALFRED: See here, Tom —

TOM: Just let me drop this 'ere hot water down the back of his neck, and decorate his cheek with a mustard plaster.

ALFRED: (*pulling* TOM *out of the way*) It's no use, I tell you — they can lock us up if we interfere.

TOM: (*discouraged; going one side*) An' I gits 'alf!

ALFRED: There, gentlemen. (*He opens door of* LANGHORNE's *room.*) You can go on with your — (*Sudden start. Shuts door with slam and stands before it.*) Death and Destruction! Evangeline!

(JOSEPHINE *turns at this, and looks.*)

TOM: (*aside*) Gee-whiffles! Wonder what struck 'im then?

BAILIFF: Say, are we goin' hin, or not?

ALFRED: Not just now. (*Glances at* JOSEPHINE.)

THOMPSON: What's the reason we can't?

ALFRED: The — the room isn't in order yet.

JOSEPHINE: (*aside*) Oh, what delicacy!

BAILIFF: Well, we'll put it in order mighty quick. (*Advances a step.*)

ALFRED: (*Motions him back.*) Stop! Wait! (*Comes forward a little.*) What's the amount of your claim?

THOMPSON: Eight pound twelve and sixpence. (*Produces bill.*)

ALFRED: (*pulling money from pockets*) I'll settle the thing. It cleans me out, but I'll settle it.

TOM: (*putting pail of water on desk; aghast; aside*) Oh, he's gone way off his head!

THOMPSON: Very well, sir. (*Takes money.*) Am much obliged — the receipt, sir.

ALFRED: Now, kindly — (*indicating door*)

BAILIFF: (*to* ALFRED) But you've forgotten one little matter, my friend. There's costs to be settled afore I goes. One pound ten and six, sir, if you please.

ALFRED: Oh, the deuce! See here, my man, I haven't got it. Can't you —

BAILIFF: No, I can't. So just stand aside now. (*He advances toward* LANGHORNE's *door, and is stopped by* ALFRED, *who is standing before it.*)

JOSEPHINE: Stop! (*She goes to* BAILIFF, *feeling in her pockets. Pays* BAILIFF.) I will not see such delicacy of sentiment trodden under foot. Here! Take your miserable costs!

ALFRED: But, my dear Mrs Bender —

JOSEPHINE: Not a word! I prefer to do it.

ALFRED: (*aside*) By Jove, if the old girl knew what she was paying for!

BAILIFF: (*having counted money*) Now we're all right, I believe. (*Starts off with* THOMPSON.)

TOM: Oh, yes, you're all right! (*Follows them.*) But where do we come in?

(*Exit* BAILIFF *and* THOMPSON *outside door. A peculiar and unearthly sound of muffled bell comes from* DABNEY's *room.* TOM *turns in surprise;* ALFRED *and* JOSEPHINE *also listen.* TOM *starts toward* DABNEY's *room.*)

TOM: Well, ef his bell ain't done an' took a spasm now! (*Seizes water pail and plaster, and rushes off. As he goes*) Comin' sir — comin'! (*Exit into* DABNEY's *room.*)

JOSEPHINE: (*to* ALFRED) I admire your delicacy so much, Mr Hastings.

ALFRED: Thanks! Thanks! But I — I really can't help it; it is an inborn instinct with me, madam. (*trying to keep her away from* LANGHORNE's *door*)

JOSEPHINE: Yes; but I don't know many people who would be willing to pay so much for a mere sentiment. Is the gentleman's apartment really in such disorder? Let me just peep in. (*Turns as if to go to* LANGHORNE's *door.*)

ALFRED: (*with a start*) No! (*Stands between her and the door.*) Ah — that is — really, Mrs Bender — consider my feelings!

JOSEPHINE: (*Looks at* ALFRED *an instant. Aside*) How he started! It can't be possible there's any — I really begin to suspect that, after all — (*A frown appears upon her face slowly. Turns to* ALFRED. *Voice changed to harder tone.*) Mr Hastings, I shall have to insist upon looking into that room.

ALFRED: Insist? Come now — that's hardly the thing, is it, for one who appreciates my delicacy of sentiment?

JOSEPHINE: Delicacy, sir, has nothing to do with it now. I am living beneath your roof with my family — my husband — and my daughter — (*On 'daughter' points to her room.* ALFRED *gives a slight start.*) If I became convinced that everything was not as it should be, I would instantly quit the house.

ALFRED: Surely, you do not suspect —

JOSEPHINE: From your actions, Mr Hastings, I know that there is some one in that room you wish to conceal. As you do not choose to relieve my mind at once by opening the door, it more than confirms my suspicions. I shall therefore wait here until the person — whoever it is — comes out. (*Seats herself in a chair at the table.*) It is a duty I owe my family.

> (ALFRED *simply stares blankly at* JOSEPHINE. *After watching her seat herself, he pulls newspaper from pocket. Draws chair before* LANGHORNE's *door and reads.*)

JOSEPHINE: (*aside*) If he thinks that affects my mind, he is the most mistaken individual on this quarter of the globe. (*She begins to hum a song, her indignation showing in it.* ALFRED *takes it up, whistling softly. She stops angrily, and looks daggers. A soft knock on* LANGHORNE's *door, from within.*)

ALFRED: (*aside*) The devil! Now Evangeline wants to get out. (*Coughs, and hitches around in his chair as if to cover up the sound made by* EVANGELINE.)

> (*Enter* LANGHORNE *from outside, running in hastily, as if pursued.*)

LANGHORNE: If that woman saw me, I am lost! (*Going to* ALFRED. *Stops, seeing situation.*)

ALFRED: (*aside*) Merciful Powers! Now he'll want to get in.

> (JOSEPHINE *starts and watches eagerly.*)

LANGHORNE: (*going quickly to his door*) You will permit me?

ALFRED: (*quickly, in an undertone to* LANGHORNE) For Heaven's sake, don't! There's a woman in there who must not be seen.

LANGHORNE: (*to* ALFRED) But see heah, deah boy — there's a woman after me, and I mustn't be seen.

ALFRED: Go into my room.

LANGHORNE: Your — oh — certainly! I don't care where I go, ye know, as long as I go somewhere. (*Dodges around* JOSEPHINE's *chair.*) Aw— chawming day! (*Exit into* ALFRED's *room.*)

JOSEPHINE: (*aside*) It's a conspiracy!
    (*Enter* BENDER *from outside, rushing in.*)
BENDER: Ha, ha! Thank Heaven, I've fixed that! (*Sees* JOSEPHINE. *Instantly turns square about, and starts toward door again and exits.*)
JOSEPHINE: (*rising quickly*) Theodore! Theodore! Stop, I say! (*She follows* BENDER.) Stop! I wish to speak with you. Theodore! (*Exit, outside door.*)
ALFRED: (*aside*) Thank Heaven for that! (*Opens* LANGHORNE's *door.*) Evangeline, quick! (*She enters.*) Quick, quick! To your room!
    (EVANGELINE *starts toward her door. Enter* JOSEPHINE *and* BENDER *from outside.* JOSEPHINE *sees* EVANGELINE *and stands in horror for an instant.*)
JOSEPHINE: (*on seeing* EVANGELINE) What! (*almost a scream*)
ALFRED: (*having fallen on ottoman; aside*) Lost!
BENDER: (*aside*) Hullo! (*Looks about to see what it is.*)
JOSEPHINE: Then you were there?
EVANGELINE: Yes, mamma. (ALFRED *starts as if to speak. She motions him not to.*) No, Alfred, I will tell them.
BENDER: 'Alfred!'
JOSEPHINE: 'Alfred!'
EVANGELINE: I had been chatting with Alfred, and I hid in that room when I heard you coming. I will not and cannot deny it.
BENDER: (*aside, admiringly*) What courage the girl has!
JOSEPHINE: And you have the hardihood to speak of this so calmly! What — what does it mean?
EVANGELINE: It means, mamma, that Alfred and I love each other. He has told me so, and I have told him so — and that's all there is about it.
BENDER: (*aside*) Magnificent! Such coolness! (*Speaks aloud without thinking, clapping hands together.*) Bravo!
JOSEPHINE: (*turning upon him*) Theodore! (JOSEPHINE *unlocks her door.*)
    (BENDER *collapses, but recovers, and claps hands together behind his back, where* JOSEPHINE *cannot see him.*)
JOSEPHINE: (*to* EVANGELINE) Go to your room at once! What course I shall take with you, I do not yet know.
EVANGELINE: (*giving* ALFRED *her hand*) Until we meet again, Alfred dear!
    (JOSEPHINE *opens her door and stands. Exit* EVANGELINE *calmly, turning at door, and throwing a kiss seriously and tenderly to* ALFRED.)
BENDER: Ha, ha! (*Chuckles — not a laugh. Crosses to* ALFRED.)
JOSEPHINE: (*at door*) Theodore! (BENDER *becomes serious at once.*) I have a few words to say to you soon. (*Exit, after giving* BENDER *a look of great significance.*)
BENDER: (*to* ALFRED, *slapping him on the shoulder*) That's a woman — eh? Now — now you can have some idea of how I feel — ha, ha, ha!
FIFI: (*opening her door*) Mr Bender!
BENDER: Eh?
FIFI: The costume has come. Do you want to see me as Prince Vladimir?
BENDER: The costume? (*Gives a glance towards his door.*) Perfectly delighted, my

dear! (*He hastens toward* FIFI, *who enters in costume of Prince Vladimir.*)
Ha, ha, ha! Charming! Charming!

FIFI: How do you like it, Mr Bender?

       (*Just as* BENDER *reaches the table,* JOSEPHINE *enters.*)

JOSEPHINE: (*above the table*) Now, Theodore, I would like to know —

       (ALFRED *gives quick exclamation of alarm.*)

BENDER: (*terrified*) Ah! (*He quickly snatches table-cover from table, and raises it high in the air, so that* FIFI *is hidden from view.*) My dear have you noticed the beautiful pattern on this table-cover? Simply divine! Exquisite! Adorable!

       (ALFRED *seizes* FIFI *at this point and hurries her off into her room an instant later. Enter* EVANGELINE *from her room. She stands at the door, trying to see what causes the excitement.* JOSEPHINE *stands astonished. While this is going on,* DABNEY *enters from his room, swaddled up with flannels, etc., as if for illness. Mustard-plaster on chest, old dressing-gown, stocking-feet, etc.*)

DABNEY: (*seeing* FIFI *as* ALFRED *hurries her off*) Ah! (*half shriek*) That creature sang in my opera, and she —

ALFRED: (*quick shout to* TOM) Stop him!

TOM: (*Entering from* DABNEY's *room, carrying plaster, bandages, etc. Jumps on* DABNEY.) Quite right, sir.

       (TOM *throws arms around* DABNEY's *neck, head, etc., so that he is effectively silenced, and they fall upon the ottoman together,* DABNEY *uttering muffled yells and shrieks,* TOM *putting plaster over his mouth.* ALFRED *snatches up newspaper, and stands reading nonchalantly before* FIFI's *door.* BENDER *drops, overcome, into a chair, the table-cover falling over him.* JOSEPHINE, *transfixed with astonishment at the behavior of the gentlemen.*)

CURTAIN

    ACT III

SCENE: *Same as in Act I. Some trifling changes in furniture.* TOM *discovered working at a large shallow pasteboard box, the empty interior of which is exposed to view of audience. He appears to have been glueing something on bottom, which is turned up stage.*

TOM: (*seated at table*) I've had enough o' that there cove as yells down them stairs ev'ry other minit, a-wanting ter know what time it is, an' I'm a-goin' ter fix him so's he won't give us no more trouble. Ef he goes on with it, the nervous galoot in there's a-goin' ter leave, an' he'll burst up the whole business afore we know it — an' I ain't goin' ter have the business bursted now (*working*) — while I gits half. (*He picks up box, then, suddenly, turning box so that bottom is to front, he quickly hangs it to a hook on wall near foot of stairs, and immediately rushes down and to table where he gets a pot of black paint and brushes. On back of box is painted or pasted a white paper or cardboard, with an enormous clock face painted upon it, without any hands.* TOM *dashes up with the paint, and quickly paints from six to ten hands on the clock, these hands pointing in every direction. He names the time of each as he puts it in.*) Quarter-past eleving. Two minutes afore three. Seving o'clock. There! Now he can take his choice — an' no noise about it. (*Stands, viewing his work.*) That there ain't so bad, now. When I gits through with this here job, I kin go into the clock business.

> (*Enter* BENDER *from his room. He is in good spirits, and comes on whistling. Stops and looks at the clock face and at* TOM.)

TOM: What do you think of it, sir?

BENDER: Is that style of timepiece your own invention?

TOM: It's fur the feller up-stairs, sir; him as makes such a contineral hollerin' fur the time. He'd orter be out now in a minit or two — it's more'n half an hour now sence the last time.

BENDER: Well, all I can say is —

> (*Bell rings in* DABNEY'*s room.* TOM *starts toward stairs, but stops.*)

TOM: Gee-whiffles! I thought it was 'im. It was the other one. (*Goes toward* DABNEY'*s door. Bell rings above.*)

TOM *and* BENDER: There! (*They start and look.*)

VOICE: (*above*) Look here! Can't somebody down there tell me what —

> (*Sudden jangle of bell, which comes banging and rattling down the stairs from above, followed by pipe, novel, and a beer mug; noise of furniture.* TOM *and* BENDER *hold in suppressed laughter; finally burst out.*)

TOM: That there settled 'im, sir.

BENDER: That clock would settle anything. Ha, ha!

> (*Enter* ALFRED *from outside.*)

ALFRED: From appearances, one would suppose you were having quite a humorous time.

BENDER: Ah, ha, ha, ha! (*Points to clock.*) For the benefit of the second floor!

ALFRED: (*seeing clock*) Has the second floor seen it?

TOM: Yes, sir; he's just took an observation. (*Bell rings in* DABNEY'*s room.*) Gee-whiffles! I forgot all about that nervous galoot. (*Exit into* DABNEY'*s room.*)

DABNEY: (*in room*) Don't! don't!

> (BENDER *goes walking about room, smiling, and whistling snatches of things out of tune, hands behind him, etc. Half smiling now and then, as if thinking of something very pleasant.* ALFRED *watches him a while.*)

ALFRED: (*aside*) The old boy is in great spirits to-day. Wonder what's going on. As he is to be my father-in-law, I'll have to look out for him a little. (*Looks at* BENDER. BENDER *goes and looks off at his door.*) Think of it! Engaged to that little dear — yes, and as good as Engaged to my cousin Emily at the same time! A pretty position to be in! But I'm in it, and the only way is to tell Uncle Egbert the whole thing when he comes home; for I couldn't give up Evangeline. Oh, no! Anything but that! Anything but that!

BENDER: Alfred, my boy, has the post come in this morning?

ALFRED: No, not yet.

> (BENDER *walks about up and down.* ALFRED *sticks his hands in his pockets and looks at him.*)

ALFRED: I say, you must be expecting something very nice.

BENDER: (*Stops and looks at* ALFRED.) I am. (*Goes near* ALFRED. *Speaks confidentially.*) Ha, ha! It's too good to keep.

ALFRED: Don't keep it, then.

BENDER: The fact is — (*Glances around to see that no one overhears.*) I'm expecting a letter — for my wife.

ALFRED: That is, she's expecting it?

BENDER: No, no! Not by a — 'hem! (*glance*) She doesn't know anything about it.

ALFRED: Ah!

BENDER: I — (*impressively, in* ALFRED's *ear*) I wrote it myself; disguised hand, of course. Oh, she'll never know it's from me!

ALFRED: In that case, I've no doubt she'll be delighted to get it.

BENDER: No, I hardly think so, as it informs her that I have an appointment to-day, at the park, near the Marble Arch.

ALFRED: It does! You mean — a lady? (BENDER *nods emphatically, looking very jovial and pleased, and walks around a little, whistling.*) But, my dear Mr Bender —

BENDER: Perfectly true. (*Nods significantly.*) I have an appointment — but not at the park.

ALFRED: Where?

BENDER: (*confidentially*) Here.

ALFRED: By Jove! (BENDER *nods and walks as before.*) Who is the — the other party, if I may ask? (BENDER *motions significantly towards* FIFI's *door.*) Not — not the opera singer!

BENDER: Sh! Yes.

ALFRED: (*after regarding* BENDER *an instant*) How very rapid you are for an elderly man.

BENDER: (*pleased*) I — I did Miss Fifi a little favor, you know; and out of gratitude she has invited me to a — ahem — a champagne breakfast. That is, she furnishes the invitation, and I — furnish the breakfast.

ALFRED: And in the meantime, Mrs Bender goes to waylay you?

BENDER: At the Marble Arch. (ALFRED *stares in astonishment.* BENDER *pauses an instant, then paces restlessly.*) Now, what the deuce delays that mail? (*His door opens.*) Careful, now! (*Enter* JOSEPHINE, *dressed for calling.* BENDER *meets her.*) Why, Josephine, love, are you going — anywhere in particular?

JOSEPHINE: Do you forget that we were to make several calls to-day with our dear Alfred and Evangeline?

ALFRED: Oh, Heavens!

JOSEPHINE: Alfred, dear, not dressed yet?

ALFRED: Well, it seemed to me — that — er — the weather —

JOSEPHINE: Why, the weather is perfect.

ALFRED: Yes; but the — the reports say there's another blizzard on the way from America. (*holding up a newspaper*) Do you know what a frightful thing a blizzard from America is?

JOSEPHINE: No; and I don't care. (*severely*) We are to make these calls.

> (ALFRED *stands an instant looking at her.* BENDER *smothers a laugh, but quickly catches himself, and looks solemn.*)

ALFRED: (*at his door; aside*) Anything but calling on her relatives! (*Turns and looks at* JOSEPHINE. *She is still looking at him. He exits into his room.*)

JOSEPHINE: (*Looks severely at* BENDER.) Theodore, you are to come with us.

BENDER: I? Oh, of course — of course. (*aside*) Now what is the matter with that damned postman!

> (*Enter* TOM *from* DABNEY'*s room with a demijohn and several bottles.*)

JOSEPHINE: Thomas! Thomas!

TOM: Yes'm — one minute, mum. (*Puts things down and turns to* JOSEPHINE.)

JOSEPHINE: Come here.

TOM: I am here, mum.

> (*Double knock of postman, outside*)

BENDER: (*start of relief*) Tom — letters.

TOM: (*going to door*) Quite right, sir. (*Disappears an instant and returns at once.* BENDER *fills time with a pleased smile and glance at* JOSEPHINE. TOM *goes quickly to* BENDER.) Paper for you, sir.

BENDER: (*alarmed*) Is that — all?

TOM: (*Goes to* JOSEPHINE.) Letter fur you, mum.

> (JOSEPHINE *takes it and opens it.*)

BENDER: (*Sits at table, opening the paper, and looking over the top at* JOSEPHINE: *aside, chuckling*) That's the one.

> (JOSEPHINE *looks up.* BENDER *instantly opens and plunges into his paper.*)

TOM: (*aside*) Gee-whiffles! The old duck's got somethin' on hand again; I kin tell it every time. (*Exit through arch.*)

JOSEPHINE: What wretched writing! (*Reads.*)

BENDER: (*aside*) Sorry she doesn't like it.

JOSEPHINE: (*Reads.*) 'Respected Madam. Pray do not consider me too presuming, but I think it my duty to — warn you.' (*She looks closer, interested.*) What's this! (*Reads more excitedly, repeating aloud only the important parts.*) 'At Hyde Park; Marble Arch, between ten and eleven o'clock — a well-meaning Friend.' Ah! (*subdued gasp, dropping the letter to the floor*)

BENDER: (*Who has had his eye on* JOSEPHINE *over or under his paper during the above, rises to* JOSEPHINE, *laying aside paper.*) Now, what they wanted to send me that for — er — Good Heavens, Josephine! (*as if noticing her strained expression*) No unpleasant news, I hope?

JOSEPHINE: (*Starts; assumes a smile which is rather ghastly.*) Oh, no. Very pleasant — very — ha, ha! Yes.

BENDER: (*as if suspicious*) Um! Looks like a man's handwriting.

JOSEPHINE: (*assumed indifference*) Does it? (*Smiles.*)

BENDER: (*assuming some warmth*) I said it did.

JOSEPHINE: Oh — really!

BENDER: (*Makes a motion as if to pick the letter up;* JOSEPHINE, *with sudden exclamation of alarm, snatches it from floor. They stand looking at each other.*) There's something in that letter.

JOSEPHINE: That's quite possible, as you didn't write it.

BENDER: Your actions are very suspicious, madam. I'd have you understand that, as your husband, I have a right —
> (*Enter* ALFRED, *dressed for calling. He stops on seeing situation, turns away, chuckling to himself.*)

JOSEPHINE: (*to* ALFRED, *very pleasantly, yet showing the bitter feeling beneath*) Oh, Alfred, I have changed my plans a little; I feel a headache coming on — and (*Glances at* BENDER.) — and — I think I'd better lie down quietly for a little while.

BENDER: (*approaching* JOSEPHINE; *speaks sympathetically*) Oh, my dear Josephine, I —

JOSEPHINE: (*Shoots a glance at* BENDER *which stops him instantly. To* ALFRED) You and Evangeline are to go to the Dickermans' without me, and I will call there for you later.

BENDER: Oh, so we aren't to go with them? In that case, my dear, I will take the opportunity to call on an old business friend of mine in Upton Street.

JOSEPHINE: (*looking calmly and stonily at* BENDER) You will call on an old business friend of yours in Upton Street?

BENDER: Yes. You remember Barton Briggs? Dear old fellow! Shall I give him your regards?

JOSEPHINE: Oh, do. By all means. (*showing savageness in spite of herself*) Give the dear old fellow my regards.

BENDER: (*cheerfully*) Yes, my angel, I will. Good-bye for a little while. (*Exit outside door, whistling or humming.*)
> (*Enter* EVANGELINE *from her room, very tastefully dressed.*)

ALFRED: (*going quickly to her*) My little darling, how enchanting you look!

EVANGELINE: (*looking up to him; pleased*) Do I? But you ought not to say so, you know.

ALFRED: Can't help it. (*He glances at* JOSEPHINE, *and seeing her turned away, steals a kiss from* EVANGELINE. JOSEPHINE *turns quickly and comes toward them.*)

EVANGELINE: Where is papa?

JOSEPHINE: (*significantly*) He has gone to call upon a dear old business friend.

EVANGELINE: But I thought —

JOSEPHINE: No matter what you thought. Come — we will start.

ALFRED: Start! Aren't you going to lie down after all?

JOSEPHINE: I have decided it would be better for me to take the air.

ALFRED: Oh!
> (JOSEPHINE *suddenly turns, as if she had thought of something. Marches down to her door, and, reaching in, gets an umbrella. Enter* TOM *through arch; he looks at the party.* ALFRED *and* EVANGELINE *watch* JOSEPHINE's *movements. She walks back, carrying umbrella with peculiar fierceness of manner.* TOM, *coming slowly down, slides back off, watching* JOSEPHINE *with evident concern.*)

EVANGELINE: (*surprised*) But, mamma, dear, you don't want an umbrella to-day!

JOSEPHINE: (*at outside door; turns*) Oh, I don't know about that. The report says there's a blizzard coming from America, and it's just as well to be prepared. (*Marches out, gripping the umbrella ferociously.*)

EVANGELINE: (*looking at* ALFRED) What does she mean, Alfred?

ALFRED: She means business. (*Exits with* EVANGELINE, *outside door.*)

TOM: (*Gives a whistle indicative of 'whew!'*) Gee-whiffles, but ef it's old Bender she's got in her mind, they'll have to bring 'im 'ome in baskets! (*Exit through arch into hall.*)

BENDER: (*entering from outside door*) Everything is working like a charm! My wife safely down the street, and making a bee-line for Hyde Park. I hope she'll enjoy the walk. If she doesn't — 'hem — perhaps she'll enjoy the walk back. (*Chuckles.*)

> (*Enter* TOM *through arch with two bottles of champagne. Crosses to* DABNEY's *door.*)

BENDER: (*meeting* TOM) Ah, Tom!

TOM: Yes, sir!

BENDER: They are to send in a little breakfast from Torino's. When it comes, take care of it.

TOM: I've had breakfast, sir.

BENDER: No, no! It's for Miss Oritanski. Ha, ha! I am invited to join her. I say — I suppose there's no objection — to — 'hem — a — quiet little breakfast here?

TOM: None whatsomever, sir. We aims to give our lodgers 'all the comforts of home'.

BENDER: Good! When it comes, just take it to her room.

TOM: She locked it up, sir, when she went out.

BENDER: (*thunderstruck*) Went — went out!

TOM: Yes, sir.

BENDER: Where?

TOM: To the theatre, sir. She had a sudden call for rehearsal — somebody sick. She told me to tell you as she was werry sorry indeed — werry sorry.

BENDER: Why — confound it — I was to breakfast with her! Why — (*speechless with vexation*)

> (*Knock outside;* TOM *rushes off, and exits outside door.*)

BENDER: That's probably the breakfast. What infernal, confounded, outrageous luck!

> (*Enter* TOM *with breakfast hamper, which he sets near* FIFI's *door on a chair. This hamper contains two bottles of champagne, some very fancily done up French chops, a salad dressed in the highest style of art, and other fancy dishes. Rolls, wine-glasses, knives, plates, napkins, etc., for two; and two bunches of flowers for button-hole and corsage. Chops, rolls, champagne, and two or three small things should be practical for business.*)

BENDER: (*Looks dubiously at the breakfast.*) What the deuce can I do?

TOM: Ef it wuz me, sir, I'd hop into a cab an' drive to the theatre.

BENDER: Good idea. I'll do it. (*Exits outside door.*)

TOM: (*looking after* BENDER) Ef he'd a seen his ole lady a-goin' out with that there umbrella o' hern, he'd be takin' a cab for the railway station.

> (*Knock on outside door.* TOM *exits through arch.*)

VOICE: (*outside*) Telegram, sir.

TOM: (*outside*) Telegram?

VOICE: Yes, sir.

TOM: (*entering with telegram, reading*) To Alfred Hastin's, esq. Gee-whiffles! Ef people ain't commencin' a-telegraphin' fur rooms! This here house is gittin' pop'lar. (*Puts envelope in his pocket.*)

ALFRED: (*entering hastily, through arch*) See here, Tom! Miss Bender dropped her bracelet — she thinks it was in this room. Help me look, quick!

TOM: Yes, sir. (*They look about on floor.*)

ALFRED: (*seeing envelope sticking out of* TOM'*s pocket*) What have you got there?

TOM: (*quickly handing envelope — innocent and official manner, as if he had just arrived with it*) Telegram for you, sir.

ALFRED: (*snatching and opening it*) Good Heavens, why didn't you say so!

TOM: I did, sir. I just said so.

ALFRED: (*reading telegram*) Good Heavens!

TOM: (*staring at* ALFRED *an instant; without emotion*) Anybody dead, sir?

ALFRED: Yes — we're dead.

TOM: W'en is the funeral?

ALFRED: You'd better get ready for it now. My aunt is coming home. 'Sent from Venice. Mr Pettibone gone to Hamburg on business. Am coming home with Emily. Must see you. Very important matter. Rosalind Pettibone.' (*Sits down on chair, overcome.* TOM *goes and sits on the ottoman.* ALFRED *suddenly jumps up.*) Here — get me some paper — quick now — no time to waste. (ALFRED *takes pen from his pocket.*)

TOM: Yes, sir! (*Jumps up, snatches paper from desk.*)

ALFRED: (*seated at table*) I'll try to stop them. Not much chance, but I'll try. (*Writes quickly, reading aloud.*) 'Mrs Egbert Pettibone, Venice. In mercy's sake, don't come. Impossible. Dangerous. House — (*Thinks.*) What the devil can I say is the matter with the house?

TOM: Burnt down.

ALFRED: Hang it, they'd come all the sooner!

TOM: Blown up. (*Bell rings from* DABNEY'*s room.*) Oh, that nervous galoot has ordered more wine. (*Rushes off with the two bottles into* DABNEY'*s room.*)

ALFRED: Oh, no — no. Ah! (*Writes rapidly.*) 'House just painted. Painter's colic. Pipes burst. Influenza epidemic. Small-pox next door. Alfred.' (*Enter* TOM *from* DABNEY'*s room.*) Here, quick, Tom! Telegraph office! (*Rises and hurries* TOM *up toward outside door.*) Run all the way!

TOM: (*Starts off.*) Yes, sir. (*Stops.*) Pay it, sir?

ALFRED: No, hang it! Collect!

TOM: Correct! (*Exit, outside door.*)

ALFRED: They'll never get it. (*Looks at his telegram.*) N — probably started already. Only one thing to do. Get our lodgers out — and Evangeline — and Emily — Oh, the deuce! And how in Heaven's name I am to evict my parents-in-law, is more than I —

(*Enter* FIFI *from outside door, jauntily dressed.*)

ALFRED: (*aside*) And here's another one. Oh, Lord, if my aunt should find her here! I must get her out first.

FIFI: (*very bright and vivacious*) Ah, Doctor, how charmed I am to meet you!
(*Begins to take off her gloves.*)
ALFRED: Thanks, I'm sure.
FIFI: Dear me! (*Imitates his tone.*) 'Thanks, I'm sure.' Something gone wrong with
my fascinating landlord?
ALFRED: Your fascinating landlord has a confession to make.
FIFI: (*in mock alarm, motioning him to stop with one hand, and going toward her
door*) Mercy, please don't, doctor! (*Takes key and unlocks her door.*) At least
not until I've had something to sustain me. This dreadful rehearsal made me
miss a most delightful breakfast that — (*Sees hamper near her door.*) Ah!
(*delighted*) Why, it's here! Poor Mr Bender! (*Laughs merrily.*) He couldn't
wait.
ALFRED: But my dear Miss Oritanski —
FIFI: (*Almost screams with sudden idea.*) Oh, stop! You shall breakfast with me.
ALFRED: But, my dear Miss Oritanski —
FIFI: There — there — that will do. That table (*pointing to it*), bring it down here.
(*She stamps her foot. ALFRED does not notice what she says.*) Bring that
table here.
> (ALFRED *drags table down as if not knowing what he is doing, all
> the time trying to speak. Through the whole scene ALFRED acts as
> if unconscious of what he is about. No sign of the slightest enjoy-
> ment or spirit appears; acts mechanically.* FIFI *places hamper on
> ottoman, instantly going to work to get things out, throwing table-
> cloth to* ALFRED.)
FIFI: Spread it out — spread it out! (ALFRED *does so.*) And then you can confess
all you like. An immense saving of time. Breakfast — confess — all in one.
ALFRED: But, my dear young lady —
FIFI: (*pushing something into his hand*) Just put that there. (*Flies about, quickly
and vivaciously.*)
ALFRED: (*putting article in wrong place on table, not knowing where*) You don't
understand — what I was going to —
FIFI: No, no! not there. There! (*Changes it.*) Oh, dear! you're not much assistance,
I must say! That goes there. (*Puts another article into his hand.*) That's it!
You actually got that right!
ALFRED: Now, Miss Oritanski, — listen. This is a matter of vital importance.
FIFI: If you want a matter of vital importance, open this! (*Tosses bottle of
champagne to* ALFRED, *and corkscrew from hamper.*)
ALFRED: But look here, there's no time to lose.
FIFI: Well — I'm not losing any, am I?
ALFRED: (*aside*) By Jove, I should say not! (*Holds bottle mechanically, as he
caught it.*)
FIFI: You're the one that's losing time. Why don't you open it?
ALFRED: Open what? (FIFI *points to bottle.*) Oh, you want that opened?
FIFI: Of course, Mr Stupid.
ALFRED: But first —
FIFI: Nothing first. I won't hear a word, unless you do as I say.
ALFRED: Oh, Lord! (*Opens bottle as if it were a nuisance.*)

FIFI: (*Gets chair and pushes* ALFRED *into it, then kneels herself on back of the ottoman.*) That's it! You're coming to your senses at last.

ALFRED: On the contrary, I am losing them.

FIFI: There! (*Finishes setting table.*)

ALFRED: But you said you'd listen if —

FIFI: There! (*Delicately gives* ALFRED *a French chop with her fingers.*) Just try this. It's from Torino's. I know it by the style. (ALFRED, *confused for an instant, holds chop.*) Eat it. You don't know how nice it is. (ALFRED, *seated, confused, with the chop in one hand, and champagne bottle in the other.*) Pour the wine, why don't you? (ALFRED *pours the wine in the glasses.*) Pour it! Ah, isn't that lovely! You'll feel better in a moment.

ALFRED: (*aside*) Good Heavens — I must stop this!

> (*Enter* EVANGELINE *from outside door. Stops, horrified, on seeing* ALFRED *and* FIFI.)

FIFI: (*holding up glass of champagne*) Happy days, doctor!

ALFRED: But first —

FIFI: No, no! Happy days first! Happy days, doctor! then, perhaps, I'll listen.

ALFRED: (*quickly, as if to get through with it*) Happy days, then. Any kind of days you like. (*Drinks quickly.* FIFI *drains glass.*)

FIFI: That's just exquisite, isn't it?

ALFRED: Now, will you listen?

FIFI: (*Picks up a rose.*) Ah, how sweet! This is for your button-hole. (*Reaches over to put it in* ALFRED's *coat.*)

ALFRED: (*catching* FIFI's *hand*) You must listen now. I have something to ask you — and you will promise not to refuse me. My happiness depends upon it. It may be my life-long happiness. You will not refuse me when you know how much —

EVANGELINE: (*Cries out.*) Oh! (*Sinks swooning on chair.* ALFRED *springs to his feet and looks round.*)

ALFRED: Evangeline! (*Hastens to her.*)

FIFI: (*aside*) Ah, a little love episode! (*Goes on with her breakfast tranquilly.*)

ALFRED: What a cursed coincidence!

FIFI: Yes, doctor. It was unfortunate, I admit.

ALFRED: Evangeline!

> (EVANGELINE *revives and rises with difficulty.* ALFRED *tries to assist her, but she will not permit it.*)

FIFI: (*aside*) I'm almost sorry for the little innocent. (*Drinks champagne cheerfully.*)

EVANGELINE: (*Walks slowly and weakly toward her door.* ALFRED *again tries to assist her, but she repulses him.*) No!

ALFRED: Believe me, I am innocent!

FIFI: (*rising from ottoman; aside*) O, yes, they are always innocent.

ALFRED: You are mistaken, if you think — that I — that we — Miss Oritanski, I beg you to tell her how it was.

FIFI: My dear doctor (*wiping her fingers daintily with napkin, and tossing it down*), I would be charmed to do so — charmed (*Moves backward to her door.*); but there's one quite serious objection — the young lady evidently saw how it was herself. (*Exits into her room.*)

ALFRED: (*realizing that* FIFI *has made matters a hundred times worse*) Good Heavens! (*Turns to* EVANGELINE *in desperation.*) Evangeline! You must listen, my darling.

EVANGELINE: (*at her door*) No — I would rather not — now —

ALFRED: But, my darling, you must hear me! You must listen, Evangeline, for I can explain exactly how — how —

EVANGELINE: Yes, of course you have excuses. But, O Alfred! what difference could it make — what difference could anything make — when I saw (*voice full of emotion*) — the dreadful affair — with my own eyes? (*Turns, and exits into her room.*)

ALFRED: Oh, this is a crime — this is — this is simply — oh — (*Paces back and forth once.*) I can't stand it — I — I'll go and walk the streets. (*Starts off, then stops, listening at door.*) Mrs Bender! I hear her familiar panting on the stairs. (*Starts toward arch; stops.*) I can't meet her now. I'll walk the streets some other time. I must get this out of the way. (*Moves the table back.*) They'll be sure to look for me in my room. Dabney's room! That's the thing! (*Exits into* DABNEY's *room.*)

>   (DABNEY's *voice heard in incoherent revelry as* ALFRED *goes in;*
>   *Enter* JOSEPHINE *from outside with umbrella; puts it in hat rack.*
>   *Very excited, exhausted, disarranged, dusty, bedraggled, hot, and*
>   *out of breath. She looks fiercely around the room, then drops into*
>   *a chair.*)

JOSEPHINE: No one there. Not a sign — not a vestige of the man — or of anyone looking for him, excepting me — I was looking for him — tramping up and down around that miserable Arch — in all the heat — and dust — and noise. Oh, there's something at the bottom of all this! (DABNEY's *voice heard in his room.*) What can be going on in there? (*Rises to go.* EVANGELINE *opens her door a little.*) Is that you, Evangeline? Come here! (EVANGELINE *comes out, giving an anxious glance about the room. Her eyes are red from weeping, and she is very pale.*) Why, my child — why Evangeline — what has happened? (*She rises and meets* EVANGELINE.)

EVANGELINE: Oh, nothing! (*Wipes a tear away quickly.*)

JOSEPHINE: Where is Alfred? (EVANGELINE *tries to speak. Cannot. Shakes head. Suddenly buries head on* JOSEPHINE's *breast.*) Something has gone wrong. You have quarrelled.

EVANGELINE: (*Shakes head negatively; raises head a little.*) We have parted — forever. (*head down again, and stifled sobs*)

JOSEPHINE: This is all foolishness. One of you is to blame. If it's Alfred, then he must apologize. If it's you — 'hem — he must apologize just the same.

EVANGELINE: (*shaking head emphatically*) No! I never — want to see him again (*Raises head.*), mamma. He left me — at the Dickermans' — to look for my lost bracelet — and I found him here — breakfasting with the opera singer. Yes, and worse than breakfasting.

JOSEPHINE: Worse!

EVANGELINE: Hundreds and hundreds of times worse. He was — he was holding her hands — and telling her — that — that — Oh! (*Breaks down and sobs.*)

JOSEPHINE: I must look into this.

EVANGELINE: It won't — do any good — I've looked into it. That was enough.

BENDER: (*entering from outside, rushing in hurriedly and excitedly; as he comes in*) Not at the theatre! Where the dev — Thunder and lightning — my wife!

    (JOSEPHINE *leads* EVANGELINE *to her door in silence and motions her to go in.* EVANGELINE *exits.* JOSEPHINE *turns and faces* BENDER.)

BENDER: (*trying to command a cheerful tone*) Ah, my angel! Been out — or just going?

JOSEPHINE: I have a few words to say to you. (BENDER *looks a trifle apprehensive.* JOSEPHINE *takes letter from pocket and extends it toward him.*) Do you see this?

BENDER: (*rather weakly*) Oh, yes — I — I see it. (*As* JOSEPHINE *still holds it out, he takes it.*) Looks like the one you snatched up so nervously this morning.

JOSEPHINE: It is.

BENDER: Ah! May I — read it?

JOSEPHINE: May you read it?

BENDER: (*slight start*) I believe I — suggested —

JOSEPHINE: (*commandingly*) Read it.

BENDER: (*quite subdued*) Yes — that was the idea that I — (JOSEPHINE *motions him; he stops and reads the letter calmly.*)

JOSEPHINE: (*watching closely; aside*) He does not move an eye-lash. He is innocent. (*aloud*) Well?

BENDER: Quite amusing, my dear. (*Hands her the letter.*) Ha, ha, ha! (*rather a forced laugh*)

JOSEPHINE: Yes, isn't it? Ha, ha, ha! (*rather a bitter laugh*)

BENDER: I only wish you had gone there.

JOSEPHINE: I did go there.

BENDER: Ha? You really went? Ha, ha, ha! Then I wish I'd gone.

JOSEPHINE: What!

BENDER: (*seriously*) No — that is, only to see you, my love — to see you enjoy yourself.

JOSEPHINE: Oh! (*Though still frowning darkly, she is somewhat mollified. She turns and looks toward* ALFRED's *door, as if with a new thought. Looks sharply at* BENDER.) Theodore, do you think I do not know who wrote that letter? (*Shakes letter in her hand.*)

BENDER: (*blankly*) You — you don't say!

JOSEPHINE: I do say — and I say that the person is not ten steps from me at this instant.

BENDER: (*beginning to show considerable alarm, though he turns so that* JOSEPHINE *does not observe it; aside*) My soul!

JOSEPHINE: Now, shall I tell you why this person wrote it?

BENDER: (*thoroughly unnerved and aghast*) Oh — er — perhaps there's no need of going into that, my dear.

JOSEPHINE: (*hotly*) There is need of going into that. He wrote it, Bender, to get me out of the way, so that he could enjoy a breakfast tête-à-tête here with our comic opera young woman. (*pointing to* FIFI*'s door indignantly*)

BENDER: (*aside*) There's no escape from this, but to confess and beg forgiveness. (*aloud*) My dear, I shall have to admit —

JOSEPHINE: I don't want you to admit. I want you to act.

BENDER: (*Stares with blank face at* JOSEPHINE.) Where would you like to have me act?

JOSEPHINE: Here!

BENDER: (*Stares again, then gives an uncertain glance around the room. Weakly*) Here?

JOSEPHINE: Here; and now you must see him.

BENDER: See — whom?

JOSEPHINE: Stupid, stupid! Alfred, of course — who wrote this letter — got me out of the way — left Evangeline at the Dickermans', and then came here and breakfasted and flirted with this creature from the theatre.

BENDER: (*suddenly comprehending*) Eh! (*Looks about savagely.*) My breakfast! My — (*Stamps foot in indignation, after seeing the remains of the breakfast.*)

JOSEPHINE: (*turning quickly*) What!

BENDER: (*recovering himself*) My — son-in-law, I say.

JOSEPHINE: Isn't it shameful! (*going up to her door*)

BENDER: Shameful? It's — it's beyond words.

JOSEPHINE: Come here. Evangeline will tell you everything.

BENDER: Yes, my dear. (*aside*) Saved for the present — but how the deuce will it end?

(*Noises as before in* DABNEY*'s room*)

ALFRED: (*entering from* DABNEY*'s room, turning and starting quickly towards outside door*) Now, to get out before —

JOSEPHINE: (*commandingly*) Wait! (ALFRED *stops.*) My husband has something to say to you.

BENDER: (*aside; in agony*) If I abuse him, he'll betray me.

JOSEPHINE: Come, come! (ALFRED *looks away an instant.*)

BENDER: 'Hem! (*Tries to assume a severity of attitude and expression.*) Sir — (ALFRED *turns to him;* BENDER *instantly melts; very meekly*) Sir — I said — sir —

ALFRED: Well? What is it?

BENDER: (*turning to* JOSEPHINE) He wants to know what it is.

JOSEPHINE: Pooh!

BENDER: (*to* ALFRED) Yes, pooh! Now, you mustn't take offence, my boy —

JOSEPHINE: Stop! If you can't do better, I'll interfere.

BENDER: (*aside*) Oh — that would end everything! He'd let it all out. (*to* ALFRED) Your — your behavior, sir, was — er —

JOSEPHINE: (*to* BENDER, *spitefully*) Outrageous!

BENDER: (*rather tamely*) Outrageous.

JOSEPHINE: (*to* BENDER) Ungentlemanly!

BENDER: Um — 'hem! (*Turns to* JOSEPHINE.) Eh?

JOSEPHINE: (*to* BENDER) We are furious at you!

BENDER: Yes, we are. (*tamely*) Very furious.

JOSEPHINE: (*speaking directly to* ALFRED) You ought to be ashamed of yourself – engaged to one lady, and flirting and breakfasting with another.

BENDER: (*with sudden animation and seriousness*) Yes – breakfasting with another – at my ex – er – 'hem! (*Suddenly checks himself.*)

ALFRED: (*Puts both hands on his shoulders, and checks* BENDER *suddenly.* JOSEPHINE *has turned away for the instant.*) Mrs Bender, I have flirted with no one – breakfasted with no one. I simply –

JOSEPHINE: (*quickly*) What – you dare to deny it? Mercy on us! Perhaps you will go so far as to deny that you sent me this letter?

ALFRED: Letter? I – sent? (*Looks at* JOSEPHINE *and then at* BENDER.)

BENDER: (*Sits down; aside*) Now is my time to die.

JOSEPHINE: (*pushing the letter into* ALFRED'*s hands*) Take the vile fabrication! Take it!

ALFRED: (*aside*) His letter! (*Looks at* BENDER.) Jove! I have an idea – I'll do it! For Evangeline's sake, I'll do it!

JOSEPHINE: No wonder you are speechless!

ALFRED: No – I can't be expected to say much – under the circumstances.

JOSEPHINE: Then you did write it?

ALFRED: (*nonchalantly*) O yes.

JOSEPHINE: (*almost a scream of triumph*) Ah! (*to* BENDER) I told you! (BENDER *stands an instant paralyzed;* ALFRED *stands with bowed head.*) Did you hear what he said? He confessed it!

BENDER: Confessed – that – he – ?

JOSEPHINE: Yes. (BENDER *goes to* ALFRED *precipitately. Thinking* BENDER *means to assault* ALFRED.) Oh! (*Catches* BENDER *by the arm.*)

BENDER: (*to* ALFRED) You jewel!

JOSEPHINE: No violence, Theodore!

BENDER: (*to* JOSEPHINE) Unhand me, Josephine! This is my affair.

ALFRED: (*quick aside to* BENDER) That's it! Play the indignant!

BENDER: (*violently*) So – you were the cowardly wretch who stooped to such a villainous, underhand trick as this. Fie! – (*threateningly*) I say – Fie!

ALFRED: (*aside to* BENDER) Go on. Fie some more.

JOSEPHINE: (*aside*) Dear me! I'm afraid Theodore will do him some injury. I must reconcile them.

BENDER: Is nothing on earth sacred to you? Neither my stainless past nor the future welfare of my innocent child? (*advancing upon* ALFRED; *very threateningly*) Have you forgotten that a father's –

JOSEPHINE: (*to* BENDER) Theodore, you must not forget yourself!

BENDER: I will forget myself! I forget everything but the vengeance that is due –

JOSEPHINE: (*rushing between the two men with a cry of alarm; to* BENDER) No, you shall not hurt him! (*to* ALFRED) Have you no excuse to offer for your conduct, Alfred? Nothing to say?

ALFRED: My dear Mrs Bender, believe me, I was not taking a breakfast with the lady – I only happened to be there.

BENDER: (*aside*) I wish I'd happened to be there.

JOSEPHINE: Well, I will try to believe what you say. Time brings all things to light.

BENDER: (*aside*) I hope it won't this time.

JOSEPHINE: So I will do what I can to reconcile Evangeline. But first you must beg my husband's pardon.

ALFRED: What? O yes — of course. (*to* BENDER) You'll overlook it, I trust?
(BENDER *stands stonily, partly turning his back, and folds his arms.*)

JOSEPHINE: Theodore, you must forgive him.

BENDER: He has wronged me too deeply.

JOSEPHINE: (*Puts* ALFRED*'s hand in* BENDER*'s, and goes up to her door.*) Now, make up and be friends. (*She nods encouragingly, and exits into her room.*)

BENDER: (*calling after her*) Don't leave me alone with him — something will happen. (*Short pause.* BENDER *and* ALFRED *look around cautiously, then fall into each other's arms.* BENDER, *effusively, feelingly, wringing* ALFRED*'s hands*) My dear boy, I am overwhelmed with gratitude!

ALFRED: (*drily*) Well, by Jove, you ought to be! She'd have torn you limb from limb.

BENDER: Is there anything I can do for you in return?

ALFRED: Certainly. That's the precise reason I've done all this. You must do something in return.

BENDER: What is it?

ALFRED: Move out of the house with your family this very day.

BENDER: What? Move — move out?

ALFRED: And not only that, but you must persuade the opera singer to go. She's paid her rent, so I can't do anything. But you can.

BENDER: You're mad, my boy.

ALFRED: Not in the least — but I will be if you don't go.

BENDER: But how am I to —

JOSEPHINE: (*entering with* EVANGELINE *from their room*) Here she is, Alfred, ready to make peace with you.
(EVANGELINE *stands with her eyes downcast;* BENDER *joins* JOSEPHINE.)

ALFRED: (*going to* EVANGELINE) Evangeline, I hope your mother has convinced you that there was a mistake.

EVANGELINE: I knew there was a mistake — of some kind. (*After a short struggle with herself, gives* ALFRED *her hand.*) I will try to forget it, Alfred, but I could not remain in the house — it would be impossible while that dreadful person is permitted to live here.

ALFRED *and* BENDER: What! (*They exchange glances.*)

EVANGELINE: Oh, yes, she must go away! Papa will have to see that she does it. And until then we will take rooms at the hotel near the corner of Southgate Street. It isn't far, you know.

ALFRED: (*aside*) By Jove — if this isn't luck!

EVANGELINE: Mamma and I have arranged it all — and I'm going over there now to engage the rooms. Perhaps — perhaps you would like to come with me.

ALFRED: (*going up to* EVANGELINE) I shall be delighted. Ah, Evangeline! (*near door; gets hold of her hand*) You must believe me innocent of any —

EVANGELINE: (*finger to lips*) Sh! (*Points to* FIFI*'s room.*)

ALFRED: Oh, the deuce! (*They exit.*)

JOSEPHINE: Well – you see what must be done. I could not pacify Evangeline in any other way. The woman must be got rid of.

BENDER: But it can't be done, my dear – she's paid in advance.

JOSEPHINE: (*Starts slightly; gives* BENDER *a quick look.* BENDER *starts; looks alarmed.* JOSEPHINE, *sternly*) How do you know that?

BENDER: The fact is, Josephine, Alfred himself just spoke to me about getting her to leave. He asked me to – to help him arrange it.

JOSEPHINE: Oh, he did! (*Thinks.*) Then we must do it.

BENDER: All very well to say – but how? That's the question.

JOSEPHINE: If I only had some excuse, I could very soon make her pack up.

BENDER: Oh, yes. If you had some excuse.

JOSEPHINE: (*sudden idea*) Ah! (*Nods her head as if it would do.*) Theodore, you shall furnish me one.

BENDER: I? How can I –

JOSEPHINE: By making love to ner.

BENDER: (*in an injured tone*) Oh, my dear!

JOSEPHINE: No nonsense, now! It is just the thing, and we will do it at once. (*Glances around as if surveying the room.*) You must meet her here – in this room – alone. You must be very attentive – in fact, affectionate.

BENDER: Heavens, Josephine, what do you – !

JOSEPHINE: Sh! You can do it. In the meantime I will use that small ladder and observe the whole affair from the transom there, over our door.

BENDER: (*aside; alarmed*) My soul!

JOSEPHINE: At the proper time – just when it has gone far enough – I will scream, rush in, and make such a scene that the creature will be glad to escape with her life.

BENDER: (*aside*) I'll be glad to escape with mine.

JOSEPHINE: (*Takes the hamper off ottoman, and places it on chair, between the doors.*) This will work beautifully.

BENDER: (*aside*) Great Caesar! The opera singer will betray me.

JOSEPHINE: I read of just such a case in a book, and it worked beautifully. (*She knocks on* FIFI's *door.*)

BENDER: (*to* JOSEPHINE) Hold on – what – what are you doing?

JOSEPHINE: (*hurrying across to her door*) You have simply to do as I told you – leave the rest to me. (*Exits, shutting the door after her carefully.*)

BENDER: Heavens and earth and – and the other place – I'm in for it now!

JOSEPHINE: (*appearing at the transom over her door, opening it*) Now, be careful.

BENDER: (*with deep meaning*) I will.

FIFI: (*entering from her room, looking about inquiringly*) Did any one knock? (*Sees* BENDER; *speaks very sweetly.*) Oh, Mr Bender, are you there? (*Comes down slowly in front of ottoman.*)

BENDER: Yes, I'm here. (*a glance of misery at his room*) I thought – perhaps – you'd join in a little – er – chat –

FIFI: A chat? Oh, certainly, Nothing could be more charming. (*aside*) How awkward the man is. (*She sits on ottoman, facing her room.*)

BENDER: (*Goes round at back of ottoman and seats himself left of* FIFI.) Now if she'll only keep quiet about the breakfast – and the dressmaker's bill!

FIFI: (*Laughs out merrily.*) Why, Mr Bender, what is the matter with you to-day? You don't seem like the same man I –

BENDER: (*quickly*) 'Hem – 'hem – (*Coughs to cover up her remark.*) Oh, nothing, my dear! I dare say you've heard me going about whistling and – and – carolling with joy; but you know we have different moods.

FIFI: Perhaps you have had a little matrimonial scene with Mrs Bender, eh?

BENDER: No – no – impossible! We are like turtle doves.

FIFI: Dear me! I didn't know that turtle doves suffered so much. (*Laughs lightly.*)

JOSEPHINE: (*aside*) Oh, the little fiend!

FIFI: (*archly*) What do you think the other turtle dove would say if she saw this turtle dove sitting here with me?

BENDER: (*confused*) Ahem – I – (JOSEPHINE *motions him to go on. He nods to his wife, and suddenly takes* FIFI's *hand.*) Ah, my dear young lady –

FIFI: (*smiling*) There – now you're more like yourself again.

BENDER: (*jumping half up, and trying to cover up* FIFI's *remark*) Ah, 'hem – yes – as you say – the – er – weather is more like itself again. (*He still has her hand.*)

> (*Enter* AUGUSTUS McSNATH *abruptly from outside door. He stops and stands looking at* BENDER. JOSEPHINE *begins to motion to* BENDER *violently, from the transom.* BENDER *finally sees her, and looks toward the door. Seeing* McSNATH, *he instantly drops* FIFI's *hand, and starts back.* FIFI *looks around and sees* McSNATH, *but is perfectly composed.*)

FIFI: Ah, we have an audience.

McSNATH: (*Stops on seeing the situation.*) Beg pardon, my name is McSnath.

BENDER: Is it?

McSNATH: (*looking at* BENDER *suspiciously*) It is – I said it was.

BENDER: Well, I didn't say it wasn't.

McSNATH: I didn't say you did. (*pause*)

JOSEPHINE: (*motioning to* BENDER; *loud whisper; aside to him*) Get him away – get him away.

McSNATH: I'm an old friend of Mr Pettibone. We haven't met for years.

BENDER: Don't say?

McSNATH: I do say. I said we hadn't met –

BENDER: I heard you.

McSNATH: Is he at home?

BENDER: No.

McSNATH: I'm sorry.

BENDER: So am I.

McSNATH: Stayed over a day, just to see my dear old Pettibone.

BENDER: Well, there's no such a person as your dear old Pettibone here.

McSNATH: (*Looks suspiciously at* BENDER; *aside*) Something out of the way going on. Very suspicious looking – I'll hunt him up, and tell him about it. He ought to know.

BENDER: Good day, sir.

McSNATH: I'll call again.

BENDER: We shall enjoy a visit from you at any time.

(McSNATH *goes toward outside door. Turns at door and looks back.* BENDER *keeps his eye on* McSNATH. *Exit* McSNATH.)

BENDER: (*taking* FIFI's *hand passionately*) Thank Heaven, he's gone! You dear little — (*Starts back; aside*) Oh, Lord! I forget my wife. (*Sinks on seat beside* FIFI.)

JOSEPHINE: (*aside*) He's doing splendidly now.

FIFI: Oh, Mr Bender, you must excuse me for not waiting breakfast for —

BENDER: (*sudden endeavor to interrupt*) Ah, ahem! (*at the same time seizing a book from table near at hand and throwing it on floor*) Yes. (*Seizes her hand.*) No words can express it. (FIFI *stares in surprise.*)

JOSEPHINE: (*aside*) What is the matter with the man?

FIFI: And after you had been so good about the dressmaker's little —

BENDER: (*This time, more excited, he sends a vase crashing to the floor. Rises and exclaims in a loud voice, to drown* FIFI's *remarks.*) Oh — ah — yes — my dear! Have you ever seen this album — ahem? (*He seizes a portfolio from desk, throwing several books down, and opens it suddenly before* FIFI. *He stands trembling and wipes perspiration from his brow.*)

FIFI: (*aside*) I wonder if he's been drinking! (*She glances at the book which* BENDER *shoved before her. Aloud*) Why, that isn't an album, Mr Bender!

BENDER: Eh? (*Snatches it away.*) Oh! (*aside*) This is killing me. The only way is to plunge in, and bring matters to a climax. (*aloud; sinking and kneeling beside* FIFI, *putting his arm around her*) Miss Oritanski — I cannot conceal the beating of my heart — I cannot hide from you the fact, guilty though it is, that I love —

> (*Enter* ALFRED *from outside, hastily, anticipating cue a little. He stops an instant in astonishment.* BENDER *sees* ALFRED, *and signs to him frantically to go away.*)

ALFRED: (*coming into room quickly*) Look here, Bender, you must be crazy! I can't get you out of another scrape as I did with that confounded letter of yours, by taking it on myself —

> (BENDER *jumps up with a shout of alarm.* JOSEPHINE *utters a ghastly shriek, and disappears from transom. Sound inside her door of crash, bang, and clatter of falling step-ladder; and at same time door opens, and* JOSEPHINE *falls swooning into the room, with ladder fallen partly in door near her.* FIFI *screams and runs to her door where she stands frightened.*)

FIFI: His wife!

> (TOM *rushes on from outside door.* EVANGELINE *runs behind him, and falls on her knees by* JOSEPHINE, *with exclamation of alarm.*)

EVANGELINE: Oh, what is it, mamma?

ALFRED: Good Heavens, what have I done!

BENDER: You've wrecked the entire family.

TOM: Gee-whiffles! Now, he'll get all the comforts of home.

CURTAIN.

ACT IV

SCENE: Same as in Act I. BENDER *is discovered sitting on the bottom stair, with his head buried in his hands as if in mental agony, and in such a way that he does not at first attract attention.*

BENDER: It was kind of Alfred and Evangeline to intercede for me — but — (*shaking head*) — no use — no use. (*Turns up sadly. Speaks meditatively, in a low voice.*) My wife — was never in such a state — before — never.

> (*Enter* ALFRED *and* EVANGELINE *from her room, with a subdued quietness as if a dead body lay in the room. They close the door quietly and carefully.* BENDER *turns to them, looking for a gleam of hope.*)

BENDER: (*low voice*) Well?

ALFRED: (*Shakes head.*) She won't listen to anything.

EVANGELINE: We reasoned with her all we could, papa. She is going to move to the hotel, and has already ordered the trunks taken over. She — she is to meet a lawyer there at four o'clock.

BENDER: A lawyer? (*They nod sadly.*)

ALFRED: Yes — Tom has gone out to bring one.

BENDER: And — what did she say — about me?

EVANGELINE *and* ALFRED: Nothing.

> (BENDER *repeats 'nothing' with his lips alone — no sound. He looks at* ALFRED. ALFRED *shakes his head.*)

EVANGELINE: Oh papa — if a divorce could be avoided! (*She puts her head down on* ALFRED's *shoulder to hide her tears.*)

BENDER: (*after pause*) And — you really think she would be so cruel — so heartless as to — !

> (*Enter* JOSEPHINE. BENDER, *seeing her, breaks off with 'Ahem' and a cough, and looks wanderingly toward other parts of the room.*)

JOSEPHINE: (*between* ALFRED *and* BENDER) I am glad, children, that you are alone, for I have something to say.

> (BENDER *turns slowly and looks at* JOSEPHINE *in ghastly astonishment.* ALFRED *looks at* JOSEPHINE *in surprise also.*)

EVANGELINE: But, mamma dear — we're not alone.

JOSEPHINE: Indeed! I fail to see any one else.

BENDER: (*aside*) I must be growing thin.

JOSEPHINE: I wished to inform you that I have decided not to go home, but to find some quiet watering-place where no prying eyes will intrude upon my widow's sorrow.

BENDER: (*suddenly breaking out*) Oh, look here! This is going a little — a — a —

JOSEPHINE: (*Looks sternly and coldly at* BENDER, *freezing him into silence. He is frozen. She turns to* EVANGELINE.) It is singular that a stranger should have the audacity to address us.

EVANGELINE: A stranger, mamma?

JOSEPHINE: I said a stranger. (*Darts an indignant glance at* BENDER. *He quails.*)

You will of course come with me Evangeline, and you, Alfred, must join us as soon as you can. Then the whole family will be united again.

ALFRED: (*rather timidly*) And — and your husband — ?

JOSEPHINE: My husband — my — ? (*stops and stands as if holding back tears.*) We will sometimes think of him. He was a man who had some good qualities.

EVANGELINE: (*with new hope; eagerly*) Yes, mamma.

JOSEPHINE: But they were few and far between.

BENDER: (*forgetting himself again*) Josephine, you'll do me the credit of —

JOSEPHINE: (*Glances as before, stopping* BENDER *in the midst of his line.*
BENDER *again frozen.*) I wish to do justice to the memory of one who has passed away.

BENDER: (*aside*) Thunder and lightning! This is not pleasant at all.

JOSEPHINE: I wish this person wouldn't disturb us. (*Goes toward her room; after looking at* BENDER *an instant, turns to* EVANGELINE.) Evangeline, my child, you had better go over to our rooms at the hotel for the present. I will come soon.

EVANGELINE: Yes, mamma.

(BENDER *stops pacing and looks at them.* EVANGELINE *looks uncertainly at him. Slight pause.*)

JOSEPHINE: (*To* EVANGELINE; *speaks in a cold, calm voice.*) Children, if you desire to take leave of your former father, I have no objection. (*Goes slowly into her room.*)

(*Slight pause. All three draw long breaths.*)

BENDER: There goes my widow.

ALFRED: (*sympathetically*) Yes (*taking* BENDER*'s hand and pressing it*), so far as I see, you're a dead man.

BENDER: (*to* EVANGELINE) Evangeline, you received permission to take a last look at the remains. (*Holds out hand to her.*)

EVANGELINE: (*going quickly to* BENDER *and embracing him*) Oh, papa, I am so sorry!

BENDER: Thank you! Thank you!

EVANGELINE: (*Looks round at her door; then more confidentially*) You shall come with me to the hotel, and we will try to think of some way to appease her.

BENDER: Alfred, my boy, let me know when I am to be buried.

EVANGELINE: (*as they go off; shocked*) Oh!

ALFRED: (*Sits on ottoman; laughs a little.*) Poor papa Bender! Heaven only knows how he'll get out of this scrape. But I've got my own affairs to get out of — I can't be expected to worry about his. Thank the Lord, the house is nearly empty — and yet — that telegram! It gives me the cold shivers when I think of it. Oh, nonsense! They'd be here before this if they were coming. I dare say they got my dispatch. That ought to stop them. (*He starts toward outside door. Seeing* MRS PETTIBONE *and* EMILY *enter, he sits in chair at the table. Enter* MRS PETTIBONE *and* EMILY, *in travelling rig, carrying satchels, parcels, etc. They come in very abruptly, and see* ALFRED *at once. They put down satchels, etc., on table.*)

MRS PETTIBONE: Ah, Alfred! (*She goes toward him.*)

EMILY: Is that — ? (*Goes toward him.*) Why, so it is!

MRS PETTIBONE: Yes, here he is — as large as life. (MRS PETTIBONE *and*
EMILY *shake his hands.* ALFRED*'s arms hang limp.*)

EMILY: Goodness! What's the matter with him? He must be asleep. Here! Wake
up! (*She shakes him.*)

ALFRED: (*recovering himself*) Oh — yes — how-dy'-do? Glad to see you.

EMILY: Well, it's about time!

MRS PETTIBONE: You received our telegram, of course?

ALFRED: (*quickly*) Yes — but you didn't get mine?

EMILY: Yours? No.

ALFRED: And I sent it 'collect'.

MRS PETTIBONE: What did you say in it?

ALFRED: I told you not to — oh — well — it's of no consequence now, you
know.

EMILY: You told us — not to — ?

ALFRED: Not to — er — delay a moment. (*aside*) Hang it, I hate to lie like that.

EMILY *and* MRS PETTIBONE: (*relieved*) Oh!

MRS PETTIBONE: And, now, Alfred, it is best for you to know at once why we
are here, without my husband's knowledge, for it concerns you and Emily
very deeply — very deeply.

(ALFRED *looks at the ladies anxiously.*)

EMILY: Oh, mamma, dear, you're making such a tragic affair out of it!

MRS PETTIBONE: (*cuttingly*) Indeed! Perhaps you can break the intelligence with
more levity?

EMILY: (*going to* ALFRED, *laughing*) I'm sure there's no breaking about it. You
see, Alfred — cousin Alfred (*laughs.*), you and I have been about half or three-
quarters engaged to each other for some time. Now, although we're very fond
of each other — aren't we? — still, we both know it isn't exactly the kind
required. (ALFRED *says nothing.*) I know you do — and I know I do — so,
don't you think it is about time the engagement was — 'hem — (*burlesque
comedy gesture*) frustrated?

ALFRED: (*rising; suddenly seizing* EMILY*'s hand*) You don't mean it!

EMILY: (*Laughs; turns to* MRS PETTIBONE.) See that? What did I tell you! The
boy is so delighted, he hasn't the politeness to conceal it.

ALFRED: Oh, no!

EMILY: Oh, yes! And I really believe (*an idea coming to her; slowly raises her
finger and points it at him*) — Alfred! You have been falling in love, too!

ALFRED: Too!

EMILY: (*catching herself*) Oh! (*hand over mouth an instant*)

ALFRED: Then you — then she — ha, ha, ha! (*Looks from one to the other. Both
nod their heads affirmatively.*) Really! Ha, ha! Bless you! I congratulate you.
(*Seizes* EMILY*'s hand, and then, in his enthusiasm,* MRS PETTIBONE*'s
also.*) I — I — oh, this is joyful! ha, ha, ha! (*Falls in chair.*)

EMILY: Well — upon my word! (*piqued*)

ALFRED: Who is the unfortunate man? (*Rises.*)

EMILY *and* MRS PETTIBONE: What!

ALFRED: No, fortunate, of course — ha, ha, ha! We must be friends. I'll treat him royally – a drive – down the Strand – o' na'bus – Aquarium – Why don't you tell me his name? (*to* EMILY)

MRS PETTIBONE *and* EMILY: (*They have been in vain trying to stop the flow of* ALFRED's *enthusiasm.*) Victor Smythe.

ALFRED: Ha – Vic – (*aside*) By George!

MRS PETTIBONE: Yes; he has been devoted to Emily for a long time; but for some reason, your uncle seems to have a particular aversion to the young man.

ALFRED: (*meaningly*) Yes – he has.

MRS PETTIBONE: I have done all I could to smooth matters over.

> (ALFRED *smothers a laugh. Enter* DABNEY *from his room, towel around his head, nursing his head still, and in evident misery.*)

MRS PETTIBONE: Why, who is that person?

EMILY: Dear me!

ALFRED: That – ah – yes! You mean – oh! That? (*Speaks confidentially.*) Poor fellow, he has seen better days. A victim of cruel misfortune – drunken wife – starving children – and all that. I took pity on him. He helps me, 'hem – keep the house in order. (*aside*) That's true.

> (DABNEY *sinks on ottoman.*)

MRS PETTIBONE: (*pityingly*) How sad the poor fellow seems.

EMILY: Yes – but come, mamma; it would hardly do to have Mr Smythe find us looking like this.

ALFRED: Smythe! He isn't coming here!

MRS PETTIBONE: Yes – we sent word to him from the station.

> (ALFRED *gives a look of resignation.* DABNEY *catches sight of the ladies, and rises quickly, hurriedly trying to arrange his collar and conceal the towel he had against his head.*)

DABNEY: I most humbly crave pardon. I was not aware there were ladies present.

MRS PETTIBONE: Ah – do not speak of it, dear sir. We know all.

> (DABNEY *is astonished.* ALFRED *picks up book or paper and watches over the top of it.*)

EMILY: Yes – and you mustn't be down-hearted. Things will be better by-and-by.

DABNEY: (*involuntary motion toward head*) I hope so, I'm sure.

MRS PETTIBONE: (*suddenly putting money into* DABNEY's *hand*) Pray accept that. Only a trifle, but it may relieve you. (*She quickly goes up to* FIFI's *door, and exits.*)

> (DABNEY, *overcome with surprise, turns and watches her off.*)

EMILY: (*impulsively giving* DABNEY *money*) For your starving little ones. (*Goes quickly up to* FIFI's *door and exits.*)

> (ALFRED *sits at the table.* DABNEY, *amazed, watches* EMILY *off. He goes to* ALFRED *in a state of blank astonishment.* ALFRED *has picked up a book, which he pretends to be reading as he stands up.*)

DABNEY: (*looking at money in his hands*) What does all this mean?

ALFRED: (*looking up from book*) All what, mean?

DABNEY: Why did they give me money for my starving children?

ALFRED: Who?

DABNEY: Those ladies.

ALFRED: (*looking around room*) What ladies?

DABNEY: Who were here a moment ago.

ALFRED: (*shaking head*) Haven't been any ladies here. (*Resumes perusal of book.*)

DABNEY: Ha! (*Rubs eyes. Feels head. Looks at money.*) Perhaps I'd better go out and get some air.

ALFRED: Yes, do.

> (DABNEY *goes toward stairs. Just as he gets near stairway, the outside door opens, and he stands back a little. Enter* MR PETTIBONE *hurriedly. He sees* ALFRED *at once.*)

PETTIBONE: Ugh! Alfred! (*He is evidently laboring under great excitement. Mechanically tosses his umbrella, rugs, etc., to* DABNEY, *without looking at him, and comes down into the room.* DABNEY *catches the articles thrown to him, and stands an instant in still deeper and blanker bewilderment. Puts hand to head. Blinks. Then turns and exits through the arch, carrying the luggage in his arms.*)

ALFRED: (*aside*) Merciful powers! (*Drops into chair.*)

PETTIBONE: (*putting hat and coat on hat rack*) You didn't expect to see me, I dare say.

ALFRED: (*face indicating that this is the end of everything*) O yes – I thought you'd come.

PETTIBONE: (*Shakes* ALFRED's *hand very hurriedly, and without show of feeling.*) I came here to sell this house.

ALFRED: (*gasp*) Sell it!

PETTIBONE: Yes – sell it – sell it. I will never live in the neighborhood. What do you think? Letters have come to her – while we were away. I am going to dispose of everything I own – everything – and then take her to America – or some other half-civilized country. I'll see you again in a moment – I must draw up some papers regarding the sale and put them in the hands of my attorney.

ALFRED: Yes – of course. Ahem! Where did you leave the family?

PETTIBONE: The family? Don't ask – no matter. Venice – I believe it was. I told them I was going to Hamburg on business. That was a lie. (*Exits into* DABNEY's *room.*)

ALFRED: (*Sits on ottoman; aside*) This is the finishing stroke. It doesn't make any difference what happens now. Things have gone beyond me – but there's (*Rises.*) Emily and Auntie. I'll warn them. (*Goes to* FIFI's *door.*) It may do some good yet. (*Knocks on door. Speaks in low voice.*) Say – you two – come out, quick.

> (EMILY *and* MRS PETTIBONE *enter.* ALFRED *signs them to be quiet.*)

EMILY *and* MRS PETTIBONE: What's the matter, Alfred?

ALFRED: Sh – Uncle's here!

EMILY *and* MRS PETTIBONE: What!

ALFRED: Just arrived. Going to sell the house. Fact is, the reason he has been going on so lately is that he thinks this Smythe chap has been paying attentions to you. (*indicating* MRS PETTIBONE)

MRS PETTIBONE: Me! Me! (*Both ladies are surprised.*)

EMILY: (*indignantly*) The idea!

MRS PETTIBONE: Emily, I have said all along that this concealment was perfectly absurd. Now I shall have a talk with Mr Pettibone. Alfred, do hurry to Mr Smythe's lodgings, 251 Wells Court Road, and tell him not to come here on any account, until I send him word.

ALFRED: Very well. (*Goes to the outside door. Turns to them.*) Lock yourself in that room – don't stir until I get back. (*Exits.*)

(*Door of* DABNEY's *room opens.*)

EMILY: (*seeing door open*) Oh – it's papa!

MRS PETTIBONE: Hurry! (*They run hastily into* FIFI's *room and close and lock the door.*)

PETTIBONE: (*entering from* DABNEY's *room, with papers, etc., and plasters*) Alfred! What has the boy been doing? I never saw such horrible confusion in my life. Everything upside down. Full of medicine bottles, plasters, music-scores – (*throwing plasters off*) I can't do any work there. (*A knock on the outside door.* PETTIBONE *stops.*) Who is it?

(*Enter* McSNATH *from outside door.*)

McSNATH: Ah! My dear Pettibone! I'm glad to find you at last.

PETTIBONE: Find me? What do you – who are you?

McSNATH: Why, McSnath – your ancient friend McSnath. You haven't forgotten? (*Holds out hand.*)

PETTIBONE: (*shaking* McSNATH's *hand mechanically, and dropping it at once*) Oh, McSnath. Ancient friend. Yes. Glad to see you – sit down. (*Walks about absently.*)

McSNATH: (*astonished; follows* PETTIBONE *with eyes; sits; aside*) Odd sort of welcome this is, I must say. Something's wrong with him. (*aloud*) You've been out of town, I believe?

PETTIBONE: Eh? Oh – yes – yes – I believe so.

McSNATH: I called here only a short time ago.

PETTIBONE: Yes – I dare say you did.

McSNATH: I did. That's what I say. And although I didn't find you at home, I had the pleasure of seeing your wife.

PETTIBONE: (*suddenly aroused; turns*) Eh!

McSNATH: (*aside*) Ah! That's what is troubling him. (*Rises.*)

PETTIBONE: You say you saw – ?

McSNATH: My dear friend – calm yourself; but take my advice and don't go off on a journey again.

PETTIBONE: What are you talking about?

McSNATH: Now, be calm, I say! No wonder her behavior enrages you.

PETTIBONE: Ah! How do you know that?

McSNATH: Good Heavens! Couldn't I see?

PETTIBONE: See what?

McSNATH: What was going on a couple of hours ago – in this room. Your wife seated there – enjoying the society of a gentleman, and, from all appearances, enjoying it very much.

PETTIBONE: (*half choking in effort to stop* McSNATH) Aw – gig – stop! Nonsense! Absurd! I left my wife in Venice — day before yesterday. Venice! Do you hear? (*He walks about savagely.*)

McSNATH: Oh, you did!

PETTIBONE: Yes, I did.

McSNATH: (*picking up shawls or satchels*) Whose are these?

PETTIBONE: (*Turns and looks. Rushes up and seizes luggage, looking wildly at it. Screams, dropping things on table.*) Ah — !

McSNATH: Venice, I think you said?

PETTIBONE: (*choking with rage*) What does — who — ah — where — Oh — I'll sift this thing to the bottom now! (*Walks about excitedly.*) The bottom! The bottom!

McSNATH: That's right. The bottom.

PETTIBONE: (*Suddenly seizes McSNATH's hand.*) Old friend — you will stand by me? Say you will.

McSNATH: I will. (*They wring each other's hands. A knock at the outside door causes them both to look up suspiciously.*)

PETTIBONE: Come in!

                (*Enter VICTOR SMYTHE. He comes into the room inquiringly.*)

SMYTHE: I beg pardon —

PETTIBONE: Ah! (*Rushes toward SMYTHE, who retreats.*) There he is! By what right do you enter this house? Answer, before I strangle you where you stand!

SMYTHE: Really, sir — I — I — came in response to a request from a — lady.

PETTIBONE: Say it! Say it, sir! From my wife!

SMYTHE: It was the lady I once supposed to be your wife —

PETTIBONE: Ah! (*as if faint*) A chair! (McSNATH *assists him to ottoman.*)

SMYTHE: I'm really very sorry, sir. I had no idea it would affect you so painfully, considering that you never were married to her —

PETTIBONE: (*springing up*) What do you mean? Never mar — Who the devil told you that?

SMYTHE: T'was your servant who gave me the distressing information.

PETTIBONE: Servant! (*Stamps about.*) Which servant? The scoundrel! It's the most scandalous falsehood ever breathed.

SMYTHE: Falsehood? Falsehood! Oh, sir, this makes me very happy.

PETTIBONE: (*coming and facing* SMYTHE) Oh, sir! It doesn't make me happy at all. (*Stamps about.*) I'll — I'll get a divorce — a divorce, do you hear? — and then you can marry the woman, for all I care.

SMYTHE: (*alarmed*) I — ?

PETTIBONE: You! You! As you've been paying her such infernally-devoted attentions —

McSNATH: (*aside to* PETTIBONE; *interrupting quickly*) No, no! That wasn't the one.

PETTIBONE: Not the one?

McSNATH: No. It was another man.

PETTIBONE: What! Is there another? My soul! (*Walks about more excited than ever.*) Why doesn't he come, so that I can kill him? Why —

(*Enter* BENDER.)

McSNATH: (*seeing* BENDER) There! There he is! That is the one!

PETTIBONE: Ha! That? (McSNATH *nods.* PETTIBONE *rushes at* BENDER.) So, sir! You are here!

BENDER: I seem to be. What of it?

PETTIBONE: This of it! I want your life! I'll have satisfaction out of you! Satisfaction — you hear?

BENDER: What for?

PETTIBONE: I am the husband of the lady you have made love to. Now, do you understand?

BENDER: You have made a mistake — my name is Bender.

PETTIBONE: You'd better change it to Breaker. This good friend of mine came in here this morning, and saw you sitting there by her side.

BENDER: (*aside*) Thunder and lightning!

PETTIBONE: Now, sir! I shall call you to account, sir!

BENDER: I'm happy to hear it, sir. And while we talk of accounts, since you are the lady's husband, you can pay this little dressmaker's bill for your wife. (*Pulls out bill.*)

PETTIBONE: (*in high whining key*) What — my wife — has allowed you to pay her debts? (*Paces floor in agony.*)

BENDER: (*shoving bill into* PETTIBONE's *hand*) There's the receipt — can't you read?

PETTIBONE: (*seizing the bill*) Ha, ha, ha! A pretty game! It says (*beating finger on bill excitedly*) Fifi Oritanski. My wife's name is Pettibone.

BENDER: It doesn't matter — she's probably called herself that, as Pettibone was such a damned ugly name.

PETTIBONE: (*in high rage*) Ha! (*Paces about.* BENDER *paces about excitedly also.*) I'll have no more words!

BENDER: Neither will I!

> (*Enter* ALFRED, *hurrying in from outside door.* SMYTHE, *on* ALFRED's *entrance, runs with fright up the staircase, and returns in a moment.*)

ALFRED: Smythe wasn't — (*Sees* PETTIBONE, BENDER, *etc., and turns at once, going toward the outside door.*)

PETTIBONE: (*rushing and catching* ALFRED) Here — here — stop! (*Brings* ALFRED *back.*) I demand an explanation. An explanation. My wife — my wife is here.

ALFRED: You've seen her, then!

PETTIBONE, McSNATH, *and* BENDER: (*a subdued exclamation together*) Ah!

ALFRED: (*going to* FIFI's *door; knocks*) Come out, auntie — he knows you're here.

> (*Sound of unlocking door. Enter* MRS PETTIBONE.)

MRS PETTIBONE: (*motioning back to* EMILY) Wait until I've spoken to him. (*Turns to* PETTIBONE.)

PETTIBONE: Madam, I have discovered everything — everything!

MRS PETTIBONE: (*with a cheerful look at* SMYTHE) Oh, I'm very glad he told you. I hope you are satisfied with my choice.

PETTIBONE: Satis — ! (*Stops in utter amazement.*)

MRS PETTIBONE: Yes. Mr Smythe is a most deserving young man, and of a very good family.

PETTIBONE: (*becoming wild*) What in the devil's name do I care for his family!

MRS PETTIBONE: Have you any objection to him?

PETTIBONE: (*with scathing irony*) Oh — not at all — not at all. And the other (*Looks at* BENDER.) how about his family?

MRS PETTIBONE: What other?

PETTIBONE: Allow me. (*Takes* MRS PETTIBONE *by the hand rather roughly, and leads her up to* BENDER.) Here is the other! Quite a gathering of your agreeable friends!

BENDER: (*having risen; politely to* PETTIBONE) May I beg the honor of an introduction?

PETTIBONE: You mean to say you don't know my wife?

           (*Slight pause; all quiet.* McSNATH *comes down to* PETTIBONE.)

McSNATH: (*low but earnest voice*) Look here! Is that your wife?

PETTIBONE: (*looking at* MRS PETTIBONE) Certainly.

           (McSNATH *gives one look, then turns abruptly about and walks off at the outside door rapidly. The others watch his exit.*)

PETTIBONE: (*turning to* MRS PETTIBONE) Rosabelle — how am I to explain your presence here?

MRS PETTIBONE: Very simply. I took advantage of your absence in Hamburg —

PETTIBONE: Ahem!

MRS PETTIBONE: — to come here with Emily and bring about an understanding between her and Mr Smythe, who have loved each other a long time, but were afraid to speak to you.

PETTIBONE: Rosabelle — you will forgive me — I have been behaving like a lunatic — because I thought that he —

MRS PETTIBONE: Yes — I know.

           (PETTIBONE *shakes hands with* SMYTHE. MRS PETTIBONE *stands with them.*)

EMILY: (*peeping out at* FIFI's *door*) I can come now, can't I?

MRS PETTIBONE: Yes — yes.

           (EMILY *enters and goes quickly to* SMYTHE. PETTIBONE *kisses her.*)

PETTIBONE: (*to* ALFRED) But wait. Wait, I say. How about Alfred?

ALFRED: Yes — you've overlooked me entirely.

PETTIBONE: You — you were going to marry her, weren't you?

ALFRED: (*Pulls out the paper used in Act I.*) That is my impression. And this little document you signed just before you left, will answer very well in a law-suit.

PETTIBONE, MRS PETTIBONE, *and* EMILY: Law-suit! Mercy on us! Dear me!

ALFRED: But on the whole, I'll let it go, and resign myself to my fate. (*Meets* SMYTHE *and* EMILY; *shakes hands and congratulates them both.*)

BENDER: Yes — and the reason is, if you'll permit me to speak, that his fate is to become my son-in-law. (*The* PETTIBONE *family is surprised.*)

MRS PETTIBONE: Ah — this noble resignation!

           (*Enter* EVANGELINE *from the outside door. As she comes on,*

JOSEPHINE *enters from her room, meeting her.* BENDER *rises and stands stiffly and unmoved.*)

JOSEPHINE: Evangeline, I will go to the hotel —

EVANGELINE: Mamma! (*stopping her, and indicating the gathering in the room*)

ALFRED: Mrs Bender, Evangeline — my uncle, my aunt, my cousin, and Mr Smythe.

(*Enter* TOM, *from outside, running on with great noise and slam, so that all look around.*)

TOM: Mrs Bender! Mrs Bender! I've got that there lawyer fur ye at last. He's comin' up the steps. (TOM *stops, looking at the crowd.*)

ALFRED: (*entreatingly*) Ah — Mrs Bender — be merciful!

EVANGELINE: (*with feeling*) Mamma — think of papa — think of us all.

JOSEPHINE: (*Looks at* BENDER. *She begins to smile as if her stern resolve were melting.* BENDER *still stands rigid. She comes to* BENDER.) Theodore —

BENDER: I'm dead!

JOSEPHINE: That depends upon me, Theodore.

BENDER: Do you think of resurrecting me?

JOSEPHINE: For the children's sake, I do.

BENDER: Then I forgive you.

(JOSEPHINE *sits in chair;* BENDER *kneels to the left of her; simpering forgiveness, etc.*)

PETTIBONE: Look here, Alfred, how in the world did all this come about — eh?

MRS PETTIBONE *and* EMILY: Yes — how was it? We'd like to know.

ALFRED: (*seizing* TOM *and bringing him forward*) Through a little idea of mine in which I was ably assisted by taking this young man into partnership on the sole condition —

TOM: That I gits half.

CURTAIN

SECRET SERVICE

A romance of the Southern Confederacy
A drama in four acts

First produced in its original form, under the title of *The Secret Service*, at the Broad Street Theatre, Philadelphia, on 13 May 1895, with the following cast:

CAPTAIN RALPH CHALLONER	Maurice Barrymore
MR BENTON ARRELSFORD	William Harcourt
MAJOR GENERAL RANDOLPH	H.B. Bradley
WILFRED VARNEY	Edwin Arden
DR HORACE GARNET	R.F. McClannin
HENRY DUMONT	M.L. Alsop
JONAS	T.E. Jackson
LILLIAN VARNEY	Mary Hampton
CAROLINE MITFORD	Odette Tyler
MRS GENERAL VARNEY	Ida Vernon
MARTHA	Alice Leigh
ELEANOR FAIRFAX	Elaine Eillson
MISS KITTRIDGE	Lulu Hopper
MISS FARRINGTON	Meta Brittain

The production was unsuccessful and was immediately withdrawn. After radical revision, it was produced at the Garrick Theatre, New York, on 5 October 1896, with the following cast:

GENERAL NELSON RANDOLPH	Joseph Brennan
MRS GENERAL VARNEY	Ida Waterman
EDITH VARNEY	Amy Busby
WILFRED VARNEY	Walter Thomas
CAROLINE MITFORD	Odette Tyler
LEWIS DUMONT/CAPTAIN THORNE	William Gillette
HENRY DUMONT	M.L. Alsop
MR BENTON ARRELSFORD	Campbell Gollan
MISS KITTRIDGE	Meta Brittain
LIEUTENANT MAXWELL	Francis Neilson
MARTHA	Alice Leigh
JONAS	H.D. James
LIEUTENANT FORAY	William B. Smith
LIEUTENANT ALLISON	Louis Duval
SERGEANT WILSON	I.N. Drew

SERGEANT ELLINGTON   Henry Wilton
CORPORAL MATSON   H.A. Morey
CAVALRY ORDERLY
ARTILLERY ORDERLY
HOSPITAL MESSENGER
FIRST WAR DEPT. MESSENGER
SECOND WAR DEPT. MESSENGER
THIRD WAR DEPT. MESSENGER
FOURTH WAR DEPT. MESSENGER
TELEGRAPH OFFICE MESSENGER A
TELEGRAPH OFFICE MESSENGER B
EDDINGER

An evening in Richmond during the war of the rebellion at a time when the Northern forces were entrenched before the city and endeavoring by all possible means to break down the defenses and capture the Confederate capital. While no special effort has been made in the direction of historical accuracy, the City of Richmond at the time set forth in SECRET SERVICE was in a state of the utmost excitement and confusion. Wounded and dying were being brought in from the defenses by the car-load. Churches, libraries and public buildings were converted into hospitals. Owing to the scarcity of surgeons and medical attendants women and even young girls assisted at the dressing of wounds and nursed the sufferers day and night. Other women were occupied sewing coarse and heavy sand bags for the strengthening of the fortifications. Strict military discipline was impossible. Courts martial if held at all were composed of any available material, even private citizens serving if necessary. Troops were being hurried in from the South and no careful scrutiny was attempted. This made it possible for many Northern secret service men to enter the city and remain there in various disguises. In the midst of this trouble a brave attempt at gaiety was kept up — chiefly by the young people in a desperate endeavor to distract their minds from the terrible situation. There were dances and 'starvation parties' so called because of the necessarily limited fare provided and the booming of the great siege guns often sounded above the strains of a dreamy waltz or the lively beat of a polka.

V *Secret Service*, Act III: 'The Telegraph Office'. Gillette is in the foreground

ACT I

Drawing-room in GENERAL VARNEY's *house — Franklin Street — Richmond.
Eight o'clock. Richly furnished. Southern characteristics. Fire-place on left side.
Wiᵈe doors or arch up left set diagonally open to a front hall. Portieres on these
doors or arch to draw, completely closing opening. Stairway seen through these
doors or arch, in the hall, at back, ascending from a landing a few steps high back of
center of opening, and rise off to the left. Entrance to street off left below stairs.
Entrance to dining room and kitchen off right below stairs. Both of these openings
are back of double doors or arch up left center. Wide door at center opening to a
back parlor which is being used for women who come there to sew and work for
hospitals. Two double French windows on right side, one up stage set oblique, and
one down, both opening to a wide veranda. Shrubbery, etc., beyond the veranda
and vines, etc., on balustrade and posts of veranda — which must be in line of sight
for whole house outside the upper of these two windows. Both these windows are
'French' extending down to floor, and to open and close on hinges. They also have
curtains or draperies which can easily be drawn to cover them. Below window down
right a writing desk and chair. Between these windows stand a pedestal and vase of
flowers to be knocked over by* THORNE *in* ACT IV. *Chair near pedestal — chair
and cabinet right of center door against wall. Table left of center door against wall
with lamp and vase of flowers. Couch down right center. Table and two chairs left
center. Chair each side of the fireplace. Hall seat in hall. Pedestal and statue on
landing in hall. Dark or nearly dark outside windows with strong moonlight effect.
Lights on in hall and in room up center, but not glaring — light in the room itself
full on but shaded so that it gives subdued effect. No fire in fireplace. Portieres on
both windows closed at rise. Windows closed at rise. As curtain rises low distant
boom of cannonading rolls in distance and quiets down — then is heard again.* MISS
KITTRIDGE, *one of the women who is sewing for the hospitals, enters from the
center doors. Stops, listens to the sound of cannon — with worried look — crosses
to window and looks out. Flashes on her face, then turns and goes toward table at
left. She gathers up pieces of cloth and linen rags that are on the table, looks
toward window again, then takes them off at center door, closing the door carefully
after her. Sounds of a heavy door closing outside left. Enter at door up left*
WILFRED VARNEY, *a boy of about sixteen — impetuous — Southern — black-
eyed — dark hair. He is fairly well dressed, but in a suit that has evidently been
worn some time. Dark shade. He comes rapidly into the room looking about. Goes
to door up center, opens it a little way and looks off. Closes it. Goes to window.
Throws open portieres and windows and looks anxiously off. Red flashes on backing. Distant boom and low thunder of cannon. Enter* MARTHA, *a negro servant,
coming from door at foot of stairs.* WILFRED *turning sees her, and crosses toward
her.*

WILFRED: Where's mother?

MARTHA: She's up staars with Mars Howard sah.

WILFRED: Ah've got to see 'er!

MARTHA: Mars Howard he's putty bad dis ebenin' — Ah dunno's she'd want to
leave 'im. — Ah'll go up an' see what she says. (*Exit door up left and up the
stairway.*)

(WILFRED *left alone, moves restlessly about, especially when low rumble of distant cannon is heard. Effect of passing artillery in the street outside. On hearing it he hurries to the window and looks out, continuing to do so while the sounds of the passing guns, horses and men are heard. While he is at the window* MRS VARNEY *enters, coming down the stairway and on at door up left. She is quiet, pale, with white or nearly white hair and a rather young face. Her dress is black and though rich, is plain. Not in the least 'dressy' or fashionable. In manner she is calm and self-possessed. She pauses and looks at* WILFRED *a moment. He turns and sees her.* MARTHA *follows her down and exits door at foot of stairway.*)

WILFRED: (*Goes toward her.*) Howard isn't worse is he?

MRS VARNEY: Ah'm afraid so.

WILFRED: Anything Ah can do?

MRS VARNEY: (*Shakes head.*) No — no. — We can only wait — and hope. (WILFRED *walks away a little as if he could not quite say the thing on his mind.*) Ah'm thankful there's a lull in the cannonading. Do they know why it stopped? (*boom of cannon — a low distant rumble*)

WILFRED: It hasn't stopped altogether — don't you hear?

MRS VARNEY: Yes, but compared to what it was yesterday — you know it shook the house — and Howard suffered dreadfully!

WILFRED: (*suddenly facing her*) So did I mother! (*low boom of cannon*)

MRS VARNEY: You!

WILFRED: When Ah hear those guns and know the fighting's on, it makes me —

MRS VARNEY: (*Goes toward table left center, interrupting quickly.*) Yes, yes — we all suffered — we all suffered, dear! (*Sits right of table.*)

WILFRED: Mother, Ah want to speak to you! You may not like it but you must listen — you must let me — (*Goes toward her.*)

MRS VARNEY: (*Motioning so that he stops; slight pause. She soon speaks in a low voice. She takes his hand in a motherly way.*) I know — what it is.

WILFRED: Ah can't stay back here any longer! It's worse than being shot to pieces! Ah can't do it mother! (MRS VARNEY *looks steadily into* WILFRED*'s face but says nothing. Soon she turns away a little as if she felt tears coming into her eyes.*) Why don't you speak?

MRS VARNEY: (*turning to him with a faint attempt to smile*) Ah don't know what to say.

WILFRED: Say you won't mind if Ah go down there and help 'em!

MRS VARNEY: It wouldn't be true!

WILFRED: I can't stay here!

MRS VARNEY: You're so young Wilfred!

WILFRED: No younger than Tom Kittridge — no younger than Ell Stuart — nor cousin Stephen — nor hundreds of the fellows fighting down there! — See mother — they've called for all over nineteen — that was weeks ago! The eighteen call may be out any minute — the next one after that takes me! Do I want to stay back here till they order me out! Ah should think not! (*Walks about, stops and speaks to* MRS VARNEY.) If Ah was hit with a shell an' had to stay it would be different! But Ah can't stand this — Ah can't do it mother!

MRS VARNEY: (*rising and going to him*) I'll write to your father.

WILFRED: Why that'll take forever! You don't know where his Division is — They change 'em every day! I can't wait for you to write.

MRS VARNEY: (*Shakes head and speaks finally.*) I couldn't let you go without his consent! You must be patient! (WILFRED *starts slowly toward door with head lowered in disappointment, — but not ill-naturedly.* MRS VARNEY *looks yearningly after him a moment as he moves away, then goes toward him.*) Wilfred! (WILFRED *turns and meets her and she holds him and smooths his hair a little with her hand.*) Don't feel bad that you have to stay here with your mother a little longer!

WILFRED: Aw — It isn't that!

MRS VARNEY: My darling boy — I know it! You want to fight for your country — and I'm proud of you! I want my sons to do their duty! But with your father commanding a brigade at the front and one boy lying wounded — perhaps mortally — (*Pause —* MRS VARNEY *moves away a few steps.*)

WILFRED: (*After pause — goes to her.*) Well you'll write to father tonight, won't you?

MRS VARNEY: Yes — yes!

(*Door bell is heard ringing in distant part of the house.* WILFRED *and* MRS VARNEY *both listen.* MARTHA *crosses outside door up left from right, on her way to open the front door. Heavy sound of door off left. In a moment she returns and appears at door up left.*)

MARTHA: Hit's one o' de men fum de hossiple ma'am. (WILFRED *hurries to door and exits to see the messenger.*)

MRS VARNEY: We've just sent all the bandages we have.

MARTHA: He says de's all used up, an' two more trains juss come in crowded full o' wounded sojers — an' mos' all of 'em drefful bad!

MRS VARNEY: Is Miss Kittridge here yet?

MARTHA: Yaas'm.

MRS VARNEY: Ask her if they've got enough to send. Even if it's only a little, let them have it. What they need most is bandages.

MARTHA: (*crossing toward door up center*) Yaas'm. (*Exits.* MRS VARNEY *goes toward the door up left, stops near the door.*)

MRS VARNEY: Oh — (*beckoning*) Come in. (*She moves toward center.* MESSENGER *appears at the door. He is a crippled soldier in battered Confederate uniform. His arm is in a sling.*) What hospital did you come from?

MESSENGER: (*Remains up near door left.*) The Winder ma'am.

MRS VARNEY: Have you been to St Paul's? You know the ladies are working there tonight.

MESSENGER: Yes — but they hain't a-workin' for the hospitals, ma'am — they're making sandbags for the fortifications.

MRS VARNEY: Well, I hope we can give you something.

MISS KITTRIDGE: (*Enters at door up center bringing a small bundle of lint, etc.*) This is all there is now. (*Hands package to the* MESSENGER.) If you'll come back in an hour, we'll have more for you. (MESSENGER *takes package and exits door left. Sound of front door closing outside.*) We're all going to stay

tonight, Miss Varney. There's so many more wounded come in it won't do to
stop now.

MRS VARNEY: (*on sofa*) No, no — we mustn't stop.

MISS KITTRIDGE: Is — is your son — is there any change?

MRS VARNEY: Ah'm afraid the fever's increasing.

MISS KITTRIDGE: Has the Surgeon seen him this evening?

MRS VARNEY: No — oh, no! (*shaking her head*) We couldn't ask him to come
twice — with so many waiting for him at the hospital.

MISS KITTRIDGE: But they.couldn't refuse you Mrs Varney! There's that man
going right back to the hospital! I'll call him and send word that — (*starting
toward the door*)

MRS VARNEY: No, no — I can't let you! (*Rises.*)

MISS KITTRIDGE: Not for — your own son?

MRS VARNEY: Think how many sons must be entirely neglected to visit mine
twice! (*Sound of door outside left. Enter* EDITH VARNEY, *a light quick
entrance, coming from outside — hat in hand as if just taking it off as she
enters.*) Edith dear! How late you are! You must be tired out!

EDITH: Ah'm not tired at all! Besides, I haven't been at the hospital all day. Good-
bye, Miss Kittridge! I want to tell Mama something.

MISS KITTRIDGE: O dear! I'll get out of hearing right quick! (*Exit.*)

EDITH: (*up to door lightly and calling after* KITTRIDGE) I hope you don't mind.

MISS KITTRIDGE: Mercy, no!

> (EDITH *closes the door and goes to* MRS VARNEY, *taking her
> down stage to chair right of table.* MRS VARNEY *sits in chair and
> EDITH on stool close to her in front of table.*)

EDITH: Mama — what do you think? What do you think?

MRS VARNEY: What is it, dear?

EDITH: Ah've been to see the President!

MRS VARNEY: What! — Mr Davis!

EDITH: Yes! An' Ah asked him for an appointment for Captain Thorne for the War
Department Telegraph Service — an' he gave it to me — a Special Commission!
Appointing him to duty here in Richmond — a very important position — so
now he won't have to be sent back to the front — an' it'll be doing his duty
just the same.

MRS VARNEY: But Edith — you don't —

EDITH: Yes it will, Mama! The President told me they needed a man who understood telegraphing and who was of high enough rank to take charge of the
Service! And you know Cap'n Thorne is an expert! Since he's been here in
Richmond he's helped 'em in the telegraph office very often — Lieutenant
Foray told me so! (MRS VARNEY *slowly rises and moves away — slight
pause.*) Now, Mama, Ah feel you're going to scold — an' you mustn't because
it's all fixed, an' the commission'll be sent over here in a few minutes — just
as soon as it can be made out! An' the next time he comes Ah'm to hand it
to him myself.

MRS VARNEY: He's coming this evening.

EDITH: (*Looks at* MRS VARNEY *an instant before speaking — then in low voice*)
How do you know?

MRS VARNEY: (*going back of table*) This note came half an hour ago. (*about to hand note from table to* EDITH, *who sees note and anticipates her action, picking it up and going quickly right with it*)

EDITH: Has it been here — all this time? (*Opens envelope eagerly, and reads note.*)

MRS VARNEY: (*after a moment*) You see what he says? This'll be his last call. — He's got his orders to leave. (*Sits right of table left center.*)

EDITH: (*Sits on sofa.*) Why, it's too ridiculous! Just as if the commission from the President wouldn't supersede everything? It puts him at the head of the Telegraph Service! He'll be in the command of the Department! — He says — (*glancing at note*) good-bye call does he! All the better — it'll be that much more of a surprise! (*rising and going toward* MRS VARNEY) Now Mama, don't you breathe — Ah want to tell him myself!

MRS VARNEY: But Edith dear — Ah don't quite approve of your going to the President about this.

EDITH: (*changing from light manner to earnestness*) But listen, Mama — Ah couldn't go to the War Department people — Mr Arrelsford's there in one of the offices — and ever since Ah refused him you know how he's treated me! — (*slight deprecatory motion from* MRS VARNEY) If Ah'd applied for the appointment there he'd have had it refused — and he'd have got them to order Cap'n Thorne away right off — Ah know he would — and — (*Stands motionless as she thinks of it.*) That's where his orders to go came from!

MRS VARNEY: But my dear —

EDITH: It is, Mama! (*slight pause*) Isn't it lucky I got that commission today!
(*Door bell rings in distant part of the house.* JONAS *goes across hall to the door up left.* MRS VARNEY *moves up stage a little waiting to see who it is.* EDITH *listening. Heavy sound of door off left.* JONAS *enters at the door up left.*)

JONAS: (*coming to* MRS VARNEY) It's a officer, ma'am. He says he's fum de President — an — (*Hands a card to* MRS VARNEY.) he's got ter see Miss Edith pussonully.

EDITH: (*low voice*) It's come, Mama!

MRS VARNEY: (*Rises and goes up center.*) Ask the gentleman in. (*Hands card to* EDITH. JONAS *exits left.*)

EDITH: (*overjoyed but keeping voice low*) It's the Commission!

MRS VARNEY: (*low voice*) Do you know who it is?

EDITH: No! But he's from the President — it must be that!
(*Enter* JONAS *at door up left. He comes on a little bowing someone in. Enter* LIEUT. MAXWELL *at door up left. He is a very dashing young officer, handsome, polite and dressed in a showy and perfectly fitting uniform.* JONAS *exits.* MRS VARNEY *advances a little.*)

LT MAXWELL: Good evening. (*Bows;* MRS VARNEY *and* EDITH *bow slightly. To* MRS VARNEY) Have Ah the honah of addressing Miss Varney?

MRS VARNEY: I am Mrs Varney, sir. (*emphasizing 'Mrs' a little*)

LT MAXWELL: (*bowing to* MRS VARNEY) Madam — Ah'm very much afraid this looks like an intrusion on my part, but Ah come from the President and he desires me to see Miss Varney personally!

MRS VARNEY: Anyone from the President could not be otherwise than welcome. This is my daughter. (*indicating* EDITH)

    (LIEUT. MAXWELL *bows to* EDITH *and she returns the salutation. He then walks across to her, taking a large brown envelope from his belt.*)

LT MAXWELL: Miss Varney, the President directed me to deliver this into your hands — with his compliments. (*handing it to* EDITH) He is glad to be able to do this not only at your request, but as a special favor to your father, General Varney.

EDITH: (*taking envelope*) Oh, thank you!

MRS VARNEY: Won't you be seated, Lieutenant?

EDITH: O yes — do! (*Holds envelope pressed very tight against her side.*)

LT MAXWELL: Nothing would please me so much, ladies — but Ah have to be back at the President's house right away. Ah'm on duty this evening. — Would you mind writing me off a line or two, Miss Varney — just to say you have the communication?

EDITH: Why certainly — (*Takes a step or two toward desk at right.*) You want a receipt — I — (*Turns and crosses toward door up left.*) I'll go upstairs to my desk — it won't take a moment! (*Turns at door.*) And — could I put in how much I thank him for his kindness?

LT MAXWELL: Ah'm sure he'd be more than pleased! (EDITH *exits and hastens up the stairway.*)

MRS VARNEY: (*moving forward slowly*) We haven't heard so much cannonading today, Lieutenant. Do they know what it means?

LT MAXWELL: (*going forward with* MRS VARNEY) Ah don't think they're quite positive, ma'am, but they can't help lookin' for a violent attack to follow.

MRS VARNEY: I don't see why it should quiet down before an assault!

LT MAXWELL: It might be some signal, ma'am, or it might be they're moving their batteries to open on a special point of attack. They're tryin' ev'ry way to break through our defenses, you know.

    (*Door bell rings in distant part of house.*)

MRS VARNEY: It's very discouraging! (*Seats herself at table.*) We can't seem to drive them back this time!

LT MAXWELL: We're holding 'em where they are though! They'll never get in unless they do it by some scurvy trick — that's where the danger lies!

    (*Heavy sound of door off left.*)

EDITH: (*Enters, coming lightly and quickly down the stairway, with a note in her hand, and without the official envelope, which she has left in her room.*) Is Lieutenant Maxwell — (*seeing him down stage with* MRS VARNEY *and going across toward them*) O yes!

    (JONAS *enters at door up left as* EDITH *reaches up center, showing in* CAPTAIN THORNE.)

JONAS: (*low voice*) Will you jess kinely step dis way, suh!

    (MRS VARNEY *rises and moves down in front of and then up left of table.* MAXWELL *turns and meets* EDITH *up right center.*)

EDITH: (*meeting* MAXWELL) I didn't know but you — (*She stops — hearing* JONAS *and quickly turns, looking off left.*) Oh! — Captain Thorne!

(*Enter* CAPTAIN THORNE *at door up left meeting and shaking hands with* EDITH. THORNE *is dressed as a Confederate Captain of Artillery. It is somewhat worn and soiled.* LIEUT. MAXWELL *turned and moved up a little on* EDITH's *entrance, remaining a little right of center.* JONAS *exits left.*)

EDITH: (*giving* THORNE *her hand briefly*) We were expecting you! — Here's Captain Thorne, Mama!

(MRS VARNEY *moves up left center meeting* THORNE *and shaking hands with him graciously.* — EDITH *turns away and goes to* LIEUT. MAXWELL. THORNE *and* MRS VARNEY *move up center near small table and converse.*)

EDITH: I wasn't so very long writing it, was I lieutenant? (*She hands him the note.*)

LT MAXWELL: Ah've never seen a quicker piece of work, Miss Varney. (*putting note in belt or pocket*) When you want a clerkship ovah at the Government offices you must shorely let me know!

EDITH: (*smilingly*) You'd better not commit yourself — Ah might take you at your word!

LT MAXWELL: Nothing would please me so much Ah'm sure! All you've got to do is just to apply!

EDITH: Lots of the girls are doing it — they have to, to live! Aren't there a good many where you are?

LT MAXWELL: Well we don't have so many as they do over at the Treasury. Ah believe there are more ladies there than men!

MRS VARNEY: (*Comes down a little.*) Perhaps you gentlemen have met! (*glancing toward* MAXWELL)

(THORNE *shakes head a little and steps forward, looking at* MAXWELL.)

MRS VARNEY: Cap'n Thorne — Lieutenant Maxwell.

THORNE: (*slight inclination of head*) Lieutenant.

LT MAXWELL: (*returning bow pleasantly*) I haven't had the pleasure — though Ah've heard the Cap'n's name mentioned several times!

THORNE: Yes? (MRS VARNEY *and* EDITH *are looking at* MAXWELL.)

LT MAXWELL: (*as if it were rather amusing*) In fact Cap'n, there's a gentleman in one of our offices who seems mighty anxious to pick a fight with you!

(EDITH *is suddenly serious and a look of apprehension spreads over* MRS VARNEY's *face.*)

THORNE: (*easily*) Pick a fight! Really! Why what office is that, Lieutenant?

LT MAXWELL: (*slightly annoyed*) The War Office, sir!

THORNE: Dear, dear! Ah didn't suppose you had anybody in the War Office who wanted to fight!

LT MAXWELL: (*almost angry*) An' why not, sir?

THORNE: (*easily*) Well if he did he'd hardly be in an office would he — at a time like this?

LT MAXWELL: (*trying to be light again*) Ah'd better not tell him that, Cap'n — he'd certainly insist on havin' you out!

THORNE: (*moving down with* MRS VARNEY) That would be too bad — to interfere with the gentleman's office hours! (THORNE *and* MRS VARNEY *move down near table — in conversation.*)

LT MAXWELL: (*to* EDITH) He doesn't believe it, Miss Varney, — but it's certainly true, an' I dare say you know who the —

EDITH: (*quickly interrupting* MAXWELL — *low voice*) Please don't Lieutenant! — I — (*an apprehensive glance toward* THORNE) I'd rather not — (*with a slight catch of breath*) — talk about it!

LT MAXWELL: (*after short pause of surprise*) Yes, of course! — Ah didn't know there was any —

EDITH: (*interrupting again, with attempt to turn it off*) Yes! (*a rather nervous effort to laugh lightly*) — You know there's always the weather to fall back on!

LT MAXWELL: (*picking it up easily*) Yes — Ah should say so! An' mighty bad weather too — most of the time!

EDITH: (*laughingly*) Yes — isn't it! (*They laugh a little and go on talking and laughing to themselves, moving toward right upper window for a moment and soon move across toward door up left as if* MAXWELL *were going.*)

MRS VARNEY: (*back of table with* THORNE) From your note Captain Thorne, I suppose you're leaving us soon. Your orders have come.

THORNE: Yes — Mrs Varney, they have. — Ah'm afraid this'll be my last call.

MRS VARNEY: Isn't it rather sudden? It seems to me they ought to give you a little time.

THORNE: Ah well (*slight smile*) we have to be ready for anything, you know!

MRS VARNEY: (*with a sigh*) Yes — I know! — It's been a great pleasure to have you drop in on us while you were here. We shall quite miss your visits.

THORNE: (*a slight formality in manner*) Thank you. I shall never forget what they've been to me.

> (MAXWELL *is taking leave of* EDITH *up center.*)

EDITH: Lieutenant Maxwell is going, Mama!

MRS VARNEY: So soon! Excuse me a moment, Captain! (*Goes hurriedly toward* MAXWELL — THORNE *goes near mantel.*) Ah'm right sorry to have you hurry away, Lieutenant. We shall hope for the pleasure of seeing you again.

LT MAXWELL: Ah shall certainly call, Mrs Varney — if you'll allow me. — Cap'n! (*saluting* THORNE *from near the door up left*)

THORNE: (*turning from mantel; half salute*) Lieutenant!

LT MAXWELL: Miss Varney! Mrs Varney! (*Bowing to each. Exits.* MRS VARNEY *follows* MAXWELL *off at door up left — speaking as she goes.*)

MRS VARNEY: Now remember Lieutenant, you're to come sometime when duty doesn't call you away so soon!

> (EDITH *turns and moves slowly to table up center on* MAXWELL'*s exit.*)

LT MAXWELL: (*outside — voice getting more distant*) Trust me to attend to that, Mrs Varney.

> (*Heavy sound of door off left*)

THORNE: (*moving toward* EDITH *who is up center near small table*) Shall I see Mrs Varney again?

EDITH: (*getting a rose from vase on table*) Oh yes — you'll see her again! — But not just now.

THORNE: I haven't long to stay.

EDITH: (*down center a little*) Well — do you know — Ah think you have more time than you really think you have! It would be odd if it came out that way — wouldn't it? (*playing with flower in her hand*)

THORNE: Yes — but it won't come out that way.

EDITH: Yes — but you — (*She stops as* THORNE *is taking the rose from her hand — which she was holding up in an absent way as she talked.* THORNE *at the same time holds the hand she had it in. She lets go of the rose and draws away her hand.*)

EDITH: (*a little embarrassed*) You know — you can sit down if you want to! (*indicating chair at left of table*)

THORNE: Yes — I see.

EDITH: (*Sits at right of table.*) You'd better! — Oh, I've a great many things to say!

THORNE: Oh — you have!

EDITH: (*Nodding — her left hand is on the table.*) Yes.

THORNE: I have only one.

EDITH: (*looking up at him*) And — that is — ?

THORNE: (*taking her left hand in both of his*) Good-bye.

EDITH: But Ah don't really think you'll have to say it!

THORNE: (*looking tenderly down at her*) I know I will!

EDITH: (*low voice — more serious*) Then it'll be because you want to!

THORNE: (*quickly*) No! It will be — because I must.

EDITH: (*rising slowly and looking at him a little mischievously as she does so*) Oh — because you must! (THORNE *nods a little.* EDITH *walks toward center thinking whether to tell him or not. He watches her. She suddenly turns back and goes again to table left center.*) You don't know some things I do!

THORNE: (*laughing a little at first*) Ah think that's more than likely, Miss Varney! (*Goes to left of table.*) Would you mind telling me a few so Ah can somewhat approach you in that respect?

EDITH: (*seriously*) Ah wouldn't mind telling you one, and that is, it's very wrong for you to think of leaving Richmond yet!

THORNE: Ah — but you don't —

EDITH: (*Sits in chair right of table, breaking in quickly.*) Oh, yes, Ah do!

THORNE: (*Sits in chair left of table, looking up at her amused.*) Well — what?

EDITH: Whatever you were going to say! Most likely it was that there's something or other Ah don't know about! — But Ah know this — (*looking away front — eyes lowered a little*) you were sent here only a few weeks ago to recover from a very bad wound — (THORNE *looks down and little front quickly.*) — and you haven't nearly had time for it yet!

THORNE: (*as if amused*) Ha, ha — yes. (*looking up at* EDITH *with usual expression*) Ah do look as if the next high wind would blow me away, don't I?

EDITH: (*turning to him earnestly — half rising*) No matter how you look, you ought not — Oh — (*rising fully and turning away from him*) You're just making fun of it, like you always do! (*Goes up center, turns to* THORNE *again.*) No matter! You can make all the fun you like, but the whole thing is settled, and you aren't going away at all!

(THORNE *has risen when* EDITH *did.*)

THORNE: Oh — Ah'm not!

EDITH: No!

THORNE: Well, that's quite a change for me! (*Puts hat on table and moves up near* EDITH *going back of table.*) Perhaps you wouldn't mind telling me what I am going to do?

EDITH: (*turning to him*) Ah wouldn't mind at all — an' it's this — you see Ah've been to the — (*Hesitates.*) Now! Ah'm almost afraid to tell you!

THORNE: (*near* EDITH) Don't tell me Miss Varney — because it's really true. I've got my order — I'm leaving tonight.

(EDITH *looks at* THORNE *an instant — then turns and goes right and sits on couch, looking at him from there.*)

EDITH: (*after an instant*) Where — to the front?

THORNE: (*Moves over to* EDITH.) We can't always tell where orders'll take us. (*Sits on the couch beside her.*)

EDITH: But listen! Supposing there were other orders — from a higher authority — appointing you to duty here?

THORNE: (*eyes lowered before him*) It wouldn't make any difference.

EDITH: (*sudden alarm*) You don't — you don't mean you'd go — in spite of them? (THORNE *raises his eyes to hers in slight surprise and looks at her an instant. Then he nods affirmatively.*) But if it proved your first order was a mistake — and — (*In her earnestness she makes a little motion with her left hand within his reach.*)

THORNE: (*taking her hand in his*) It wasn't a mistake (*Hesitates, looks up in her face an instant — then releasing her hand rises and moves up a little standing faced up toward window.*)

EDITH: (*After watching* THORNE *until he is motionless, rises and comes up to him with a new apprehension.*) Is it — something dangerous?

THORNE: (*turning to* EDITH *and speaking lightly*) Oh, well — (*slight laugh*) enough to make it interesting!

EDITH: (*low voice*) Don't be angry if I ask you again about your orders — I must know!

THORNE: Why?

EDITH: No matter — tell me!

THORNE: I can't do that Miss Varney.

EDITH: You needn't! Ah know! (THORNE *with a sudden apprehensive glance to front; looks back at her once.*) They're sending you on some mission where death is almost certain. They'll sacrifice your life because they know you are fearless and will do anything! There's a chance for you to stay here and be just as much use — and Ah'm going to ask you to do this! It isn't your life alone — there are other lives to think of — that's why I ask you! — It may not sound well — but — you see —

THORNE: (*catching her hands passionately*) Ah my — (*suddenly recovering and partly turning away — not, however, releasing her hands*) No no! — You shan't have this against me too!

EDITH: Against you! Why? Why? What do you mean? Why is it against you?

THORNE: (*holding her hands close*) Because I must go — my business is elsewhere — I ought never to have seen you or spoken to you — but I had to come to this house — and you were here — and how could I help it? Oh — I couldn't — for my whole — it's only you in the — (*Stops, releases her hands, and turns blindly right. Then, as if to go left, speaks.*) Your mother — I'll say good-bye to her!

EDITH: (*going quickly in his way*) No! — You must listen! They need you here in Richmond! — The President told me so himself! — Your orders are to stay! You are given a Special Commission on the War Department Telegraph service, and you —

THORNE: (*quickly, decisively, but in subdued voice*) No! No! I won't take it! I couldn't take it Miss Varney!

EDITH: You'll do that much for me!

THORNE: (*holding her hands*) It's for you that I'll do nothing of the kind! If you ever think of me again remember I refused it!

EDITH: (*breaking into* THORNE's *last few words*) You can't refuse! It's the President's request — it's his order! (*leaving him and going toward door*) Please wait a minute! I left it upstairs and you'll see —

THORNE: No! Don't get it! (*following her*) Don't get it! I won't look at it!

EDITH: (*Stops and turns.*) But I want you to see what it is! It puts you at the head of everything! You have entire control! When you see it Ah know you'll accept! Please wait! (*Exits at door up left and runs up the stairway.*)

THORNE: (*as she goes*) Miss Varney — I can't —

EDITH: (*as she goes*) Oh yes you can!

> (THORNE *stands looking off after* EDITH *for an instant. Then turns and hurries down to table and seizing his hat, starts rapidly up toward door up left as if to go. As* THORNE *starts down for hat sound of heavy door outside left, closing with a bang. Enter at door up left* CAROLINE MITFORD, *skipping in lightly, crossing back of* THORNE *to up center. She is breathless from having run across the street. Her dress is made of what is supposed to have been a great grandmother's wedding gown as light and pretty as possible, with a touch of the old-fashioned in cut and pattern. She is very young and attractive.*)

CAROLINE: (*Comes quickly on — stops abruptly.*) Oh! — Good evening!

THORNE: (*mechanical salute*) Miss Mitford! (*Turns and looks up the stairs.*)

CAROLINE: (*saluting*) Yes of co'se — Ah forgot! — How lucky this is! You're just the very person Ah wanted to see! (*going toward couch*) Ah'll tell you all about it in just a minute! Goodness me! (*Sits.*) Ah'm all out o'breath — just runnin' ovah from our house! (*Devotes herself to breathing for an instant.*)

THORNE: (*going quickly down to her*) Miss Mitford — would you do something for me?

CAROLINE: Why of co'se Ah would!

THORNE: (*rapidly*) Thank you very much! — Tell Miss Varney when she comes down — Just say good-night for me and tell her I've gone!

CAROLINE: (*pretending astonishment*) Why Ah wouldn't do such a thing for the wide, wide world! It would be a wicked dreadful lie — because you won't be gone!

THORNE: I'm sorry you look at it that way — Good-night Miss Mitford! (*Turns to go.*)

CAROLINE: (*jumping to her feet and coming round on his left between him and the door*) No no! — You don't seem to understand! Ah've got something to say to you!

THORNE: (*hurriedly*) Yes — but some other time — (*trying to go*)

CAROLINE: (*detaining him*) No no no! — Wait! (THORNE *stops.*) There isn't any other time! It's tonight! — We're going to have a starvation party!

THORNE: Good heavens — another of those things!

CAROLINE: Yes — we are! It's goin' to be ovah at mah house this time! Now we'll expect you in half an hour. (*her fingers up to emphasize the time*)

THORNE: Thank you, Miss Mitford, but I can't come! (*indicating off*) I've got to be —

CAROLINE: (*interrupting*) N — n — n — (*until she quiets him*) Now that wouldn't do at all! You went to Mamie Jones's! Would you treat me like that?

THORNE: Mamie Jones — that was last week Thursday — (CAROLINE *trying to stop him with 'now — now — now!' etc.*) Her mother — (CAROLINE *louder with 'now — now!' THORNE raises his voice above the din.*) Her mother — (*As* CAROLINE *is still going on he gives it up and looks front in despair.*)

CAROLINE: (*when quiet has come, very distinctly*) Now there isn't any use o' talkin'!

THORNE: (*Nods.*) Yes I see that!

CAROLINE: Didn't you promise to obey when Ah gave orders? Well, these are orders!

THORNE: (*turning to her for a last attempt*) Yes, but this time —

CAROLINE: This time is just the same as all the other times only worse! (*Turns away and goes to back of table left center and picks up flowers; THORNE turns and goes a little way toward up right center as if discouraged. CAROLINE speaks without turning.*) Besides that, she expects it.
(THORNE *turns at once and looks across at* CAROLINE.)

THORNE: What did you say? (*Moves toward her.*)

CAROLINE: (*smelling a flower daintily, facing front*) Ah say — she expects it — that's all!

THORNE: Who do you mean?

CAROLINE: (*Turns and looks at him.*) Who?

THORNE: (*assent*) Um-hm!

CAROLINE: (*innocently*) Who expects you?

THORNE: (*assent again*) Ah ha!

CAROLINE: Why Edith of co'se! Who did you s'pose Ah was talkin' about all this time?

THORNE: Oh! She expects me to — (*gesture up toward door left*)

CAROLINE: Why of co'se she does! Just to take her ovah! — Goodness me! You needn't stay if you don't want to! Now Ah'll go an' tell her you're waiting — that's what Ah'll do. (*Starts up toward stairs, stops and turns at door.*) You won't go now?

THORNE: If she expects it Miss Mitford (*moving up toward her*), I'll wait an' take her over — but I can't stay a minute!

CAROLINE: Well Ah thought you'd come to your senses some time or other! You don't seem to quite realize what you've got to do! — See here, Mr Captain — (*bringing him down center a little with her, on her right*) Was she most ready?

THORNE: Well — e — how do I — how —

CAROLINE: What dress did she have on?

THORNE: Dress?

CAROLINE: Oh, you men! Why she's only got two!

THORNE: (*relieved*) Yes — well then very likely this was one of them, Miss Mitford!

CAROLINE: (*starting up toward door*) Oh, no mattah — Ah'm going up anyway! (THORNE *moves up center as* CAROLINE *goes up left center.* CAROLINE *stops near door and turns to* THORNE.) Cap'n Thorne — you can wait out there on the veranda! (*pointing to window up right*)

THORNE: (*Glances where she points — then to her.*) I know — but if I wait right here she'll —

CAROLINE: (*majestically*) Those are orders! (THORNE *looks at her an instant — then salutes and wheels about making complete turn to right and starts toward the window.* CAROLINE *is watching him admiringly. As* THORNE *reaches right center*) It's cooler outside you know!

THORNE: (*turning to her and standing in stiff military attitude*) Pardon me, Miss Mitford — orders never have to be explained!

CAROLINE: That's right — I take back the explanation! (*taking one step to her right as she gives odd little salute*)

THORNE: (*with deferential salute in slight imitation of hers — but with step to his left*) That's right Miss Mitford — take it back! (*Turns and is reaching to pull aside curtains of window with right hand.*)

CAROLINE: And — oh yes! — Cap'n!

    (THORNE *turns to her again questioningly — right hand still holding curtain behind him.*)

CAROLINE: (*a peremptory order*) Smoke!

    (*For an instant* THORNE *does not understand. Then he sees it and relapses at once into easy manner, stepping forward a little and feeling with right hand in coat front for cigar — turning somewhat to front.*)

THORNE: Oh — ha — ha — (*smiling*) you mean one of those Nashville sto —

CAROLINE: Silence sir! (THORNE *looks at her quickly.*) Orders never had to be explained!

THORNE: (*with salute*) Right again Miss Mitford — orders never have to be explained! (*Exits at window up right.*)

CAROLINE: (*Looks admiringly after* THORNE.) He's splendid! If Wilfred was only like that! (*Thinks.*) But then — our engagement's broken off anyway so what's the diff! — Only — if he was like that — Ah'd — no! Ah don't think Ah'd — (*Shakes head.*)

    (*Enter* MRS VARNEY *at door left.* CAROLINE *does not notice her until she comes near, then breaks off in middle of sentence and goes right on in same breath.*)

Why how dy do!

MRS VARNEY: Why Caroline dear! What are you talking about all to yourself?

CAROLINE: (*confused*) Oh — just — Ah was just saying you know — that — why Ah don't know — Ah don't really know what Ah was goin' to — e — Do you think it's goin' to rain?

MRS VARNEY: Dear me, child — I haven't thought about it! — Why what have you got on? Is that a new dress?

CAROLINE: New dress! Well Ah should think so! These are my great grand-mother's mother's weddin' clothes! Aren't they just the most beautiest you ever saw! Just in the nick of time too! Ah was on my very last rags, an' Ah didn't know what to do — an' Mama gave me a key and told me to open an old horsehair trunk in the garret — an' Ah did — and these were in it! (*Takes a dance step or two, holding dress out.*) Just in time for the starvation party tonight! Ran ovah here to show it to Edith — where is she?

MRS VARNEY: She won't be over tonight, I'm afraid. (*Crosses to right center.*)

CAROLINE: Oh yes she will!

MRS VARNEY: But I've just come down dear!

CAROLINE: Yes — but Ah'm just going *up* dear!

(CAROLINE *turns and runs quickly up the stairs and off.* MRS VARNEY *alone a moment. After a little she moves down front in thought. She turns to desk and prepares to write a letter. Suddenly* CAROLINE *races down the stairs again and runs lightly on at door up left.* MRS VARNEY *looks up surprised.* CAROLINE *hurries across toward window as if going out.*)

MRS VARNEY: You see Caroline, it was no use!

CAROLINE: (*turning*) No use! (*Comes down in front of couch near* MRS VARNEY.)

MRS VARNEY: Why you don't mean — in this short time —

CAROLINE: Goodness me! Ah didn't stop to argue with her — Ah just told her!

MRS VARNEY: Told her what, child!

CAROLINE: Why — that Cap'n Thorne was waitin' for her out yere on the v'randah!

MRS VARNEY: She isn't going is she?

CAROLINE: Well, Ah wouldn't like to say for sure (*moving nearer* MRS VARNEY *and lower voice*) but you just watch which dress she has on when she comes down! Now Ah'll go out there an' tell him she'll be down in a minute — then the whole thing's finished up all round! Ah have more trouble getting people fixed so they can come to my party than it would take to run a blockade into Savannah every fifteen minutes! (*Goes around couch and runs off at window up right.*)

(MRS VARNEY *looks after* CAROLINE *with a smile for a moment, and then taking some paper and envelopes in her hand, rises, and moves as if to go to door up left. Enter* WILFRED *at door up left, coming in as if he wished to avoid being seen, and looking off up stairway as he enters. He carries a package under his coat, which is done up in a paper loosely. He turns quickly seeing* MRS VARNEY *and makes a very slight movement as if to conceal the package he carries. He stands looking at her.*)

MRS VARNEY: What have you got there Wilfred?

WILFRED: Here? (*Brings out package.*) O — it's only — (*Looks at her a little guiltily.*) Have you written that letter yet?

MRS VARNEY: No dear — I've been too busy. But I'm going to do it right now. (*Goes across to door at left. Near the door she glances round a little anxiously at* WILFRED. *He is looking at her. Then she exits and goes up the stairs.*)

(WILFRED *turns away after she has gone. Glances round room, goes down to table left center and begins to undo the package cautiously. He has hardly got the paper loosened — just enough to enable audience to see that it contains a pair of military trousers — when* CAROLINE *appears at window.*)

CAROLINE: (*speaking off at window right*) Those are orders Cap'n — an' orders never have to be explained!

(WILFRED *hurriedly stuffs the trousers inside his coat and buttons it over them.*)

THORNE: (*outside, at a little distance*) Perfectly right Miss Mitford!

(CAROLINE *enters through window, closing it after her, but does not close portieres.* WILFRED *is about to start toward down left.* CAROLINE *turning from window sees* WILFRED.)

CAROLINE: Good evening Mr Varney.

WILFRED: (*coldly*) Good evening Miss Mitford! (*Both now start rapidly toward door up left but as it brings them toward each other they stop simultaneously in order to avoid meeting.*)

CAROLINE: Excuse me — Ah'm in a hurry!

WILFRED: That's plain enough! (*Looks at her.*) Another party Ah reckon!

CAROLINE: You reckon perfectly correct — it is another party!

WILFRED: Dancing!

CAROLINE: (*Speaks emphatically.*) What of it? What's the matter with dancing Ah'd like to know?

WILFRED: Nothing's the matter with it — if you want to *do* it!

CAROLINE: Well Ah want to *do* it fast enough if that's all you mean! (*Turns away.*)

WILFRED: But I must say it's a pretty way to carry on — with the sound of the cannon not six miles away!

(WILFRED *is dead in earnest not only in this scene but in all his scenes.*)

CAROLINE: (*Turns back to him.*) What do you want us to do? Sit down and cry about it? — That would do a heap o' good now wouldn't it?

WILFRED: Oh — I haven't time to talk about it! (*Starts to go.*)

CAROLINE: Well it was you who started out to talk about it — Ah'm right sure Ah didn't!

WILFRED: (*After glance to see that no one is near, turns on her.*) Oh — you needn't try to fool me! Ah know well enough how you've been carrying on since our engagement was broken off! Half a dozen officers proposing to you — a dozen for all Ah know!

CAROLINE: What difference does it make? Ah haven't got to marry 'em have I?

WILFRED: Well — (*twist of head*) it isn't very nice to go on like that Ah must say — proposals by the wholesale! (*turning away*)

CAROLINE: Goodness gracious — what's the use of talking to me about it? *They're* the ones that propose — *Ah* don't!

WILFRED: (*turning on her*) Well what do you let 'em do it for?

CAROLINE: How can Ah help it?

WILFRED: Ho! (*sneer*) Any girl can help it! You helped it with me all right!

CAROLINE: Well, that was different! (*a queer look at him*)

WILFRED: And ever since you threw me ovah —

CAROLINE: (*indignantly*) Oh! — Ah *didn't* throw you ovah — you just *went* ovah! ❨*Turns away a little.*❩

WILFRED: Well, Ah went over because you walked off alone with Major Sillsby that night we were at Drury's Bluff an' encouraged him to propose — (CAROLINE *looks round in wrath.*) Yes — encouraged him!

CAROLINE: Of co'se Ah did! Ah didn't want 'im hangin' round forever did Ah? That's the on'y way to finish 'em off!

WILFRED: You want to finish too many of 'em off! Nearly every officer in the 17th Virginyah Ah'll be sworn!

CAROLINE: What do you want me to do — string a placard round my neck saying 'No proposals received here — apply at the office!' Would that make you feel any better?

WILFRED: (*throwing it off with pretended carelessness*) Oh, it doesn't make any difference to me what you do!

CAROLINE: Well if it doesn't make any difference to you, it doesn't even make as much as that to me! (*Turns and sits on left end of couch.*)

WILFRED: (*turning on her again*) Oh — it doesn't! Ah think it *does* though! You looked as if you enjoyed it pretty well while the 3rd Virginyah was in the city!

CAROLINE: Enjoyed it! Ah should think Ah did! (*jumping up*) Ah just love every one of 'em! They're on their way to the front! They're going to fight for us — an' — an' die for us — an' Ah love 'em. (*Turns away.*)

WILFRED: Well why don't you accept one of 'em an' have done with it!

CAROLINE: How do you know but what Ah'm going to?

WILFRED: (*Goes toward her a little.*) Ah suppose it'll be one of those smart young fellows with a cavalry uniform!

CAROLINE: It'll be *some* kind of a uniform! It won't be anyone that stays in Richmond — Ah can tell you that!

WILFRED: (*After looking at her — unable for a moment to speak — looks round room helplessly, then speaks in a low voice.*) Now I see what it was! I had to stay in Richmond — an' so you —

CAROLINE: (*in front of couch*) Well — (*looking down, playing with something with her foot*) that made a heap o' difference! (*Looks up — different tone.*) Why Ah was the on'y girl on Franklin Street that didn't have a — a — someone she was engaged to at the front! The on'y one! Just think what it was — to be out of it like that! (WILFRED *simply looks at her.*) Why you've no idea what Ah suffered! Besides, it's our — our duty to help all we can!

WILFRED: (*hoarsely*) Help! (*thinking of his trousers*)

CAROLINE: Yes — help! There aren't many things we girls can do — Ah know that well enough! But Colonel Woodbridge — he's one o' Morgan's men you know — well he told Mollie Pickens that the boys fight *twice* as well when they have a — a sweetheart at home! (WILFRED *glances about quickly*.)

WILFRED: He said that did he?

CAROLINE: Yes — an' if we can make 'em fight twice as well — why we just ought to do it — that's all! We girls can't do much but we can do something!

WILFRED: (*Short pause — He makes an absentminded motion of feeling the package under his arm.*) You're in earnest are you?

CAROLINE: Earnest!

WILFRED: You really want to help — all you can!

CAROLINE: Well Ah should think so!

WILFRED: An' if Ah was — (*Glances around cautiously.*) If I was going to join the army would you help me?

CAROLINE: (*looking front and down; slight embarrassment*) Why of co'se Ah would — if it was anything Ah could do!

WILFRED: (*earnestly — quite near her*) Oh it's something you can do all right — Ah'm sure o' that!

CAROLINE: (*hardly daring to look up*) What is it?

WILFRED: (*unrolling a pair of old gray army trousers, taking them from under his coat so that they spread before her on cue*) Cut these off! (*Short pause; CAROLINE looking at trousers. WILFRED looks at her; soon goes on very earnestly holding them before his own legs to measure.*) They're about twice too long! All you got to do is to cut 'em off about there — an' sew the ends so they won't ravel out!

CAROLINE: (*the idea beginning to dawn on her*) Why they're for the Army! (*taking trousers and hugging them to her — legs hanging down*)

WILFRED: Sh! — Don't speak so loud for heaven's sake! (*a glance back as if afraid of being overheard*) Ah've got a jacket here too! (*Shows her a small army coat.*) Nearly a fit — came from the hospital — Johnny Seldon wore it — he won't want it any more you know — an' he was just about my size!

CAROLINE: (*low voice*) No — he won't want it any more. (*Stands thinking.*)

WILFRED: (*after a slight pause*) Well! — Ah thought you said you wanted to help!

CAROLINE: (*quickly*) Oh yes — Ah do! Ah do!

WILFRED: Well go on — what are you waiting for?

CAROLINE: (*near end of couch*) Yes! Yes! (*Hurriedly drops on knees on floor and takes hold, spreading trousers out exactly and patting them smooth.*) This is the place isn't it? (*pointing to near the knees*)

WILFRED: No — not up there — Here! (*indicating about three inches from the bottom of the trouser leg*)

CAROLINE: Oh yes! Ah see! (*Hurriedly snatches pins from her dress; puts one in mouth and one in place WILFRED indicates — all very rapid and earnest. Takes hold of other leg of trousers, speaking as if pin in mouth — innocently and without looking up.*) The other one just the same? (*A musical rise to voice at end of this. WILFRED does not deign to reply. CAROLINE hearing nothing looks up at him.*) Oh yes, o' co'se! (*She quickly puts pin in other leg of trousers.*)

> (*From trouser business* CAROLINE'*s demeanor toward* WILFRED *is entirely changed. It is because he is going to join the army.*)

(CAROLINE *on floor with trousers and coat takes hold of the work with enthusiasm.*) Do you see any scissors around anywhere? (WILFRED *dashes about looking on tables, after putting jacket on end of couch.*) This won't never tear — (*trying to tear off trousers' leg*) — for all Ah can do!

WILFRED: (*First looking on table down left center and picking up paper jacket was wrapped in. He gets a work-basket from table up center and quickly brings it.*) There must be some in here! (*Hands the scissors out of the basket to* CAROLINE. *As she reaches up from her position on the floor to take them, she looks in* WILFRED'*s face an instant — then quickly down to work again. Then she works with head down.* WILFRED *leaves wrapping paper up stage out of the way.*)

CAROLINE: (*slight pause — on her knees near couch; low voice, not looking up at him*) When are you goin' to wear 'em?

WILFRED: When they're cut off!

CAROLINE: (*Looks up at him; thread or scissors in mouth.*) You mean — you're really —

WILFRED: Um hm! (*assent*)

CAROLINE: But your mother —

WILFRED: She knows it.

CAROLINE: Oh!

WILFRED: She's going to write the General tonight.

CAROLINE: But how about if he won't let you?

WILFRED: (*with boyish determination, but keeping voice down*) Ah'll go just the same!

CAROLINE: (*Suddenly jumps to her feet dropping everything on the floor and catches his hand.*) Oh Ah'm so glad! Why it makes another thing of it! When Ah said that about staying in Richmond Ah didn't know! Oh, Ah do want to help all I can!

WILFRED: (*who has been regarding her burst of enthusiasm rather coldly*) You do!

CAROLINE: Indeed — indeed Ah do!

WILFRED: Then cut those off for Heaven's sake!

CAROLINE: Oh yes! (*She catches up trousers, jacket, etc., and sits quickly on couch and excitedly paws them over.*) Where shall Ah cut 'em?

WILFRED: The same place — Ah haven't grown any!

CAROLINE: Dear me — Ah don't know where it was!

WILFRED: You stuck some pins in!

CAROLINE: (*finding pins*) Oh yes — here they are! (*seizing the trousers and going to work, soon cutting off one of the trousers' legs*)

WILFRED: That's it!

CAROLINE: When did you say she was going to write?

WILFRED: Tonight.

CAROLINE: (*looking up with distrust*) She doesn't want you to go does she?

WILFRED: Ah don't reckon she does — very much!

CAROLINE: She'll tell him not to let you!

WILFRED: (*Looks at her with wide open eyes.*) No!

CAROLINE: That's the way they always do!

WILFRED: The devil!

CAROLINE: Ah should think so!

WILFRED: What can Ah do!

CAROLINE: Write to him yourself.

WILFRED: Good idea!

CAROLINE: Then you can just tell him what you like!

WILFRED: Ah'll tell him Ah *can't* stay here!

CAROLINE: (*excitedly rising, letting the jacket fall on floor*) Tell him you're coming anyhow!

WILFRED: Ah will!

CAROLINE: Whether he says so or not!

WILFRED: Then he'll say so, won't he?

CAROLINE: O' co'se he will — there ain't anything else to say!

WILFRED: Ah'll do it! (*Starts to go up left; stops and goes back to* CAROLINE.) Say — you're pretty good! (*Catching one of* CAROLINE'*s hands impulsively.* CAROLINE *looks down at work in her hand.*) Ah'll go upstairs an' write it now! (*Starts toward door.* CAROLINE *watches him. He turns back and she looks quickly down at her work again.*) Finish those things as soon as you can an' leave 'em here — in the hall closet! (*indicating outside left*)

CAROLINE: (*nodding her head*) Yes!

WILFRED: An' don't let anyone see 'em whatever you do!

CAROLINE: (*shaking her head*) No!

> (WILFRED *hurries off at door up left.* CAROLINE *looks after him with expression of ecstasy — lapsing into dreaminess as she turns to front. Suddenly bethinks herself with a start and a little 'O' and slipping down on floor near chair she goes excitedly to work on the trousers, cutting at the other leg with violence and rapidly, getting it nearly cut through so that later it dangles by a few threads. Suddenly she stops work and listens. Then with great haste she gathers up all the things she can, leaving the jacket however where it fell, and jumps to her feet with them in her arms, hugging the confused bundle close against her and hastily tucking in portions that hang out so that MRS VARNEY won't see what it is.*)

MRS VARNEY: (*Enters from up left coming down the stairway and into the room.*) Oh — you haven't gone yet!

CAROLINE: Not quite! I mean not yet! It doesn't begin for an hour you know!

MRS VARNEY: What doesn't begin?

CAROLINE: The party!

MRS VARNEY: Oh — then you have plenty of time! (*turning as if to go up center*)

CAROLINE: (*hastening across toward door left with her arms full of things*) Yes — but Ah'll have to go now sure enough! (*She drops the scissors.*)

MRS VARNEY: (*turning*) You dropped your scissors dear!

CAROLINE: Oh! (*coming back for them*) I — I thought I heard something! (*In picking them up she lets the cut-off end of a trouser leg fall but does not notice it and goes toward door up left.*)

MRS VARNEY: (*coming down stage*) What are you making, Caroline?

CAROLINE: (*turning near door*) Oh — Ah was just altering a dress, that's all! (*turning to go*)

MRS VARNEY: (*stooping and picking up the piece of trouser leg*) Here, Carrie! — you dropped a — a — (*Looks at it.*)

CAROLINE: (*hurrying to* MRS VARNEY *and snatching the piece — stuffing it in with rest*) Oh yes! — (*Looks at* MRS VARNEY *an instant. The other piece of trouser leg is hanging by its shred in full sight.*) That — that was one of the sleeves! (*Turns and hurries off at door up left and exits door below stairway.*)

(MRS VARNEY *after a moment turns and goes toward door up center. Seeing something on the couch she stops and goes to pick it up. On coming to it she finds the little gray soldier's jacket left by* CAROLINE *in her hasty scramble.* MRS VARNEY *stoops and picks it up and stands looking at it facing front. After a brief pause the loud sound of hurried opening of front door outside left and tramp of heavy feet on the floor is heard.* MRS VARNEY *looks up and across left, letting the coat fall on the couch. Enter* MR BENTON ARRELSFORD *up left, a tall fine looking Southern man of about thirty-five or forty dressed in citizen's clothes — black frock coat — rather distinguished appearance. He is seen outside door up left hurriedly placing a guard of Confederate soldiers at doors outside up left, also at foot of stairs, and at any other exit in sight.* MRS VARNEY, *much surprised, moves toward door left.* MR ARRELS-FORD *at the same time and as noiselessly as possible, hastens into the room.*)

MRS VARNEY: Mr Arrelsford! (*Goes toward center, up a little.*)

ARRELSFORD: (*Comes quickly across to* MRS VARNEY. *Speaks in a low voice and rapidly.*) Ah was obliged to come in without ceremony, Mrs Varney. You'll understand when I tell you what it is!

MRS VARNEY: And those men — (*Motions toward guards.*)

ARRELSFORD: They're on guard at the doors out there!

MRS VARNEY: (*low voice*) On guard! — You mean —

ARRELSFORD: Ah'm very much afraid we've got to put you to a little inconvenience, Mrs Varney! (*Glances about cautiously.* MRS VARNEY *stands astonished.*) Is there anybody in that room? (*pointing to door up center*)

MRS VARNEY: Yes — a number of ladies sewing for the hospitals.

ARRELSFORD: Kindly come this way a little. (*going down stage with* MRS VARNEY) One of your servants has got himself into trouble, Mrs Varney, an' we're compelled to have him watched!

MRS VARNEY: What kind of trouble?

ARRELSFORD: (*low voice*) Pretty serious, ma'am! That's the way it looks now! — You've got an old white-haired niggah her —

MRS VARNEY: You mean Jonas?

ARRELSFORD: Ah believe that's his name!

MRS VARNEY: You suspect him of something!

ARRELSFORD: (*keeping voice down*) We don't suspect — we *know* what he's done! (*Glances round before going on.*) He's been down in the Libby Prison under pretense of selling something to the Yankees we've got in there, an' he now has on his person a written communication from one of them which he intends to deliver to some Yankee agent here in Richmond! (*Goes around in front of table and up near door up left center.*)

MRS VARNEY: (*motionless a second looking at* ARRELSFORD *but soon recovers*) Send for the man! (*starting to move up stage and toward left*) Let us see if this —

ARRELSFORD: (*quickly stopping her*) No! Not yet! (*Glances quickly round at doors and windows — then speaks in lowered voice but with great intensity and clearness.*) Ah've got to get that paper! If he's alarmed he'll destroy it! Ah've got to have it! It'll give us the clue to one o' their cursed plots! They've been right close on this town for months — trying to break down our defenses and get in on us. This is some rascally game they're at to weaken us from the inside! Two weeks ago we got word from our agents that we keep over there in the Yankee lines telling us that two brothers — Lewis and Henry Dumont — have been under Secret Service orders to do some rascally piece of work here in Richmond. We had close descriptions of these fellows but we've never been able to lay our hands on 'em till last night!

MRS VARNEY: (*near* ARRELSFORD, *intense whisper*) You've got them?

ARRELSFORD: (*low voice but intense*) We've got one o' them! An' it won't take long to run down the othah!

MRS VARNEY: The one — the one you caught — was he here in Richmond?

ARRELSFORD: No — he was brought in last night with a lot o' men we captured making a raid.

MRS VARNEY: Taken prisoner!

ARRELSFORD: (*Nods affirmatively, glances round.*) Let himself be taken! That's one of their tricks for getting through our lines when they want to bring a message or give some signal.

MRS VARNEY: You mean, they get into Libby Prison?

ARRELSFORD: Yes! Damn them! (*this oath indistinctly between his teeth*) But we were on the lookout for this man and we spotted him pretty quick. I gave orders not to search him or to take away his clothes but to put him in with the others and keep the closest watch on him that was ever kept on a man! We knew from his coming in that his brother must be here in the city and he'd send a message to him the first chance he got.

MRS VARNEY: But Jonas! How could he —

ARRELSFORD: Easy enough! He comes down to Libby to sell goubers to the prisoners — we let 'im pass — he fools around awhile until he gets a chance to brush against this man Dumont — we're watching an' we see a bit of paper pass between 'em! The old rascal's got that paper now ma'am, an' besides these men in heah I've got a dozen more on the outside watching him through the windows! (*Turns and moves up, glancing off left with some anxiety.*)

MRS VARNEY: (*After slight pause, turns and speaks in intense but subdued voice, almost a whisper.*) The man he gives it to! *He's* the one you want!

ARRELSFORD: (*approaching her quickly, low voice but intense*) Yes! But I can't wait long! If the Niggah sees a man or hears a sound he'll destroy it before we can jump in on 'im — an' I must have that paper! (*Strides quickly up,* MRS VARNEY *following a step or two; speaks off up left in low but sharp voice.*) Corporal!

(*Enter* CORPORAL *at door up left; he salutes and stands.*)

How is it now?

CORPORAL: (*low voice*) All quiet sir!

(ARRELSFORD *and* MRS VARNEY *face each other.*)

ARRELSFORD: (*low, intense*) It won't do to wait — I've got to get that paper! It's the key to the game they're trying to play against us!

MRS VARNEY: (*half whisper*) No no! The man he's going to give it to! Get him!

ARRELSFORD: That paper might give us a clue! If not I'll make the niggah tell! Damn it — I'll shoot it out of him! (*Turns to* CORPORAL.) How quick can you get at him from that door! (*pointing off up left*)

CORPORAL: (*no salute, low voice*) It's through a hallway — and across the dining-room.

ARRELSFORD: Well, take two men and —

MRS VARNEY: (*interrupting, touching* ARRELSFORD *to stop him*) Why not keep your men out of sight and let me send for him — here?

ARRELSFORD: (*after a second's thought*) That's better! We'll get 'im in here! While you're talking to him they can nab him from behind! (*Turns to* CORPORAL.) You heard?

CORPORAL: Yes, sir.

ARRELSFORD: Keep your men out of sight — get 'em back there in the hall — an' while we're making him talk send a man down each side and pin him! Hold 'im stiff! He mustn't destroy any paper he's got!

(CORPORAL *salutes and exits with men off left.* MRS VARNEY *turns to* ARRELSFORD, *who is well up center, with her hand on the bell rope.*)

MRS VARNEY: Now, Mr Arrelsford?

ARRELSFORD: Yes.

(MRS VARNEY *rings the bell. Short pause. Enter* MARTHA *at door up left. She stands in the doorway.*)

MRS VARNEY: (*near mantel*) Is there anyone I can send to the hospital, Martha?

MARTHA: Luther's out yere, ma'am.

MRS VARNEY: Luther? (*Considers.*) No — he's too small. I don't want a boy.

MARTHA: Jonas is yere, mam — if you want him.

MRS VARNEY: Oh, Jonas — yes! Tell 'im to come in here right away.

MARTHA: Yaas'm. (*Exit.*)

(MRS VARNEY *crosses and sits on couch.* ARRELSFORD *waits up center.* OLD JONAS *appears at the door up left coming from door below stairs. He is a thick-set gray-haired old negro. He comes a few steps into the room.* MRS VARNEY *looks at* JONAS *and he at her — at first he is entirely unsuspecting, but in a moment, seeing* ARRELS-FORD *standing up center his eyes shift about restlessly for an instant.*)

MRS VARNEY: Jonas —

JONAS: Yes ma'am.

MRS VARNEY: Have you any idea why I sent for you?

JONAS: Ah heers you was wantin' to sen' me to de hossiple ma'am.

> (CORPORAL *and* MEN *enter behind* JONAS.)

MRS VARNEY: Oh — then Martha told you.

> (CORPORAL *motions to* MEN *and they instantly step forward —
> one on each side of* JONAS, *and stand motionless.*)

JONAS: Waal she didn't ezzackly say whut you — (*Sees man each side of him and
stops in the midst of his speech. He does not start, but is frozen with terror.
Stands motionless. Expression of face scarcely changes. Soon he lowers his
eyes and then begins stealthily to get his right hand toward his inside breast
pocket.*)

> (CORPORAL *gives a sharp order. The men instantly seize* JONAS.
> CORPORAL *quickly feels in his pocket.* JONAS *struggles desper-
> ately but in an instant the* CORPORAL *has the paper which he
> hands — with a salute — to* ARRELSFORD. MRS VARNEY *rises as
> men seize* JONAS.)

ARRELSFORD: See if there's anything more!

CORPORAL: (*Quickly searches* JONAS. MEN *still holding him, raising his arms
above his head, etc. After the search* MEN *release* JONAS *and stand guard
one on each side of him.* CORPORAL *salutes.*) That's all sir.

ARRELSFORD: (*Turns to lamp on table up center, opening the paper as he does
so, while* CORPORAL *is searching* JONAS. MRS VARNEY *watches him
intently.* ARRELSFORD *reads the paper quickly and at once wheels round
on* JONAS, *speaks in low voice but sharp and telling.*) Who was this for?
(JONAS *stands silent.*) If you don't tell it's going to be mighty bad for you!
(JONAS *stands silent looking at* ARRELSFORD, *who, after pause, turns to*
MRS VARNEY.) I'm right sorry ma'am, but it looks like we've got to shoot
'im! (*Eyeing* JONAS; *goes down center.*) Corporal! (*Motions him to approach
—* CORPORAL *steps to* ARRELSFORD *on salute;* ARRELSFORD *speaks in
low voice.*) Take him outside and get it out of him! String him up till he
talks! You understand! (CORPORAL *salutes and is about to turn.*) Here!
(CORPORAL *turns to* ARRELSFORD *on salute;* ARRELSFORD *glances
toward window at right and back left.*) Go down on that side — back of the
house! (*pointing left*) And keep it quiet! Nobody must know of this! Not a
soul!

> (CORPORAL *salutes again, goes up to* MEN, *and gives an order.*
> MEN *turn on order and march* JONAS *off at door up left, all very
> quick with military precision.* CORPORAL *goes with them.*
> ARRELSFORD *stands watching exit until they are gone and the
> sound of the closing of heavy front door is heard, then turns to* MRS
> VARNEY. *They keep voices down to nearly a whisper in the follow-
> ing scene, but with utmost force and intensity.*)

MRS VARNEY: (*indicating paper in his hand*) Was there anything in that —

ARRELSFORD: (*near* MRS VARNEY) We've got the trick they want to play!

MRS VARNEY: But not the man — not the man who is to play it!

ARRELSFORD: I didn't say that!

MRS VARNEY: There's a clue?

ARRELSFORD: There *is* a clue!

MRS VARNEY: Will it answer? Do you know who —

ARRELSFORD: As plain as if we had his name!

MRS VARNEY: Thank God! (*Motionless an instant, then extends her hand for the paper.*) Let me see it! (ARRELSFORD *momentary hesitation — then hands her the paper, which she looks at and then reads aloud.*) 'ATTACK TONIGHT — PLAN 3 — USE TELEGRAPH' — (*slight motion or sound from* ARRELSFORD *to quiet her and a quick glance round*) What does it mean?

ARRELSFORD: (*Takes paper.*) They attack tonight! — The place where they strike is indicated by 'Plan 3'. (*finger on the words on paper*)

MRS VARNEY: Plan three?

ARRELSFORD: He knows what they mean by that! It's arranged beforehand!

MRS VARNEY: And — the last — the last there! (*quick look at paper*) 'Use Telegraph'?

ARRELSFORD: He's to use our War Department Telegraph Lines to send some false order and weaken that position — the one they indicate by 'Plan Three' — so they can break through and come down on the city!

MRS VARNEY: Oh! (*pause, then suddenly*) But the one — the man who is to do this — there's nothing about *him*!

ARRELSFORD: There *is* something about him!

MRS VARNEY: (*rapidly — almost run together*) What? Where? I don't see it!

ARRELSFORD: 'Use Telegraph!' (*The two stand looking at one another.*) We know every man on the Telegraph Service — and every man of them's true! But there's some who want to get into that service that we don't know quite so well!

MRS VARNEY: He would be one!

ARRELSFORD: There aren't so very many! (*These speeches given suggestively — with slight pause after each.*) It isn't every man that's an expert! — The niggah brought this paper to your house, Mrs Varney?

MRS VARNEY: My — (*Hesitates, beginning to realize.*)

ARRELSFORD: For more than a month your daughter has been working to get an appointment for someone on the Telegraph Service — perhaps *she* could give us some idea —

> (*A moment's pause, the two looking at one another, then suddenly* MRS VARNEY *turns and hurries to window up right and quickly pulls curtains together, turning and facing back to* ARRELSFORD *at same instant.*)

IS HE THERE? (MRS VARNEY *nods affirmatively and comes toward* ARRELSFORD.) Could he hear what we said?

MRS VARNEY: (*Shakes head negatively.*) He's at the further end! (ARRELSFORD *glances at windows nervously;* MRS VARNEY, *after a pause, speaks in low voice.*) You have a description you say!

ARRELSFORD: Yes — at the office.

MRS VARNEY: Then this man — this Captain Thorne —

ARRELSFORD: (*with vehemence*) There *is* no Captain Thorne! This fellow you have in your house is Lewis Dumont! (*short pause*)

MRS VARNEY: You mean — he came here to —

ARRELSFORD: (*with vindictive fury breaking through in spite of himself – yet voice subdued almost to a sharp whisper*) He came to this town – he came to this house – knowing your position and the influence of your name – for the sole purpose of getting some hold on our Department Telegraph line! He's corrupted your servants – he's thick with the men in the telegraph office – what he hasn't done God A'mighty knows! But Washington ain't the only place where there's a Secret Service! We've got one here in Richmond! Oh – (*a shake of his head*) two can play at that game – an it's my move now! (*Goes up right center a few steps.*)

> (*Enter* EDITH VARNEY *running rapidly down stairway and calling out excitedly as she comes. She wears a white dress and has in her hand the large official envelope which she took upstairs in earlier scene.* ARRELSFORD *goes toward windows up right.*)

EDITH: Mama! Mama! – Quick Mama! (MRS VARNEY *hurries toward door up left to meet her.* ARRELSFORD *turns in surprise looking toward door.*) Under my window – in the bushes – they're hurting someone frightfully! Ah'm sure they are! Oh – come! (*starting toward door to lead the way;* MRS VARNEY *stands looking at* EDITH, *who stops surprised that she does not follow.*) If you aren't coming Ah'll go myself! (*turning to go*)

MRS VARNEY: Wait, Edith! (EDITH *stops and turns back to* MRS VARNEY.) I must tell you something – it'll be a terrible shock I'm afraid! (EDITH *goes toward* MRS VARNEY, ARRELSFORD *turns away a little – standing near right center watching window.*) A man we trusted as a friend has shown himself a treacherous conspirator against us!

EDITH: (*after a slight pause – low voice*) Who? (*Pause.* MRS VARNEY *cannot bring herself to speak the name. After a slight pause, in the same low voice*) Who is it?

ARRELSFORD: (*swinging round on her; low voice but with vindictiveness*) It is the gentleman, Miss Varney, whose attentions you have been pleased to accept in the place of mine!

> (*Short pause.* EDITH *looking at* ARRELSFORD, *white and motionless. Then she turns her face appealing to her mother;* MRS VARNEY *nods slowly in affirmation.* EDITH *puts the envelope with Commission in belt or bosom of dress in an absent manner.*)

EDITH: (*low voice*) Is it Mr Arrelsford who makes this accusation?

ARRELSFORD: (*breaking out hotly but keeping voice down*) Yes, since you wish to know! From the first I've had my suspicions that this – (*Stops on seeing* EDITH'*s move toward the window up right.*)

> (EDITH *turns on 'Since you wish to know' and goes quickly toward the window.* ARRELSFORD *steps before her; speaks rapidly in low voice.*)

Where are you going?

EDITH: (*low voice*) For Captain Thorne.

ARRELSFORD: (*low voice*) Not now!

EDITH: (*turning with flashing indignation on* ARRELSFORD; *low voice*) Mr Arrelsford, if this is something you're afraid to say to him – don't you *dare* say it to me!

ARRELSFORD: (*indignantly; low voice*) Miss Varney, if you —

MRS VARNEY: (*interrupting quickly, low voice*) Edith, he has good reason for not meeting Captain Thorne now!

EDITH: (*turning quickly to* MRS VARNEY) Ah should think he had! The man who said that to his face wouldn't live to speak again!

MRS VARNEY: My dear, you don't —

EDITH: Mama — this man has left his desk in the War Department so that he can have the pleasure of persecuting me! He's never attempted anything in the active service before! And when I ask him to face the man he accuses he turns like a coward!

ARRELSFORD: (*angrily, but keeping voice subdued*) Mrs Varney, if she thinks —

EDITH: (*low voice*) I think nothing! I know a man of Captain Thorne's character is above suspicion!

ARRELSFORD: (*low voice*) His character! Ha ha! (*a sneer*) Where did he come from? — Who is he?

EDITH: Who are you?

ARRELSFORD: That's not the question.

EDITH: (*low voice*) Neither is it the question who is he! If it were I'd answer it — I'd tell you he's a soldier who has fought and been wounded for his country!

ARRELSFORD: (*low voice but incisive*) We're not so sure of that!

EDITH: (*after a pause of indignation*) He brought us letters from General Stonewall Jackson and —

ARRELSFORD: (*quick and sharp*) General Jackson was killed before his letter was presented!

EDITH: What does that signify if he wrote it?

ARRELSFORD: Nothing — *if* he wrote it!

EDITH: Mr Arrelsford, if you mean — (MRS VARNEY *goes to* EDITH *putting her hands on* EDITH'*s arm.*)

MRS VARNEY: (*low voice*) Listen Edith! They have proofs of a conspiracy on our Government Telegraph Lines. (ARRELSFORD *says 'Sh' and goes to window up right;* EDITH *turns from* ARRELSFORD *and looks before her, listening on mention of 'Telegraph Lines';* MRS VARNEY *leads* EDITH *a little left of center.*) Two men in the Northern Secret Service have been sent here to do this work. One is in Libby Prison. Our old Jonas went there today — secretly took a message from him and brought it here — to the other! (EDITH *turns toward* MRS VARNEY *sharply.*) We've just had Jonas in here and found that paper on him!

   (ARRELSFORD *comes down right looking off through curtains of windows.*)

EDITH: (*rapidly, desperately, in low voice*) But he hasn't said it was for —
   (*Dull heavy sound of front door closing outside left.*)

ARRELSFORD: (*low voice but incisively*) Not yet — but he will! (EDITH *looks at him not comprehending; enter* CORPORAL *at door up left who stands on salute;* LADIES *turn to him,* EDITH *breathless with anxiety,* MRS VARNEY *calm but intent.* ARRELSFORD *goes to* CORPORAL *and speaks in low voice.*) Well, what does he say?

CORPORAL: (*low voice*) Nothing sir — he won't speak!

ARRELSFORD: (*sharply, but voice subdued*) What have you done?

CORPORAL: Strung him up three times and —

ARRELSFORD: (*enraged but keeping his voice down*) Well string him up again! If he won't speak shoot it out of him! Kill the dog! (*Comes blindly down left; CORPORAL salutes and exits; ARRELSFORD turns to LADIES and goes back of table, gets hat from table.*) We don't need the niggah's evidence — there's enough without it!

EDITH: (*low voice*) There's nothing!

ARRELSFORD: (*at table, low voice*) By twelve o'clock tonight you'll have all the proof you want!

EDITH: There's no proof at all!

ARRELSFORD: I'll show it to you at the telegraph office! Do you dare go with me?

EDITH: (*low voice*) Dare! (*Moves toward him.*) I *will* go with you!

ARRELSFORD: (*low voice*) I'll call for you in half an hour! (*Goes up toward left door.*)

EDITH: Wait! — what are you going to do?

ARRELSFORD: (*Comes down back of table; low voice but incisive*) I'm going to let him get this paper! He'll know what they want him to do — and then we'll see him try to do it!

EDITH: You're going to spy on him — hound him like a criminal!

ARRELSFORD: I'm going to prove what he is!

EDITH: (*low voice*) Then prove it openly! Prove it at once! It's a shame to let a suspicion like that rest on an honorable man! Let him come in here and —

ARRELSFORD: (*low voice*) Impossible!

EDITH: (*low voice*) Then do something else but do it now! (*Turning away a little, speaks desperately.*) We must know that he is — that he's innocent! We must know that! (*a thought; turns to ARRELSFORD.*) You say the prisoner in Libby is his brother — that's what you said — his brother! Bring him here! Go to the prison and bring that man here!

ARRELSFORD: (*speaking across table, subdued exclamation*) What!

EDITH: Let them meet! Bring them face to face! Then you can see whether —

ARRELSFORD: (*low voice, speaks rapidly*) You mean — bring them together here?

EDITH: Yes!

ARRELSFORD: As if the prisoner was trying to escape?

EDITH: Any way you like — but end it!

ARRELSFORD: When?

EDITH: Now!

ARRELSFORD: (*after instant's thought*) I'm willing to try that! — Can you keep him here? (*with a motion toward windows*)

EDITH: (*scarcely more than a movement of lips*) Yes.

ARRELSFORD: It won't be more than half an hour. Be out there on the veranda. When I tap on the glass bring him into this room and leave him alone!

EDITH: (*hardly more than nod and a whisper*) Yes. (*Turns away toward front.*)

ARRELSFORD: (*Goes rapidly toward door up left, stops and turns near door.*) I rely on you Miss Varney to give him no hint or sign that we suspect —

(MRS VARNEY *and* EDITH *both turn indignantly on him,* MRS
VARNEY *with slight exclamation.*)

EDITH: (*interrupting* ARRELSFORD) Mr Arrelsford!

(ARRELSFORD *stands an instant — then bows stiffly and exits at
door up left.* EDITH *stands where she was as if stunned.* MRS
VARNEY *looks after* ARRELSFORD, *then turns to* EDITH.)

EDITH: (*after pause, not looking round, nearly whisper*) Mama! (*Reaches out her
hand as if feeling for help or support;* MRS VARNEY *comes to* EDITH *and
takes her hand.*) Mama!

MRS VARNEY: (*low voice*) I'm here, Edith!

EDITH: (*pause,* EDITH *thinking of something, her eyes wide open, staring vacantly
before her and holding tight to* MRS VARNEY's *hand*) Do you think — do
you think — that could be what he meant? (MRS VARNEY *looking intently
at* EDITH) The Commission I got for him — this afternoon.

MRS VARNEY: (*low voice*) Yes — yes!

EDITH: The Commission you know — from the President — for the — for the Telegraph Service! He — he — refused to take it!

MRS VARNEY: Refused!

EDITH: (*nodding a little, hardly able to speak*) He said — he said it was for me that
he could not!

MRS VARNEY: It's true then!

EDITH: (*turning quickly to her and trying to stop her by putting her hand over her
mouth, speaking rapidly, breathlessly, yet not in a loud voice*) No no! Don't
say it!

MRS VARNEY: (*putting* EDITH's *hand away*) Yes!

EDITH: Oh, no!

MRS VARNEY: Infamous traitor! They ought to lash him through the streets of
Richmond!

EDITH: (*impulsively trying to stop* MRS VARNEY) No Mama! No — no — no!
(*She stops — a moment's pause, she realizes the truth; speaks in almost a
whisper.*) Yes — yes — (*Stops, pauses, stands erect, looks about, motions
MRS VARNEY to go.*)

(MRS VARNEY *turns quietly and leaves the room, going out at the
door up left.* EDITH *stands supporting herself without knowing that
she does so — one hand on a table or back of chair. Soon coming to
herself she turns and goes toward the window up right. When near
center she stops. Stands there a moment looking toward the window.
Then brushes her hand quickly across her eyes and takes the President's Commission from the bosom of dress. She looks at it as if
thinking, folds it slowly and puts it back again, and then walks to
the window, throws aside the curtains and pushes it open.* CAPTAIN
THORNE, *outside at some distance, makes sound with chair as
though he rose and pushed or set it back and the sound of his footsteps outside approaching briskly follows at once.* EDITH *moves
back away from the window and near table and stands there looking
at the window. After footsteps and after* EDITH *is motionless,*

CAPTAIN THORNE *walks briskly and unsuspiciously into the room at window up right, glancing about as he does so — not seeing* EDITH *until he is a little way in. Upon seeing her he stops an instant where he is, and then goes directly across to her and is about to take her hand as he speaks.*)

THORNE: Miss Varney —

EDITH: (*as she snatches her hand away and shrinks back slightly; breathless*) No — don't touch me! (*A second's pause; she recovers almost instantly.*) Oh — it was you! (*smiling as if at her own stupidity*) Why how perfectly absurd I am! (*crossing in front of* THORNE *lightly and going to window at up right*) Ah'm sure Ah ought to be ashamed of myself! (*Turns to him.*) Do come out a minute — on the veranda — Ah want to talk to you about a whole lot o' things! There's half an hour yet before the party! (*turning to go*) Isn't it a lovely night! (*Exits at the window up right with forced gaiety of manner disappearing in the darkness.*) Oh, come along!

(THORNE *stands looking at* EDITH *when she first speaks. As she crosses he is looking down a little but looks slowly up toward front and turns a little after her cross, looking at her as she stands for a moment in the window. After her exit he slowly turns toward front and his eyes glance about and down once as he weighs the chances.*)

EDITH: (*after brief pause for above, calling gaily from outside, not too near the window*) Oh, Cap'n Thorne!

(THORNE *turns quickly looking off right again; hesitates an instant; makes up his mind; walks rapidly to window — a slight hesitating there, without stopping. Exits at window.*)

CURTAIN

ACT II

The same room as in Act I; strong moonlight outside both windows at right. Portieres are closed at both windows. Nine o'clock. MRS VARNEY *discovered seated at desk down right. She is not busy with anything but sits watching that no one goes out to the veranda. Sound of closing of door outside left; enter* MISS KITTRIDGE *at door up center, which stands ajar as if she had recently come out.*

MRS VARNEY: Was it the same man?

MISS KITTRIDGE: No; they sent another one this time.

MRS VARNEY: Did you have anything ready?

MISS KITTRIDGE: Oh yes — Ah gave 'em quite a lot. We've all been at the bandages — that's what they need most. (MRS VARNEY *rises; seems preoccupied; goes across to left and looks off.* MISS KITTRIDGE *watches her rather anxiously a moment.*) Did you want anything, Mrs Varney?

MRS VARNEY: (*turning*) No — I — nothing, thank you. (MISS KITTRIDGE *is turning to go but stops when* MRS VARNEY *speaks again.* MRS VARNEY *goes nearer to* MISS KITTRIDGE.) Perhaps it would be just as well if any of the ladies want to go, to let them out the other way. You can open the door into the dining-room. We're expecting someone here on important business.

MISS KITTRIDGE: Ah'll see to it, Mrs Varney.

MRS VARNEY: Thank you. (*Exit* MISS KITTRIDGE *at door up center. MRS VARNEY stands a moment, then goes down left and rings bell, crosses to right center, going back of table, then goes slowly up center, waiting. Enter* MARTHA *at door up left from door right of stairway.*) Did Miss Caroline go home?

MARTHA: (*near door*) No'm. She's been out yere in de kitchen fur a while.

MRS VARNEY: In the kitchen!

MARTHA: Yaas'm.

MRS VARNEY: What is she doing?

MARTHA: She's been mostly sewin' and behavin' mighty strange about sumfin a great deal o' de time. Ah bleeve she's gittin' ready to go home now.

MRS VARNEY: Ask her to come here a moment.

MARTHA: Yaas'm. (*Turns and exits up left.* MRS VARNEY *waits a little, then goes forward a few steps. Enter* CAROLINE *at left door from door right of stairway. She comes into the room trying to look very innocent.*)

MRS VARNEY: Caroline — (CAROLINE *goes down center with* MRS VARNEY. *She is expecting to hear something said about the sewing she has been doing.*) Are you in a hurry to get home? Because if you can wait a few minutes while I go upstairs to Howard it'll be a great help.

CAROLINE: (*looking around in some doubt*) You want me to — just wait? Is that all?

MRS VARNEY: I — (*Hesitates a little.*) — I don't want anyone to go out on the veranda just now. (CAROLINE *looks toward veranda.*) Edith's there — with —

CAROLINE: (*suddenly comprehending*) Oh yes! (*Glances toward windows.*) Ah know how that is — Ah'll attend to it! (*Crosses to up right center.*)

MRS VARNEY: Just while I'm upstairs — it won't be long! (*Goes to door left and turns.*) Be careful won't you dear! (*Exit and up the stairway.*)

CAROLINE: Careful! Well Ah should think so! As if Ah didn't know enough for that! (*Goes toward window up right and pauses. Her face is radiant with the imagined romance of the situation; peeps out slyly through curtains. After a moment she turns, an idea having occurred to her, and quickly rolls the couch up across before the window, kneels on it with her back to the audience, and tries to peep through curtains. Enter* WILFRED *door up left, coming in cautiously and if he had been watching for an opportunity. He stops just within the door and looks back up stairway. He has on trousers which* CAROLINE *fixed for him and also the jacket.* CAROLINE *rises and turns from the couch and sees* WILFRED, *startled at first. He turns to her; she stands adoring him in his uniform, which, though showing strange folds and awkwardness at the bottom of the trousers from being cut off and sewed by an amateur, do not appear grotesque or laughable.*)

CAROLINE: (*subdued exclamation, seeing* WILFRED *in uniform*) Oh!

WILFRED: (*low voice, speaking across from door*) Mother isn't anywhere around is she?

CAROLINE: (*coming to center*) She — she just went upstairs.

WILFRED: (*down a little*) Ah'm not running away — but if she saw me with these things on she might feel funny.

CAROLINE: (*half to herself*) She might not feel so very funny!

WILFRED: Well — you know — (*going over to desk down right and taking papers and letters from pockets*) how it is with a feller's mother. (CAROLINE *nods;* WILFRED *hurriedly searches for letter among others, feeling in different pockets, so that he speaks without much thinking what he says.*) Other people don't care — but mothers — well — they're different.

CAROLINE: (*Speaks absently.*) Yes — other people don't care! (*Moves toward up left, the thought of* WILFRED *actually going giving her a slight sinking of the heart at which she herself is surprised.*)

WILFRED: Ah've written that letter to the General! — Here it is — on'y Ah've got to end it off some way! (*Pulls a chair sideways to desk and half sits, intent on finishing the letter; prepares pen and runs hand into his hair impetuously.*) Ah'm not going to say 'Your loving son' or any such rubbish as that! It would be an almighty let-down! Ah *love* him of course — but this isn't that kind of a letter! (*pointing out writing on letter and speaking as if he supposed* CAROLINE *was at his shoulder*) Ah've been telling him — (*Looking round sees that* CAROLINE *is standing at a considerable distance looking at him.*) — What's the matter?

CAROLINE: Nothing — !

WILFRED: Ah thought you wanted to help!

CAROLINE: (*quickly*) Oh yes — Ah do! Ah do! (*Goes to* WILFRED *at desk; he looks in her face an instant, followed by a pause; then* CAROLINE *stammeringly asks*) The — the (*indicating his trousers by a little gesture*) — are they how you wanted 'em?

WILFRED: What?

CAROLINE: Those things. (*pointing to trousers*)

WILFRED: (*Glances at legs.*) Oh — they're all right! Fine! — Now about this letter — tell me what you think! (*turning to letter again*)

CAROLINE: Tell me what you said!

WILFRED: Want to hear it?

CAROLINE: Ah've got to haven't I? How could Ah help you if I didn't know what it was all about!

WILFRED: You're pretty good! (*Looks at her briefly.*) You *will* help me won't you? (*catching hold of her hand as she stands near him*)

CAROLINE: Oh' co'se Ah will — (*After an instant's pause draws hand away from him.*) about the letter!

WILFRED: That's what I mean! — It's mighty important you know! Everything depends on it!

CAROLINE: Well Ah should think so! (*Gets chair from between windows and pulls it near* WILFRED *on his left and sits looking over the letter while he reads — showing deep interest.*)

WILFRED: Ah just gave it to him strong!

CAROLINE: That's the *way* to give it to him!

WILFRED: You can't fool round with *him* much! He means business! But he'll find out Ah mean business too!

CAROLINE: That's right — everybody means business! — What did you say?

WILFRED: Ah said this! (*Reads letter.*) 'General Ransom Varney — Commanding

Division Army of the Northern Virginia — Dear Papa — This is to notify you
that Ah want you to let me come right now! If you don't Ah'll come anyhow
— that's all! The eighteen call is out — the seventeen comes next an' Ah'm not
going to wait for it! Do you think Ah'm a damned coward? Tom Kittridge
has gone! He was killed yesterday at Cold Harbor. Billy Fisher has gone. So
has Cousin Stephen and he ain't sixteen. He lied about his age but Ah don't
want to do that unless you make me. Answer this right now or not at all!'

CAROLINE: That's splendid!

WILFRED: Do you think so?

CAROLINE: Why it's just the thing!

WILFRED: But how'm Ah going to end it?

CÅROLINE: Just end it!

WILFRED: How?

CAROLINE: Sign your name.

WILFRED: Nothing else?

CAROLINE: What else is there?

WILFRED: Just 'Wilfred'?

CAROLINE: O'co'se!

WILFRED: (*Looks at her an instant then turns suddenly to desk and writes his
name.*) That's the thing! (*Holds it up.*) Will the rest of it do?

CAROLINE: Do! Ah should think so! (*rising*) Ah wish he had it now! (*Goes toward
center.*)

WILFRED: (*rising*) So do I! — It might take two or three days! (*Moves toward
CAROLINE.*) Ah can't wait that long! Why the Seventeen call might —
(*Stops; thinks frowningly.*)

CAROLINE: (*suddenly turning*) Ah'll tell you what to do! — Telegraph!
(WILFRED *looks at her — she at him. After an instant he glances at the
letter.*)

WILFRED: Whew! (*a whistle*) Ah haven't got money enough for that!

CAROLINE: 'Twon't take so very much!

WILFRED: Do you know what they're charging now? Over seven dollars a word!

CAROLINE: Let 'em charge! We can cut it down so there's only a few words an'
it means just the same! (*They both go at the letter each holding it on his or
her side.*) The address won't cost a thing!

WILFRED: Won't it?

CAROLINE: No! They never do! There's a heap o' money saved right now! We can
use that to pay for the rest! (WILFRED *looks at her a little puzzled.*) What
comes next? (*Both look over the letter.*)

WILFRED: 'Dear Papa' —

CAROLINE: Leave that out! (*Both scratch at it with pens or pencils.*)

WILFRED: Ah didn't care much for it anyway!

CAROLINE: He knew it before.

WILFRED: Ah'm glad it's out!

CAROLINE: So'm I! What's next? (*reading*) 'This — is — to — notify — you — that
— Ah — want — you — to — let — me — come — right — now.' We might leave
out that last 'to'.

WILFRED *and* CAROLINE: (*reciting it off together experimentally to see how it reads without the 'to'*) 'Ah—want—you—let—me—come—right—now.' (*after instant's thought both shake heads.*)

WILFRED: No!

CAROLINE: No!

WILFRED: It doesn't sound right.

CAROLINE: That's only a little word anyhow!

WILFRED: So it is. What's after that? (*Both eagerly look at letter.*)

CAROLINE: Wait — here it is! (*Reads.*) 'If — you — don't — Ah'll — come — any- how — that's — all.' (*They consider.*)

WILFRED: We might leave out 'that's all'.

CAROLINE: (*quickly*) No! Don't leave that out! It's very important. It doesn't seem so but it is! It shows — (*Hesitates.*) Well — it shows that's all there is about it! That one thing might convince him!

WILFRED: We've got to leave out something!

CAROLINE: Yes — but not that! Perhaps there's something in the next! (*Reads.*) 'The—eighteen—call—is—out—' That's got to stay!

WILFRED: (*Reads.*) 'The—seventeen—comes—next.'

CAROLINE: That's got to stay!

WILFRED: (*shaking head*) Yes!

CAROLINE: (*taking it up*) 'Ah'm—not—going—to—wait—for—it!' (*shaking head without looking up*) No! No!

WILFRED: (*shaking head*) No!

CAROLINE: We'll find something in just a minute! (*reading*) 'Do—you—think— Ah'm—a—damned—coward!' (*Both look up from the letter simultaneously and gaze at each other in silence for an instant.*)

WILFRED: (*after pause*) We might leave out the —

CAROLINE: (*breaking in on him with almost a scream*) No no! (*They again regard each other.*)

WILFRED: That 'damn''s going to cost us seven dollars and a half!

CAROLINE: It's worth it! Why it's the best thing you've got in the whole thing! Your papa's a general in the army! He'll *understand* that! What's next? Ah know there's something now.

WILFRED: (*Reads.*) 'Tom—Kittridge—has—gone. He—was—killed—yesterday—at— Cold—Harbor.'

CAROLINE: (*slight change in tone, a little lower*) Leave out that about his (*very slight catch of breath*) about his being killed.

WILFRED: (*looking at her*) But he was!

CAROLINE: (*suddenly very quiet*) Ah know he was — but you haven't got to tell him the news — have you?

WILFRED: That's so! (*They both cross off the words.*)

CAROLINE: (*becoming cheerful again*) How does it read now? (*both looking over the letter*)

WILFRED: It reads just the same — except that about Tom Kittridge.

CAROLINE: (*looking at* WILFRED *astonished*) Just the same! After all this work!
(*They look at one another rather astounded for an instant, then suddenly turn to the letter again and study over it earnestly. Sound of door bell in distant part of house. Soon after* MARTHA *crosses*

outside left coming from door right of stairway to go to door. Sound of door off left. A moment later she is seen going up the stairway carrying a large envelope. WILFRED and CAROLINE are so absorbed in work that they do not observe the bell or MARTHA's movements.)

CAROLINE: (*looking up from letter*) Everything else has got to stay!

WILFRED: Then we can't telegraph — it would take hundreds of dollars!

CAROLINE: (*with determination*) Yes we can! (WILFRED *looks at her; she takes the letter.*) Ah'll send it! (*backing up a little toward door up left*)

WILFRED: How can you —

CAROLINE: Never you mind!

WILFRED: (*Follows her up a little.*) See here! (*taking hold of letter*) Ah'm not going to have you spending money!

CAROLINE: Ha! There's no danger! Ah haven't got any to spend!

WILFRED: (*Releases hold on letter.*) Then what are you going to do?

CAROLINE: (*turning up toward door up left with letter*) Oh — Ah know! (*Turns toward* WILFRED.) Ah reckon Douglass Stafford'll send it for me!

WILFRED: (*quickly to her*) No he won't! (*They face each other; CAROLINE surprised.*)

CAROLINE: What's the reason he won't?

WILFRED: (*slight pause*) If he wants to send it for *me* he can — but he won't send it for *you*!

CAROLINE: What do you care s'long as he sends it?

WILFRED: (*looking at* CAROLINE — *slight change of tone — softer*) Well — Ah care! That's enough! (*They look at each other, then both lower eyes, looking in different directions.*)

CAROLINE: Oh, well — if you feel like that about it — ! (*Turns away.*)

WILFRED: (*eyes lowered*) That's the way Ah feel! (*Pause; WILFRED looks up at her — goes down toward her.*) You — you won't give up the idea of helping me because I feel like that — will you?

CAROLINE: (*impulsively, with start and turn toward* WILFRED) Mercy no — Ah'll help you all I can! (WILFRED *impulsively takes her hand as if in gratitude and so quick that she draws it away and goes on with only a slight break.*) About the letter!

WILFRED: That's what Ah mean! (*They stand an instant,* CAROLINE *looking down,* WILFRED *at her.*)

CAROLINE: (*suddenly turning toward desk*) Ah'm going to see if we can't leave out something else! (*Sits at desk; WILFRED goes near her and stands looking over her, intent on the letter.*)

(*Enter MRS VARNEY, coming down the stairway and into the room at door up left. She has an open letter in her hand. She also brings a belt and cap rolled up together. She pauses at the door and motions someone who is outside left to come in. MARTHA follows her down and exits through door right of stairway. Enter an orderly up left just from his horse after a long ride. Dusty, faded and bloody uniform; yellow stripes; face sunburned and grim. He stands near the door waiting, without effort to be precise or formal, but nevertheless being entirely soldierly.* MRS VARNEY *waits until he enters.*)

MRS VARNEY: (*Comes down center a little.*) Wilfred! (WILFRED *and* CAROLINE *turn quickly. They both stare motionless for a moment.*) Here's a letter from your father. He sent it by the orderly. (WILFRED *moves a step or two toward* MRS VARNEY *and stands looking at her.* CAROLINE *slowly rises with her eyes on* MRS VARNEY, *who speaks calmly but with the measured quietness of one who is controlling herself.*) He tells me – (*Stops a little but it is only her voice that falls; she does not break down or show emotion; holds letter toward* WILFRED.) You read it!

   (WILFRED, *after glance at* CAROLINE, *steps quickly to* MRS VARNEY *and takes the letter. Reads it –* MRS VARNEY *looking away a little as he does so.* CAROLINE's *eyes upon* WILFRED *as he reads. The* ORDERLY *faced to right on obliqued line of door.* WILFRED *finishes very soon. He glances at the* ORDERLY, *then hands the letter to his mother as he steps across to him.*)

WILFRED: (*standing before the* ORDERLY) The General says Ah'm going back with you!

ORDERLY: (*saluting*) His orders, sir!

WILFRED: When do we start?

ORDERLY: Soon as you can sir – Ah'm waiting!

WILFRED: We'll make it right now! (*Turns and walks quickly to his mother.*) You won't mind, mother.

   (MRS VARNEY *does not speak, but quietly strokes the hair back from his forehead with a trembling hand – and only once. She then hands him the belt that has seen service and the cap that is old and worn.*)

MRS VARNEY: (*low voice*) Your brother wanted you to take these – I told him you were going; (WILFRED *takes them; puts on the belt at once.*) He says he can get another belt – when he wants it. You're to have his blankets too – Ah'll get them. (*Crosses* WILFRED *and goes off at door up left and off to left going back of orderly.*)

WILFRED: (*finishing adjusting the belt;* CAROLINE *motionless but now looking down at the floor;* WILFRED *suppresses excitement.*) Fits as if it was made for me! (*to* ORDERLY) Ah'll be with you in a jiffy! (*Goes to* CAROLINE.) We won't have to send that now – (*indicating letter*) will we? (CAROLINE *shakes her head a little without looking up – then slowly raises hand in which she has the letter and holds it out to him, her eyes still on the floor.* WILFRED *takes the letter mechanically and keeps it in his hand during the next few lines, tearing it up absent-mindedly.*) You're pretty good – to help me like you did! You can help me again if you – if you want to! (CAROLINE *raises her eyes and looks at him.*) Ah'd like to fight twice as well if – (*Hesitates.* CAROLINE *looks at him an instant longer and then looks down without speaking.*) Good-bye! (WILFRED *holds out his hand.* CAROLINE *puts her hand in his without looking at him.*) Perhaps you'll write to me about – about helping me fight twice as well! Ah wouldn't mind if you telegraphed! That is – if you telegraphed that you would! (*Slight pause.* WILFRED *holding* CAROLINE's *hand boyishly;* CAROLINE *looking down.* WILFRED *tries to say something but can't find the words. Enter* MRS VARNEY *at door up left;* WILFRED *hears her and turns — leaving* CAROLINE *and meeting his mother near center. She brings an army blanket rolled and tied.* WILFRED *takes it and slings it over his shoulder.*) Good-bye mother! (*Kisses her rather hurriedly;* MRS VARNEY *stands passive.*) You won't mind, will you. (*Crosses at once to* ORDERLY *with eagerness and enthusiasm.*) Ready sir! (*saluting;* ORDERLY *turns and marches off at door up left,* WILFRED *following.*)

> (*The opening and closing of the door outside is heard, and then it is still.* MRS VARNEY *is the first to move. She turns and walks slowly up a few steps, her back to the audience, but with no visible emotion. It is as if her eyes filled with tears and she turned away. When she stops,* CAROLINE *moves a little, her eyes still down, walking slowly across toward door left, but not with emphasized deliberation.* MRS VARNEY *hears her going and turns in time to speak just before she reaches the door.*)

MRS VARNEY: Going, dear? (CAROLINE *nods her head a little without looking around.*) Oh yes! (*Speaks with a shade of forced cheerfulness.*) Your party, of course! You ought to be there! (CAROLINE *stops and speaks back into the room without looking at* MRS VARNEY.)

CAROLINE: (*subdued voice; with a sad little shake of head*) There won't — (*Shakes head again a little.*) There won't be any party tonight. (*Exit door left.*)

MRS VARNEY: (*After an instant's wait starts toward door up left.*) Caroline! Stop a moment! (*at door*) I don't want you to go home alone! (*Goes down left and rings the bell.*)

CAROLINE: (*outside*) Oh Ah don't mind!

> (*Sounds of front door and heavy steps of men outside, up left.* MRS VARNEY *goes up left, looks off and then retires back a little into the room. Enter* ARRELSFORD *and two soldiers at the door up left. He motions men to stand at the door and goes quickly to* MRS VARNEY.)

ARRELSFORD: (*low voice*) Is he — ? (*a motion toward window at right*)

MRS VARNEY: (*hardly above a whisper*) Yes! (*Glances round toward window.*)
> (*Enter* CAROLINE *at door up left from off left.*)

CAROLINE: Oh Mrs Varney — there's a heap o' soldiers out yere! You don't reckon anything's the mattah do you?

> (*Enter* MARTHA *at door up left from door right of stairway.* ARRELSFORD *goes back to* MRS VARNEY *to window up right, looks through curtains.*)

MRS VARNEY: (*hastening to* CAROLINE) Sh! — No — there's nothing the matter! Martha, I want you to go home with Miss Mitford — at once! (*urging* CAROLINE *off*) Good night dear! (*kissing her*)

CAROLINE: Good night! (*Looks up in* MRS VARNEY's *face.*) You don't reckon she could go with me to — (*Hesitates.*) somewhere else, do you?

MRS VARNEY: Why where do you want to go?

CAROLINE: Just to — just to the telegraph office!
>(ARRELSFORD *turns sharply and looks at* CAROLINE *from window.*)

MRS VARNEY: Now! At this time of night!

CAROLINE: Ah've got to! Oh, it's very important business!
>(ARRELSFORD *watching* CAROLINE)

MRS VARNEY: Of course, then Martha must go with you! Good night!

CAROLINE: Good night! (*Exit* CAROLINE *and* MARTHA *at door up left and off.*)

MRS VARNEY: (*calling off to* MARTHA) Martha, don't leave her an instant!

MARTHA: No'm — Ah'll take care! (*heavy sound of door outside up left*)

ARRELSFORD: (*going up center quickly — low, sharp voice*) What is she going to do at the telegraph office?

MRS VARNEY: (*going down left center a little; low voice*) *I've* no idea!

ARRELSFORD: Has she had any conversation with him? (*Motions toward right.*)

MRS VARNEY: Why — they were talking together here — early this evening! But it isn't possible she could —

ARRELSFORD: Anything is possible! (*Goes over to* CORPORAL *at up left quickly, passing back of* MRS VARNEY, *who moves up to right center as he crosses.*) Have Eddinger follow that girl! Don't let any dispatch go out until I see it! Make no mistake about that! (CORPORAL *exits with salute at door up left; brief pause;* ARRELSFORD *turns to* MRS VARNEY.) Are they both out there? (*Motions toward window.*)

MRS VARNEY: (*glance back at right first*) Yes! Did you bring the man from Libby Prison?

ARRELSFORD: The guard's holding him in the street. When we get Thorne in here alone I'll have him brought up to that window (*pointing*) an' shoved into the room!
>(CORPORAL *reappears at the door and waits for further orders.*
>ARRELSFORD *and* MRS VARNEY *continue in low tones.*)

MRS VARNEY: Where shall I —

ARRELSFORD: Out there (*pointing up left and going toward door a little*) where you can get a view of this room!

MRS VARNEY: But if he sees me —

ARRELSFORD: He won't if it's dark in the hall! (*Turns to* CORPORAL *and gives order in low distinct voice.*) Shut off those lights out there! (*indicating lights outside the door or archway up left.* CORPORAL *exits; lights off*) We can close these curtains can't we?

MRS VARNEY: Yes. (ARRELSFORD *draws curtains at door up left.*)

ARRELSFORD: I don't want much light in here! (*indicating drawing-room.* CORPORAL *and* MEN *exit up left.* ARRELSFORD *goes to table up left center and turns gas or lamp down;* MRS VARNEY *turns down lamp on desk — stage in half light.* ARRELSFORD *carefully moves couch away from window up right and opens portieres of window, and then speaks almost in a whisper.*) Now open those curtains! Carefully! Don't attract attention! (*indicating window down right*)
>(MRS VARNEY *very quietly draws back the curtains to window*

*down right — moonlight through the window covers as much of
stage as possible, as well as backing up right.*)

ARRELSFORD: (*moving over to up left center and speaking across to* MRS
VARNEY *after lights are down*) Are those women in there yet? (*indicating
door up center*)

MRS VARNEY: Yes.

ARRELSFORD: Where's the key? (MRS VARNEY *moves noiselessly to the door.*)
Is it on the inside? (MRS VARNEY *turns and nods affirmatively.*) Lock the
door!

       (MRS VARNEY *turns the key as noiselessly as possible.* EDITH
*suddenly appears at window up right coming on quickly and closing
the windows after her.* MRS VARNEY *and* ARRELSFORD *both
turn and stand looking at her.* EDITH *turns to them and stands an
instant.*)

EDITH: (*going toward* MRS VARNEY *with hand stretched out — very low voice —
but breathlessly and with intensity*) Mama! (MRS VARNEY *hurries forward
with her center;* ARRELSFORD *remains up left center looking on.*) I want to
speak to you!

ARRELSFORD: (*low tone, stepping forward*) We can't wait!

EDITH: You must! (ARRELSFORD *moves back protestingly.* EDITH *turns to*
MRS VARNEY — *almost a whisper*) I can't — I can't do it! Oh — let me go!

MRS VARNEY: (*very low voice*) Edith! You were the one who —

EDITH: (*almost a whisper*) I was sure then!

MRS VARNEY: Has he confessed?

EDITH: (*quickly*) No no! (*glance toward* ARRELSFORD)

ARRELSFORD: (*low voice — sharp*) Don't speak so loud!

MRS VARNEY: (*low voice*) What is it Edith — You must tell me!

EDITH: (*almost a whisper*) Mama — he loves me! (*breathless with emotion*) — Yes
— and I — Oh — let someone else do it!

MRS VARNEY: You don't mean that you — (ARRELSFORD *comes forward
quickly.*)

EDITH: (*seeing* ARRELSFORD *approach and crossing to him*) No no! Not now!
Not now!

MRS VARNEY: More reason now than ever!

ARRELSFORD: We *must* go on!

EDITH: (*turning desperately upon* ARRELSFORD *in low voice*) Why are you
doing this?

ARRELSFORD: Because I please!

EDITH: (*low voice but with force*) You never pleased before! Hundreds of
suspicious cases have come up — hundreds of men have been run down — but
you preferred to sit at your desk in the War Department.

MRS VARNEY: Edith!

ARRELSFORD: We won't discuss that now!

EDITH: No — we'll end it! I'll have nothing more to do with the affair!

ARRELSFORD: You won't!

MRS VARNEY: You won't!

EDITH: Nothing at all! — Nothing! — Nothing!

ARRELSFORD: (*low voice but with vehemence*) At your own suggestion Miss Varney, I agreed to a plan by which we could criminate this friend of your – or establish his innocence. At the critical moment – when everything's ready you propose to withdraw – making it a failure and perhaps allowing him to escape altogether!

MRS VARNEY: You mustn't do this Edith!

EDITH: (*desperately*) He's there! The man is there – at the further end of the veranda! What more do you want of me!

ARRELSFORD: (*low voice, sharp, intense*) Call 'im into this room! If anyone else should do it he'd suspect! He'd be on his guard!

EDITH: (*after pause*) Very well – I'll call 'im into this room. (*Moves as if to do so.*)

ARRELSFORD: One thing more! I want 'im to have this paper! (*holding out paper taken from* JONAS *in Act I*) Tell 'im where it came from – tell 'im the old niggah got it from a prisoner in Libby!

EDITH: (*quietly*) Why am I to do that?

ARRELSFORD: (*low but very strong*) Why not? If he's innocent where's the harm? If not – if he's in this plot – the message on that paper will send 'im to the telegraph office tonight and that's just where we want him!

EDITH: I never promised that!

ARRELSFORD: (*hard sharp voice though subdued*) Do you still believe him innocent?

EDITH: (*pause; slowly raises her head erect, looks* ARRELSFORD *full in the face; almost whisper*) I still – believe him – innocent!

ARRELSFORD: Then why are you afraid to give him this? (*indicating paper*)
(*Pause.* EDITH *turns to* ARRELSFORD, *stretches out her hand and takes the paper from him. She pauses a moment.* ARRELSFORD *and* MRS VARNEY *watch her. She turns and moves up a few steps toward the window; stops and stands listening; noise of chair off right.*)

EDITH: Captain Thorne's coming.

ARRELSFORD: (*going to door up left and holding curtain back*) This way Mrs Varney! Quick! Quick! (ARRELSFORD *and* MRS VARNEY *hasten off at the door up left, closing portieres after them.*)
(EDITH *moves and stands near table. Sound of* THORNE'*s footsteps on veranda outside windows.* EDITH *slowly turns toward the window and stands looking at it with a fascinated dread.* THORNE *opens the window and enters at once, coming a few steps into the room, when he stops and stands an instant looking at* EDITH *as she looks strangely at him. Then he goes to her.*)

THORNE: (*low voice, near* EDITH) Is anything the matter?

EDITH: (*slightly shakes her head before speaking; nearly a whisper*) Oh *no*!

THORNE: You've been away such a long time!

EDITH: Only a few minutes!

THORNE: Only a few years. ·

EDITH: (*easier*) Oh – if that's a few years – (*turning away front a little*) what a lot of time there is!

THORNE: No. – There's only tonight!

EDITH: (*turning to him; a breathless interrogation*) What!

THORNE: (*taking her hands*) There's only tonight and you in the world! — Oh — see what I've been doing! I came here determined not to tell you I love you — and for the last half hour I've been telling you nothing else! Ah, my darling — there's only tonight and you!

EDITH: (*suddenly moving back a little from him; nearly a breathless whisper*) No no — you mustn't! (*a quick apprehensive glance around down toward left and back; speaks very quickly, as if afraid she would be overheard*) — not now! (*Stands turned away from* THORNE.)

> (THORNE *holds position he was in an instant. Then moves back slightly, and as she is looking front he darts a quick suspicious glance toward curtains up left and instantly back to her.* EDITH *moves forward a little,* THORNE *slowly releasing her hand.* — *After looking at her there an instant* THORNE *darts another swift glance* — *this time toward the window up right and the same instant back to her again.*)

THORNE: (*low voice, from where he stands, above her*) Don't mind what I said Miss Varney — I must have forgotten myself. (*brief pause; steps down to her*) Believe me I came to make a friendly call and — and say good-bye. (*bowing slightly*) Permit me to do so now. (*Turns up at once and walks toward door up left.*)

EDITH: (*quickly across to right center as* THORNE *goes up*) Oh! — Cap'n Thorne! (*This is timed to stop him just before he reaches the closed portieres of door up left.* THORNE *turns and looks at* EDITH — *moonlight across from window right on him.* EDITH *tries to be natural, but her lightness somewhat forced.*) Before you go I — (*slight quiver in her voice*) — I wanted to ask your advice about something! (*Stands turned a little to front.*)

THORNE: (*Looks at her motionless an instant longer, then turns his head slowly toward the portieres on his left; turns back to* EDITH *again and at once moves down to her.*) Yes?

EDITH: What do you think this means? (*Holds the piece of paper out toward him but avoids looking in his face.*)

THORNE: (*stepping quickly to her and taking the paper easily*) Why, what is it? (*a half-glance at the paper as he takes it*)

EDITH: It's a — (*Hesitates slightly; recovers at once and looks up at him brightly.*) That's what I want you to tell me.

THORNE: (*looking at the paper*) Oh — you don't know!

EDITH: (*shaking head slightly*) No. (*Stands waiting, eyes averted.* THORNE *glances quickly at her an instant on peculiar tone of 'no'.*)

THORNE: (*looking again at the paper*) A note from someone?

EDITH: It might be.

THORNE: (*glancing about*) Well, it's pretty dark here! (*Glances toward low-turned lamp on desk; crosses to it.*) If you'll excuse me I'll turn up this lamp a little more — (*going to desk*) then we can see what it is. (*Turns up lamp.*) There we are! (*Looks at paper; as soon as he sees it, looks front quickly showing that he recognizes it, without a start; slow turn to* EDITH, *then looks at the paper again — reads as if with difficulty.*) 'Attack . . . tonight' — There's something about 'Attack tonight' — (*Turns to* EDITH.) Could you make out what it was?

> (EDITH *shakes head negatively. Her lips move, but she cannot speak. She turns away.* THORNE *looks at her a second, then a slow turn of head, looking up stage, then turns to examine the paper again.*)

'Attack . . . tonight . . . plan . . . three.' (*Looks up front as if considering; repeats.*) Plan three! (*considering again, slight laugh*) Well — this thing must be a puzzle of some kind, Miss Varney. (*turning to her*)

EDITH: (*slowly, strained voice, as if forcing herself*) It was taken from a Yankee prisoner!

THORNE: (*instantly coming from former easy attitude into one showing interest and surprise; looks at* EDITH) So! Yankee prisoner eh? (*While speaking he is instinctively holding paper in right hand as if to look at it again when he finishes speaking to* EDITH.)

EDITH: Yes — down in Libby! — He gave it to one of our servants — old Jonas!

THORNE: (*Turns quickly to paper.*) Why here! This might be something — (*Looks again at the paper.*) 'Attack tonight — plan three — use Telegraph — ' (*second's pause; he looks up front*) Use Telegraph! (*Turns quickly to* EDITH *and goes toward her.*) This might be something important Miss Varney! Looks like a plot on our Department Telegraph Lines! Who did Jonas give it to?

EDITH: No one!

THORNE: Well — how — how —

EDITH: We took it away from him!

THORNE: Oh! (*long 'Oh' of 'How could you!' Starting at once as if to cross above* EDITH *to left*) That was a mistake!

EDITH: (*detaining him; speaks rapidly, almost a whisper*) What are you going to do?

THORNE: (*strong; determined*) Find that nigger and make him tell who this paper was for — he's the man we want! (*crossing back of her to left and up toward door*)

EDITH: (*turning quickly to him*) Cap'n Thorne — they've lied about you!

THORNE: (*wheeling round like a flash and coming down quickly to her*) Lied about me! What do you mean? (*seizing her hands and looking in her face to read what it is*)

EDITH: (*quick, breathless, very low, almost whisper*) Don't be angry — I didn't think it would be like this!

THORNE: (*with great force*) Yes — but what have you done?

EDITH: (*breaking loose from him and crossing to left*) No! (*almost a quick cry spoken close on his speech*)

THORNE: (*as she crosses before him, trying to detain her*) But I must know!

> (*Heavy sound of door outside left and of steps and voices in the hall — 'Here! This way!' etc.*)

CORPORAL: (*off left, speaking outside door*) This way! Look out on that side will you?

> (THORNE *stands near center listening.*)

EDITH: Oh! (*going rapidly up left*) — I don't want to be here! (*Exits door up left and goes up stairs out of the way of the soldiers; THORNE instantly backs away, drawing revolver and stands ready for attack from up left.*)

> (*Enter at once on exit of EDITH, CORPORAL with two MEN at door up left. They cross rapidly toward window up right — CORPORAL leading, carrying a lighted lantern. THORNE, seeing CORPORAL, at once breaks position and moves across towards up center as MEN cross, watching CORPORAL, who is up right center.*)

CORPORAL: (*near window*) Out here! Look out now!

> (*MEN exit at window up right.*)

THORNE: (*quick on CORPORAL's speech so as to stop him*) What is it Corporal? (*putting revolver back into holster*)

> (*THORNE stands up center in moonlight from window facing CORPORAL.*)

CORPORAL: (*turning and saluting*) Prisoner sir — broke out o' Libby! We've run him down the street — he turned in here somewhere! If he comes in that way would you be good enough to let us know! (*pointing to the window down right*)

THORNE: Go on, Corporal! (*Starts across to window.*) I'll look out for this window! (*Exit CORPORAL window up right.*)

> (*THORNE strides rapidly to window down right, pushes curtain back each side and stands within the window looking out. Right hand on revolver, left hand holding curtains back. Moonlight on through windows across stage. Dead pause for an instant. Suddenly the two men who crossed with CORPORAL appear at window up right holding HENRY DUMONT. With a sudden movement they force him on through the window and disappear quickly outside. DUMONT stands where he landed, looking back through window not comprehending what is going on. He gives a quick glance about the room. DUMONT wears uniform of United States Cavalry, worn with service. He is pale as from lack of food — but not emaciated or ill. THORNE down right standing motionless near window waiting — DUMONT up right center, holding position he struck on entrance. Enough light on him to show the blue United States uniform. After a second's pause DUMONT turns from the window and looks slowly about the room, taking in the various points like a caged animal, turning his head very slowly as he looks one way and another. Soon he moves a few steps down and pauses. Turns and makes out a doorway up left, and after a glance round, he walks rapidly toward it. Just before he reaches the door there is a slight sound outside, and the blades of two or three bayonets come down into position through the curtains, showing at the door and barring his exit. He stops on seeing the bayonets. Slight click of bayonets striking together as they come into position. Light outside window right strikes across blades of bayonets. On noise of bayonets, THORNE turns quickly and moves a few steps into the room, trying to see who is there. He sees DUMONT and stands looking across at him.*)

Bayonets withdrawn at once after they are shown. DUMONT *turns from the door and begins to move slowly down stage at left, along the wall. Just as he is coming around table down left toward center he sees* THORNE *and stops dead. Both men motionless, their eyes upon each other.* DUMONT *makes a start as if to escape through window up right, moving across toward it.*)

THORNE: (*quick and loud order as* DUMONT *starts toward window*) Halt — You're a prisoner!

(DUMONT, *after instant's hesitation on* THORNE'*s order, starts rapidly toward window up right.* THORNE *heads him off, meeting him and seizes him.*)

THORNE: Halt! I say!

(*The two men struggle together, moving quickly down stage very close to front — getting as far as possible from those who are watching them.*)

THORNE: (*loud voice, as they struggle down stage*) Here's your man Corporal! What are you doing there?

DUMONT: (*when down as far as possible — holding* THORNE *motionless an instant and hissing out between his teeth, without pause or inflection on words*) ATTACK TONIGHT — PLAN THREE — TELEGRAPH — DO YOU GET IT?

THORNE: (*quick*) YES!

(*This dialogue in capitals shot at each other with great force and rapidity — and so low that people outside door could not hear.*)

DUMONT: (*low voice, almost whisper*) They're watching us! Shoot me in the leg!

THORNE: (*holding* DUMONT *motionless*) No no! I can't do that!

DUMONT: You must!

THORNE: I can't shoot my own brother!

DUMONT: It's the only way to throw 'em off the scent!

THORNE: Well I won't do it anyhow!

DUMONT: If you won't do it I will! Give me that revolver! (*pushing left arm out to get revolver*)

THORNE: (*holding* DUMONT'*s arm back motionless*) No no Harry! You'll hurt yourself!

DUMONT: (*beginning to struggle to get revolver*) I don't care! Let me have it!

(*They struggle quickly and move into light from window down right.*)

THORNE: (*calling out as he struggles with* DUMONT) Here's your man Corporal! What's the matter with you!

DUMONT: (*holding* THORNE *motionless in light and trying to get at his revolver*) Give me that gun!

THORNE: (*as* DUMONT *holds him and is just getting revolver; loud, aspirated, sharp*) Look out Harry! You'll hurt yourself! (*Gets his right hand on revolver to hold it;* DUMONT *manages with his left to wrench* THORNE'*s hand loose from the revolver and hold it up while he seizes the weapon with his right hand and pulls it out of the holster. At the same time he shoves* THORNE *off.*)

THORNE: Look out! (*as* DUMONT *throws him off and attempts to fire the gun at himself. Before* THORNE *can recover and turn* DUMONT *fires. There is a quick sharp scream from ladies outside left.* DUMONT *with a groan, staggers down toward center and falls mortally wounded holding the revolver in his hand until he is down and then releasing it, so that* THORNE *can find it near.*) Harry — you've shot yourself! (*on shot and scream; instantly dives for the revolver and gets it, coming up on same motion with it in right hand and stands in careless attitude just over* DUMONT's *body. Men's voices heard outside up left;* ARRELSFORD *gives an order.*)

> (*Enter* ARRELSFORD *and* MEN *from door up left, followed by* EDITH, MRS VARNEY *and* MISS KITTRIDGE. *Enter* CORPORAL *and men from the window up right.* ARRELSFORD *runs at once to table up center and turns up lamp. Others stand on tableau —* MRS VARNEY *and* EDITH *at left,* MISS KITTRIDGE *up left;* MEN *in doorway and up right center near window.*)

ARRELSFORD, MRS VARNEY, EDITH, MISS KITTRIDGE, CORPORAL, MEN: (*as they enter*) Where is he! What has he done! He's shot the man! This way now! etc. (*Exclamations stop at once on lights on.*)

THORNE: (*with careless swing of revolver across him toward center as he brings it up to put back into holster — as the people stop quiet*) There's your prisoner Corporal — look out for him! (*Stands putting revolver back into holster.*)

CURTAIN

ACT III

The War Department Telegraph Office. Ten o'clock. A plain and somewhat battered and grimy room on the second floor of a public building; stained and smoky walls. Large windows — the glass covered with grime and cobwebs. Plaster off walls and ceiling in some places. All this from neglect — not from bombardment. It is a room which was formerly somewhat handsome. Moldings and stucco-work broken and discolored. Very large and high door or double doors up right center obliqued. This door opens to a corridor showing plain corridor-backing of a public building. This door must lead off well to right so that it shall not interfere with window showing up left center. Three wide French windows up left and left center obliques a little, with balcony outside extending right and left and showing several massive white columns, bases at balcony and extending up out of sight as if for several stories above. Backing of windows showing night view of city roofs and buildings as from height of second floor. Large disused fireplace with elaborate marble mantel in bad repair and very dirty on right side behind telegraph tables. Door up center opening to cupboard with shelves on which are Battery Jars and Telegraph Office truck of various kinds. Room lighted by gas on right above right telegraph table, several burners branching from a main pipe and all to turn on and off easily by means of one cock in main pipe, just above the telegraph table. Show evening through window up left — dark, with lights of buildings very faint and distant, keeping general effect outside window of darkness. (Moonlight at window on the massive white columns and the characters who go out on the balcony.) Corridor outside

door up right center not strongly illuminated. In the room itself fair light but not brilliant. Plain, solid table with telegraph instruments down right center. Another table with instruments along wall at right side. Table down right braced to look as if fastened securely to the floor. Also see that wire connections are properly made from all the instruments in the room to wires running up the wall on right side, thence across along ceiling to up left and out through broken panes in upper part of windows up left. This large bunch of wires leading out, in plain sight, is most important. Large office clock over mantel set at 10 o'clock at opening and to run during the Act. Two instruments A. and D. on table right center — A. is at right end of table and is only one used at that table, D. being for safety. B. and C. on long table against fireplace. B. is at lower end of table, C. at upper end; one chair at table down right center. Two chairs at table right. One chair up center. No sound of cannonading in this Act. At opening there are two OPERATORS *at work, one at table down right center, one at table on right side. They are in old gray uniform, but in shirt sleeves. Coats are hung up or thrown on chairs one side. Busy click-effects of instruments. After first continued clicking for a moment there are occasional pauses.* MESSENGERS A. *and* B. *near door up right center.*
MESSENGER 3 *in front of door center talking to* MESSENGER 4. MESSENGER 2 *is looking out of middle window over left.*

SECOND OPERATOR (LT ALLISON): (*at table right, instrument B., finishing writing a dispatch*) Ready here! (MESSENGER A. *steps quickly forward and takes dispatch.*) Department! The Secretary must have it tonight! (MESSENGER *salutes and exits quickly at door up right with dispatch. Short pause. Other* MESSENGER *standing on attention.*)

FIRST OPERATOR (LT FORAY): (*at table down right center, instrument A.*) Ready here! (MESSENGER B. *steps quickly down and takes dispatch from* LT FORAY.) To the President — General Watson — marked private! (MESSENGER B. *salutes and off quickly door up right.*)

    (LT ALLISON *at right moves to another instrument when it begins to click and answers call.*)

MESSENGER 1: (*Enters hurriedly at door up right and comes down to table right center with dispatch.*) Major Bridgman!

LT FORAY: (*looking up from work*) Bridgman! Where's that?

MESSENGER 1: (*Glances at dispatch.*) Longstreet's Corp.

LT FORAY: That's yours Allison. (*Resumes work.*)

    (LT ALLISON *holds out hand for dispatch.* MESSENGER 1 *gives it to him and exits at door up right.* ALLISON *sends message on instrument B. Sound of band of music in distance increasing very gradually.* MESSENGERS *to go windows left and look out but glance now and then at operators.*)

MESSENGER 2: (*opening center window and looking out*) What's that going up Main Street?

MESSENGER 3: (*Looks out.*) Richmond Grays!

MESSENGERS 2 *and* 4: No!

    (*All look out through middle window up left.*)

MESSENGER 2: That's what they are sure enough!

MESSENGER 3: They're sending 'em down the river!

MESSENGER 2: Not tonight!

MESSENGER 4: Seems like they was, though!

MESSENGER 3: I didn't reckon they'd send the Grays out without there was something going on!

MESSENGER 4: How do you know but what there is?

MESSENGER 2: Tonight! Why good God! It's as quiet as a tomb!

MESSENGER 4: Ah reckon that's what's worrying 'em! It's so damned unusual!
>   (*Sound of band gradually dies away. Before music dies away,* LT FORAY *finishes a dispatch and calls.*)

LT FORAY: Ready here! (MESSENGER 3 *down to him and takes dispatch.*) Department — from General Lee — duplicate to the President!
>   (MESSENGER 3 *salutes and exits quickly up right. Enter an* ORDERLY, *door up right; goes quickly down to* LT FORAY. MESSENGERS 2 *and* 4 *stand, talking near windows left.*)

ORDERLY: (*Salutes.*) The Secretary wants to know if there's anything from General Lee come in tonight?

LT FORAY: Just sent one over an' a duplicate went out to the President.

ORDERLY: The President's with the Cabinet yet — he didn't go home! They want an operator right quick to take down a cipher.

LT FORAY: (*calling out to* LT ALLISON) Got anything on, Charlie?

LT ALLISON: Not right now!

LT FORAY: Well go over to the Department — they want to take down a cipher.
>   (LT ALLISON *gets coat and exits door up right, putting coat on as he goes, followed by the* ORDERLY *who came for him. Door up right is opened from outside by a couple of* YOUNG OFFICERS *in showy and untarnished uniforms, who stand in most polite attitudes waiting for a lady to pass in.* LT FORAY *very busy writing at table right center, taking message from instrument A. but stops this message for* CAROLINE *scene.*)

FIRST YOUNG OFFICER: Right this way, Miss Mitford!

SECOND YOUNG OFFICER: Allow me, Miss Mitford! This is the Department Telegraph office!
>   (*Enter at the door up right* CAROLINE. *The young officers follow her in.* MARTHA *enters after the officers, and waits near door well up stage.*)

CAROLINE: (*Coming down center, speaks in rather subdued manner and without vivacity, as if her mind were upon what she came for.*) Thank you!

FIRST YOUNG OFFICER: Ah'm afraid you've gone back on the Army, Miss Mitford!

CAROLINE: (*Looks at* FIRST YOUNG OFFICER *questioningly.*) Gone where?

SECOND YOUNG OFFICER: Seems like we ought to a' got a salute as you went by!

CAROLINE: Oh yes! (*Salutes in perfunctory and absent-minded manner and turns away glancing about room and moving down a step or two.*) Good evening!
>   (*nodding to one of the* MESSENGERS *waiting up left*)

MESSENGER 2: (*touching cap and stepping quickly to* CAROLINE) Good evening, Miss Mitford! Could we do anything for you in the office tonight?

(MESSENGER A. *remains up near upper window left.*)

CAROLINE: Ah want to send a telegram!

> (*The three officers stand looking at* CAROLINE *quieted for a moment by her serious tone.*)

SECOND YOUNG OFFICER: Ah'm afraid you've been havin' bad news, Miss Mitford?

CAROLINE: No — (*shaking her head*) no!

FIRST YOUNG OFFICER: Maybe some friend o' yours has gone down to the front!

CAROLINE: (*beginning to be interested*) Well — supposing he had — would you call that bad news?

FIRST YOUNG OFFICER: Well Ah didn't know as you'd exactly like to —

CAROLINE: Then let me tell you — as you didn't know — that *all* my friends go down to the front!

SECOND YOUNG OFFICER: I hope not *all* Miss Mitford!

CAROLINE: Yes — all! If they didn't they wouldn't *be* my friends.

FIRST YOUNG OFFICER: But some of us are obliged to stay back here to take care of you.

CAROLINE: Well there's altogether too many trying to take care of me! You're all discharged! (*Crosses to down left.*)

> (MESSENGER 3 *enters door up right center and joins* MESSENGER 4 *up left center near upper window.* OFFICERS *fall back a little, looking rather foolish but entirely good-natured.*)

SECOND YOUNG OFFICER: If we're really discharged Miss Mitford, looks like we'd have to go!

FIRST YOUNG OFFICER: Yes — but we're mighty sorry to see you in such bad spirits Miss Mitford!

SECOND YOUNG OFFICER *and* MESSENGER 2: Yes indeed we are, Miss Mitford!

CAROLINE: (*turning*) Would you like to put me in real good spirits?

FIRST YOUNG OFFICER: Would we!

SECOND YOUNG OFFICER: You try us once!

MESSENGER 2: Ah reckon there ain't anything we'd like bettah!

CAROLINE: Then Ah'll tell you *just* what to do! (*They listen eagerly.*) Start out this very night and never stop till you get to where my friends are — lying in trenches and ditches and earthworks between us and the Yankee guns!

SECOND YOUNG OFFICER, FIRST YOUNG OFFICER, MESSENGER 2: (*remonstrating*) But really, Miss — you don't mean —

CAROLINE: Fight Yankees a few days and lie in ditches a few nights till those uniforms you've got on look like they'd been some *use* to somebody! If you're so mighty anxious to do something for me, *that's* what you can do! (*turning away*) It's the only thing Ah want!

> (*The* YOUNG OFFICERS *stand rather discouraged an instant.*)

LT FORAY: (*business*) Ready here! (MESSENGER 3 *steps quickly down to him.*) Department! Commissary General's office! (MESSENGER 3 *salutes, takes dispatch and exits up right center.* MESSENGER 2 *returns to* MESSENGER 4 *during this, and stands with him near window up left center.*)

(MESSENGER A. *enters quickly at door up right center and comes down to* LT FORAY, *handing him a dispatch and at once makes his exit by same door.* FIRST *and* SECOND YOUNG OFFICERS *exit dejectedly after* MESSENGER.)

CAROLINE: (*going across with determined air near* LT FORAY *when she sees an opportunity*) *Oh* Lieutenant Foray!

LT FORAY: (*Turns and rises quickly with half salute.* CAROLINE *gives a little attempt at a military salute.*) I beg your pardon, Miss! (*Grabs at his coat which is on a chair near at right and hastily starts to put it on.*) I didn't know —

CAROLINE: (*remonstrating*) No no — don't! Ah don't mind. You see — Ah came on business!

LT FORAY: (*Puts on coat.*) Want to send something out?

CAROLINE: Yes!

LT FORAY: (*going to her*) 'Fraid we can't do anything for you here! This is the War Department, Miss.

CAROLINE: Ah know that — but it's the on'y way to send, an' Ah — (*sudden loud click of instrument on instrument B.* LT FORAY *turns and listens.*)

LT FORAY: (*crossing back of table right center*) Excuse me a minute, won't you? (*going to instrument on lower table right and answering; writing down message, etc.*)

CAROLINE: Yes — Ah will. (*a trifle disconcerted, stands uneasily*)

LT FORAY: Ready here! (MESSENGER 2 *down quickly to table*) Department! Quick as you can — they're waiting for it! (MESSENGER 2 *takes dispatch, salutes, and exits.* LT FORAY *rises and crosses to* CAROLINE.) Now what was it you wanted us to do, Miss?

CAROLINE: Just to (*short gasp*) to send a telegram.

LT FORAY: I reckon it's private business?

CAROLINE: (*looking at him with wide open eyes*) Ye — yes! It's — private!

LT FORAY: Then you'll have to get an order from some one in the department. (*Goes down to back of table right center and picks up papers.*)

CAROLINE: That's what Ah thought (*taking out a paper*) so Ah got it. (*Hands it to him.*)

LT FORAY: (*glancing at paper*) Oh — Major Selwin!

CAROLINE: Yes — he — he's one of my —

LT FORAY: It's all right then! (*Instrument B. calls. He quickly picks up a small sheet of paper and a pen and places them on table near* CAROLINE *and pushes chair up with almost the same movement.*) You can write it here Miss.

CAROLINE: Thank you. (*Sits at table — looks at paper — picks out sheet — smooths it out and writes, pausing an instant to think once or twice and a nervous glance toward* LT FORAY, *who returns to table and answers call and sits, taking down dispatch hurriedly.* MARTHA *standing motionless up stage, waiting — her eyes fixed on the telegraph instruments.* CAROLINE *starts and draws away suspiciously on loud click of instrument A. near her; moves over to left side of table, looking suspiciously at the instrument — puts pen in mouth — gets ink on tongue — makes wry face. She carefully folds up her dispatch when she has written it, and turns down a corner.* LT FORAY *when nearly through, motions to* MESSENGER 4.)

LT FORAY: (*still writing, speaks hurriedly*) Here! (MESSENGER 4 *comes down quickly.*) Department! Try to get it before the President goes! (*handing* MESSENGER 4 *dispatch, who salutes and exits.* LT FORAY *rising, to* CAROLINE) Is that ready yet, Miss?

CAROLINE: (*rising, hesitating*) Yes, but I — (*Finally starts to hand it to him.*) Of course you've — (*Hesitates.*) You've got to take it!

LT FORAY: (*brief puzzled look at her*) Yes, of course.

        (*She hands him the dispatch. He at once opens it.*)

CAROLINE: (*sharp scream*) Oh! (*Quickly seizes the paper out of his hand. They stand looking at one another.*) Ah didn't tell you to *read* it!

LT FORAY: (*after look at her*) What did you want?

CAROLINE: Ah want you to *send* it!

LT FORAY: How am I going to send it if I don't read it!

CAROLINE: (*after looking at him in consternation*) Do — you — mean — to — say —

LT FORAY: I've got to spell out every word! Didn't you know that?

CAROLINE: (*sadly, and shaking her head from side to side*) Oh — Ah must have — but Ah — (*Pauses trying to think what to do.*)

LT FORAY: Would there be any harm in my —

CAROLINE: (*turning on him with sudden vehemence*) Why Ah wouldn't have you see it for worlds! My gracious! (*Soon opens the dispatch and looks at it.*)

LT FORAY: (*good-naturedly*) Is it as bad as all that!

CAROLINE: Bad! It isn't bad at all! On'y — Ah only don't want it to get out all over the town — that's all.

LT FORAY: It won't ever get out from this office, Miss. (CAROLINE *looks steadfastly at* LT FORAY.) We wouldn't be allowed to mention anything outside!

CAROLINE: (*doubtful look at him*) You wouldn't!

LT FORAY: No Miss. All sorts of private stuff goes through here.

CAROLINE: (*with new hope*) Does it?

LT FORAY: Every day! Now if that's anything important —

CAROLINE: (*impulsively*) O yes — it's — (*recovering herself*) — it is!

LT FORAY: Then I reckon you'd better trust it to me.

CAROLINE: (*Looks at him for a moment.*) Ye — yes — Ah reckon Ah had! (*Hesitatingly hands him her telegram.*)

        (LT FORAY *takes the paper and at once turns away to the table as if to go to business of sending it on instrument B.*)

CAROLINE: (*quickly*) Oh stop! (LT FORAY *turns and looks at her from table.*) Wait till I — (*going up stage toward door hurriedly*) Ah don't want to be here — while you *spell out every word*! Ah couldn't stand *that*!

        (LT FORAY *stands good-naturedly waiting.* CAROLINE *takes hold of* MARTHA *to start out of door with her. Enter* EDDINGER — *a private in a gray uniform — at door up right.* CAROLINE *and* MARTHA *stand back out of his way. He glances at them and at once goes down to* LT FORAY, *salutes and hands him a written order and crosses to left center, wheels and stands at attention.* LT FORAY *looks at the order, glances at* EDDINGER, *then at* CAROLINE. CAROLINE *and* MARTHA *move as if to go out at door up right.*)

LT FORAY: Wait a minute, please! (*standing near table down right.* CAROLINE *and* MARTHA *stop and turn toward him.*) Are you Miss Mitford?

CAROLINE: Yes — Ah'm Miss Mitford!

LT FORAY: I don't understand this! Here's an order just come in to hold back any dispatch you give us.

CAROLINE: (*after looking speechless at him a moment*) Hold back any — hold back —

LT FORAY: Yes Miss. And that ain't the worst of it!

CAROLINE: Wh — what else is there? (*Comes down a little way looking at* LT FORAY *with open eyes;* MARTHA *remains near door.*)

LT FORAY: This man has orders to take it back with him. (*slight pause*)

CAROLINE: Take it back with him? Take what back with him?

LT FORAY: Your dispatch Miss. (CAROLINE *simply opens mouth and slowly draws in her breath.*) There must be some mistake, but that's what the order says.

CAROLINE: (*with unnatural calmness*) And where does it say to take it back to?

LT FORAY: (*Looks at the order.*) The name is Arrelsford! (*brief pause*)

CAROLINE: The order is for that man (*indicating* EDDINGER) to take my dispatch back to Mr Arrelsford?

LT FORAY: Yes Miss.

CAROLINE: An' does it say anything in there about what Ah'm goin' to be doin' in the meantime?

LT FORAY: No.

CAROLINE: That's too bad!

LT FORAY: I'm right sorry this has occurred Miss, and —

CAROLINE: Oh — (*shaking head*) there isn't any occasion for your feeling sorry — because it hasn't occurred! And besides that it isn't goin' to occur! (*becoming excited*) When it does you can go aroun' bein' sorry all you like! Have you got the faintest idea that Ah'm goin' to let him take my telegram away with him and show it to that man! Do you suppose —

MARTHA: (*coming forward a step and breaking in in a voice like a siren*) No, sir! You ain't a goin' ter do it — you can be right sure you ain't!

LT FORAY: But what can I do, Miss?

CAROLINE: (*advancing*) You can either send it or hand it back to me — that's what you can do!

MARTHA: (*calling out*) Yes suh — that's the very best thing you can do! An' the sooner you do it the quicker it'll be done — Ah kin tell you that right now!

LT FORAY: But this man has come here with orders to —

CAROLINE: (*going defiantly to* EDDINGER *and facing him*) Well this man can go straight back and report to Mr Arrelsford that he was unable to carry out his orders! (*defiant attitude toward* EDDINGER) That's what he can do!

MARTHA: (*now thoroughly roused and coming to a sense of her responsibility*) Let 'im take it! Let 'im take it ef he wants to so pow'fle bad! Just let the other one there give it to him — an' then see 'im try an' git out through this do' with it! (*standing solidly before door up right center with folded arms and ominously shaking head; talks and mumbles on half to herself*) Ah want to see him go by! Ah'm just a' waitin' fur a sight o' him gittin' past dis do'!'

That's what ah'm waitin' fur! (*Goes on talking half to herself, quieting down gradually.*) Ah'd like to know what they s'pose it was Ah come'd round yere for anyway — these men with their orders an' fussin' an' —

LT FORAY: (*down right when quiet is restored*) Miss Mitford, if I was to give this dispatch back to you now it would get me into a heap o' trouble.

CAROLINE: (*looking at him*) What kind of trouble?

LT FORAY: Might be put in prison — might be shot!

CAROLINE: You mean they might —

LT FORAY: Sure to do one or the other!

CAROLINE: Just for givin' it back to me?

LT FORAY: That's all.

CAROLINE: (*after looking silently at him for a moment*) Then you'll have to keep it!

LT FORAY: (*sincerely, after a pause*) Thank you Miss Mitford!

CAROLINE: (*a sigh, reconciling herself to the situation*) Very well — that's understood! You don't give it back to me — an' you can't give it to him — so nobody's disobeying any orders at all! (*going up and getting a chair from up center and bringing it forward*) And that's the way it stands! (*Banging chair down to emphasize her words close to* EDDINGER *and directly between him and* LT FORAY, *then plumps herself down on the chair and facing right, looks unconcerned.*) Ah reckon Ah can stay as long as he can! (*half to herself*) Ah haven't got much to do!

LT FORAY: But Miss Mitford —

CAROLINE: Now there ain't any good o' talkin'! If you've got any telegraphin' to do you better do it. Ah won't disturb you!

> (*Rapid steps heard in corridor outside. Enter* ARRELSFORD *door up right coming in hurriedly, somewhat flushed and excited. He looks hastily about, and goes at once toward* LT FORAY.)

ARRELSFORD: What's this! Didn't he get here in time?

LT FORAY: Are you Mr Arrelsford?

ARRELSFORD: Yes. (*sharp glance at* CAROLINE) Are you holding back a dispatch?

LT FORAY: Yes sir.

ARRELSFORD: Why didn't he bring it?

LT FORAY: Well, Miss Mitford — (*Hesitates, with a motion toward* CAROLINE.)

ARRELSFORD: (*comprehending*) Oh! (*Crosses back of* CAROLINE *and* EDDINGER *to left.*) Eddinger! (EDDINGER *wheels to left facing him.*) Report back to Corporal Matson. Tell him to send a surgeon to the prisoner who was wounded at General Varney's house — if he isn't dead by this time! (*Moves over to left as* EDDINGER *goes up;* CAROLINE *turns and looks at him on hearing 'prisoner', rising at same time and pushing chair back up center.* EDDINGER *salutes and exits quickly up right center.* ARRELSFORD *turns and starts toward* LT FORAY.) Let me see what that dispatch —

> (LT FORAY *stands right with* CAROLINE'*s dispatch in his hand.*
> CAROLINE *steps quickly in front of* ARRELSFORD, *who stops in some surprise at her sudden move.*)

CAROLINE: (*facing* ARRELSFORD) Ah expect you think you're going to get my telegram an' read it?

ARRELSFORD: I certainly intend to do so!

CAROLINE: Well there's a great big disappointment loomin' up right in front of you!

ARRELSFORD: (*with suspicion*) So! You've been trying to send out something you don't want us to see!

CAROLINE: What if Ah have?

ARRELSFORD: Just this! You won't send it — and I'll see it! (*about to pass* CAROLINE) This is a case where — (CAROLINE *steps in front of* ARRELS-FORD *again so that he has to stop.*)

CAROLINE: This is a case where you ain't goin' to read my private writin'. (*Stands looking at him with blazing eyes.*)

ARRELSFORD: Lieutenant — I have an order here putting me in charge! Bring that dispatch to me!

> (LT FORAY *about to move toward* ARRELSFORD; MARTHA *suddenly steps down in front of* LT FORAY *with ponderous tread and stands facing him.*)

MARTHA: Mistah Lieutenant can stay juss about whar he is! (*brief pause*)

ARRELSFORD: (*to* LT FORAY) Is that Miss Mitford's dispatch?

LT FORAY: Yes sir!

ARRELSFORD: Read it! (CAROLINE *turns with a gasp of horror.* MARTHA *turns in slow anger.* LT FORAY *stands surprised for an instant.*) Read it out!

CAROLINE: You shan't do such a thing! You have no right to read a private tele-gram —

MARTHA: (*speaking with* CAROLINE) No sah! He ain't no business to read her letters — none whatsomever!

ARRELSFORD: (*angrily*) Silence! (CAROLINE *and* MARTHA *stop talking.*) If you interfere any further with the business of this office I'll have you both put under arrest! (*to* LT FORAY) Read that dispatch!

> (CAROLINE *gasps breathless at* ARRELSFORD — *then turns and buries her face on* MARTHA's *shoulder sobbing.*)

LT FORAY: (*Reads with some difficulty.*) 'Forgive me — Wilfred darling — please — forgive me and I will help you all I can.'

ARRELSFORD: That dispatch can't go! (*Turns and moves left a few steps.*)

CAROLINE: (*turning and facing* ARRELSFORD, *almost calm with anger*) That dispatch can go! An' that dispatch will go! (ARRELSFORD *turns and looks at* CAROLINE; MARTHA *moves up on right side ready to exit, standing well up center and turning toward* ARRELSFORD.) Ah know someone whose orders even you are bound to respect and someone who'll come here with me an' see that you do it!

ARRELSFORD: I can show good and sufficient reasons for what I do!

CAROLINE: Well you'll have to show good and sufficienter reasons than you've shown to me — Ah can tell you that, Mr Arrelsford!

ARRELSFORD: I give my reasons to my superiors, Miss Mitford!

CAROLINE: Then you'll have to go 'round givin' 'em to everybody in Richmond, Mr Arrelsford! (*Saying which* CAROLINE *makes a deep curtsey and turns and sweeps out through door up right followed in the same spirit by*

MARTHA *who turns at the door and also makes a profound curtsey to*
ARRELSFORD, *going off haughtily.*)
>(LT FORAY *sits down at table right center and begins to write.*
>ARRELSFORD *looks after* CAROLINE *an instant and then goes*
>*rapidly over to* LT FORAY.)

ARRELSFORD: Let me see that dispatch!

LT FORAY: (*slight doubt*) You said you had an order, sir.

ARRELSFORD: (*impatiently*) Yes — yes! (*Throws order down on telegraph table.*)
Don't waste time!
>(LT FORAY *picks up order and looks closely at it for an instant.*)

LT FORAY: Department order sir?

ARRELSFORD: (*assenting shortly*) Yes.

LT FORAY: I suppose you're Mr Arrelsford all right?

ARRELSFORD: Of course!

LT FORAY: We have to be pretty careful sir! (*Hands him* CAROLINE*'s telegram
and goes on writing.* ARRELSFORD *takes it eagerly and reads it; thinks an
instant.*)

ARRELSFORD: Did she seem nervous or excited when she handed this in?

LT FORAY: She certainly did!

ARRELSFORD: Anxious not to have it seen?

LT FORAY: Anxious! I should say so! She didn't want me to see it!

ARRELSFORD: We've got a case on here and she's mixed up in it!

LT FORAY: But that dispatch is to young Varney — the General's son!

ARRELSFORD: So much the worse! It's one of the ugliest affairs we ever had! I
had them put me on it and I've got it down pretty close! (*going across left*)
We'll end it right here in this office inside of thirty minutes!
>(*Enter a* PRIVATE *at door up right. He comes down at once to*
>ARRELSFORD.)

ARRELSFORD: (*turning to him*) Well, what is it?

PRIVATE: The lady's here sir!

ARRELSFORD: Where is she?

PRIVATE: Waiting down below — at the front entrance.

ARRELSFORD: Did she come alone?

PRIVATE: Yes sir.

ARRELSFORD: Show her the way up. (PRIVATE *salutes and exits;* ARRELS-
FORD *comes to* LT FORAY.) I suppose you've got a revolver there? (LT
FORAY *brings up revolver in matter-of-fact way from beneath his table and
puts it on table, resuming business of writing, etc.*) I'd rather handle this thing
myself — but I might call on you. Be ready — that's all!

LT FORAY: Yes sir.

ARRELSFORD: Obey any orders you get an' send out all dispatches unless I stop
you.

LT FORAY: Very well sir.
>(*Door up right is opened by the* PRIVATE *last on, and* EDITH *is
>shown in.* ARRELSFORD *meets her.* PRIVATE *exits.*)

EDITH: (*in a low voice but under control*) I — I've accepted your invitation.

ARRELSFORD: I'm greatly obliged Miss Varney! As a matter of justice to me it was — (LT FORAY *puts revolver back on shelf under table.*)

EDITH: (*interrupting*) I didn't come to oblige you! I'm here to see that no more — murders are committed in order to satisfy your singular curiosity.

ARRELSFORD: (*low voice*) Where has he been? (*brief pause*) Is the man dead?

EDITH: (*looking at him steadily*) The man is dead. (*pause*)

ARRELSFORD: (*Turns to her; with cutting emphasis but low voice*) It's a curious thing, Miss Varney, that a Yankee prisoner more or less should make so much difference to you. They're dying down in Libby by the hundreds!

EDITH: At least they're not killed in our houses — before our very eyes!

(*Enter an* ORDERLY *who is a Special Agent of the War Department at door up right. He comes quickly in and crosses to* ARRELSFORD, *then glances around toward* LT FORAY. ARRELSFORD *moves down stage to speak to the* ORDERLY, *in a low voice.*)

ARRELSFORD: Well, have you kept track of him?

ORDERLY: (*in low voice throughout scene*) He's coming up Fourth Street, sir!

ARRELSFORD: Where has he been?

ORDERLY: To his quarters on Cary Street. We got in the next room and watched him through a transom.

ARRELSFORD: What was he doing?

ORDERLY: Working at some papers or documents.

ARRELSFORD: Could you see them? Could you see what it was?

ORDERLY: Headings looked like orders from the War Department.

ARRELSFORD: He's coming in here with forged orders!

ORDERLY: Yes sir.

ARRELSFORD: His game is to get control of these wires and then send out dispatches to the front that'll take away a battery from some vital point!

ORDERLY: Looks like it sir.

ARRELSFORD: And that vital point is what the Yankees mean by Plan Three! That's where they'll hit us. (*Glances round quickly considering — goes up left above line of middle window — turns to* ORDERLY.) Is there a guard in this building?

ORDERLY: (*going near* ARRELSFORD) Not inside — there's a guard in front and sentries around the barracks over in the square.

ARRELSFORD: They could hear me from this window, couldn't they?

ORDERLY: The guard could hear you. (*glance toward door right*) He must be nearly here sir, you'd better look out!

EDITH: (*up center, low voice*) Where shall I go?

ARRELSFORD: Outside here — on the balcony — I'll be with you!

EDITH: But — if he comes to the window!

ARRELSFORD: We'll step in at the next one. (*to* ORDERLY) See if the window of the Commissary-General's office is open.

ORDERLY: (*Steps quickly out of window up left through middle window, and goes off along balcony left. He returns at once re-entering through middle window.*) The next window's open sir.

ARRELSFORD: That's all I want of you — report back to Corporal Matson. Tell him to get the body of that prisoner out of the Varney house — he knows where it's to go!

ORDERLY: Very well sir! (*Salutes, crosses and exits door up right.*)

ARRELSFORD: (*to* EDITH) This way please! (*Conducts her out through middle window to balcony. He is closing the window to follow when he sees a* MESSENGER *enter up right and thereupon he stops just in the window keeping out of sight behind window frame.*)

> (*Enter* MESSENGER 1; *takes position up stage waiting for message as before.* ARRELSFORD *eyes him sharply an instant — then comes forward a step.*)

ARRELSFORD: Where did you come from?

MESSENGER 1: War Department sir.

ARRELSFORD: Carrying dispatches?

MESSENGER 1: Yes sir.

ARRELSFORD: You know me don't you?

MESSENGER 1: I've seen you at the office sir.

ARRELSFORD: I'm here on Department business. All you've got to do is to keep quiet about it! (*Exit* ARRELSFORD *at middle window which he closes after him and then disappears from view along balcony to left.*)

> (*Enter* MESSENGER 2; *takes his place with* MESSENGER 1 *at up left.* LT FORAY *busy at table. Moment's wait. Enter* CAPTAIN THORNE *at door up right center. As he comes down he gives one quick glance about the room but almost instantly to front again, so that it would hardly be noticed. He wears cap and carries an order in his belt.* THORNE *goes down at once to table and face* LT FORAY.)

THORNE: (*saluting*) Lieutenant! (*Hands* LT FORAY *the order which he carried in his belt.*)

LT FORAY: (*Turns, sees* THORNE, *rises, saluting briefly, takes order, opens and looks at it.*) Order from the Department. (*Moves a little to give* THORNE *chance to get to back of table.*)

THORNE: (*motionless, facing to right*) I believe so. (*Quickly glances at door up right as* LT FORAY *is looking at the order.*)

LT FORAY: They want me to take a cipher dispatch ovah to the President's house.

THORNE: (*moving to take* LT FORAY's *place at table — pulls chair back a little and then tosses cap over on table right.*) Yes — I'm ordered on here till you get back. (*Goes to place back of table right center and stands arranging things on the table.*)

LT FORAY: (*at table right, looking front*) That's an odd thing. They told me the President was down here with the Cabinet! He must have just now gone home I reckon.

THORNE: (*standing at table and arranging papers, etc. on it*) Looks like it. — If he isn't there you'd better wait. (*looking through a bunch of dispatches*)

LT FORAY: (*Gets cap from table right, puts it on.*) Yes — I'll wait! (*pause*) You'll have to look out for Allison's wires, Cap'n. He was called ovah to the Department.

> (THORNE *stops and looks front an instant on mention of* ALLISON.)

THORNE: (*easy manner again*) Ah ha — Allison!

LT FORAY: Yes.

THORNE: Be gone long? (*Throws used sheets in waste-basket and fixes a couple of large envelopes ready for quick use.*)

LT FORAY: Well, you know how it is — they generally whip around quite a while before they make up their minds what they want to do. I don't expect they'll trouble you much! It's as quiet as a church down the river. (*starting toward door up right*)

THORNE: (*seeing a cigar on the table near instrument*) See here — wait a minute — you'd better not walk out and leave a — no matter! (LT FORAY *stops and turns back to* THORNE — *comes center a little.*) It's none of my business (*tapping with the end of a long envelope on table where the cigar is*) Still, if you want some good advice, that's a dangerous thing to do!

LT FORAY: (*coming down*) What is it Cap'n?

THORNE: Leave a cigar lying around this office like that! (*Picks it up with left hand and lights a match with right.*) Somebody might walk in here any minute and take it away! (*about to light cigar*) I can't watch your cigars all day (*lighting it*).

LT FORAY: (*laughing*) Oh! Help yourself Cap'n!

THORNE: (*suddenly snatching cigar out of mouth with left hand and looking at it*) What's the matter with it? Oh well — I'll take a chance. (*Puts it in his mouth and resumes lighting.*)

LT FORAY: (*Hesitates a moment, goes down near* THORNE, *confidentially.*) Cap'n, if there's any trouble around here you'll find a revolver under there. (*indicating shelf under table.* THORNE *stops lighting cigar an instant; eyes motionless front; match blazes up.*)

THORNE: (*at once resuming nonchalance — finishing lighting cigar*) What about that? What makes you think — (*pulling in to light cigar*) there's going to be trouble?

LT FORAY: Oh well, there might be!

THORNE: (*tossing match away*) Been having a dream?

LT FORAY: Oh no — but you never can tell! (*Starts toward door.*)

THORNE: (*cigar in mouth; going at papers again*) That's right! You never can tell. But see here — hold on a minute! (*reaching down and getting revolver from shelf and tossing it on table near left end*) If you never can tell you'd better take that along with you. I've got one of my own. (*rather sotto voce*) I can tell!

(*Click of instrument A.* THORNE *answers on instrument A. at right end of table right center and slides into chair.*)

LT FORAY: Well, if you've got one here, I might as well. (*Takes revolver.*) Look out for yourself, Cap'n! (*Goes up. Instrument A. begins clicking off a message.* THORNE *sits at table listening and ready to take down what comes.*)

THORNE: Same to you old man — and many happy returns of the day! (*Exit* LT FORAY *door up right center.* THORNE *writes message, briefly addresses long envelope. Instrument A. stops receiving as* THORNE *addresses envelope. He okays dispatch.*) Ready here! (MESSENGER 1 *down to* THORNE *and salutes.*) Quartermaster-General. (*handing dispatch to* MESSENGER)

MESSENGER 1: Not at his office, sir!

THORNE: Find him! He's got to have it!

MESSENGER 1: Very well sir! (*Salutes and exits quickly up right.*)

> (THORNE *turns slowly left looking to see if there is a* MESSENGER *there; sees there is one without looking entirely around. A second's wait. Instrument C. upper end of table right begins to click.*
>
> THORNE *quickly rises and going to instrument C. answers call — on instrument — drops into chair up right and writes message — puts it in envelope and okays call.*)

THORNE: Ready here! (MESSENGER 2 *goes quickly across to* THORNE *and salutes.*) Secretary of the Treasury — marked private. Take it to his house. (*Begins to read a dispatch he twitched off from a file.*)

MESSENGER 2: He's down yere at the Cabinet, sir.

THORNE: Take it to his house and wait till he comes!

> (MESSENGER 2 *salutes and exits door up right center, closing the door after him. On the slam of door* THORNE *crushes dispatch in right hand and throws it to floor — and wheels front — his eyes on the instrument down right center. All one quick movement. Then he rises and with cat-like swiftness springs to the door up right and listens — opens the door a little and looks off. Closes it quickly, turning swiftly to center and opens the door up center glancing in. Then he goes to the window up left center — the nearest. Pushes it open a little and looks off through window and begins at same time to unbuckle belt and unbutton coat. Turns and moves down toward the telegraph table right center at same time throwing belt over to right above right table, and taking off coat. Glances back up left — looks to see that a document is in breast pocket of coat — letting audience see that it is there — and lays coat over back of chair above table right center with document in sight so that he can get it without delay. Takes revolver from hip pocket and quickly but quietly lays it on the table right center, just to right of the instrument, and then seizes key of instrument A. and gives a certain call: (−.... .. ..). Waits. A glance rapidly to left. He is standing at table — cigar in mouth. Makes the call again. Waits again. Gives the call third time. Goes to lower end of table right and half sits on it, folding arms, eyes on instrument, chewing cigar, with a glance or two up stage, but his eyes come quickly back to the instrument. Slides off table — takes cigar out of his mouth with left hand and gives the call again with right: (−.... .. ..) putting cigar in mouth again and turning and walking up stage looking about. Soon he carelessly throws papers which he took from right pocket — off up stage. Just as he throws papers — facing to left — the call is answered: (−.... .. ..). THORNE is back at the table right center in an instant and telegraphing rapidly — cigar in mouth. When he has sent for about five seconds steps are heard in corridor outside up right. He quickly strikes a match — which is close at hand to right of instrument — and sinks into the chair, appearing to be lazily lighting his cigar as a MESSENGER*

comes in at door up right center. MESSENGER 4 *enters as soon as he hears match strike and goes down at once to* THORNE *with dispatch. Salutes and extends it toward* THORNE — *on* THORNE'*s left.*)

MESSENGER 4: Secretary of War, Cap'n! Wants to go out right now! (THORNE *tosses away match, takes dispatch and opens it.* MESSENGER 4 *salutes, turns and starts up toward door.*)

THORNE: Here! Here! What's all this! (*looking at the dispatch.* MESSENGER 4 *returns to him, salutes.*) Is that the Secretary's signature?

MESSENGER 4: Yes sir — I saw him sign it.

(THORNE *looks closely at the signature. Turns it so as to get gas light. Turns and looks sharply at the* MESSENGER *and then back to dispatch again; puts it on table and writes an O.K. on it.*)

THORNE: Um hm — saw him sign it did you?

MESSENGER 4: Yes sir.

THORNE: (*writing*) Got to be a little careful tonight! (*holding dispatch up from table in left hand so that audience can see it is the same one — with the Secretary's signature*)

MESSENGER 4: I can swear to that one sir. (*Salutes, turns and goes up and exits.*)

(THORNE *listens — faced front for exit of* MESSENGER. *Dispatch in left hand. Instantly on slam of door he puts cigar down at end of table, rises, folds and very dexterously and rapidly cuts off the lower part of the paper which has the signature of the Secretary of War upon it, holds it between his teeth and tears the rest of the order in pieces, which he is on the point of throwing into waste-basket at left of table when he stops and changes his mind, stuffing the torn-up dispatch into his right hand trousers pocket. Picks up coat from back of chair and takes the document out of inside breast pocket. Opens it out on table and quickly pastes to it the piece of the real order bearing the signature, wipes quickly with handkerchief, puts handkerchief back into pocket, picks up cigar which he laid down on table and puts it in mouth, at same time sitting and at once beginning to telegraph rapidly on instrument A.; rapid click of the instrument.* THORNE *intent, yet vigilant. During business of* THORNE *pasting dispatch,* ARRELSFORD *appears outside windows up left at side of columns. He motions off toward left.* EDITH *comes into view there also.* ARRELSFORD *points toward* THORNE, *calling her attention to what he is doing. They stand at the window watching* THORNE — *the strong moonlight brings them out sharply. After a few seconds* ARRELSFORD *accidentally makes a slight noise with latch of window. Instantly on this faint click of latch* THORNE *stops telegraphing and sits absolutely motionless — his eyes front.* ARRELSFORD *and* EDITH *exit quickly and noiselessly on balcony to left. Dead silence. After a motionless pause,* THORNE *begins to fumble among papers on the table with his left hand, soon after raising the dispatch or some other paper with that hand in such a way that it will screen his right hand and the telegraph instrument*

on the key of which it rests, from an observer on the left. While he
appears to be scanning this paper or dispatch with the greatest attention, his right hand slowly slips off the telegraph key and toward his
revolver which lies just to the right of the instrument. Reading it, he
very slowly moves it over the right edge of the table, and down
against his right leg. He then begins to push things about on the table
with left hand as if looking for something and soon rises as if not
able to find it, and looking still more carefully. THORNE keeps
revolver close against right side — looks about on table, glances over
to table on right as if looking for what he wanted there, puts cigar
down on table before him — after about to do so once and taking a
final puff — and steps over to table at right still looking for something, and keeping revolver out of sight of anyone at window up left.
As he looks he raises left hand carelessly to the cock of the gas
bracket and instantly shuts off light. Stage dark. Instantly on lights
off, THORNE drops on one knee at right of table right center —
facing toward left. Revolver covering windows up left. Light from
windows gauged to strike across to THORNE at table with revolver.
After holding it a short time, he begins slowly to edge up stage, first
seizing chair with his coat on it, and crouching behind it — then
edges cautiously up on right until within reach of the door, when he
suddenly slides the heavy bolt, thus locking the doors on the inside.
From doors up right THORNE glides with a dash — throwing aside
the chair in the way — at the door of closet up center which opens
down stage and hinges on its left side. With motion of reaching it he
has it open — if not already open — and pushing it along before him
as he moves left toward window. When moving slowly behind this
door with his eyes and revolver on window the telegraph instrument
down right suddenly gives two or three sharp clicks. THORNE
makes an instantaneous turn front covering the instrument with
revolver. Sees what it was. Turns left again. Just as he gets door
nearly wide open against wall at back he dashes at windows up left
center and bangs them open with left hand covering all outside with
revolver in his right. In an instant sees that no one is there.
Straightens up — looking. Quick spring past first window stopping
close behind the upright between first and second windows, and at
same time banging these windows open and covering with revolver.
Sees no one. Looks this way and that. Makes quick dash outside and
covers over balustrade — as if someone might be below. In again
quick. Looks about with one or two quick glances. Concludes he
must have been mistaken, and starts down toward table right center
— stops after going two or three steps and looks back. Turns and
goes rapidly down to table. Picks up cigar with left hand. Puts
revolver at right end of table with right hand, and gets a match with
that hand. Stands an instant looking left. Strikes match and is about
to relight cigar. Pause — eyes front. Match burning. Listening. Looks
left — lights cigar — as he is lighting cigar thinks of gas being out, and

steps to right, turns it on and lights it. Lights full on. THORNE *turns
quickly, looking left as lights on. Then steps at once — after glancing
quickly about room — to telegraph table, puts down cigar near upper
right corner of table with left hand and begins to telegraph with left
hand, facing front. Suddenly sharp report of revolver outside
through lower window, up left with crash of glass and on it*
ARRELSFORD *springs on at middle window left with revolver in
his hand.* THORNE *does not move on shot except quick recoil from
instrument, leaning back a little, expression of pain an instant. His
left hand — with which he was telegraphing — is covered with blood.
He stands motionless an instant. Eyes then down toward his own
revolver. Slight pause. He makes a sudden plunge for it getting it in
his right hand. At same instant quick turn on* ARRELSFORD *but
before he can raise the weapon* ARRELSFORD *covers him with
revolver and* THORNE *stops where he is, holding position.*)

ARRELSFORD: Drop it! (*pause*) Drop that gun or you're a dead man! Drop it I
say! (*a moment's pause.* THORNE *gradually recovers to erect position again,
looking easily front, and puts revolver on the table, picking up cigar with
same hand and putting it casually into his mouth as if he thought he'd have a
smoke after all, instead of killing a man. He then gets handkerchief out of
pocket with right hand and gets hold of a corner of it not using his left.*
ARRELSFORD *advances a step or two, lowering revolver, but holding it
ready.*) Do you know why I didn't kill you like a dog just now?

THORNE: (*back of table right center as he twists handkerchief around his
wounded hand*) Because you're such a damn bad shot.

ARRELSFORD: Maybe you'll change your mind about that!

THORNE: (*Arranging handkerchief to cover his wounded hand — leaving fingers
free. Speaks easily and pleasantly.*) Well I hope so I'm sure. It isn't pleasant to
be riddled up this way you know!

ARRELSFORD: Next time you'll be riddled somewhere else besides the hand!
There's only one reason why you're not lying there now with a bullet through
your head!

THORNE: Only one, eh?

ARRELSFORD: Only one!

THORNE: (*still fixing hand and sleeve*) Do I hear it?

ARRELSFORD: Simply because I gave my word of honor to someone outside
there that I wouldn't kill you now!

(THORNE *on hearing 'someone outside there' turns and looks at*
ARRELSFORD *with interest.*)

THORNE: (*taking cigar out of mouth and holding it in right hand as he moves
toward* ARRELSFORD) Ah! Then it isn't a little tête-à-tête between our-
selves! You have someone with you! (*stopping near center coolly facing him*)

ARRELSFORD: (*sarcastically*) I *have* someone with me Captain Thorne! Someone
who takes quite an interest in what you're doing tonight!

THORNE: (*Puts cigar in mouth.*) Quite an interest, eh! That's kind I'm sure. (*Takes
cigar out of mouth facing front.*) Is the gentleman going to stay out there all
alone on the cold balcony, or shall I have the pleasure — (*Enter* EDITH *from*

balcony through the upper window, where she stands supporting herself by the sides. She is looking toward right as if intending to go, but not able for a moment, to move; avoids looking at THORNE.) — of inviting him in here and having a charming little three-handed — (*glancing up toward window he sees* EDITH *and stops motionless. Looks at her quietly a moment — then turns slowly and looks at* ARRELSFORD — *who has a slight smile on his lips; then turns front and holds position motionless.*)

EDITH: (*Does not speak until after* THORNE *looks front; low voice*) I'll go, Mr Arrelsford!

ARRELSFORD: Not yet, Miss Varney!

EDITH: (*coming blindly into room a few steps as if to get across to the door up right*) I don't wish to stay — any longer!

ARRELSFORD: One moment please! We need you!

EDITH: (*Stops.*) For what?

ARRELSFORD: A witness.

EDITH: You can send for me. I'll be at home. (*about to start toward door*)

ARRELSFORD: (*sharply*) I'll have to detain you till I turn him over to the guard — it won't take a moment! (*Steps to the middle window, still keeping an eye on* THORNE *and calls off in loud voice.*) Corporal o' the guard! Corporal o' the guard! Send up the guard will you!

      (EDITH *shrinks back up center not knowing what to do.*)

VOICE: (*outside in distance, as if down below in the street*) What's the matter up there! Who's calling the guard!

ARRELSFORD: (*at window*) Up here! Department Telegraph! Send 'em up quick!

VOICES: (*outside*) Corporal of the Guard Post Four! (*repeated more distant*) Corporal of the Guard Post Four! (*repeated again almost inaudible*) Corporal of the Guard Post Four! Fall in the guard! Fall in! (*These orders gruff — indistinct — distant. Give effect of quick gruff shouts of orders barely audible.*)

EDITH: (*turning suddenly on* ARRELSFORD) I'm not going to stay! I don't wish to be a witness!

ARRELSFORD: (*after an instant's look at* EDITH — *suspecting the reason for her refusal*) Whatever your feelings may be Miss Varney, we can't permit you to refuse!

EDITH: (*with determination*) I do refuse! If you won't take me down to the street I'll find the way out myself! (*Stops as she is turning to go, on hearing the* GUARD *outside running through lower corridors and coming up stairway and along hallways outside up right.* THORNE *holds position looking steadily front, cigar in right hand.*)

ARRELSFORD: (*loud voice to stop* EDITH) Too late! The guard is here! (*Steps down left center with revolver, his eye on* THORNE.)

      (EDITH *stands an instant and then as the* GUARD *is heard nearer in the corridor she moves up to window and remains there until sound of* GUARD *breaking in the door. Then she makes her exit off to left on balcony, disappearing so as to attract no attention.*)

ARRELSFORD: (*shouting across to* THORNE) I've got you about where I want you at last! (THORNE *motionless; sound of hurried tread of men outside as*

if coming on double quick toward the door, on bare floor of corridor) You thought you was almighty smart — but you'll find we can match your tricks every time!
> (*Sound of the GUARD coming suddenly ceases close outside the door up right.*)

SERGEANT OF THE GUARD: (*close outside door*) What's the matter here! Let us in!

THORNE: (*loud, incisive voice, still facing front*) Break down the door Sergeant! Break it down! (*As he calls begins to back up stage toward right center.*)
> (*Officers and men outside at once begin to smash in the door with the butts of their muskets.*)

ARRELSFORD: (*surprised*) What are you saying about it!

THORNE: You want 'im in here, don't you!

ARRELSFORD: (*Moves up a little as THORNE does, and covers him with revolver; speaks through noise of breaking door.*) Stand where you are!
> (*THORNE has backed up until nearly between ARRELSFORD and the door, so that the latter cannot fire on him without hitting others. But he must stand a trifle to right of line the men will take in rushing across to ARRELSFORD.*)

THORNE: (*facing ARRELSFORD*) Smash in the door! What are you waiting for! Smash it in Sergeant! (*Keeps up this call till door breaks down and men rush in — which must be at once. Door is quickly battered in and SERGEANT and MEN rush on. THORNE, continuing without break from last speech, above all the noise, pointing to ARRELSFORD with left hand*) Arrest that man! (*SERGEANT and six MEN spring forward past THORNE and seize ARRELS-FORD before he can recover from his astonishment, throwing him nearly down in the first struggle, but pulling him to his feet and holding him fast. As soon as quiet, THORNE moves down center.*) He's got in here with a revolver and he's playing Hell with it!

ARRELSFORD: Sergeant — my orders are —

THORNE: (*facing him*) Damn your orders! You haven't got orders to shoot every-body you see in this office! (ARRELSFORD *makes a sudden effort to break loose.*) Get his gun away — he'll hurt himself! (*Turns at once and goes to table right center putting his coat in better position on back of chair, and then getting things in shape on the table. At same time putting cigar back in mouth and smoking. SERGEANT and MEN twist revolver out of ARRELS-FORD's hands.*)

ARRELSFORD: (*continuing to struggle and protest*) Listen to me! Arrest him! He's sending out a false —

SERGEANT OF THE GUARD: Now that'll do! (*silencing ARRELSFORD roughly by hand across his mouth — to THORNE*) What's it all about, Cap'n?

THORNE: (*at table arranging things*) All about! I haven't got the slightest — (*sudden snatch of cigar out of mouth with right hand and then to SERGEANT as if remembering something*) He says he came out of some office! Sending out dispatches here he began letting off his gun at me. (*Turns back arranging things on table.*) Crazy lunatic!

ARRELSFORD: (*struggling to speak*) It's a lie! Let me speak — I'm from the —

SERGEANT: (*quietly to avoid laugh*) Here! That'll do now! (*silencing him, then to* THORNE) What shall we do with him?

THORNE: (*tossing things into place on table with one hand*) I don't care a damn — get him out o' here — that's all I want!

SERGEANT: Much hurt, Cap'n?

THORNE: (*carelessly*) Oh no. Did up one hand a little — I can get along with the other all right. (*Sits at table and begins telegraphing.*)

ARRELSFORD: (*struggling desperately*) Stop him! He's sending a — wait! Ask Miss Varney! (*Speaks until stopped; wildly, losing all control of himself*) She saw him! Ask her! Ask Miss Varney!

SERGEANT: (*breaking in*) Here! Fall in there. We'll get him out. (*The guard quickly falls in behind* ARRELSFORD, *who is still struggling.*) Forward — (*Enter quickly an* OFFICER *striding in at door up right.*)

OFFICER: (*loud voice, above the noise*) Halt! (MEN *on motion from* SERGEANT *stand back, forming a double rank behind* ARRELSFORD. *Two* MEN *hold him in front rank. All face to center,* SERGEANT *up left center.*)

(*Enter* MAJOR GENERAL HARRISON RANDOLPH *striding in at door up right center.* CAROLINE *comes to door after the* GENERAL, *and stands just within, up right center.* ARRELSFORD *has been so astonished and indignant at his treatment that he can't find his voice at first.* OFFICERS *salute as* GENERAL RANDOLPH *comes in.* THORNE *goes on working instrument at table, cigar between his teeth. He has the dispatch with signature pasted on it spread on table before him.*)

GENERAL RANDOLPH: (*Comes down center and stops.*) What's all this about refusing to send Miss Mitford's telegram! Is it some of your work Arrelsford?

ARRELSFORD: (*breathless, violent, excited*) General! They've arrested me. A conspiracy! A — (*Sees* THORNE *working at telegraph instrument.*) Stop that man — for God's sake stop him before its too late!

(CAROLINE *edging gradually up right center quietly slips out at door up right center, unnoticed.*)

GENERAL RANDOLPH: Stop him! What do you mean?

THORNE: (*back of table, quickly rising so as to speak on cue, with salute*) He means me sir! He's got an idea some dispatch I'm sending out is a trick of the Yankees!

ARRELSFORD: (*excitedly*) It's a conspiracy! He's an imposter — a — a —

THORNE: Why the man must have gone crazy General! (*Stands facing left motionless.*)

ARRELSFORD: I came here on a case for —

GENERAL RANDOLPH: (*sharply*) Wait! I'll get at this! (*to* SERGEANT *without turning to him*) What was he doing?

SERGEANT: (*with salute*) He was firing on the Cap'n sir.

ARRELSFORD: He was sending out a false order to weaken our lines at Cemetery Hill and I — ah — (*suddenly recollecting*) Miss Varney! (*looking excitedly about*) She was here — she saw it all!

GENERAL RANDOLPH: (*gruffly*) Miss Varney!

ARRELSFORD: Yes sir!

GENERAL RANDOLPH: The General's daughter?

ARRELSFORD: (*nodding affirmatively with excited eagerness*) Yes sir!

GENERAL RANDOLPH: What was she doing here?

ARRELSFORD: She came to see for herself whether he was guilty or not!

GENERAL RANDOLPH: Is this some personal matter of yours?

ARRELSFORD: He was a visitor at their house — I wanted her to know!

GENERAL RANDOLPH: Where is she now? Where is Miss Varney?

ARRELSFORD: (*looking about excitedly*) She must be out there on the balcony! Send for her!

GENERAL RANDOLPH: Sergeant! (SERGEANT *steps down to him and salutes.*) Step out there on the balcony. Present my compliments to Miss Varney and ask her to come in!

> (SERGEANT *salutes and steps quickly out through middle window on the balcony. Walks off at left, reappears walking back as far as balcony goes. Turns and re-enters room, coming down and saluting.*)

SERGEANT: No one there sir!

> (THORNE *turns and begins to send dispatch, picking up the forged order with left hand as if sending from that copy and quickly opening instrument A. and telegraphing with right, all on nearly same motion.*)

ARRELSFORD: She must be there! She's in the next office! The other window. Tell him to — (*Sees* THORNE *working at instrument.*) Ah! (*almost screaming*) Stop him! He's sending it now!

GENERAL RANDOLPH: (*to* THORNE) One moment Cap'n! (THORNE *stops. Salutes. Drops dispatch in left hand to table. Pause for an instant — all holding their positions.* GENERAL RANDOLPH *after above pause, to* ARRELSFORD) What have *you* got to do with this?

ARRELSFORD: It's a Department Case! They assigned it to me!

GENERAL RANDOLPH: What's a Department Case?

ARRELSFORD: The whole plot — to send the order — it's the Yankee Secret Service! His brother brought in the signal tonight!

> (GENERAL RANDOLPH *looks sharply at* ARRELSFORD.)

THORNE: (*very quietly, matter-of-fact*) This ought to go out sir — it's very important.

GENERAL RANDOLPH: Go ahead with it!

> (THORNE *salutes and quickly turns to instrument A. dropping dispatch on table and begins sending rapidly as he stands before the table, glancing at the dispatch as he does so as if sending from it.*)

ARRELSFORD: (*seeing what is going on*) No no! It's a —

GENERAL RANDOLPH: Silence!

ARRELSFORD: (*excitedly*) Do you know what he's telling them!

GENERAL RANDOLPH: No! Do you?

ARRELSFORD: Yes! If you'll —

GENERAL RANDOLPH: (*to* THORNE) Wait! (THORNE *stops, coming at once to salute, military position a step back from table facing front.*) Where's that dispatch? (THORNE *goes to* GENERAL RANDOLPH *and hands him the dispatch; then back a step.* GENERAL RANDOLPH *takes the dispatch. To*

ARRELSFORD) What was it? What has he been telling them? (*Looks at dispatch in his hand.*)

ARRELSFORD: (*excitedly*) He began to give an order to withdraw Marston's Division from its present position!

GENERAL RANDOLPH: That is perfectly correct.

ARRELSFORD: Yes — by that dispatch — but that dispatch is a forgery!
(THORNE *with a look of surprise turns sharply toward* ARRELSFORD.) It's an order to withdraw a whole division from a vital point! A false order! He wrote it himself! (THORNE *stands as if astounded.*)

GENERAL RANDOLPH: Why should he write it? If he wanted to send out a false order he could do it without setting it down on paper, couldn't he?

ARRELSFORD: Yes — but if any of the operators came back they'd catch him doing it! With that order and the Secretary's signature he could go right on! He could even order one of them to send it!

GENERAL RANDOLPH: How did he get the Secretary's signature?

ARRELSFORD: He tore it off from a genuine dispatch! Why General — look at that dispatch in your hand! The Secretary's signature is pasted on! I saw him do it!

THORNE: Why — they often come that way! (*Turns away nonchalantly toward front.*)

ARRELSFORD: He's a liar! They never do!

THORNE: (*Turns indignantly on 'liar' and the two men glare at each other a moment; recovering himself*) General, if you have any doubts about that dispatch send it back to the War Office and have it verified!
(ARRELSFORD *is so thunderstruck that he starts back a little unable to speak. He stands with his eyes riveted to* THORNE *until cue of telegraph click below.*)

GENERAL RANDOLPH: (*slowly, his eyes on* THORNE) Quite a good idea!
(*pause*) Sergeant! (*holding out dispatch;* SERGEANT *salutes and waits for orders.*) Take this dispatch over to the Secretary's office and — (*sudden loud click of telegraph instrument A.* GENERAL RANDOLPH *stops, listening. To* THORNE) What's that?
(ARRELSFORD *looking at the instrument.* THORNE *stands motionless, excepting that he took his eyes off* ARRELSFORD *and looked front listening on click of instrument.*)

THORNE: (*slight wait*) Adjutant General Chesney.

GENERAL RANDOLPH: From the front?

THORNE: Yes sir.

GENERAL RANDOLPH: What does he say?

THORNE: (*Turns and steps to table, stands eyes front, listening to instrument.*)
His compliments sir — (*pause — continued click of instrument*) He asks — (*pause — continued click of instrument*) for the rest — (*pause — click of instrument*) of that dispatch — (*pause — click; then stops*) It's of vital importance. (THORNE *stands motionless.*)

GENERAL RANDOLPH: (*After very slight pause abruptly turns and hands the dispatch back to* THORNE.) Let him have it! (THORNE *hurried salute, takes dispatch — sits at table and begins sending.*)

ARRELSFORD: General — if you —

GENERAL RANDOLPH: (*sharply to him*) That's enough! We'll have you examined at headquarters! (*Hurried steps in corridor outside up right and enter quickly at door* LT FORAY, *breathless and excited.*)

ARRELSFORD: (*catching sight of* LT FORAY *as he comes in*) Ah! Thank God! There's a witness! He was sent away on a forged order! Ask him! Ask him! (*pause;* LT FORAY *standing up stage looking at others surprised,* THORNE *continuing business at instrument*)

GENERAL RANDOLPH: (*after instant's pause during which click of instrument is heard*) Wait a moment, Cap'n!

> (THORNE *stops telegraphing, sits motionless, hand on the key. An instant of dead silence.* GENERAL RANDOLPH *moves up center to speak to* LT FORAY.)

GENERAL RANDOLPH: (*gruffly*) Where did you come from?

LT FORAY: (*not understanding exactly what is going on; salutes*) There was some mistake sir!

> (ARRELSFORD *gives gasp of triumph quick on cue; brief pause of dead silence.*)

GENERAL RANDOLPH: Mistake eh? Who made it?

LT FORAY: I got an order to go to the President's house, and when I got there the President — !

THORNE: (*rising at telegraph table*) This delay will be disastrous sir! Permit me to go on — if there's any mistake we can rectify it afterwards! (*Turns to instrument and begins sending as he stands before it.*)

ARRELSFORD: (*half suppressed cry of remonstrance*) No!

GENERAL RANDOLPH: (*who has not given heed to* THORNE's *speech — to* LT FORAY) Where did you get the order?

ARRELSFORD: He's at it again sir!

GENERAL RANDOLPH: (*Suddenly sees what* THORNE *is doing.*) Halt there! (THORNE *stops telegraphing.*) What are you doing! I ordered you to wait!

THORNE: (*Turns to* GENERAL RANDOLPH.) I was sent here to attend to the business of this office and that business is going on! (*turning again as if to telegraph*)

GENERAL RANDOLPH: (*temper rising*) It's not going on sir, until I'm ready for it!

THORNE: (*turning back to the* GENERAL; *loud voice, angrily*) My orders came from the War Department — not from you! This dispatch came in half an hour ago — they're calling for it — and it's my business to send it out! (*Turning at end of speech and seizing the key endeavors to rush off the dispatch.*)

GENERAL RANDOLPH: Halt! (THORNE *goes on telegraphing. To* SERGEANT) Sergeant! (SERGEANT *salutes.*) Hold that machine there! (*pointing at telegraph instrument.* SERGEANT *and two men spring quickly across to right;* SERGEANT *rushes against* THORNE *with arm across his breast forcing him over to right against chair and table on right — chair a little away from table to emphasize with crash as* THORNE *is flung against it — and holds him there. The two men cross bayonets over instrument and stand motionless. All done quickly, business-like and with as little disturbance as possible.*)

GENERAL RANDOLPH *strides down center and speaks across to* THORNE.)
I'll have you court-martialed for this!

THORNE: (*breaking loose and coming down right*) You'll answer yourself sir, for
delaying a dispatch of vital importance!

GENERAL RANDOLPH: (*sharply*) Do you mean that!

THORNE: I mean that! And I demand that you let me proceed with the business of
this office!

GENERAL RANDOLPH: By what authority do you send that dispatch?

THORNE: I refer you to the Department!

GENERAL RANDOLPH: Show me your order for taking charge of this office!

THORNE: I refer you to the Department! (*Stands motionless facing across to left.*)
(EDITH *appears at upper window up left, coming on from balcony
left, and moves a little into room.* SERGEANT *remains at right
above table when* THORNE *broke away from him.*)

GENERAL RANDOLPH: By God then I'll *go* to the Department! (*Swings round
and striding up center a little way*) Sergeant! (SERGEANT *salutes.*) Leave
your men on guard there and go over to the War Office — my compliments to
the Secretary and will he be so good as to —

ARRELSFORD: (*suddenly breaking out on seeing* EDITH) Ah! General! (*pointing
to her*) Another witness! Miss Varney! She was here! She saw it all!
(THORNE *on* ARRELSFORD's *mention of another witness glances
quickly up left toward* EDITH, *and at once turns front and stands
motionless, waiting.* GENERAL RANDOLPH *turns left and sees*
EDITH.)

GENERAL RANDOLPH: (*bluffly touching hat*) Miss Varney! (EDITH *comes
forward a little.*) Do you know anything about this?

EDITH: (*Speaks in low voice.*) About what, sir?

GENERAL RANDOLPH: Mr Arrelsford here claims that Captain Thorne is acting
without authority in this office and that you can testify to that effect.

EDITH: (*very quietly*) Mr Arrelsford is mistaken! He has the highest authority!
(ARRELSFORD *aghast*, GENERAL RANDOLPH *surprised.*
THORNE *faces left listening, motionless.*)

GENERAL RANDOLPH: (*after pause of surprise*) What authority has he?

EDITH: (*drawing the commission from her dress*) The authority of the President of
the Confederate States of America! (*handing the commission to* GENERAL
RANDOLPH, *who takes it and at once opens and examines it.* EDITH *stands
a moment where she was, looking neither at* ARRELSFORD *nor* THORNE,
then slowly retires up and stands back of others out of the way.)

GENERAL RANDOLPH: (*looking at commission*) What's this! Major's Commission! Assigned to duty on the Signal Corps! In command of the Telegraph
Department!

ARRELSFORD: (*breaking out*) That commission — let me explain how she —

GENERAL RANDOLPH: That'll do! — I suppose this is a forgery too?

ARRELSFORD: Let me tell you sir —

GENERAL RANDOLPH: You've told me enough! Sergeant — take him to headquarters!

SERGEANT: (*quick salute*) Fall in there! (*motioning men at instrument, who hurry across and fall into rank*) Forward march!

>   (SERGEANT *and* GUARD *quickly rush* ARRELSFORD *across to door up right and off.*)

ARRELSFORD: (*resisting and protesting as he is forced off*) No! For God's sake, General, listen to me! It's the Yankee Secret Service! Never mind me, but don't let that dispatch go out! He's a damned Yankee Secret Agent! His brother brought in the signal tonight!

>   (*Sound of footsteps of the* GUARD *outside dying away down the corridor and of* ARRELSFORD's *voice protesting and calling for justice. Short pause,* THORNE *motionless through above looking front;* GENERAL RANDOLPH, *who crossed to up left center on men forcing* ARRELSFORD *off, goes down center and looks across at* THORNE.)

GENERAL RANDOLPH: (*gruffly*) Cap'n Thorne! (THORNE *comes to straight military position, goes to the* GENERAL *and salutes.* GENERAL *gruffly*) It's your own fault Cap'n! If you'd had the sense to mention this before we'd have been saved a damned lot o' trouble! There's your commission! (*Hands to* THORNE, *who takes it saluting –* GENERAL *turns to go.*) I can't understand why they have to be so cursed shy about their Secret Service Orders! (*Goes up toward exit, stops and speaks to* LT FORAY *who is standing at right of door.*) Lieutenant! (LT FORAY *salutes. Very gruffly*) Take your orders from Cap'n Thorne! (*Turns and goes heavily off, very much out of temper.*)

>   (LT FORAY *goes down right and sits at telegraph table on extreme right. Busy with papers. No noise.* THORNE *stands facing left, commission in right hand, until the* GENERAL *is off. Turns right glancing round to see that he is gone, and at once glides to telegraph instrument A. and begins sending with right hand – still holding commission in it.* EDITH *comes quickly down to* THORNE.)

EDITH: (*at upper corner of table, very near* THORNE) Cap'n Thorne! (THORNE *stops and turns quickly to her, hand still on key. She goes on in low voice, hurried, breathless.*) That gives you authority – long enough to escape from Richmond!

THORNE: Escape? Impossible! (*Seizes key and begins to send.*)

EDITH: Oh! You wouldn't do it now! (THORNE *instantly stops sending and looks at her.*) I brought it – to save your life! I didn't think you'd use it – for anything else! Oh – you wouldn't.

>   (THORNE *stands looking at her. Sudden sharp call from instrument A. turns him back to it.* EDITH *looks at him – covers her face and moans, at same time turning away left. She moves up to the door up right and goes out.* THORNE *stands in a desperate struggle with himself as instrument A. is clicking off the same signal that he made when calling up the front. He almost seizes the key – then resists – and finally, with a bang of right fist on the table, turns and strides up left center, the commission crushed in his right hand.*)

LT FORAY: (*who has been listening to calls of instrument, rising as* THORNE *comes to a stand up left center*) They're calling for that dispatch sir! What shall I do?

THORNE: (*turning quickly*) Send it!

>   (LT FORAY *drops into seat at table right center and begins sending at the same time arranging dispatch at left of table for* THORNE *to seize.* THORNE *stands motionless on the order an instant. As* LT FORAY *begins to send he turns round a little up to right slowly and painfully, right arm up across eyes in a struggle with himself. Suddenly he breaks away and dashes toward table right center.*)

THORNE: No no — stop! (*Seizes the dispatch from the table in his right hand which still has the commission crumpled in it.*) I won't do it! I won't do it! (LT FORAY *rises in surprise on* THORNE *seizing the dispatch, and stands facing him.* THORNE *points at instrument unsteadily.*) Revoke the order! It was a mistake! I refuse to act under this commission! (*throwing the papers in his right hand down on the floor and standing center slightly turned away to left*)

CURTAIN

ACT IV

Drawing-room at GENERAL VARNEY's. *Same as Acts I and II. Eleven o'clock. The furniture is somewhat disordered as if left as it was after the disturbances at the close of the second act. Nothing is broken or upset. Half light on in room. Lamps lighted but not strong on. Portieres on window down right are closed. Thunder of distant cannonading and sounds of volleys of musketry and exploding shells on very strong at times during this act. Quivering and rather subdued flashes of light — as the artillery is some miles distant — shown at windows right from time to time. Violent and hurried ringing of church bells in distant parts of the city — deep, low tones booming out like a fire bell. Sounds of hurried passing in the street outside of bodies of soldiers — artillery — cavalry, etc. on cues, with many horse-hoof and rattling gun carriage and chain effects — shouting to horses — orders, bugle calls, etc. The thunder of cannonading, shelling fortifications, musketry, flashes, etc., must be kept up during the act, coming in now and then where it will not interfere with dialogue, and so arranged that the idea of a desperate attack will not be lost. Possible places for this effect are marked thus in the script: (XXX). At rise of curtain, thunder of artillery and flashes of light now and then. Ringing of church and fire bells in distance.* CAROLINE *is discovered in window up right shrinking back against curtains and looking out through window with fright. Enter* MRS VARNEY *coming hurriedly down the stairs from up left and in at door.*

MRS VARNEY: Caroline! (CAROLINE *goes to her.*) Tell me what happened? She won't speak! Where has she been? Where was it?

CAROLINE: (*frightened*) It was at the telegraph office!

MRS VARNEY: What did she do? What happened? Try to tell!

>   (*Flashes — cannonading — bells, etc., kept up strong. Effect of passing artillery begins in the distance very softly.*)

CAROLINE: Ah don't know! Ah was afraid and ran out! (*alarm bell very strong*) It's the alarm bell, Mrs Varney — to call out the reserve!

MRS VARNEY: Yes — yes! (*glance of anxiety toward windows right*) They're making a terrible attack tonight. Lieutenant Maxwell was right! That quiet spell was the signal! (*artillery effect louder*)

CAROLINE: (*Goes to window, turns to* MRS VARNEY *and speaks above noise, which is not yet on full.*) It's another regiment of artillery goin' by! They're sendin' 'em all over to Cemetery Hill! That's where the fighting is! Cemetery Hill! (*effect on loud*)

> (CAROLINE *watches from window.* MRS VARNEY *crosses over left and rings bell. As effect dies away* MARTHA *enters up left from door right of stairs.*)

MRS VARNEY: Go up and stay with Miss Edith till I come. Don't leave her a moment! (MARTHA *turns and hurries up the stairway. Alarm bell and cannon on strong*) Shut the curtains Caroline!

CAROLINE: (*Closes the window curtains at right.*) Ah'm afraid they're goin' to have a right bad time tonight! (*going to* MRS VARNEY)

MRS VARNEY: Indeed I'm afraid so! Now try to think dear, who was at the telegraph office? Can't you tell me something?

CAROLINE: (*shaking her head*) No — only they arrested Mr Arrelsford!

MRS VARNEY: Mr Arrelsford! Why, you don't mean that!

CAROLINE: Yes Ah do! An' General Randolph — he came — Ah went an' brought him there — an' oh — he was in a frightful temper!

MRS VARNEY: And Edith — now you can tell me — what — what did she do?

CAROLINE: Ah can't Mrs Varney. Ah don't know! Ah just waited for her outside — an' when she came out she couldn't speak — an' then we hurried home! That's all Ah know, Mrs Varney — truly!

> (*Loud ringing of door bell in another part of the house.* CAROLINE *and* MRS VARNEY *turn toward door up left. Noise of heavy steps outside left and* ARRELSFORD *almost immediately strides into the room, followed by two privates, who stand at the door.* CAROLINE *steps back up stage a little as* ARRELSFORD *enters, and* MRS VARNEY *faces him.*)

(XXX)

ARRELSFORD: (*roughly, as he advances on* MRS VARNEY) Is your daughter in the house?

MRS VARNEY: (*after a second's pause*) Yes!

(XXX)

ARRELSFORD: I'll see her if you please!

MRS VARNEY: I don't know that she'll care to receive you at present.

ARRELSFORD: What she cares to do at present is of small consequence! Shall I go up to her room with these men or will you have her come down?

MRS VARNEY: Neither one nor the other until I know your business.

> (*Effect of passing cavalry and artillery — strong*)

ARRELSFORD: (*excitedly*) My business! I've got a few questions to ask! Listen to that! (XXX *on strong*) Now you know what 'Attack Tonight Plan Three' means!

VI *Secret Service*, Act IV. Gillette at center stage

MRS VARNEY: (*change of manner; surprise*) Is that — the attack!

ARRELSFORD: That's the attack Madam! They're breaking through our lines at Cemetery Hill! That was PLAN THREE! We're rushing over the reserves but they may not get there in time!

(XXX)

> (CAROLINE *has crossed at back to left door as if going out, but waits to see what happens.*)

MRS VARNEY: What has my daughter to do with this?

ARRELSFORD: Do with it! She did it!

MRS VARNEY: (*astonished*) What!

> (*Noise of passing Cavalry Officer going by singly*)

ARRELSFORD: We had him in his own trap — under arrest — the telegraph under guard — when she brought in that commission!

MRS VARNEY: (*horrified*) You don't mean she —

ARRELSFORD: Yes — that's it! She put the game in his hands. He got the wires! His cursed dispatch went through. As soon as I got to headquarters they saw the trick! They rushed the guard back — the scoundrel had got away! But we're after him hot, an' if she knows where he is — (*about to turn and to toward door up left*) I'll get it out of her!

(XXX)

MRS VARNEY: You don't suppose my daughter would —

ARRELSFORD: I suppose anything!

MRS VARNEY: I'll not believe it!

ARRELSFORD: We can't stop for what you believe! (*as if to go to stairs*)
> (*Stop alarm bells.*)

MRS VARNEY: Let me speak to her!
> (*Passing cavalry effect has died away by this time.*)

ARRELSFORD: I'll see her myself! (*going up left*)

CAROLINE: (*Has stepped quietly down so that as* ARRELSFORD *turns to go toward stairway she confronts him.*) Where is your order for this?

ARRELSFORD: (*after instant's surprise*) I've got a word or two to say to you — after I've been upstairs!

CAROLINE: Show me your order for going upstairs!

ARRELSFORD: Department business — I don't require an order!

CAROLINE: (*shaking head*) Oh, you've made a mistake about that! This is a private house! It isn't the telegraph office! If you want to go up any stairs or see anybody about anything you'll have to bring an order! Ah don't know much — but Ah know enough for that! (*Exit upstairs.*)

(XXX *light*)

ARRELSFORD: (*Turns sharply to* MRS VARNEY.) Am I to understand Madam, that you —

> (*Loud ringing of door bell in distant part of house, followed almost immediately after by the sound of door outside left and tramp of many feet in the hallway*)

(XXX *cavalry effect begins again.*)

(ARRELSFORD *and* MRS VARNEY *turn. Enter quickly a*
SERGEANT *and four* MEN. MEN *are halted near left.* OFFICER
advances to MRS VARNEY. ARRELSFORD *steps back a little.*)

SERGEANT: (*touching cap roughly*) Are you the lady that lives here, ma'am?

MRS VARNEY: I am Mrs Varney.

SERGEANT: (*interrupting*) I've got an order to search the house! (*showing her the order*)

ARRELSFORD: Just in time! (*coming down*) I'll go through the house if you please!

SERGEANT: (*shortly*) You can't go through on this order — it was issued to me!

MRS VARNEY: You were sent here to —

SERGEANT: Yes, ma'am! Sorry to trouble you but we'll have to be quick about it! If we don't get him here we've got to follow down Franklin Street — he's over this way somewhere! (*Turns left about to give orders to men.*)

MRS VARNEY: Who? Who is it you —

SERGEANT: (*hurriedly*) Man named Thorne — Cap'n of Artillery — that's what he went by! (*Turns to his* MEN.) Here — this way! That room in there! (*Indicates room up center.*) Two of you outside! (*pointing to windows*) Cut off those windows.

> (*Two* MEN *run into room up center and two off at windows right, throwing open curtains and windows as they do so.* MRS VARNEY *stands aside.* SERGEANT *glances quickly round the room — pushing desk out and looking behind it, etc. Keep up cavalry effects and flashes during business; artillery strong during this. These effects distant — as if going down another street several blocks away. During business,* ARRELSFORD *goes to door left, gives an order to his men, then exits, followed by men who came with him.*)

(XXX)

> (*The two* MEN *who went off at door up center to search, re-enter shoving the old negro* JONAS *roughly into the room. He is torn and dirty and shows signs of rough handling. They force him down center a little way and he stands crouching.*)

SERGEANT: (*to* MEN) Where did you get that?

PRIVATE: Hiding in a closet sir.

SERGEANT: (*going to* JONAS) What are you doing in there? If you don't answer me we'll kick the life out of you! (*short pause; to* MRS VARNEY) Belongs to you, Ah reckon?

MRS VARNEY: Yes — but they want him for carrying a message —

SERGEANT: Well if they want him they can get him — we're looking for someone else! (*Motions to* MEN.) Throw him back in there! (MEN *shove* JONAS *off at door up center. Other* MEN *re-enter from windows at right.*) Here — this room! Be quick now! Cover that door! (*Two* MEN *have quick business of searching room down right and left. The other two* MEN *stand on guard door up left.*) Sorry to disturb you ma'am! (*Bell rings off left.*)

MRS VARNEY: Do what you please — I have nothing to conceal! (*sound of door outside up left*)

(XXX)

ORDERLY: (*outside door up left*) Here! Lend a hand will you!
>(*Two* MEN *at door up left exit to help someone outside. Enter the* ORDERLY *who took* WILFRED *away in Act II, coming on hurriedly at door up left. He stands just below door – a few steps into room – splashed with foam and mud from hard riding. He sees* SERGEANT *and salutes.* SERGEANT *salutes back and goes over, looking out of window up right.* MRS VARNEY *upon seeing the* ORDERLY *gives a cry of alarm.*)

ORDERLY: Ah've brought back the boy ma'am!

MRS VARNEY: (*starting forward*) Oh! What do you – (*breathless*) What –

ORDERLY: We never got out there at all! The Yankees made a raid down at Mechanicsville not three miles out! The Home Guard was goin' by on the dead run to head 'em off an' before I knew it he was in with 'em riding like mad! There was a bit of a skirmish an' he got a clip across the neck – nothing at all ma'am – he rode back all the way an' – (*Cavalry effects die away gradually.*)

MRS VARNEY: Oh – he's hurt – he's hurt!

ORDERLY: Nothing bad ma'am – don't upset yourself.

MRS VARNEY: (*Starts toward door.*) Where did you – (*Stops on seeing* WILFRED, *who enters supported by two* MEN. *He is pale and has a bandage about his neck.* MRS VARNEY *after the slight pause on his entrance goes to him at once.*)

MRS VARNEY: Oh Wilfred!

WILFRED: (*motioning* MRS VARNEY *off*) It's all right – you don't understand! (*Tries to free himself from the man who is supporting him.*) What do you want to hold me like that for? (*Frees himself and walks toward center a few steps a little unsteadily but not too much so.*) – You see – I can walk all right! (MRS VARNEY *comes down anxiously and holds him.* WILFRED *turns and sees his mother and takes her hand with an effort to do it in as casual a manner as possible.*) How-dy-do Mother! – Didn't expect me back so soon, did you? – Tell you how it was – (*Turns and sees* ORDERLY.) Don't you go away now – Ah'm going back with you – just wait till I rest about a minute. See here! They're ringing the bells to call out the reserves! (*starting weakly toward door left*) Ah'll go right now!

(XXX)

MRS VARNEY: (*gently holding him back*) No no Wilfred – not now!

(XXX *louder*)

WILFRED: (*weakly*) Not now! – You hear that – you hear those bells – and tell me – not now! – I – (*Sways a little.*) I – (MRS VARNEY *gives a cry of alarm seeing* WILFRED *is going to faint.*)

SERGEANT: (*quick undertone to* MEN) Stand by there! (WILFRED *faints.* MRS VARNEY *supports him, but almost immediately the two* MEN *come to her assistance.* SERGEANT *and two* MEN *push couch forward down right center and they quickly lay him on it, head to the right.* MRS VARNEY *goes to head of couch, and holds* WILFRED's *head as they lay him down.*)

(*Cannonading gradually ceases.*)

SERGEANT: (*to one of the* MEN) Find some water will you? (*to* MRS VARNEY)
Put his head down ma'am — he'll be all right in a minute!

>(*A* PRIVATE *hurries off at door up left on order to get water.*
SERGEANT *gets chair from up center and puts it back of couch.*
MRS VARNEY *goes back of couch, attending to* WILFRED. PRI-
VATE *re-enters with basin of water and gives it to* MRS VARNEY.)

SERGEANT: (*to* MEN) This way now!

>(MEN *move quickly to door up left.* SERGEANT *gives quick direc-
tions to* MEN *at door up left. All exit. One or two go right.*
SERGEANT *with most of men are seen going up the stairway.*
ORDERLY *is left standing a little below door, exactly as he was.*
MRS VARNEY *kneeling back of* WILFRED *and bathing his head
tenderly — using her handkerchief.*)

ORDERLY: (*after brief pause*) If there ain't anything else ma'am, Ah'd better
report back.

MRS VARNEY: Yes — don't wait! — The wound is dressed, isn't it?

ORDERLY: Yes'm. I took him to the Winder Hospital — they said he'd be on his
feet in a day or two — but he wants to keep quiet a bit.

MRS VARNEY: Tell the General just how it happened!

ORDERLY: (*touching cap*) Very well ma'am. (*Exit at door up left.*)

>(*Short pause.* MRS VARNEY *gently bathing* WILFRED's *head and
wrists. Alarm bells die away excepting one which continues to ring
in muffled tones.* CAROLINE *appears coming down the stairway
absent-mindedly, stopping when part way down; sees somebody in
the room. She looks more intently, then runs suddenly down the
rest of the way and into the room, stopping dead when a little way
in and looking at what is going on.* MRS VARNEY *does not see her
at first —* CAROLINE *stands motionless — face very white.* MRS
VARNEY *after a moment's pause for above, sees* CAROLINE.)

(XXX)

MRS VARNEY: (*rising quickly*) Caroline dear! (*Goes to her.*) It's *nothing!* (*Holds*
CAROLINE, *though the girl seems not to know it, her face expressionless and
her eyes fixed on* WILFRED.) He's hardly hurt at all! There — there — don't
you faint too, dear!

CAROLINE: (*very low voice*) Ah'm not going to faint! (*Sees the handkerchief in*
MRS VARNEY's *hand.*) Let me — (*Takes handkerchief and goes across
toward* WILFRED, *toward front of couch; turns to* MRS VARNEY.) — Ah
can take care of him. Ah don't need anybody here at all! (*Goes toward*
WILFRED.)

MRS VARNEY: But Caroline —

CAROLINE: (*still with a strange quiet; looks calmly at* MRS VARNEY.) Mrs
Varney — there's a heap o' soldiers goin' round upstairs — lookin' in all the
rooms. Ah reckon you'd better go an' attend to 'em.

MRS VARNEY: Yes yes — I must go a moment! (*Going up toward door, stops and
turns to* CAROLINE.) You know what to do?

CAROLINE: Oh yes! (*dropping down on the floor beside* WILFRED)

MRS VARNEY: Bathe his forehead — he isn't badly hurt! — I won't be long! (*Exit hurriedly up left closing the portieres or curtains together after her.*)

(CAROLINE *on her knees close to* WILFRED, *tenderly bathing his forehead and smoothing his hair.* WILFRED *soon begins to show signs of revival.*)

CAROLINE: (*speaking to him in low tone as he revives — not a continued speech, but with pauses, business, etc.*) Wilfred dear! — Wilfred! You're not hurt much are you? — Oh no — you're not! There there! — You'll feel better in just a minute! — Yes — just a minute!

WILFRED: (*weakly, before he realizes what has happened*) Is there — are you — (*Looks round with wide open eyes.*)

CAROLINE: Oh Wilfred — don't you know me?

WILFRED: (*Looks at her.*) What are you talking about — of course Ah know you! — Say — what am I doing anyhow — taking a bath?

CAROLINE: No no! — You see Wilfred — you just fainted a little an' —

WILFRED: Fainted! (CAROLINE *nods.*) I fainted! (*weak attempt to rise; begins to remember.*) Oh — (*Sinks back weakly.*) — Yes of course! — Ah was in a fight with the Yanks — an' got knocked — (*Begins to remember that he was wounded; thinks about it a moment, then looks strangely at* CAROLINE.)

CAROLINE: (*after looking at him in silence*) Oh, what is it?

WILFRED: Ah'll tell you one thing right yere! Ah'm not going to load you up with a cripple! Not much!

CAROLINE: Cripple!

WILFRED: Ah reckon Ah've got an arm knocked off haven't I?

CAROLINE: (*quickly*) No no! You haven't Wilfred! (*shaking head emphatically*) They're both on all right!

WILFRED: (*after thinking a moment*) Maybe I had a hand shot away?

CAROLINE: Oh — not a single one!

WILFRED: Are my — are my ears on all right?

CAROLINE: (*Looks on both sides of his head.*) Oh yes! You needn't trouble about them a minute! (WILFRED *thinks a moment, then turns his eyes slowly on her.*)

WILFRED: How many legs have Ah got left?

CAROLINE: (*Looks to see.*) All of 'em — every one!

(*Last alarm bell ceases.*)

WILFRED: (*after pause*) Then — if there's enough of me left to — to amount to anything — (*Looks in* CAROLINE's *face a moment.*) you'll take charge of it just the same? — How about that?

CAROLINE: (*after pause*) That's all right too! (CAROLINE *suddenly buries face on his shoulder.* WILFRED *gets hold of her hand and kisses it. She suddenly raises head and looks at him.*) Ah tried to send you a telegram — an' they wouldn't let me!

WILFRED: Did you? (CAROLINE *nods.*) What did you say in it? (*pause*) Tell me what you said!

CAROLINE: It was something nice! (*Looks away.*)

WILFRED: It was, eh? (CAROLINE *nods with her head turned away from him;*

WILFRED *reaches up and turns her head toward him again.*) You're sure it was something nice!

CAROLINE: Well Ah wouldn't have gone to work an' telegraphed if it was something *bad* would Ah?

WILFRED: Well if it was good, why didn't you send it?

CAROLINE: Goodness gracious! How could Ah when they wouldn't let me!

WILFRED: Wouldn't let you!

CAROLINE: Ah should think not! (*Moves back for* WILFRED*'s getting up.*) Oh they had a dreadful time at the telegraph office!

WILFRED: Telegraph office. (*Tries to recollect.*) Telegr — were you there when — (*raising himself*)

>   (*Alarm bell begins to ring again.*)

(XXX)

>   (CAROLINE *moves back a little frightened — without getting up — watching him.* WILFRED *suddenly tries to get up.*)

That was it! — They told me at the hospital! (*Attempts to rise.*)

(XXX)

CAROLINE: (*rising, trying to prevent him*) Oh, you mustn't!

WILFRED: (*Gets partly on his feet and pushes* CAROLINE *away with one hand, holding to the chair near the desk right for support with the other.*) He gets hold of our Department Telegraph — sends out a false order — weakens our defense at Cemetery Hill — an' they're down on us in a minute! An' she gave it to him! The commission! — My sister Edith!

(XXX)

CAROLINE: Oh you don't know —

WILFRED: (*imperiously*) Ah know this — if the General was here he'd see her! The General isn't here — Ah'll attend it!

(XXX)

>   (WILFRED *begins to feel a dizziness and holds on to desk for support.* CAROLINE *starts toward him in alarm. He braces himself erect again with an effort and motions her off. She stops.*)

WILFRED: (*weakly but with clear voice and commandingly*) Send her to me!

>   (CAROLINE *stands almost frightened with her eyes upon him.*)

>   (*Enter* MRS VARNEY *at door up left.* CAROLINE *hurries toward* MRS VARNEY *in a frightened way — glancing back at* WILFRED.)

CAROLINE: He wants to see Edith!

MRS VARNEY: (*going toward* WILFRED) Not now Wilfred — you're too weak and ill!

WILFRED: Tell her to come here!

MRS VARNEY: It won't do any good — she won't speak!

WILFRED: Ah don't want her to speak — Ah'm going to speak to her!

MRS VARNEY: Some other time!

WILFRED: (*Leaves the chair that he held to and moves toward door up left as if to pass his mother and* CAROLINE.) If you won't send her to me — Ah'll —

MRS VARNEY: (*stopping him*) There there! If you insist I'll call her!

WILFRED: Ah insist!

(XXX)

MRS VARNEY: (*Turns toward door and goes a few steps; stops, turns back to*
CAROLINE.) Stay with him, dear!

WILFRED: (*weak voice but commandingly*) Ah'll see her alone!

> (MRS VARNEY *looks at him an instant, sees that he means what he
> says, and motions* CAROLINE *to come.* CAROLINE *looks at*
> WILFRED *a moment, then turns and slowly goes to door up left
> where* MRS VARNEY *is waiting for her, looks sadly back at*
> WILFRED *again, and then they both go off at door.*)

(XXX)

> (WILFRED *stands motionless an instant down right center as he was
> when the ladies left. Noise of approaching men — low shouts — steps
> on gravel, etc., outside up right, begins in distance. On this*
> WILFRED *turns and moves up center looking off to right, then goes
> up into the doorway opening up center but does not open the door.*)

(XXX)

> (*Alarm bell ceases. Low sound of distant voices and the tramp of
> hurrying feet quickly growing louder and louder outside right. When
> it is on strong,* THORNE *appears springing over balustrade of
> veranda above window up right and instantly runs forward into the
> room — knocking over pedestal and vase at right, but quickly back
> against wall or curtains at right so that he will not be seen. He stands
> there panting — face pale — eyes hunted and desperate. His left hand
> is bandaged roughly. He has no hat, or coat, hair is disheveled, shoes
> dusty, trousers and shirt torn and soiled. As the noise of his pursuers
> dies away he turns into the room and makes a rapid start across
> toward left, looking quickly about as if searching for someone.*
> WILFRED, *who has been watching him from up center, darts down
> center as* THORNE *goes across and comes down right of him catch-
> ing hold of him by right arm and shoulder.*)

WILFRED: Halt! You're under arrest!

THORNE: (*with a quick glance back at* WILFRED) Wait a minute! (*shaking loose
from* WILFRED) Wait a minute an' I'll go with you! (*going up left, looking
this way and that*)

WILFRED: (*a step toward* THORNE *as if to follow*) Halt I say! You're my prisoner!

THORNE: (*turning and going quickly down to him*) All right — prisoner — anything you like! (*drawing revolver from right hip pocket and pushing it into his
hands*) Take this — shoot the life out of me — but let me see my brother first!

WILFRED: (*taking the revolver*) Your brother!

THORNE: (*Nods, breathless.*) One look in his face — that's all!

WILFRED: Where is he?

THORNE: (*quick glance about; points toward the door up center*) Maybe they
took him in there! (*striding toward door as he speaks*)

WILFRED: (*springing up between door and* THORNE *and covering him with revolver*) What is he doing?

THORNE: (*facing* WILFRED) Ha!

WILFRED: (*still covering him*) What's he doing in there?

THORNE: Nothing! . . . He's dead!

WILFRED: (*Looks at* THORNE *a moment, then begins to back slowly up to door, keeping eyes on* THORNE *and revolver ready but not aimed; opens door, takes quick look into the room, and faces* THORNE *again.*) It's a lie!

THORNE: (*turning up toward him*) What!

WILFRED: There's no one there! — It's another trick of yours! (*Starts toward window up right.*) Call in the Guard! Call the Guard! Captain Thorne is here in the house!

> (WILFRED *exits at window, calling the* GUARD. *His voice is heard outside right, becoming more and more distant.* THORNE *stands a moment until* WILFRED *is off, then springs to the door up center, opens it and looks into the room, going part way off at the door. He glances this way and that within room, then attitude of failure — left hand dropping from frame of door to his side as he comes to erect position; right hand retaining hold of knob of door, which he pushed open. On* THORNE *standing erect,* EDITH *enters through the portieres of the door up left, expecting to find* WILFRED. *She stands just within the doorway.* THORNE *turns and comes out of room, closing the door as he does so. Turning away from the door, right hand still on the knob, he sees* EDITH *and stops motionless facing her.*)

THORNE: (*going to* EDITH) You wouldn't tell me would you! He was shot in this room — an hour ago — my brother Harry! — I'd like one look in his dead face before they send me the same way! Can't you tell me that much Miss Varney? Is he in the house? (EDITH *looks in his face an instant motionless — then turns and moves slowly down left center and stands near the table there.*)

THORNE: (*Turns and moves toward window up right. A sudden burst of shouts and calls outside up right in distance on* THORNE'*s turning away to right as if* WILFRED *had reached a posse of the Guard. Turning near center, a flash of distant artillery on him from outside*) Ha ha — they're on the scent, you see! — They'll get me in a minute — an' when they do it won't take long to finish me off! (*Looks at her.*) And as that'll be the last of me Miss Varney — maybe you'll listen to one thing! We can't all die a soldier's death — in the roar and glory of battle — our friends around us — under the flag we love! — no — not all! Some of us have orders for another kind of work — desperate — dare-devil work — the hazardous schemes of the Secret Service! We fight our battles alone — no comrades to cheer us on — ten thousand to one against us — death at every turn! If we win we escape with our lives — if we lose — dragged out and butchered like dogs — no soldier's grave — not even a trench with the rest of the boys — alone — despised — forgotten! These were my orders Miss Varney — this is the death I die tonight — and I don't want you to think for one minute that I'm ashamed of it — not for one minute!

> (*Suddenly shouts and noise of many men rushing up outside up right*

and also outside up left. THORNE *swings round and walks up center in usual nonchalant manner, and stands up center waiting and faced a little to right of front, leaning on side of door with outstretched right arm.* EDITH *moves to left and stands near mantel. As shouts become nearer,* THORNE *turns and stands waiting, faced to front. No assumption of bravado. Enter from both windows on right – bursting open the one down right – and from door up left a* SQUAD OF CONFEDERATE SOLDIERS *in gray uniforms – not too old and dirty – those on right headed by the* SERGEANT *who searched the house early in this act, and those on left by a* CORPORAL. WILFRED VARNEY *with revolver still in his hand, enters at windows in lead of others, coming to right center. They rush on with a shout of exultation, and stand on charge at each side.*)

WILFRED: (*to* SERGEANT) There's your man Sergeant – I hand him over to you!

SERGEANT: (*advancing to* THORNE *and putting hand roughly on his shoulder*) Prisoner!

(XXX)

(*Enter* ARRELSFORD *hurriedly at door up left.*)

ARRELSFORD: (*breaking through between men at left and standing left center*) Where is he? (*Sees him.*) Ah! We've got him have we!

SERGEANT: Young Varney here captured him, sir! (*Enter* MRS VARNEY *up left. She goes down left side near fireplace and stands looking on.*)

ARRELSFORD: So! – Run down at last! (THORNE *pays no attention to him; he merely waits for the end of the disturbance.*) Now you'll find out what it costs to play your little game with our Government Telegraph Lines! (*to* SERGEANT) Don't waste any time! Take him down the street and shoot him full of lead! – Out with him! (*going down left center on last of speech. Low shouts of approval from* MEN, *and general movement as if to start, the* SERGEANT *at same time shoving* THORNE *a little toward left*)

SERGEANT: (*gruffly, as he starts*) Come along!

WILFRED: (*a step toward center, revolver still in hand*) No! – Whatever he is – whatever he's done – he has the right to a trial! (THORNE *turns suddenly round and looks at* WILFRED.)

ARRELSFORD: General Tarleton said to me, 'If you find him shoot him on sight!'

WILFRED: I don't care what General Tarleton said – I captured the man – he's in this house – and he's not going out without he's treated fair! (*Looks up toward* THORNE; *their eyes meet, then* THORNE *turns away up stage, resting left hand against left side of door frame.*)

ARRELSFORD: (*suddenly, angrily*) Well – let him have it! – We'll give him a drum-head, boys – but it'll be the quickest drum-head ever held on earth! (*to* SERGEANT) Stack muskets here an' run 'em in for the Court!

SERGEANT: (*stepping a little down center and facing about, back to audience*) Fall in here! (MEN *break positions each side and run up stage, falling quickly into a double rank just above* SERGEANT.) Fall in the Prisoner! (MEN *separate right and left, leaving space at center;* THORNE *steps down into position and stands.*) Stack – arms! (*Front rank* MEN *stack – rear rank* MEN

pass pieces forward. Front rank MEN *lay them on stacks. Turning right to*
MRS VARNEY *and touching cap*) Where shall we find a vacant room,
ma'am?

MRS VARNEY: At the head of the stairs — there's none on this floor.

SERGEANT: (*turning up to* MEN) Escort — left face! (MEN *left face* — THORNE
obeying the order with them.) Forward — march! — File left!

    (SOLDIERS *with* THORNE *march rapidly out of the room at door
up left and disappear up the stairway. The* SERGEANT *exits after
men.*)

(XXX)

    (*The door up center slowly opens a little way and soon the old negro*
JONAS *enters cautiously — almost crawling on. He looks this way
and that and off at door up left and up the stairway. Suddenly his
eyes light on the stacks of muskets. He goes to the one up left center
— looks about fearfully, apprehensively, hesitates an instant. During
his business, artillery and cavalry effects on strong. Cannon and
musketry fire in distance — alarm bells on strong — begin as* MEN
go upstairs. JONAS *makes up his mind. He drops down on knees by
stack of muskets — snaps the breech lock of one — without moving
it from the stack — gets out the cartridge, looks at it, bites it with
his teeth and looks at it again. Bites again and makes motions of
getting the ball off and putting it in his pocket. Puts cartridge back
in the musket, snaps the lock shut, and moves on to the next.
Repeats the movement of taking the cartridge out, but is much
quicker, biting off the ball at once. Repeats more rapidly and
quickly with another musket, crawling quickly round the stack.
Moves over to second stack; same business. As* JONAS *gets well to
work on muskets* EDITH *turns at window up right and sees him. She
stands a moment motionless — then comes down on right, and
stands looking at him without moving.* JONAS, *who began after
leaving stack left center at upper side of stack right center has
worked around down stage on the stack, and has come to the lower
side.* EDITH *stands near the desk at right and drops a book upon it
on cue to make* JONAS *look up after the last musket but one.*
JONAS *looks up and sees* EDITH *watching. He stops. Stop loud
effects as* JONAS *speaks, but keep up bells and far distant cannon.*)

JONAS: (*after pause, very low voice*) Dhey's a-goin' ter shoot 'im — shoot 'im
down like a dog, Missy — an' Ah couldn't b'ar to see 'em do dat! Ah wouldn't
like it noways! You won't say nuffin' 'bout dis — fer de sake of ole Jonas
what was always so fond o' you — ebber sense ye was a little chile! (*Sees that*
EDITH *does not appear angry, and goes on with his work of drawing the
bullets out of the last musket.*) Ye see — I jiss take away dis yer — an' den dar
won't be no harm to 'im what-some-ebber — less'n day loads 'em up again!
(*Slowly hobbles to his feet as he speaks.*) When dey shoots — an' he jiss draps
down, dey'll roll 'im over inter de gutter an' be off like dey was mad! Den Ah
can be near by — an' — (*Suddenly thinks of something; a look of conster-*

nation comes over his face. He speaks in almost whisper.) How's he goin' ter know! Ef he don't drap down dey'll shoot him agin — an dey'll hab bullets in 'em nex' time! (*Anxiously glances around an instant.*) Dey'll hab bullets in 'em next time! (*Looks about. Suddenly to* EDITH.) *You* tell 'im! *You* tell him Missy — it's de ony-est way! Tell 'im to drap down! (*supplicatingly*) Do dis fur ole Jonas, honey — do it fur me — an' Ah'll be a slabe to ye ez long ez Ah lib! (*slight pause; sudden subdued yell outside up left sounding as if from men shut inside a room on the floor above.* JONAS *starts and turns on the yell; half whisper*) Dey's a-goin' ter kill 'im!

(XXX)

> (*Noise of heavy tramp of feet outside left above, doors opening, etc.; an indistinct order or two before regular order heard.* JONAS *goes hurriedly up to door up center.*)

SERGEANT: (*outside, above*) Fall in! — Right face! — Forward — March!

JONAS: (*at door*) Oh tell 'im Missy! Tell 'im to drap down for God's sake! (*Exit at door, carefully closing it after him.*)

(XXX)

> (EDITH *crosses to left center and stands waiting, her face expressionless, in front of table.*)

(XXX)

> (*Enter* WILFRED *up left coming down the stairs. He enters the room coming down center. Enter* CAROLINE *at door up left as* WILFRED *goes down center. She hurries to him with an anxious glance up stairway as she passes.*)

CAROLINE: (*almost whisper*) What are they — going to do?

WILFRED: Shoot him!

CAROLINE: When?

WILFRED: Now.

CAROLINE: (*low exclamation of pity*) Oh!

> (WILFRED *goes below couch;* CAROLINE *stands near him looking on as* SOLDIERS *and others enter.* SERGEANT *enters first followed by escort of* SOLDIERS. *They enter room and turn right marching to position they were formerly in above the stacks of muskets. Enter* ARRELSFORD *after the men. He goes across to up right center.* MRS VARNEY *enters and goes down left.*)

SERGEANT: (*at center facing up*) Halt! (MEN *halt.*) Left face! (MEN *face front.*)

> (*Enter* THORNE *up left coming down the stairway, followed by* CORPORAL *with his carbine.* THORNE *comes into position at left of front line of men.* CORPORAL *stands left of* THORNE.)

SERGEANT: Take arms! (MEN *at once take muskets, all very quick.*) Carry arms! (MEN *stand in line waiting.*) Fall in the Prisoner! (THORNE *walks in front of* MEN *to center and falls into position.*) Left face! (THORNE *and* MEN *face to left on order, ready to march out.*) Forward —

EDITH: Wait! — (*motion of hand to stop them without looking round*) Who is the officer in command?

SERGEANT: I'm in command, Miss! (*touching cap*)

EDITH: I'd like to — speak to the prisoner!

SERGEANT: Sorry Miss, but we haven't got time! (*turning as though to give orders*)

EDITH: (*sudden turn on him*) Only a word!

SERGEANT: (*Hesitates an instant, turns to MEN, stepping up left center.*) Right face! (MEN *face to front again on order,* THORNE *obeying order with others.*) Fall out the prisoner! (THORNE *moves forward one step out of rank and stands motionless.*) Now Miss!

WILFRED: (*starting indignantly toward center*) No!
              (SERGEANT *turns in surprise.*)

CAROLINE: (*holding to WILFRED and speaking in a low voice full of feeling*) Oh Wilfred — let her speak to him — let her say good-bye!
              (WILFRED *looks at CAROLINE a moment; then with gesture to SERGEANT indicates that he may go on, and turns away with CAROLINE.*)

SERGEANT: (*turning to THORNE*) The lady!
              (*A brief motionless pause* — THORNE *looking front as before. Then he turns slowly and looks at SERGEANT. SERGEANT turns and looks meaningly toward EDITH. THORNE walks down to her, stopping close on her right, standing in military position, faced, as he walked, a little left of front. ARRELSFORD looks at EDITH and THORNE. CAROLINE with WILFRED gives an occasional awed and frightened glance at THORNE and EDITH. All this arranged so that there is no movement after SERGEANT's order to 'fall out the prisoner'. EDITH, after slight pause, speaks slowly in almost a whisper and as if with an effort, but without apparent feeling, and without turning to THORNE.*)

EDITH: (*slowly, distinctly, without inflection; an occasional tremor*) One of the servants — has taken the musket balls — out of the guns. If you care to fall on the ground when they fire — you may escape with your life!

THORNE: (*after pause, to EDITH in low voice*) Do you wish me to do this?

EDITH: (*low voice, without turning*) It's nothing to me.

THORNE: (*With slight sudden movement at the cue, turns slowly away to front; brief pause, then he turns toward her again and speaks in low voice.*) Were you responsible in any way for — (EDITH *shakes her head slightly without looking at him. He turns and walks right a step or two, makes turn there and walks up center and turns to left facing the SERGEANT, saluting.*) Sergeant — (*as if making an ordinary military report*) You'd better take a look at your muskets — they've been tampered with.

SERGEANT: (*snatching musket from man nearest him*) What the — (*Quickly snaps it open. Cartridge drops to floor. SERGEANT picks it up and looks at it.*) Here! — (*handing musket back to man. Turns to squad and gives orders quickly.*) Squad — ready! (MEN *come in one movement from 'carry' to position for loading.*) Draw — cartridge! (MEN *draw cartridges. The click and snap of locks and levers ringing out simultaneously along the line*) With ball cartridge — reload! (MEN *quickly reload.*) Carry — arms! (MEN *come to carry*

on the instant; motionless, eyes front. To THORNE — *with off-hand smile*)
Much obliged sir!

THORNE: (*low voice, off-hand as if of no consequence*) That's all right. (*Stands
facing left waiting for order to fall in.* WILFRED, *after* THORNE'*s warning
to officer about muskets, watches him with undisguised admiration.*)

WILFRED: (*suddenly walking to* THORNE) Ah'd like to shake hands with
you!

THORNE: (*Turns and looks at* WILFRED; *a smile breaks gradually over his face.*)
Is this for yourself — or your father?

WILFRED: (*earnestly*) For both of us sir! (*putting out his hand a little way — not
raising it much.* THORNE *grasps his hand, they look into each other's faces a
moment, let go hands,* WILFRED *turns away to down right center to*
CAROLINE. THORNE *looks after* WILFRED *to front an instant, then turns
left.*) That's all, Sergeant!

SERGEANT: (*lower voice than before*) Fall in the Prisoner! (THORNE *steps to
place in the line and turns front.*) Escort — left face! (MEN *with* THORNE
left face) Forward ma — (*sharp cry of 'Halt! Halt' outside up left, followed
by bang of heavy door outside*) Halt! (MEN *stand motionless at left face. On
seeing the* ORDERLY *approaching — just before he is on*) Right face!
          (MEN *with* THORNE *face to front. Enter quickly at door an* AID,
          wearing Lieutenant's uniform. SERGEANT, *faced front up left
          center just forward of his men, salutes.* AID *salutes.*)

SERGEANT: (*low voice to* MEN) Present arms! (MEN *present.*) Carry arms! (MEN
come to carry again.)

(XXX)

AID: (*standing up left center, facing right*) General Randolph's compliments sir,
and he's on the way with orders!

ARRELSFORD: (*up right center*) What orders, Lieutenant? — Anything to do with
this case?

AID: (*no salute to* ARRELSFORD) I don't know what the orders are, sir. He's
been with the President.

ARRELSFORD: I sent word to the Department we'd got the man and were going
to drum-head him on the spot.

AID: Then this must be the case sir! I believe the General wishes to be present.

ARRELSFORD: Impossible! We've held the Court and I've sent the finding to the
Secretary! The messenger is to get his approval and meet us at the corner of
Copley Street.

AID: I have no further orders sir! (*Retires up with quick military movement and
turns facing front, stands motionless.*)

(XXX)

          (*Sound of door outside up left and the heavy tread of the*
          GENERAL *as he strides across the hall.*)

SERGEANT: (*low voice to* MEN) Present — arms! (MEN *present.*)
          (SERGEANT, ORDERLY, *etc., on salute. Enter* GENERAL
          RANDOLPH *at door up left, striding on hurriedly, returning salutes
          as he goes down center glancing about. Enter, after* GENERAL

RANDOLPH, *as if he had come with him,* LT FORAY. *He stands
waiting near door, faced front, military position.*)

SERGEANT: (*low order to* MEN) Carry — arms! (MEN *come to carry again.*)

GENERAL RANDOLPH: Ah, Sergeant! — (*going to him*) Got the prisoner in here
have you?

SERGEANT: (*saluting*) Just taking him out sir!

GENERAL RANDOLPH: Prison?

SERGEANT: No sir! To execute the sentence of the Court!

GENERAL RANDOLPH: Had his trial then!

ARRELSFORD: (*stepping toward him with a salute*) All done according to regu-
lations, sir! The finding has gone to the Secretary!

GENERAL RANDOLPH: (*to* ARRELSFORD) Found guilty I judge?

ARRELSFORD: Found guilty sir! — No time for hanging now — the Court ordered
him shot!

GENERAL RANDOLPH: What were the grounds for this?

ARRELSFORD: Conspiracy against our government and the success of our arms by
sending a false and misleading dispatch containing forged orders!

GENERAL RANDOLPH: Court's been misinformed. The dispatch wasn't sent!

(EDITH *looks up with sudden breathless exclamation.* WILFRED
turns with surprise. General astonishment.)

ARRELSFORD: (*recovering*) Why General — the dispatch — I saw him —

GENERAL RANDOLPH: I say the dispatch wasn't sent! I expected to arrive in
time for the trial and brought Foray here to testify. (*Calls to* FORAY *without looking round.*) Lieutenant!

(LIEUTENANT FORAY *comes quickly down facing* GENERAL
RANDOLPH — *salutes.*)

Did Captain Thorne send out any dispatches after we left you with him in the
office an hour ago?

LT FORAY: No sir. I was just going to send one under his order, but he counter-
manded it.

GENERAL RANDOLPH: What were his words at the time?

LT FORAY: He said he refused to act under that commission.

(EDITH *turns toward* THORNE *and looks at him steadfastly.*)

GENERAL RANDOLPH: That'll do, Lieutenant! (LT FORAY *salutes and retires
up left.*) In addition we learn from General Chesney that no orders were
received over the wire — that Marston's Division was not withdrawn — and
that our position was not weakened in any way. The attack at that point has
been repulsed. It's plain that the Court has been acting under error. The
President is therefore compelled to disapprove the finding and it is set aside.

ARRELSFORD: (*with great indignation*) General Randolph, this case was put in
my hands and I —

GENERAL RANDOLPH: (*interrupting bluffly, but without temper*) Well I take it
out of your hands! Report back to the War Office with my compliments!

ARRELSFORD: (*Turns and starts toward up left, turns back again after going a
few steps.*) Hadn't I better wait and see —

GENERAL RANDOLPH: No — don't wait to see anything! (ARRELSFORD *looks
at him an instant, then turns and exits at door up left; sound of door outside*

closed with force. GENERAL RANDOLPH *in front of couch.*) Sergeant!
(SERGEANT *quickly down to him on salute*) Hold your men back there. I'll
see the prisoner. (SERGEANT *salutes, turns, marches straight up from where
he is to the right division of the escort so that he is a little to right of*
THORNE *and turns front.*)

SERGEANT: Order — arms! (*Squad obeys with precision.*) Parade — rest! (*Squad
obeys.*) Fall out the Prisoner! (THORNE *steps forward one step out of the
rank and stands.*) The General! (THORNE *starts down center to go to*
GENERAL RANDOLPH. *As he steps forward,* EDITH *starts quickly toward
center and intercepts him about two-thirds of the way down, on his left.*
 ,THORNE *stopped by* EDITH *shows slight surprise for an instant, but quickly
recovers and looks straight front.*)

EDITH: (*to* THORNE *as she meets him, impulsively in low voice*) Oh — why didn't
you tell me! — I thought you sent it! I thought you —

GENERAL RANDOLPH: (*surprised*) Miss Varney!

EDITH: (*crossing* THORNE *and to the* GENERAL) There's nothing against him,
General Randolph! — He didn't send it! — There's nothing to try him for
now!

GENERAL RANDOLPH: You're very much mistaken, Miss Varney. The fact of his
being caught in our lines without his uniform is enough to swing him off in
ten minutes.

> (EDITH *moans a little, at same time moving back from* GENERAL
> *a trifle.*)

GENERAL RANDOLPH: Cap'n Thorne — (THORNE *steps down and faces*
GENERAL.) or whatever your name may be — the President is fully informed
regarding the circumstances of your case, and I needn't say that we look on
you as a cursed dangerous character! There isn't any doubt whatever that
you'd ought to be exterminated right now! — But considering the damned
peculiarity of your behavior — and that you refused for some reason — to
send that dispatch when you might have done so, we've decided to keep you
out of mischief some other way. The Sergeant will turn you over to Major
Whitfield sir! (SERGEANT *salutes.*) You'll be held as a prisoner of war!
(*Turns and goes right a few steps.*)

> (EDITH *turns suddenly to* THORNE, *coming down before him as
> he faces right.*)

EDITH: (*looking in his face*) Oh — that isn't nearly so bad!

THORNE: (*Holds her hand in his right.*) No?

EDITH: No! — Because — sometime — (*Hesitates.*)

THORNE: (*his face nearer hers*) Ah — if it's sometime, that's enough!

> (*Slight pause.* EDITH *sees* MRS VARNEY *at left and crosses to her,*
> THORNE *retaining her hand as she crosses — a step back to let her
> pass — following her with his eyes — releasing her hand only when
> he has to.*)

EDITH: Mama, won't you speak to him?

> (MRS VARNEY *and* EDITH *talk quietly.*)

WILFRED: (*suddenly leaving* CAROLINE *and striding to* THORNE, *extending
hand*) I'd like to shake hands with you!

THORNE: (*turning to* WILFRED) What, again? (*taking* WILFRED's *hand*) All right
    — go ahead.
> (WILFRED, *shaking hands with* THORNE *and crossing him to left
> as he does so — back to audience, laughing and very happy about it.*)

CAROLINE: (*coming quickly down to* THORNE) So would I! (*holding out her
    hand*)
> (THORNE *lets go of* WILFRED's *hand — now on his left — and
> takes* CAROLINE's.)

WILFRED: Don't you be afraid now — it'll be all right! They'll give you a parole
    and —

CAROLINE: (*breaking in enthusiastically*) A parole! Goodness gracious! Why
    they'll give you hundreds of 'em! (*turning away with funny little compre-
    hensive gesture of both hands on end of her speech*)

GENERAL RANDOLPH: (*gruffly*) One moment if you please! (THORNE *turns at
    once, facing* GENERAL *near center.* CAROLINE *and* WILFRED *go up above
    couch.* EDITH *stands left center.* MRS VARNEY *near table left*) There's only
    one reason on earth why the President has set aside a certain verdict of death.
    You held up that false order and made a turn in our favor. We expect you to
    make the turn complete and enter our service.
> (*All motionless — watching the scene*)

THORNE: (*after instant's pause, quietly*) Why General — that's impossible!

GENERAL RANDOLPH: You can give us your answer later!

THORNE: You have it now!

GENERAL RANDOLPH: You'll be kept in close confinement until you come to
    our terms!

THORNE: You're making me a prisoner for life!

GENERAL RANDOLPH: You'll see it in another light before many days. And it
    wouldn't surprise me if Miss Varney had something to do with your change
    of views!

EDITH: (*coming toward center*) You're mistaken General Randolph — I think he's
    perfectly right!
> (THORNE *turns to* EDITH.)

GENERAL RANDOLPH: Very well — we'll see what a little prison life will do. (*a
    sharp order*) Sergeant! (SERGEANT *comes down stage and salutes.*) Report
    with the prisoner to Major Whitfield! (*Turns away to front.*)
> (SERGEANT *turns at once to* THORNE. — THORNE *and* EDITH
> *look in each other's eyes.*)

THORNE: (*low voice to* EDITH) What is it — love and good-bye?

EDITH: (*almost a whisper*) Oh no — only the first! — And that one every day —
    every hour — every minute — until we meet again!

THORNE: Until we meet again!

SERGEANT: Fall in the Prisoner!
> (THORNE *turns and walks up, quickly taking his place in the squad.*
> EDITH *follows him up a step or two as he goes, stopping a little left
> of center.*)

SERGEANT: (*quick orders*) Attention! (*Squad obeys order.*) Carry — arms! (*Squad obeys order.*) Escort — left — face! (*Squad with* THORNE *turn left face on order.*) Forward — march!

        (*Escort with* THORNE *marches out at door up left and off to left.*)

CURTAIN

SHERLOCK HOLMES

A drama in four acts

First produced at the Star Theatre in Buffalo, New York, on 24 October 1899;
afterwards at the Garrick Theatre, New York, on 6 November 1899, with the
following cast:

SHERLOCK HOLMES	William Gillette
DR WATSON	Bruce McRae
JOHN FORMAN	Reuben Fax
SIR EDWARD LEIGHTON	Harold Heaton
COUNT VON STAHLBURG	Alfred S. Howard
PROFESSOR MORIARTY	George Wessels
JAMES LARRABEE	Ralph Delmore
SIDNEY PRINCE	George Honey
ALFRED BASSICK	Henry Herrman
JIM CRAIGIN	Thomas McGrath
THOMAS LEARY	Elwyn Eaton
'LIGHTFOOT' McTAGUE	Julius Weyms
JOHN	Henry S. Chandler
PARSONS	Soldene Powell
BILLY	Henry McArdle
ALICE FAULKNER	Katherine Florence
MRS FAULKNER	Jane Thomas
MADGE LARRABEE	Judith Berolde
TERESE	Hilda Englund
MRS SMEDLEY	Kate Ten Eyck

VII *Sherlock Holmes*, Act I. Gillette's first entrance as Holmes

FIRST ACT

SCENE. *Drawing room at Edelweiss Lodge. An old house – gloomy, decayed, situated in a lonely street in a little-frequented part of London. Wide door or open columns up left and left center to an entrance hall. Heavily carved fireplace, in large wide alcove up center. By window up right center window seats, etc. Old furniture, decayed, worn – though once very magnificent. Old carpet. A new piano. A new heavy desk down right, very solid. Door in front of lower part which opens showing a strong box or safe with combination lock. Heavily beamed ceiling, dark color. Many places out of repair in walls, ceiling. Carvings broken some – as if by age not violence. MADGE LARRABEE discovered anxiously waiting, then moving about the stage. A strikingly handsome woman, but with a somewhat hard face. Black hair. Richly dressed. She moves nervously from place to place, remaining briefly here and there and then moving again, as if nervously waiting for something. She tries to see out of the window up right, but it is dark outside. MADGE LARRABEE, seeing FORMAN, moves at once toward center as if expecting something. Enter FORMAN at door center with evening paper. He is a quiet, perfectly trained servant or butler. MADGE takes paper from him quickly.*

FORMAN: (*Speaks always very quietly.*) I beg pardon ma'am, but one of the maids wishes to know if she could speak with you.

MADGE: (*Not looking from paper, scanning it eagerly; sinks on to seat near piano.*) I can't spare the time now.

FORMAN: Very well ma'am. (*Turns to go.*)

MADGE: (*without looking up*) Which maid was it?

FORMAN: (*turning toward MADGE again*) Terese ma'am.

MADGE: (*looking up; very slight surprise in her tone*) Terese!

FORMAN: Yes ma'am.

MADGE: Have you any idea what she wants?

FORMAN: Not the least ma'am.

MADGE: She must tell you. I'm very busy, and can't see her unless I know.

FORMAN: I'll say so ma'am. (*Turns and exits, carefully and quietly closing the door after him.*)

> (MADGE *finds what she has been looking for in the paper and starts eagerly to read it. As if not seeing the print well she leans near light and resumes reading with the greatest avidity. Enter FORMAN quietly at door up center. He stands a moment at the door looking at MADGE as she reads. This is somewhat prolonged; he is not waiting for her to finish from mere politeness. His eyes are upon her sharply and intensely, yet he does not assume any expression otherwise. She finishes and angrily rises, casting the paper violently down on the floor and stamping her foot. She turns and goes near the large heavy desk, her eyes upon it. Pauses there, then turns away angrily. Sees FORMAN. Calms herself at once. FORMAN times it so that just as MADGE turns he seems to be coming into room and moves down a little.*)

FORMAN: I could get nothing from her ma'am. She insists that she must speak to you yourself.

MADGE: Tell her to wait till tomorrow. (*Turns and moves toward window up right.*)

FORMAN: I asked her to do that ma'am, as you had mentioned you were very busy this evening, and she said that she would not be here tomorrow.

MADGE: (*Turns toward* FORMAN *with some surprise.*) What does she mean by that?

FORMAN: You'll pardon me for mentioning it, ma'am, but she is a bit singular — as I take it.

MADGE: Tell her to come here — I'll see her myself. (FORMAN *bows and turns to go.* MADGE *goes toward chair she occupied and near which the paper lies. Stops with hand on piano.*) Oh — Judson! (FORMAN *stops and comes down. Everything quiet, subdued, catlike in his methods. Their eyes meet.*) How did you happen to know that I would be interested in this marriage announcement?

FORMAN: I could 'ardly 'elp it ma'am. (MADGE *turns and looks hard at him an instant.* FORMAN *stands deferentially.* MADGE *puts paper on piano — still looking at* FORMAN.)

MADGE: I suppose you have overheard certain references to the matter — between myself and my brother? (*Sits on chair near piano.*)

FORMAN: I 'ave ma'am, but I never would 'ave referred to it in the least if I did not think it might be of some importance to yourself, ma'am, to know it.

MADGE: Oh, no — of no special importance! We happen to know the parties concerned and are naturally interested in the event. Of course you do not imagine there is anything more. (*She does not look at him as she says this.*)

FORMAN: (*not looking at* MADGE — *eyes front*) Certainly not, ma'am. And may I add, that if I *did* imagine there was anything more (*look*) I'm sure you'd find it to your interest, ma'am, to remember my faithful services in 'elpin to keep it quiet.

MADGE: (*after slight pause, during which she looks steadily to front*) Judson, what sort of a fool are you? (FORMAN *turns to her with feigned astonishment.* MADGE *speaks with sharp, caustic utterance, almost between her teeth. Turns to him.*) Do you imagine I would take this house, bring this girl and her mother here, and keep up this establishment for nearly two years without protecting myself against the chance of petty blackmail by my own servants?

FORMAN: (*protestingly*) Ah — ma'am — you misunderstand me — I —

MADGE: (*rising*) I understand you too *well*! Now I beg you to understand me. I have had a trifle of experience in the selection of my servants and can recognize certain things when I see them! It was quite evident from your behavior that you had been in something yourself, and it didn't take me long to get it out of you. You are a *self confessed forger.*

FORMAN: (*quick movement of apprehension*) No! (*apprehensive look around*) Don't speak out like that! — (*Recovers a little.*) It was — it was in confidence — I told you in confidence, ma'am!

MADGE: Well I'm telling *you* in confidence that at the slightest sign of any underhand conduct on *your* part this little episode of yours will —

FORMAN: (*hurriedly, to prevent her from speaking it*) Yes, yes! I — will bear it in mind, ma'am!

MADGE: (*after a cold sharp look at him as if satisfying herself that he was now reduced to proper condition*) Very well . . . Now as to the maid — Terese — (FORMAN *inclines head for instruction.*) Do you think of anything which might explain her assertion that she will not be here tomorrow?

FORMAN: (*His eyes turned away from* MADGE. *He speaks in low tones and his behavior is subdued as if completely humiliated.*) It has occurred to me, ma'am, since you first asked me regarding the matter, that she may 'ave taken exceptions to some occurrences which she thinks she 'as seen going on in this 'ouse.

MADGE: You may raise her wages if you think it necessary. If it isn't money she wants — I'll see her myself.

FORMAN: Very well, ma'am. (*He turns and exits quietly at door up center.*)
(*Sounds of heavy door outside left.* MADGE *makes a quick motion, listening. Hurries to door up left, looking off. Enter* JIM LARRABEE, *door up left, passing her in some excitement. He is a tall heavily built man, with a hard face, full of determination, and with a strong character. He is well dressed and attractive in some respects — may be a fine looking man. Dark hair and eyes, but the hard sinister look of a criminal.*)

MADGE: Didn't you find him?

LARRABEE: No. (*Goes to the heavy desk safe and throws open the wooden doors of lower part showing the iron door and combination lock of a safe or strong box. Gives knob a turn or two nervously, and works at it.* MADGE *follows up near piano watching him.*) He wasn't there! (*Rises from desk.*) We'll have to get a locksmith in.

MADGE: No, no! We can't do that! It isn't safe!

LARRABEE: We've got to do something, haven't we? (*down quick before door of safe again, and nervous furtive tries at it*) I wish I knew a bit about these things. There's no time to be lost either! They've put Holmes on the case!

MADGE: Sherlock Holmes?

LARRABEE: Yes. (*at safe; trying knob*)

MADGE: How do you know?

LARRABEE: I heard it at Leary's. They keep track of him down there, and when he's put on something they give notice round.

MADGE: Why? What could he do?

LARRABEE: (*Rises and faces her.*) I don't know — but he'll make some move — he never waits long! It may be any moment! (*Moves about restlessly. Stops when* MADGE *speaks.*)

MADGE: Can't you think of some one else — if we can't find Sid?

LARRABEE: Sid may turn up yet! I left word with Billy Rounds and he's on the hunt for him. (*between his teeth*) Oh! — it's damnable! After holding on for two good years just for this — and now the time comes — and she's blocked us! (*Looks off and up the stairway from where he stands.*) Look here! I'll just get at her for a minute! (*Starts off.*) I have an idea I can change her mind. (*going*)

MADGE: (*quickly*) Yes — but wait, Jim! (LARRABEE *stops and turns to her; she goes near him.*) What's the use of hurting the girl? We've tried all that!

LARRABEE: Well, I'll try something else! (*Pushing* MADGE *away, he turns and goes to door left.*)

MADGE: (*quick half-whisper*) Jim! (LARRABEE *turns at door;* MADGE *approaches him.*) Remember — nothing that'll *show*! *No marks*! We might get into trouble!

LARRABEE: (*going; doggedly*) I'll look out for that. (*Exit* LARRABEE *at door left, and is seen running up stairs with a fierce haste.*)

> (*As* MADGE *looks after him with a trifle of anxiety, at door left enter* TERESE. *She is a quiet looking French maid. Pleasant face. She stands near the door up center.* MADGE *turns into the room and sees her. Stands an instant, then moves toward center and seats herself.*)

MADGE: Terese — come here! (TERESE *comes down a little way — with slight hesitation.*) Well, what is it?

TERESE: Meester Judson said I vas to come.

MADGE: I told Judson to arrange with you himself.

TERESE: He could not, madame. 1 do not veish longer to *re*-main!

MADGE: What is it? You must give me some reason!

TERESE: It is zat I *veesh* to go!

MADGE: But — you've been here for months and have made no complaint!

TERESE: Ah, madame, — it is not so before! — It is now beginning zat I do not like!

MADGE: (*Rises and turns on her sharply.*) What? What is it that you do not like?

TERESE: (*with some little spirit, but low voice*) *I do not* like *eet* madame — *eet* — *hare* — *zis place* — what you do — ze young lady you have up zere. (*indicating above*) Eet eez not well! I cannot remain to see!

MADGE: You know nothing about it! The young lady is ill — she is not right here — (*touching forehead*) — She is a great trouble to us, but we take every care of her, treat her with the utmost kindness and —

> (*A piercing scream, as if muffled by something, is heard in a distant part of the house, above. Pause. Both motionless.* TERESE *does not assume a horrified expression; she simply stands motionless. Enter at door up left, coming down stairway rapidly,* MRS FAULKNER, *a white haired lady, dressed in an old black gown which is almost in shreds.*)

MRS FAULNKER: My child! My child! They're hurting my child! (*She stands just within door looking vacantly, helplessly at* MADGE. MADGE *sees her and goes quickly to her.*)

MADGE: (*between her teeth*) What are you doing here? Didn't I tell you *never* to come down? (*The old lady simply stares vacantly, but a vague expression of trouble is upon her face.*) Come with me. (*Takes* MRS FAULKNER *by the left arm and draws her toward door. The old lady hangs back in a frightened way. The scream is heard again — more muffled — from above.*) Come, I say! (*sudden change; tenderly*) Don't be alarmed dear, your poor daughter's head is bad to-day. She'll be better soon! (*Turns to* TERESE.) Terese — come to me in the morning! (*to old lady*) Come along, dear! (*then, angrily, in low threatening voice*) Do you hear me? Come! (*Takes* MRS FAULKNER *off with some force at door left and up the stairway.*)

(TERESE *stands looking after them. Enter* FORMAN *quietly at door up center. He looks toward door up left a moment;* TERESE *is also looking the same way.* FORMAN *goes to* TERESE; *they look at one another for an instant in silence.*)

FORMAN: (*low voice*) She's made it quite satisfactory, I suppose. (TERESE *looks at him.*) You will not leave her — *now*?

TERESE: More zen evaire before! Do you hear ze young ladee? What is it that they make to her?

FORMAN: (*low voice*) It may be she is ill.

TERESE: Indeed I sink it is so zat zey make hair eel! I weel not remain to see! (*turning a little*) I can find another place; eet eez not so difficult.

FORMAN: Not so difficult if you know where to go.

TERESE: Ah — what eez *eet*!

FORMAN: I have one address —

TERESE: (*Turns to him quickly.*) Bien! — You know one? (*He nods and looks quickly off left.*) Est-ce serieux? What you call re-li-ah-ble?

FORMAN: Here — on this card — (*Quickly takes card from pocket and pushes it into her hands.*) — Go to that address! — Don't let anyone see it! (*Looks left.*)

TERESE: (*Quickly looking at card while he looks away; begins slowly to read.*) — Meester — Sheer-lock —

FORMAN: (*With a quick warning exclamation and sudden turn, seizes her, covering her mouth with one hand. They stand a moment. He looks slowly around to left without releasing her.*) Some one might hear you! Go to that address *in the morning.* (*Sound of cab outside left, driving madly up and stopping. Doorbell rings.* FORMAN *releases* TERESE *and both listen. He motions her off with a quick, short motion. She exits at door up center. He exits at door up left to open the house door. Sound of house door outside left; a solid, heavy sound — not sharp.*)

(*Enter* SID PRINCE, *walking in quickly at door up left. He is a short, stoutish, dapper little fellow. He carries a small black satchel, wears overcoat and hat, gloves, etc., and is well dressed and jaunty. He wears diamond scarf pin, rings, etc. He is quick in his movements and always on alert.* FORMAN *follows him on, standing near door at left.*)

PRINCE: (*going toward piano*) Now, then, don't waste toime, you fool — tell 'em I'm 'ere, can't yer?

FORMAN: Did you wish to see Mr Chetwood, or was it Miss Chetwood, sir?

PRINCE: (*stopping and turning to* FORMEN) Well, I'll be blowed! One would think I'd never been 'ere before! 'Ow do you know that I wasn't born in this 'ere 'ouse? Go an' tell 'em as it's Mr Sidney Prince, Esq. (*He puts satchel, which is apparently heavy, on ottoman near piano.*)

FORMAN: Oh, yes, sir — I beg pardon, sir! I'll announce you immediate, sir. (*Exits at door up left and up stairs.*)

PRINCE: (*Takes off hat, gloves, etc., laying them on a chair so as to cover the satchel. Looks about room. Walks over to the heavy desk and glances at it. Swings lower door open in easy, businesslike way.*) Ah! (*As if he had found what he was looking for. Not an exclamation of surprise. Drops on one knee*

and gives the lock a turn. Rises and goes over to his satchel, which he
uncovers and opens. Feels about for something.)
            (LARRABEE *and* MADGE *come down stairway and enter at door*
            up left. PRINCE *sees them but does not stop what he is doing.*)
MADGE: (*going over toward him*) Oh — is that you, Sid! I'm so glad you've come!
LARRABEE: Hullo, Sid! Did you get my note?
PRINCE: (*going right on with what he was doing*) Well, I'm 'ere, ain't I? (*at satchel*)
            . . . That's wat it is, I take it! (*motion toward desk*)
MADGE: Yes . . . We're awfully glad you turned up, Sid. We might of had to get in
            some stranger to do it! (*going in front of* PRINCE)
PRINCE: (*standing up and looking at them*) That would be nice, now, wouldn't it?
            If your game 'appens to be anything off color!
LARRABEE: Oh, — it isn't so specially dark.
PRINCE: That's different. (*Goes across to desk with tools from satchel.*) I say,
            Larrabee — (*quick 'Sh!' from* MADGE *just behind him*)
LARRABEE: (*at same time*) Shut up! (*They look round.* PRINCE *looks up sur-*
            prised.) For heaven's sake, Sid — remember! (*down to him*) My name is
            Chetwood here!
PRINCE: Oh! Beg your pardon — my mistake — old time wen we was learnin' the
            trade together — eh!
LARRABEE: Yes, yes!
PRINCE: What I was goin' to ask you, *Chetty*, old man — (MADGE *and*
            LARRABEE *glance round a little nervously.*) — was ware you picked up such
            a relic as this 'ere box! . . . (*about to try some tools on lock, looks about*) All
            clear, you say? No danger lurking?
LARRABEE: (*Shakes head.*) Not in the least! (MADGE *moves away a little,*
            glancing cautiously about. PRINCE *tries tools.* LARRABEE *remains near*
            piano.)
PRINCE: (*At lock. They watch him as he tries tools.*) You're not robbing *your-*
            selves, I trust?
LARRABEE: (*Remains near* PRINCE.) Well, it looks a bit like it!
PRINCE: I knew you was on some rum lay — squatting down in this 'ere place for
            over a year; but I never could seem to — (*Works.*) — get a line on you. (*He*
            works a moment and then crosses to get a tool out of satchel, which is near
            end of piano. Goes near light and begins to adjust it. Stops and looks sharply
            at MADGE *and* LARRABEE.) What do we get here — specie, I trust?
LARRABEE: Sorry to disappoint you, but it isn't.
PRINCE: That's too bad! (*near lamp on piano; light on him*)
MADGE: (*Shakes head.*) Only a bundle of papers, Sid.
PRINCE: (*Works at tool an instant before speaking.*) Pipers!
LARRABEE: Um.
PRINCE: Realize, I trust?
MADGE: Well, we can't tell — it may be something — it may be nothing. It won't
            be *much* at the best.
PRINCE: Well, if it's something, I'm in it, I trust? (*Goes a step or two toward*
            MADGE.)
MADGE: Why, of course, Sid — Whatever you think is due you for opening the box.

PRINCE: Fair enough! (*as if it was all settled to go on*) Hold, 'ere! (*Glances round quickly.*) 'efore we starts 'er goin' — what's the general surroundin's?

LARRABEE: Oh! What's the good of wasting time? (*going near* PRINCE)

PRINCE: (*up to him*) If I'm in this I'm *in* it, ain't I? An' I want to know *wat* I'm in.

MADGE: Why don't you tell him, Jim?

PRINCE: If anything 'appened, 'ow'd I get a line on 'em to shy out for?

LARRABEE: Well — I'm willing to give him an idea of what the matter is, but I won't give the name of the — (*Hesitates.*)

PRINCE: That's all I ask — *wat it is.* I don't want no names.

LARRABEE: (*nearer* PRINCE, *speaking lower*) Well, you know we've been working the continent — resorts and all that.

PRINCE: So I've 'eard.

> (MADGE *motions them to wait. Goes up center and left center looking off quietly. Nods to them to proceed.*)

LARRABEE: It was over there — Hamburg was the place. We came across a young girl who'd been having trouble. Her sister just died. Her mother seemed wrong here. (*Touches forehead.*)

PRINCE: Well — you run across 'er.

LARRABEE: Madge took hold of her and found that this sister of hers had been having some sort of a love affair with a man of exceedingly high rank — or at least — expectations that way.

PRINCE: 'Ow much was there to it?

LARRABEE: Promises of marriage.

PRINCE: Broke it, of course.

LARRABEE: Yes — and her heart with it. I don't know what more she expected — anyway she *did* expect more. She and her child died together.

PRINCE: Oh — dead!

> (MADGE *turns to* LARRABEE *and* PRINCE, *listening.*)

LARRABEE: Yes, but the *case isn't*! There are letters, photographs, jewelry with inscriptions that he gave her. The sister's been keeping them! . . . (*a glance about*) We've been keeping the sister! . . . You see?

PRINCE: (*Whistles.*) It's the sister you've got here? — An' what's 'er game?

LARRABEE: To get even! She waits till he wants to marry. Then she shows them up. That ends it!

PRINCE: Oh, ho! That's the lay!

LARRABEE: Precisely!

PRINCE: They ought to be worth a little something!

LARRABEE: I tell you it wouldn't be safe for him to marry until he gets them out of the way! He knows it very well. But what's more, the *family* knows it!

PRINCE: Oh — family! . . . Rich, I take it.

LARRABEE: Rich isn't the word. There's something else.

PRINCE: Why, you don't mean — (*down a step;* LARRABEE *moves nearer* PRINCE *and whispers a name in his ear.*) My Gawd! Which of 'em?

LARRABEE: (*Shakes head.*) I won't tell you that.

PRINCE: Well, we are a-movin' in 'igh society! (*Thinks about it. Turns toward* LARRABEE.) How did you manage the — (*Motions above.*)

LARRABEE: We did the generous friendly.

MADGE: Oh! I picked her up, of course, and sympathized and consoled. I invited her to stop with me at my house in London — Jimmy came on and got this place — and when I brought her along a week later it was all ready — including a private desk safe for the package of letters and jewelry.

LARRABEE: (*Turns.*) Yes — combination lock and all! . . . Everything went well till a couple of weeks ago, when we began to hear from the solicitors. Some veiled proposals were made which showed the time was coming. They wanted the things out of the way. Suddenly all negotiations on their part ceased. The next thing for me to do was to threaten. I wanted the letters for that, but when I went to get them I found that by some means the girl had changed the lock. The numbers were wrong — and we couldn't frighten or starve her into opening the thing.

PRINCE: Oh — I see it now! You've got the stuff in there! (*indicating safe*)

LARRABEE: That's what I'm telling you! It's in there and we can't get it out! She's juggled the lock!

PRINCE: (*going at once to safe*) Oh, well — it won't take long to rectify that triflin' error . . . (*Stops, looking front.*) But wot gets over me is wy they broke off with their offers that way — can you make head or tail of that?

LARRABEE: Ah! (*Goes nearer to* PRINCE.) It's simple enough. (PRINCE *turns to him for explanation.*) They've given it up themselves, and got Sherlock Holmes on the case.

PRINCE: (*suddenly starting up*) Wot's that! (*pause*) Is 'Olmes in this!

LARRABEE: So they told me!

MADGE: But what can he *do*, Sid? We haven't —

PRINCE: 'Ere! Don't stand talkin'! I'll get the box open. (*Goes to piano in front of* LARRABEE.) You send a telegram, that's all I want. (*Tears page out of note-book. Hurriedly writing, the other two watching.* LARRABEE *remains at right, a little suspiciously.*) Where's your nearest telegraph office?

MADGE: Round the corner on Rincon Street.

PRINCE: Alright, half a minute. (*Goes down to* LARRABEE *and gives him the telegram he has written.*) Run for it! Mind what I say — *run for it*! (LARRABEE *is looking at him hard.*) That's to Alf Bassick — he's Professor Moriarty's confidential man. Moriarty is the king of 'em all in London. Runs everything that is shady — an 'Olmes 'as been settin' lines all round him for months — and he didn't know it — Now he's beginning to find out that 'Olmes is trackin' 'im down there's the devil to pay! 'E wants any case 'Olmes is on — it's a dead fight between 'em! 'E'll take the case just to get at 'Olmes! 'E'll kill him before he gets through, you can lay all you've got on it.

LARRABEE: What are you telling him?

PRINCE: Nothing whatever except I've got a job on as I wants to see 'im about in the mornin'! Here! Read it yourself! (LARRABEE *looks at what* PRINCE *has written.*) Don't take all night to do it! You cawn't tell wat might 'appen! (*Crosses to safe.*)

MADGE: Go on, Jim! (LARRABEE *crosses to door left,* MADGE *following him.*)

LARRABEE: (*to* MADGE, *near door*) You keep your eyes open!

MADGE: Don't you worry!

  (*Exit* LARRABEE. MADGE *at door left looks after him. Quick sound of door closing outside left.* PRINCE *has dropped down to work — real work now — at desk. Short pause.* MADGE *stands watching* PRINCE *a moment. She moves over to near piano and picks up a book carelessly, which she glances at with perfect nonchalance.*)

MADGE: (*Speaks without taking eyes from book.*) I've heard of this Professor Moriarty.

PRINCE: If you 'aven't then you've been out in the woods!

MADGE: You say he's king of them all.

PRINCE: (*working*) Bloomin' h'emperor — that's wot I call 'im!

MADGE: He must be in a good many different things!

PRINCE: Ah, you might see it that way if you looked around an' didn't breathe too 'ard!

MADGE: What does he do?

PRINCE: I'll tell you one thing he does! (*Turns to her and rests a moment from work.*) Sits at 'ome — quiet an' easy — an' runs nearly every big operation that's on. All the clever boys are under 'im in one way or another, an' 'e 'olds 'em in his 'and without movin' a muscle! But if there's a slip and the police get wind of it there ain't never any 'old on *'im* — they can't touch 'im — an wot's more, they wouldn't want to do it if they could.

MADGE: Why not?

PRINCE: Because they've tried it — that's wy! An' the men as did try it was always found shortly after a-floatin' in the river — that is, if they was found at all! The moment a man's marked there ain't a street that's safe for 'im! No — nor yet an alley! (*Resumes drilling.*)

MADGE: (*after a pause*) How about him?

PRINCE: Square as a die, an' liberal into the bargain!

MADGE: But this isn't such a big case. He might not want —

PRINCE: (*Turns to her.*) I tell yer 'e'll take *anything* that gives him a chance at 'Olmes! He wants to trap him — that's what it is! An' that's just what he'll do! (*Resumes working rapidly, drill going in suddenly as if he had one hole sunk. He tries a few tools in it and quickly starts another hole with drills.*)

MADGE: (*Starts forward, then retreats, carelessly.*) Have you got it, Sid?

PRINCE: Not yet — but I'll be there soon. I know where I am now.

(*Sound of door closing outside left.* LARRABEE *enters at door up left hurriedly. He is breathless from running.*)

LARRABEE: How goes it?

PRINCE: So so.

LARRABEE: Now what about this Professor Moriarty? (*Gets chair from near piano and sits behind* PRINCE.)

PRINCE: Oh, ask 'er.

MADGE: It's all right, Jim. It was the proper thing to do! He can get twice as much on the things as *we* could!

(MADGE *and* LARRABEE *move near* PRINCE, *looming over him eagerly.* PRINCE *quickly introduces small punch and hammers rapidly. Sound of bolts falling inside lock as if loosened. Eagerness of all three increases with final sound of the loose iron work inside lock, and* PRINCE *at once pulls open the iron door. All three give a quick look within.* MADGE *and* LARRABEE *start back with subdued exclamations.* PRINCE *looks in more carefully, then turns to them. Pause.*)

MADGE: (*Turns to* LARRABEE.) Gone!

(*The dialogue drops to low excited tones, almost whispers, as they would if it were a robbery. Force of habit in their intense excitement.*)

LARRABEE: (*to* MADGE) She's taken 'em out!

PRINCE: (*Rises to his feet.*) What do you mean?

LARRABEE: The girl!

MADGE: (*Stops and goes quickly to safe in front of* PRINCE *and, dropping down, feels carefully about inside. Others watch her closely;* PRINCE *gives back a little for her. Rises and turns to* LARRABEE.) She's got them!

PRINCE: 'Ow can you tell if she's 'asn't done the trick already!

LARRABEE: (*Strides across to door left.*) I'll just get her down! She'll give them up now or strangle for it! (*Turns at door hurriedly.*) When I get her in, don't give her time to think. (*Exits.*)

(*Brief pause;* MADGE *glances nervously left.*)

PRINCE: Wot's 'e goin' to do?

MADGE: There's only one thing for it, Sid — we've got to get it out of her, or the whole two years' work is wasted.

(*Muffled cry of pain from* ALICE *in distance outside left.* MADGE *goes toward left nervously. Pause.*)

PRINCE: (*Glances off anxiously.*) I don't so much fancy this sort of thing. (*He goes to safe and collects tools.*)

MADGE: Don't you worry — we'll attend to it!

(*Sound of* LARRABEE *approaching and speaking angrily, nearer and nearer. Footsteps heard just before entrance.* LARRABEE *drags or pushes* ALICE FAULKNER *on at left, throwing or shoving her across him well onto the stage.*)

LARRABEE: (*as he brings* ALICE *on*) We'll *see* whether you will or not. (*Hold scene an instant.* LARRABEE *comes down a little.*) Now tell her what we want.

ALICE: (*low voice; slight shake of head*) You need not tell me. I know well enough.

MADGE: (*Drawing nearer to* ALICE *with quiet cat-like glide. Smiles.*) Oh, no, dear, you *don't* know! It isn't anything to do with locks, or keys, or numbers this time! (*Points slowly to the open safe at right.*) We want to know what you've *done* with them! (*Pause.* ALICE *looks at* MADGE *calmly, no defiance or suffering in her expression.* MADGE *comes closer and speaks with set teeth.*) Do you hear? We want to know what you've done with them!

ALICE: (*low voice, but clear and distinct*) You will not know from me.

LARRABEE: (*sudden violence, yet subdued, as if not wishing servants to overhear*) We *will* know from you — and we'll know before — (*as if to cross past* MADGE *to* ALICE)

MADGE: (*motioning him*) Wait, Jim! (*down with him a little*)

LARRABEE: (*to* MADGE *violently*) Why, they're in this room — she couldn't have got them out — and I'm going to make her — (*Turns as if to seize* ALICE.)

MADGE: (*detaining him*) No! Let me speak to her first! (LARRABEE *after an instant's sullen pause turns and walks away. Watches sullenly.* MADGE *turns to* ALICE *again.*) Don't you think, dear, it's about time to remember that you owe *us* a little consideration? Wasn't it something — just a little something, that we found you friendless and ill in Hamburg and befriended you?

ALICE: It was only to rob me!

MADGE: Wasn't it something that we brought you and your mother across to England with us — and have kept you here — in our own home — and supported and cared for you —

ALICE: So that you could rob me!

MADGE: My dear child — you have nothing of value — Why, that package of letters wouldn't bring sixpence —

ALICE: Then why do you want it? Why do you persecute me and starve me to get it? (*Pause;* MADGE *looks at her cruelly.*) All your friendship to me and my mother was a pretense — a sham. It was only to get what you wanted away from me when the time came!

MADGE: Why, we had no idea of such a thing!

ALICE: I don't believe you!

LARRABEE: (*who has controlled himself with difficulty, coming down to* ALICE) Well, believe me, then! (ALICE *turns to him, frightened but calm, with no forced expressions of pain and despair anywhere in this scene.*) You're going to tell us what you've done with that package before you leave this room to-night! (MADGE *backs away a step or two.*)

ALICE: Not if you kill me!

LARRABEE: (*seizing* ALICE *violently by the arms in back of her*) It isn't killing that's going to do it — but it's something else! (*He gets both her arms behind her, and holds her as if wrenching or twisting them from behind.* ALICE *gives slight cry of pain;* MADGE *comes to her side.* PRINCE *looks away during the following, appearing not to like the scene, but not moving.*)

MADGE: (*sharp, hard voice*) Tell us where it is! Tell us, and he'll stop!

LARRABEE: (*as if wrenching her arms*) Out with it!

ALICE: (*suppressed cry or moan*) Oh! (*She has as little expression of pain on her face as possible. The idea is to be game.*)

MADGE: Where is it?

LARRABEE: Speak quick, now! I'll give you a turn this time that'll take it out of you!

MADGE: Be careful, Jimmy!

LARRABEE: (*angry*) Is this any time to be careful? I tell you we've got to get it out of her — and we will! Will you tell? Will you tell? Will you —
(*Loud ringing of door bell in distant part of house*)

PRINCE: (*Turns quickly; short sharp whisper as he starts up.*) Look out!
(*All stand, listening an instant.* ALICE, *however, heard nothing, as the pain has made her faint, though not unconscious.*)

LARRABEE: (*to* MADGE; *low hoarse half whisper*) See who it is!
(*He pushes* ALICE *into chair facing fireplace, hiding her.* MADGE

*goes quickly down left side and cautiously draws picture away from
a small concealed window on left. LARRABEE stands near ALICE.
Steps heard outside. LARRABEE turns quickly.)*

LARRABEE: *(speaking off left)* Here! *(Enter FORMAN at door left; he stands
waiting.)* Don't go to that door! *(FORMAN simply waits; no surprise, no
looks, nothing. LARRABEE stands so that FORMAN will not see ALICE.)*

MADGE: *(standing on ottoman, speaking in a low but clear voice)* Tall slim man in
a long coat — soft hat — smooth face — carries a hunting crop.

PRINCE: *(Breaks in with quick exclamation under breath.)* Sherlock 'Olmes! *(Pause;
PRINCE quickly conceals his satchel at right above safe, closing safe door.)*

LARRABEE: Here! Put out the lights! *(Moves as if to do so.)* We won't answer the
bell.

PRINCE: *(Turns from tools, etc., and stops him quickly.)* No! No! That won't do,
ye know! Looks crooked at the start!

LARRABEE: You're right! We'll have him in — and come the easy innocent!

MADGE: But here's the girl!

PRINCE: Get her away — quick!

        (ALICE is beginning to notice what goes on in a dreamy way.)

LARRABEE: Take her up the back stairway!

MADGE: *(Takes ALICE quickly and forces her back to door up center as they
speak. Stops to speak to LARRABEE. Distinctly)* She's in very poor health
and can't see anyone — you understand?

LARRABEE: Yes! Yes! Lock her in the room — and stay by the door! *(MADGE
and ALICE quickly exit at door up center which LARRABEE closes at once
and stands front, uncertain for an instant. Pause. Doorbell rings again in
distance. Pause. LARRABEE opens lid of settle up near fireplace and gets a
loaded club, an ugly looking weapon, and shoves it into PRINCE's hand.)*
You get out that window! *(Indicates.)* Keep quiet there till he gets in the
house, then come round to the front.

PRINCE: I come round to the front after 'e's in the 'ouse — that's plain!

LARRABEE: Be ready for 'im when he comes out! If he's got the things in spite of
us, I'll give you two sharp whistles! If you don't hear them, let him pass!

PRINCE: But if I do 'ear the two wistles — ?

LARRABEE: Then let 'im have it! *(Gets PRINCE off at window up right which he
closes at once and moves rapidly down, kicking door of desk shut as he
passes. Stands at piano, leaning on it carelessly. Turns to FORMAN.)* Go on,
answer the bell.

        *(FORMAN bows slightly and exits at door up left. LARRABEE
strolls about, trying to get into an attitude of coolness. Picks up
book off piano. Sound of heavy door closing outside left. Brief
pause. Enter SHERLOCK HOLMES at door up left, hat and stick
in his hand, wearing a long coat or ulster and gloves. He lingers near
the door apparently seeing nothing in particular and slowly drawing
off gloves. Then moves toward a chair close at hand not far from the
door and well up stage. After quite a time LARRABEE turns, throws
book on piano, and saunters toward HOLMES in rather an osten-
tatious manner.)*

LARRABEE: Mr Holmes, I believe.

HOLMES: (*turning to* LARRABEE *as if mildly surprised*) Yes, sir.

LARRABEE: Who did you wish to see, Mr Holmes?

HOLMES: (*Looking steadily at* LARRABEE *an instant. Speaks very quietly.*)
Thank you so much, I sent my card — by the butler.

LARRABEE: (*Stands motionless an instant. After an instant's pause*) Oh — very
well. (*Turns and strolls about.*)
> (*Long pause. Enter* FORMAN, *coming down the stairway and to the
> door at up left.* LARRABEE *moves up near piano and turns to hear
> what* FORMAN *says.*)

FORMAN: (*to* HOLMES) Miss Faulkner begs Mr Holmes to excuse her. She is not
well enough to see anyone this evening.

HOLMES: (*Takes out note book and pencil and writes a word or two on a card or
leaf of the book. Tears it out. Pulls out watch and glances at it. Hands the
card to* FORMAN.) Hand Miss Faulkner this — and say I have —

LARRABEE: (*near piano*) I beg your pardon, Mr Holmes, but it's quite useless —
really!

HOLMES: (*Turns quietly to* LARRABEE *and looks at him.*) Oh — I'm so sorry to
hear it!

LARRABEE: (*a trifle affected by* HOLMES' *quiet scrutiny*) Miss Faulkner is — I
regret to say — quite an invalid — and can see no one.

HOLMES: Did it ever occur to you that she might be confined to the house too
much? (*an instant's pause*)

LARRABEE: (*suddenly, in low threatening tone, but not too violent*) Well, how
does that concern you?

HOLMES: (*easily*) It doesn't — I simply made the suggestion. (*The two look at one
another an instant.* HOLMES *turns quietly to* FORMAN.) That's all. (*Motions
him slightly.*) Go on. Take it up.
> (*Exit* FORMAN *at left and up stairway.*)

LARRABEE: (*Turns after a moment, breaking into hearty laughter.*) Why, of
course he can take up your card — or your note, — or whatever it is, if you
wish it so much! I merely desired to save you the trouble!

HOLMES: (*watching him through foregoing speech*) Oh! Thanks — it's very little
trouble to send a card. (*Seats himself in an easy, languid way — picks up
'Punch'.*)

LARRABEE: (*Turns; endeavors to be easy, careless, and patronizing.*) Do you
know, Mr Holmes, you interest me very much!

HOLMES: (*easily*) Ah!

LARRABEE: We've all heard of your wonderful methods — (*coming toward
HOLMES*) — your marvelous insight — your ingenuity in picking up and
following clues — and the astonishing manner in which you gain evidence
from the most trifling details — Now I dare say — in this brief moment or two
you've discovered all sorts of things about me!

HOLMES: Oh, nothing of consequence, Mr Chetwood. I've hardly more than asked
myself why you rushed off and sent that telegram in such a frightful hurry —
what possible excuse you could have had for gulping down a half a tumbler of
raw brandy at the Lion's Head on your way back — why your friend with the

auburn hair left so suddenly by the terrace window, − and what there can possibly be about the empty safe in the lower part of that desk that causes you such painful anxiety.

> (*Pause.* LARRABEE *stands motionless looking at* HOLMES. HOLMES *picks up a paper and reads.*)

LARRABEE: Ha! Ha! − very good! If those things were only true I'd be wonderfully impressed. It would be absolutely − (*Breaks.*)

> (*Enter* FORMAN, *coming down stairway and on at door left. He quietly crosses to* LARRABEE *who is watching him and extends salver with a note upon it.* HOLMES *is looking over paper languidly.*)

LARRABEE: (*Takes note.*) You'll excuse me, I trust. (HOLMES *remains silent, glancing over paper.* LARRABEE *reads the note hastily. First a second's thought after reading − as he sees that* HOLMES *is not observing him. Then he speaks.*) Ah − it's from Miss Faulkner! She begs to be allowed to see you, Mr Holmes. She actually implores it. (HOLMES *looks slowly up as though scarcely interested.*) Well, I suppose I must give way. (*Turns to* FORMAN.) Judson − *ask Miss Faulkner* to come down to the drawing room. Say Mr Holmes is waiting to see her. (FORMAN *bows and exits left and up the stairway.* LARRABEE *tries to get on the free and easy style again.*) This is most remarkable, upon my word! May I ask (*Turns toward* HOLMES.), if it's not an impertinent question, what message you sent up that could have so aroused Miss Faulkner's desire to come down?

HOLMES: (*looking up at* LARRABEE *innocently*) Merely that if she wasn't down here in five minutes I'd go up.

LARRABEE: (*slightly knocked*) Oh, that was it! (*Goes into fireplace alcove.*)

HOLMES: Quite so. (*Rises. Watches out easily.*) An if I'm not (*in front of* LARRABEE) mistaken, I hear the young lady on the stairs. In which case she has a minute and a half to spare. (*Goes near piano; takes opportunity to look at keys.*)

> (*Enter* MADGE, *coming down the stairway as if not quite strong, and entering the room at door up left. She has made her face pale, and steadies herself a little by columns, side of arch, furniture, etc., as she comes on. She gives the impression of a person who is a little weak, but endeavoring not to let it be seen.*)

LARRABEE: (*advancing to* MADGE) Alice − or − that is, Miss Faulkner, let me introduce Mr Sherlock Holmes.

> (HOLMES *is near piano.* MADGE *goes a step to him with extended hand.* HOLMES *meets* MADGE *and takes her hand in the utmost confidence.* LARRABEE *quietly draws away behind piano.*)

MADGE: Mr Holmes!

HOLMES: Miss Faulkner!

MADGE: I'm more than charmed to meet you − although it does look as if you had made me come down in spite of myself, doesn't it? But it isn't so at all, Mr Holmes; I was more than anxious to come, only the doctor has forbidden my seeing anyone − but when Cousin Freddie said I might come, why of course that fixed the responsibility on him, so I have a perfectly clear conscience!

HOLMES: I thank you very much indeed for consenting to see me, Miss Faulkner, and I'm particularly pleased that any possible damage to your health may be charged to Cousin Freddie.

MADGE: (*slight gasp*) Oh — yes — certainly! Charged to Cousin Freddie! (*Crosses near* LARRABEE.) That's one on you, isn't it?

LARRABEE: Yes — you'd have heard another on me if you'd been here a moment sooner. Mr Holmes has been telling me some extraordinary things!

MADGE: (*enthusiastic delight, turning to* HOLMES) Oh! How interesting! (*to* LARRABEE) Do tell me! What did he say? Was it right? (*Sits in seat at end of piano.* HOLMES *crosses slowly and sits on settle, giving a sharp glance to picture.*)

LARRABEE: Not absolutely correct — but interesting, nevertheless.

MADGE: (*forced enthusiasm*) Well, what did he say? Do tell me!

LARRABEE: I'm not sure that I can recall it — precisely — the first was something about sending a telegram — and taking a drink somewhere. But the other was the thing. He wanted to know what there was in the safe in the lower part of that desk that caused me such horrible anxiety!

MADGE: Why, there isn't anything. (*to* HOLMES) Is there? (*to* LARRABEE)

LARRABEE: That's just it! Ha! Ha! Ha! (*With a quick motion, swings back the doors.*) There's a safe there — but there's nothing in it!

MADGE: (*Joins him in laughter.*) Oh, really, Mr Holmes, this is too grotesque!
(HOLMES, *easily seated among the cushions, regards* MADGE *and* LARRABEE *with a peculiar whimsical look.*)

LARRABEE: (*laughing*) Yes, perhaps you'll do better next time!

MADGE: Yes, next time — (HOLMES *looks at them.*) you might try on me, Mr Holmes. (*Looks playfully at* HOLMES, *as if greatly enjoying the lark.*)

LARRABEE: What do you think of her?

HOLMES: It's very easy to discern one thing about Miss Faulkner — and that is, that she is particularly fond of the piano — her touch is exquisite, her expression wonderful and her technique extraordinary. While she likes light music very well, she is extremely fond of some of the great masters among whom may be mentioned Chopin, Liszt, and Schubert. She plays a great deal; indeed, I see it is her chief diversion — which makes it all the more remarkable that she has not touched the piano for three days! (*pause*)

MADGE: (*Turns to* LARRABEE, *a trifle disconcerted by* HOLMES' *last words, but nearly hiding it with success.*) Why, that's quite surprising, isn't it?

LARRABEE: Certainly better than he did for me. (*Remains leaning on chair, crossing legs, near piano.*)

HOLMES: I'm glad to more nearly approach your views, Mr Chetwood — (*rising*) — and as a reward will Miss Faulkner be so good as to play me something of which I am particularly fond?

MADGE: Why, I shall be delighted — if I can! (*Looks questioningly at* HOLMES.)

HOLMES: If you can! Ah! Something tells me that Chopin's Prelude Number Fifteen is at your finger ends. (LARRABEE *moves down with a look of uneasiness.*)

MADGE: Oh, yes! (*rising and forgetting her illness, going to keyboard, crossing in front of piano*) I can give you that!

HOLMES: It would please me so much.

MADGE: (*Stops suddenly as she is about to sit at piano.*) Oh, but tell me, Mr Holmes, how did you know so much about my playing — my expression — my technique?

HOLMES: Your hands.

MADGE: And my preference for the composers you mentioned?

HOLMES: Your music rack.

MADGE: Oh! How simple! But you said I hadn't played for three days — how did —

HOLMES: The keys.

MADGE: The keys?

HOLMES: A touch of London's smoky atmosphere.

MADGE: Dust! Oh dear me! (*handkerchief on keyboard*) Why, I never knew Terese to forget before. (*to* HOLMES) You must think us very untidy, I'm sure?

HOLMES: (*near bell crank*) Quite the reverse. One can easily see from many things that you're not untidy in the least, and therefore I am compelled to conclude that the failure of Terese was due to something else.

MADGE: (*a little under breath, and hesitatingly, yet compelled by* HOLMES' *pointed statement to ask*) Wh-what?

HOLMES: To some unusual excitement or disturbance that has recently taken place in this house.

MADGE: (*after an instant's pause*) Ph! You're doing very well, Mr Holmes — and you deserve your Chopin. (*Sits and makes preparations to play rather hurriedly in order to change the subject.*)

HOLMES: (*near bell*) How kind you are!

> (LARRABEE *looks to safe, far from easy in his mind; leans on piano.* MADGE *strikes a few preliminary chords during above, and soon begins to play the piece. Shortly after the music begins, and while* LARRABEE *is looking to front or elsewhere,* HOLMES *reaches quietly back and pulls the bell crank. No sound of bell is heard; the music makes it inaudible. He then sinks into seat. After a short time* FORMAN *enters at door up left and stands waiting just within door.* LARRABEE *does not see* FORMAN *at first, but happening to turn, discovers him standing there and speaks a warning word to* MADGE *under his breath.* MADGE *looks up, sees* FORMAN, *and stops playing in midst of a bar. A hesitating stop. Looks at* FORMAN *a moment.*)

MADGE: What are you doing here, Judson?

FORMAN: (*Brief pause; seems surprised.*) I came to see what was wanted, ma'am.
> (*Brief pause*)

MADGE: What was wanted?
> (*Brief pause*)

LARRABEE: No one sent for you.

FORMAN: I beg pardon, sir. I answered the bell!

LARRABEE: (*becoming savage*) What bell?

FORMAN: The drawing-room bell, sir.

LARRABEE: (*threateningly*) What do you mean, you blockhead?

FORMAN: I'm quite sure it rung, sir!

LARRABEE: (*loud voice*) Well, I tell you the bell did not ring!
>   (*Pause. The* LARRABEES *look angrily at* FORMAN.)
HOLMES: (*quietly; after slight pause. Clear, incisive voice.*) Your butler is right, Mr
>   Chetwood — the bell *did* ring.
>   (*Brief pause;* LARRABEE *and* MADGE *look at* HOLMES. MADGE
>   — *after short pause — rises slowly at piano.*)
LARRABEE: How do you know?
HOLMES: I rang it.
LARRABEE: (*roughly*) What do you want?
HOLMES: (*Rises, takes card from case.*) I want to send my card to Miss Faulkner.
>   (*Gives card to* FORMAN, *who stands apparently paralyzed.*)
LARRABEE: (*angrily approaching* HOLMES) What right have you to ring for
>   servants and give orders in my house! (MADGE *moves down right a little.*)
HOLMES: (*Turns on* LARRABEE.) What right have you to prevent my cards from
>   reaching their destination — and how does it happen that you and this woman
>   are resorting to trickery and deceit to prevent me from seeing Alice Faulkner?
>   (*Pause an instant. Turns quietly to* FORMAN.) Through some trifling over-
>   sight, Judson, neither of the cards I handed you has been delivered. See that
>   this *error* — does not occur again.
FORMAN: (*Stands apparently uncertain what to do.*) My orders, sir —
HOLMES: (*quick — sharp*) Ah! you have orders! (*a sudden sharp glance at*
>   LARRABEE *and back in an instant*)
FORMAN: I can't say, sir, as I —
HOLMES: (*Breaks in quickly.*) You were told not to deliver my card!
LARRABEE: (*step or two up*) What business of yours is this, I'd like to know!
HOLMES: I'll satisfy your curiosity on that point in a very short time!
LARRABEE: You'll understand in a very short time it isn't safe to meddle with
>   me! It wouldn't be any trouble at all for me to throw you into the street!
HOLMES: (*Saunters toward him.*) Possibly not — but trouble would swiftly follow
>   such an experiment on your part!
LARRABEE: (*Turns and goes down a few steps.*) It's a cursed lucky thing for you
>   I'm not armed!
HOLMES: Yes — well, when Miss Faulkner comes down you can go and arm your-
>   self.
LARRABEE: (*Faces front.*) Arm myself! I'll call for the police! And what's more
>   I'll do it now!
HOLMES: (*Faces* LARRABEE.) You will *not* do it now! You will remain precisely
>   where you are till the young lady I came to see has entered this room!
LARRABEE: What makes you so sure of that?
HOLMES: (*in his face*) Because you will infinitely prefer to avoid an investigation
>   of your very suspicious conduct, Mr James Larrabee — (*a sharp start from*
>   LARRABEE *as well as* MADGE *on hearing* HOLMES *address them by their*
>   *proper names*) — an investigation that shall certainly take place if you or your
>   wife presume further to interfere with my business. (HOLMES *turns and goes*
>   *to* FORMAN.) As for you, my man — it gives me pleasure to recall the
>   features of an old acquaintance. Your recent connection with the signing of
>   another man's name to a small piece of paper, has made your presence at

headquarters much desired. You will either deliver that card to Miss Faulkner at once — or you'll sleep in the police station tonight. It's a matter of small consequence to me which you do. (*Turns and strolls up near fire.*)

FORMAN: (*Motionless but torn with conflicting fears. Finally, in a low, painful voice, whispers hoarsely.*) Shall I — shall I go, sir?

      (MADGE *moves near* LARRABEE.)

LARRABEE: Take up the card — it makes no difference to me.

      (*Exit* FORMAN.)

MADGE: (*quick, sharp, aside to* LARRABEE) If she comes down, can he get them away from her?

LARRABEE: (*to* MADGE) If he does, Sid Prince'll break his head open. (*Turns away and goes to piano.* MADGE *moves near him.* HOLMES *is a step or two down from the fireplace. A pause. No one moves.*)

      (*Enter* ALICE FAULKNER *at door up left. She comes down a little, very weak, looking at* HOLMES *and leaning on table.*)

HOLMES: (*Above piano. After brief pause, turns to* LARRABEE.) A short time since you displayed an acute anxiety to leave the room — Pray do not let me detain you or your wife any longer.

      (*The* LARRABEES *do not move; they are turned away. After brief pause* HOLMES *shrugs shoulders slightly and goes to* ALICE. *They regard each other a moment.*)

ALICE: This is Mr Holmes?

HOLMES: Yes.

ALICE: And you wished to see me?

HOLMES: Very much indeed, but I am sorry to see that — (*placing a chair near her*) — you are far from well.

      (LARRABEE *gives a quick glance across at her threateningly, possibly making a gesture of warning.*)

ALICE: (*Comes a step down.*) Oh no — I — (*Stops as she catches* LARRABEE's *angry glance.*)

HOLMES: (*Pauses as he is about to place chair and looks at her.*) No? (HOLMES *lets go of chair.*) I really beg your pardon, Miss Faulkner, but — (*Goes to her and takes her hand delicately — looks at red marks on wrist. Looks up at her.*) What does this mean?

ALICE: (*Shrinking a little; sees* LARRABEE's *cruel glance.*) Oh — nothing.

HOLMES: (*Looks steadily at her an instant.*) Nothing!

ALICE: (*shaking hand*) No!

HOLMES: And the — (*pointing lightly*) — mark here on your neck plainly showing the clutch of a man's fingers? (*Indicates a place on her neck where more marks appear.*) — Does that mean nothing — also? (*Pause. He looks straight before him to front.*) It occurs to me that I should like to have an explanation of this . . . Possibly . . . (*Turns slowly toward* LARRABEE.) you can furnish one, Mr Larrabee! (*pause*)

LARRABEE: (*doggedly*) How should I know?

HOLMES: It seems to have occurred in your own house.

LARRABEE: (*Advances a little; becomes violently angry.*) What if it did? You'd better understand it isn't safe to meddle with my business.

HOLMES: (*quickly; incisively*) Ah! Then it *is* your business! We have that much at least. (LARRABEE *stops suddenly and holds himself in.* HOLMES *turns to* ALICE.) Pray be seated, Miss Faulkner. (*placing chair*)
> (ALICE *hesitates an instant, then decides to remain standing for the present.* LARRABEE *moves near end of piano and openly stands watching and listening to interview between* HOLMES *and* ALICE.)

ALICE: I do not know who you are, Mr Holmes, or why you are here.

HOLMES: I shall be very glad indeed to explain. So far as the question of my identity is concerned, you have my name and address as well as the announcement of my profession upon the card, which I observe you still hold clasped tightly in the fingers of your left hand.

ALICE: (*At once looks at the card in her hand, then looks at* HOLMES.) A — detective!

HOLMES: (*Draws chair near her and sits.*) Quite so. And my business is this. I have been consulted as to the possibility of obtaining from you certain letters and other things which are supposed to be in your possession, and which — I need not tell you are a source of the greatest anxiety.

ALICE: (*Her manner changes. She is no longer timid and shrinking.*) It is true that I have such letters, Mr Holmes, but it will be impossible to get them from me. *Others* . . . have tried — and failed!

HOLMES: What others have or have not done, while possibly instructive in certain directions, can in no way affect my conduct, Miss Faulkner. I have come to you, frankly and directly, to beg you to pity and forgive.

ALICE: There are some things, Mr Holmes, that are beyond pity — beyond forgiveness.

HOLMES: But there are other things that are not. (ALICE *looks at him.*) I am able to assure you of the sincere penitence — the deep regret — of the one who inflicted the injury and of his earnest desire to make — any reparation in his power.

ALICE: How can reparation be made to the dead?

HOLMES: How indeed! And for that very reason whatever injury you yourself may be able to inflict by means of these things can be no reparation — no satisfaction — no indemnity to the one no longer here. You will be acting for the *living* — not the dead! For your *own* gratification — your own revenge!
> (ALICE *starts slightly at the idea suggested. Pause.* HOLMES *rises, moves his chair back a little, standing with hand on it.*)

ALICE: (*Rises; stands a moment. Very quiet, low voice.*) I know — from this — and from other things that have happened — that a marriage is — contemplated.

HOLMES: It is quite true.

ALICE: I cannot give up what I mean to do. There are other things besides revenge — there is punishment. If I cannot communicate with the family — to which this man proposes to ally himself — in time to prevent such a thing — the punishment will come later. But you may be perfectly sure it will come! (HOLMES *is about to speak; she motions him not to.*) There is nothing more to say! (HOLMES *gives signal. She looks up at* HOLMES *an instant.*) Good night, Mr Holmes! (*She turns and goes toward door up left.*)

HOLMES: But my dear Miss Faulkner, before you —

(*A confused noise of shouting and terrified screams from below
followed by sounds of people running up a stairway and through the
halls*)

HOLMES: What's that? (*Goes up to door right center.* ALICE, *hearing noise, stops
and comes down.*)

(*All stop and listen. Noise louder. Enter* FORMAN *at door up left,
running to door breathless and white. At same time, smoke pours in
through door up left and from doors of entrances up stage.*)

FORMAN: (*gasping*) Mr Chetwood! Mr Chetwood!

MADGE *and* LARRABEE: (*moving across toward him*) What is it? Speak out!

(HOLMES *moves quietly up above piano, keeping his eyes sharply
on* ALICE. *She stands back alarmed.*)

FORMAN: The lamp — in the kitchen, sir! It fell off the table — an' everything
down there is blazin', sir!

(ALICE *gives a scream and looks quickly at a chair up center at the
same time making an involuntary start toward it. She stops upon
seeing* HOLMES, *and stands.*)

MADGE: Oh! The house — is on fire! (*She gives an involuntary start and glance
toward safe, forgetting that the package is gone. Instantly recovers and
hurries toward door left.*)

(LARRABEE *with one bound exits at door up left.* MADGE *exits
after him, followed by* FORMAN. *Noise of people running down
stairs, growing less and dying away outside left and below.*)

HOLMES: Don't alarm yourself, Miss Faulkner (*slight shake of head*), there is no
fire!

ALICE: (*a step back, showing by her tone that she fears something*) No fire!
(*Stands dreading what may come.*)

HOLMES: The smoke was all I arranged for. (*slight pause*)

ALICE: Arranged for? (*Looks at* HOLMES.)

(HOLMES *moves up to large upholstered chair which* ALICE
glanced at and made start toward a moment since.)

ALICE: What does it mean, Mr Holmes? No! No! No!

(HOLMES *feels rapidly over chair. Rips away upholstery.* ALICE
*attempts to stop him, but is too late and backs to piano almost in a
fainting condition.* HOLMES *stands erect with a package in his
hand.*)

HOLMES: That I wanted this package of papers, Miss Faulkner.

(ALICE *stands looking at* HOLMES *speechless, motionless. She
meets his gaze for a moment and then covers her face with her
hands, and there is a very slight motion of convulsive sob or two.*
HOLMES *with a quick motion steps quickly and in a business-like
way to the chair where his coat, hat, and cane are and picks up coat,
throwing it over his arm, as if to go at once. As he is about to take
his hat he catches sight of* ALICE's *face and stops dead where he is.
Stands looking at her motionless. She soon looks up at him again,
brushing hand across her face as if to clear away any sign of crying.
Pause.* HOLMES' *eyes leave her face and he glances downward. After*

a moment he lays his coat back on chair, keeping cane in hand. Pauses an instant, then turns toward her.)

HOLMES: (*low voice*) I won't take them, Miss Faulkner. (*He looks down an instant. Her eyes are upon his face steadily.*) As you – (*still looking down*) – as you – very likely conjecture, the – alarm of fire was only to make you betray their hiding place – which you did. And I – availed myself of that betrayal – as you see. But now that I witness your great distress – I find that I cannot keep them. Unless – (*looking up at her*) – you can – possibly – change your mind and let me have them – of your own free will . . . (*He looks at her a moment. She shakes her head very slightly.*) I hardly supposed you could. (*Looks down a moment, then up.*) I will therefore – return them to you. (*Very slight pause and he is about to start toward her as if to hand her the package.*)

(*Sound of quick footsteps outside. Enter* LARRABEE *at door up left with a revolver in his hand, followed by* MADGE.)

LARRABEE: You've got them, have you? And now I suppose we're going to see you walk out of the house with them! (*Handles revolver with meaning.*)

HOLMES: (*Looks quietly at* LARRABEE *an instant.*) On the contrary, you're going to see me return them to their rightful owner.

LARRABEE: (*with revolver*) Yes – I think that's about the safest thing for Mr Sherlock Holmes to do!

HOLMES: (*Stops dead and looks at* LARRABEE. *Walks quietly down facing him.*) You flatter yourself, Mr Larrabee. The reason I do not leave the house with this package of papers is not because of you, or what you may do – or say – or think – or feel! It's on account of this young lady! I care *that* for you and your cheap bravado! (HOLMES *looks quietly in his eyes an instant, then turns and goes to* ALICE.) Miss Faulkner, permit me to place this in your hands. (*Gives her the package. She takes it with sudden eagerness, then turns and keeps her eyes steadily on* HOLMES.) Should you ever change your mind and be so generous – so forgiving as to wish to return these letters to the one who wrote them, you have my address. In any event rest assured there will be no more cruelty, no more persecution in this house. You are perfectly safe with your property now – for I shall so arrange it that your faintest cry of distress will be heard! And if that cry *is* heard – it will be a very unfortunate thing for those who are responsible! Good night, Miss Faulkner.

(*Pause.* ALICE *looks at* HOLMES *an instant, uncertain what to do. He makes a slight motion indicating her to go. After a slight pause she crosses in front of* HOLMES *and exits at door up left.* HOLMES *waits, motionless, eyes on* ALICE *until her exit, and he looks off after her for a moment, then turns and takes his coat and hat. Turns to* LARRABEE *and* MADGE, *coming down to them.*)

HOLMES: As for you, sir, and you, madam, I beg you to understand that you continue your persecution of that young lady *at your peril*! (*Looks at them an instant.*) Good evening. (*Walks out at door up left, and the sound of heavy outside door closing is heard outside left.*)

(*Pause.* LARRABEE *and* MADGE *stand where* HOLMES *left them. Sound of window right opening.* PRINCE *hurries in.*)

PRINCE: (*sharp but subdued*) 'E didn't get it did 'e? (LARRABEE *shakes head;*
PRINCE *looks at him puzzled and then turns toward* MADGE.) Well — wat is
it? — Wat's the pay if 'e didn't?

MADGE: He gave it to *her!*

PRINCE: What! — 'E found it! (MADGE *indicates yes by slight movement.*) An'
gave it to the girl! (MADGE *repeats slight affirmative motion.*) Well 'ere — I
say! — Wat are you waitin' for! Now's your chance — before she 'ides it again!
(*Starts as if to go off left.*)

MADGE: (*Stops* PRINCE.) No! — Wait! (*She glances round nervously.*)

PRINCE: Wat's the matter! (*going to* LARRABEE) Do you want to lose it!

LARRABEE: (*Turns suddenly.*) No! — You're right! It's all a cursed bluff! (*Starts
as if to go off left.*)

MADGE: (*Meets them, as if to stop them.*) No, no, Jim!

LARRABEE: I tell you now's our time to get it — and we will!

(*Just as* PRINCE *and* LARRABEE *reach door left a distant sound of
three heavy blows as if struck from underneath up against the floor,
reverberates through the house. All stop motionless. Pause.*)

LARRABEE: (*low voice*) What's that?

MADGE: (*low voice*) Someone at the door!

LARRABEE: No — it was on that side! (*Indicates up stage.*)

(PRINCE *glances round alarmed.* MADGE *rings the bell. Pause.
Enter* FORMAN *at door up center. All stand easily as if nothing is
out of the usual.*)

MADGE: I think someone knocked, Judson.

(FORMAN *at once crosses quietly but quickly to left and exits.
Sound of door outside closing again.* FORMAN *re-enters.*)

FORMAN: I beg pardon, ma'am, there's no one at the door.

MADGE: That's all. (*Exit* FORMAN *at door left.*)

PRINCE: (*Speaks almost in whisper.*) 'E's got us watched! Now wat we want to do
is to leave it alone an' let the Hemperor 'ave it!

MADGE: (*low voice; taking a step or two toward* PRINCE) Do you mean —
Professor Moriarty? (LARRABEE *turns to* PRINCE.)

PRINCE: That's 'oo I mean! Once let *'im* get at it an 'e'll settle it with 'Olmes
pretty quick! (*Turns to* LARRABEE.) Meet me at Leary's — nine sharp
— in the morning. (*Looks at door left quickly and turns to them again.*)
Don't you worry a minute! I tell you the Professor'll get at 'im before
to-morrow night! 'E don't wait long either! An wen 'e strikes — it means
death.

(PRINCE *exits at window up right. Brief pause.* MADGE *crosses
stage and looks after him from above piano.* LARRABEE *crosses
slowly and, suddenly feeling revolver in his hip pocket, snatches it
out and makes a start for door where* HOLMES *went out. Stops
suddenly, thinks it hopeless, throws revolver away, and with a
despairing look on his face, sinks on to ottoman as light fades
away.*)

CURTAIN

SECOND ACT

First Scene

Scene. *Professor Moriarty's underground office. A large vault-like room, with rough masonry walls, and vaulted ceiling. The general idea of this place is that it has been converted from a cellar room of a warehouse into a fairly comfortable office or headquarters. No windows. Solid large door up left center in flat. Dark stone basement corridor backing. This door has various mechanical and electric devices for bolting, opening, closing, to operate as described in Act. A smaller door down right. Both these doors with very deep thickness; setting them back in wall, and then showing its solidity. Up right an archway has been planked up solid (all painted work), planks dark and grimy. Maps and charts have been tacked to this planking as high up as one could reach. Large heavy writing-desk up center against flat. Books, ledgers, etc., in cases above it. Railway guides hanging. Heavy swinging desk chair. Other chairs. Telephones, speaking tubes, push buttons at right end of desk. A long writing table at left against wall. Racks of papers, books. Room lighted by gas brackets. The color or tone of this set must not be similar to the 3rd Act set, which is a gloomy and dark bluish brown. Effect in this set of masonry that has long ago been whitewashed and is now old, stained and grimy. Maps on wall are railroad maps of England, France, Germany, Russia. Also a marked map of London – heavy spots upon certain localities. Also many charts of buildings, plan of floors, possible tunnelings. Many books about on impoverished shelves. Doyle's description of* PROFESSOR MORIARTY: *Extremely tall and thin. His forehead domes out in a white curve and his two eyes are deeply sunken in his head. Clean-shaven, pale, ascetic looking. Shoulders rounded, and his face protrudes forward and is forever slowly oscillating from side to side in a curiously reptilian fashion. 'He peered at me with his curiously puckered eyes.' Deep hollow voice.*

PROFESSOR ROBERT MORIARTY *is seated at a large desk up center with his back to audience. He is looking over letters, telegrams, papers, as if morning mail. He is a middle aged man, with massive head, gray hair, and a face full of character, overhanging brow, heavy jaw. A man of great intellectual force.* JOHN, *a clerk, is working at desk left, posting up accounts. He faces the wall.*

JOHN: The whole amount comes to fourteen hundred eighteen and six.

MORIARTY: Take out the half and divide the rest between the three.

JOHN: Yes, sir.

MORIARTY: (*Looks up.*) Wait. (JOHN *looks at him.*) Who was in that?

JOHN: Leary, O'Hagan, and The Seraph.

MORIARTY: I'll not take half. It was a hard piece of work – and Leary got a bullet in his shoulder while they were getting out with the haul. Put me down for one quarter of it. What did Davidson turn in last week from that Railway office haul at Chibley?

JOHN: (*Quickly turns leaves of a book, looking for item.*) Four hundred twenty-eight, fourteen-four.

MORIARTY: That man is holding back on us. Make a note for Bassick.

JOHN: Yes, sir.

(*Peculiar signal ring of electric bell or strong bell-buzzer*)

JOHN: He's here now, sir.

> (MORIARTY *touches a lever on his desk and a bolt slides back on the door. Door opens. Enter* ALFRED BASSICK, *with packet of papers, which he puts on desk; a solid fine-appearing man of 40 or so. Black hair and eyes; alert; strong; yet showing by some sinister trait or look what his character is. He goes at once to* MORIARTY *at desk and is about to speak upon some important business.*)

MORIARTY: Before we go into anything else I want to refer to Davidson.

BASSICK: I've got him down myself, sir. He's holding back!

MORIARTY: Something like six hundred short on that last haul, isn't it?

BASSICK: Certainly as much as that.

MORIARTY: Have him attended to. Craigin is the one to do it. (BASSICK *sitting at end of* MORIARTY's *desk writing a memo quickly*) And see that his disappearance is noticed. Have it spoken of. That finishes Davidson. Now as to this Blaisdell matter — did you learn anything more?

BASSICK: The whole thing was a trap!

MORIARTY: What do you mean?

BASSICK: A trap set and baited by an expert —

MORIARTY: But those letters and papers of instructions — you brought them back or destroyed them, I trust?

BASSICK: I could not do it, sir — Manning has disappeared and the papers are gone!

MORIARTY: (*Looks at him. Rises. Brief pause.*) This is Sherlock Holmes again. (*Turns and paces the floor heavily a moment; moves up to* BASSICK.) That's bad for the Underwood trial!

BASSICK: I thought Shackelford was going to get a postponement!

MORIARTY: (*Stops; shakes head. Slight pause before speaking and stops and faces front.*) He tried to — found he was blocked!

BASSICK: Who could have done it? (MORIARTY *turns and looks at him almost hypnotically, his head vibrating from side to side as if making him speak the name.*) Sherlock Holmes!

MORIARTY: Sherlock Holmes again. (*He nods slowly several times, his eyes still fixing* BASSICK. JOHN *looks up from his work, and both look at* MORIARTY *awe-struck during following speech.* BASSICK *as if fascinated by* MORIARTY. *Slight affirmative motion.*) He's got hold of between twenty and thirty papers and instructions in as many different jobs, and some as to putting a man or two out of the way — and he's gradually completing chains of evidence that if we let him go on will reach to me as sure as I stand here! Reach to me! Ha! (*Sneer. He turns away to front.*) He's playing rather a dangerous game, Bassick! Inspector Wilson tried it seven years ago. Wilson is dead. Two years later Henderson took it up. We haven't heard anything of Henderson, lately. Eh?

BASSICK: (*Shakes head.*) Not a thing, sir!

MORIARTY: Ha! (*sneer*) This Holmes is rather a talented man, but he doesn't realize what can happen between now and Monday! He doesn't know that there isn't a street in London that'll be safe for him if I whisper his name to Craigin! A van may strike him as he crosses the street — a piece of timber may fall from a scaffold — a little push from an underground platform — I might even make him a little call myself — just for the satisfaction of it. (BASSICK *watches* MORIARTY *with some anxiety, then comes down to him.*) Bassick! Baker Street, isn't it? His place — Baker Street — eh?

BASSICK: Baker Street, sir.

MORIARTY: We could make it safe. We could make it absolutely secure for three squares each way.

BASSICK: Yes, sir, but —

MORIARTY: We could! We've done it over and over again elsewhere! Police decoyed. Men in every doorway! (*sudden turn to* BASSICK) Do this to-night — in Baker Street! At nine o'clock call his attendants out on one pretext and another and keep them out — you understand! I'll see this Sherlock Holmes myself! I'll give him a chance for his life. If he declines to treat with me —
> (*Pause. He takes a savage looking bull dog revolver from a cabinet drawer and examines it carefully, slowly placing it in breast pocket. Peculiar ring of telephone bell.* MORIARTY *looks quickly around, gives a nod to* BASSICK *indicating him to attend to it.* BASSICK *at desk stands and picks up ear piece of telephone.* MORIARTY *stands looking at papers.*)

BASSICK: (*Speaks into receiver and listens as indicated.*) Yes — Yes, Bassick — what name did you say? Oh, Prince, yes. He'll have to wait. — Yes — I got his telegram last night. — Well, tell him to come and speak to me at the phone. (*longer wait*) Yes — I got your telegram, Prince, but I have an important matter on. You'll have to wait. — Who? — (*Suddenly becomes very much interested.*) What sort of a game is it? — Where is he now? — Wait a moment. (*to* MORIARTY) Here's something, sir. Sid Prince has come here with some job, and he says he's got Holmes fighting against him.

MORIARTY: (*quick turn to* BASSICK) Eh! Ask him what it is. Ask him what it is! (BASSICK *is about to speak on the telephone.* MORIARTY, *quickly*) Wait! (BASSICK *stops.*) Let him come here!

BASSICK: (*surprised; alarmed*) You don't mean —

MORIARTY: Precisely! (*up to desk*) — Precisely! I mean that precisely!

BASSICK: It's dangerous!

MORIARTY: It is to help me avoid a greater danger!

BASSICK: No one sees you — no one knows you. That has meant safety for years!

MORIARTY: (*near desk*) No one sees me now! No one! You talk with him — I'll listen from the next room. (BASSICK *looks at him an instant hesitatingly.*) This is *your office* — you understand. *Your office.* I'll be there! (BASSICK *turns to telephone.* MORIARTY *stands listening in characteristic attitude of intense concentration.*)

BASSICK: (*Speaks into telephone.*) Is that you, Prince? — Yes, I find I can't come out — but I'll see you here. — Come with you, you say? What interest have they got? What's the name? (*Listens a moment; looks round to* MORIARTY.) He says there's two with him — a man and a woman named Larrabee. They won't consent to any interview unless they're present.

MORIARTY: Larrabee. I remember them. Send them all in! (*A motion toward the telephone;* MORIARTY *stands listening.*)

BASSICK: (*Speaks into telephone.*) Eh, Prince — ask Beads to come to the telephone. — Beads — oh — (*lower voice*) Those people with Prince — do they
seem to be all right? Look close — yes — well — take them out through the
warehouse and down by the circular stairway and then bring them here by
the long tunnel. — Yes, here! — Look them over as you go along to see
they're not carrying anything! — And watch that no one sees you come
down! — Yes. — (*Hangs up ear piece. Turns and looks at* MORIARTY, *then
goes toward him before speaking.*) I don't like this, sir!

MORIARTY: (*Turns on him.*) I tell you it's certain death unless we can settle with
this man Holmes! I'll hear everything!

> (MORIARTY *starts toward door right. Buzzer rings three times.*
> BASSICK *looks at* MORIARTY. MORIARTY, *without the least
> haste, moves to door right and exits, leaving the door ajar. Pause.*
> BASSICK *turns a little.*)

BASSICK: (*low voice*) John. (*Motions him to come down.*)

JOHN: (*Goes to* BASSICK. *Low voice but alert.*) Yes, sir.

BASSICK: Keep your eyes on them from behind. If you see anything suspicious,
drop your pencil. If it's the man, pick it up — if it's the woman, leave it on
the floor.

JOHN: Yes, sir. (*Goes back to table.*)

> (BASSICK *pushes the lever at desk, and the bolt slides back from
> door up left center. The door slowly swings open. Enter* SID
> PRINCE *followed by* MADGE *and* LARRABEE. BASSICK *leaves
> the desk and meets them.*)

BASSICK: Ah, Prince!

PRINCE: How d'y're do, Mr Bassick, let me introduce my friends Mr and Mrs
Larrabee.

> (BASSICK *and others bow.* JOHN *quietly and unobtrusively closes
> the door up left center, sliding bolt, after which he resumes his seat
> with back to others, but soon turns and appears to be reading a
> book. Keeps watch on the* LARRABEES *over the top of it, holding
> a pencil in his hand.* SID PRINCE, *between introductions, gives a
> few sharp glances about.* BASSICK *hands chair for* MADGE.
> PRINCE *stands facing front;* LARRABEE *gets chair from* BASSICK
> *and sits left above* MADGE.)

LARRABEE: You don't get any too much daylight in here.

BASSICK: We have no use for it. (*Laughs with* LARRABEE *quietly. All very brief
and subdued.*) Can I offer you anything, madam?

MADGE: (*low voice*) Thank you, no. Nothing at all.

PRINCE: (*low voice; somewhat awed*) I suppose this is the 'eadquarters — eh?

BASSICK: This is my private office.

PRINCE: An' 'ow about 'im?

BASSICK: Who?

PRINCE: Wy — 'im — The Guv'nor. The — e —

BASSICK: Professor Moriarty never comes up to town. (PRINCE *is glancing about
with his sharp quick squint. To* PRINCE) Of course you understand I do not
usually see anyone here, but from what little you gave me through the tele-

phone it looked as if you might have something — interesting — so I thought it just as well to come in where we wouldn't be disturbed. (BASSICK *motions* PRINCE *to sit. Both sit,* BASSICK *in desk chair.*)

PRINCE: We 'ave got something interesting — there can't be any doubt o' that!

BASSICK: You said Holmes was in it, I believe.

PRINCE: 'Olmes was cert'nly in it last night. 'Ow much he's going to stay in we ain't quite sure!

BASSICK: Kindly let me have the particulars.

        (LARRABEE *gives 'H'm!' indicating that he wants to hear.*)

PRINCE: It won't take long to lay it out for you. Jim and Madge Larrabee 'ere which I used to know in early days — they picked up a girl at 'Amburg, ware 'er sister had been 'avin' a strong affair of the 'eart with a very 'igh young nob who promised to marry 'er — but the family stepped in and threw the whole thing down. E'd be'aved very bad to 'er an' had let 'imself out, an' written 'er letters an' given 'er rings an' tokens, ye see — and there was photographs, too — an' as these various things showed 'ow 'e'd deceived an' betrayed 'er, they wouldn't look nice at all considerin' of wat the young man was, an' wat 'igh titles 'e was comin' into. So wen this girl ups an' dies of it all, these letters an' things all falls into the 'ands of the sister — which is the one my friends 'ere 'as been nursin' along — together with 'er mother.

BASSICK: (*to* LARRABEE) Where have you had these people?

LARRABEE: (*Rises and goes toward* BASSICK.) We took a house up the Norrington Road where we'd be out of the way.

BASSICK: How long have you been there?

LARRABEE: Two years the fourteenth of next month.

BASSICK: And when will those letters and — other evidences of the young man's misconduct — when will they reach their full value?

PRINCE: (LARRABEE *is about to answer, but he jumps in quickly.*) It's *now*, don't you see! It's *now*! — There's a marriage comin' on an' there's been offers an' the problem is to get the papers in our 'ands.

BASSICK: Where are they?

PRINCE: The girl's got 'old of 'em, sir!

        (BASSICK *turns for explanation of this to* LARRABEE.)

LARRABEE: We had a safe for her to keep them in, supposing that when the time came we could open it, but the lock was out of order and we got Prince in to help us. He opened it last night and the package containing the things was gone. — She had taken them out herself.

BASSICK: What did you do when you discovered this?

PRINCE: Do! — I 'adn't any more than got the box open, sir, an' given one look in it, when Sherlock 'Olmes rings the front doorbell!

BASSICK: (*intent*) There — at your house?

LARRABEE: At my house.

BASSICK: He *didn't get those letters*?

LARRABEE: Well, he did get them, but he passed them back to the Faulkner girl.

BASSICK: (*in surprise*) What did that mean?

LARRABEE: (*slight shrug of shoulders*) There's another thing that puzzles me. There was an accident below in the kitchen — a lamp fell off the table and scattered burning oil about, the butler came running up yelling fire! We ran down there and a few buckets of water put it out right enough.

BASSICK: Did Holmes go down with you?

LARRABEE: No.

BASSICK: And of course the girl did not.

LARRABEE: No. He and the girl were in the drawing room.

MORIARTY: (*loud exclamation of impatience or anger outside*) Oh! Why did you do that? (*Enters at door right.*)

> (*All look in surprise.* BASSICK *rises from chair by desk.*
> LARRABEE *and* MADGE *also rise.*)

MORIARTY: The first thing we must do is to get rid of your butler — not discharge him — *get rid of him.* (*up to* BASSICK) Craigin for that! To-day! As soon as it's dark. Give him two others to help — Mr Larrabee will send the man into the cellar for something — they'll be ready for him. (MADGE *shudders slightly.*) It need not inconvenience you at all, madam. We do these things quietly. (*to* BASSICK, *who is writing orders at desk*) What's The Seraph doing?

BASSICK: He's on the Reading job tomorrow night.

MORIARTY: (*touching* BASSICK *on shoulder and marking the fact by almost looking into* BASSICK*'s face*) Put him with Craigin to-day to help with that butler. (*to* LARRABEE) But there's something else we want! Have you seen those letters — the photographs and whatever else there may be? Have you seen them? Do you know what they're like?

MADGE: I have, sir! I've looked them through carefully several times.

MORIARTY: (*going to her*) Ah — that is well! (*Brings her a little forward by the arm, but still among the rest.*) Now, could you make me a counterfeit set of these things and tie them up so they will look precisely like the package Sherlock Holmes held in his hand last night?

MADGE: I could manage the letters — but —

MORIARTY: If you can manage the letters I'll send someone who can manage the rest — from your description. Bassick — that old German artist.

BASSICK: Leuftner?

MORIARTY: Precisely. Send Leuftner to Mrs Larrabee at eleven. (*Looks at watch.*) Quarter past ten — that gives you three quarters of an hour to reach home. (*to* BASSICK) Take her address. (LARRABEE *goes up to* BASSICK *and whispers the address, leaning on desk.* BASSICK *writes.* MORIARTY, *to* MADGE) I shall want that counterfeit package at eleven tonight. Twelve hours to make it!

MADGE: It will be ready, sir.

MORIARTY: Good! Bassick — notify the Lascar that I may require the Gas Chamber at Stepney to-night.

BASSICK: The Gas Chamber?

MORIARTY: The one back of the river; and have Craigin there at a quarter before twelve with two others. Mr Larrabee (*turning slightly to him*) I shall want you to write a letter to Mr Sherlock Holmes which I shall dictate. — And to-night I may require a little assistance from you both. (*taking in* PRINCE *with his glance*) Meet me here at eleven.

LARRABEE: (*Goes forward a little.*) This is all very well, sir, but you have said nothing about — the business arrangements. I'm not sure that I —

MORIARTY: (*Turns front.*) You have no choice. (PRINCE *goes near* MADGE.)

LARRABEE: No choice!

MORIARTY: (*Looks at him.*) No choice. *No choice! No choice!* (MADGE *turns in surprise;* PRINCE *aghast.*) I do what I please! It pleases me to take hold of this case!

LARRABEE: (*angry*) Well, what about pleasing me? (BASSICK *rises and comes down on* MORIARTY's *right.*)

MORIARTY: (*Looks at* LARRABEE *an instant.*) I am not so sure but I shall be able to do that as well! I will obtain the letters from Miss Faulkner and negotiate them for much more than you could possibly obtain. In addition — if nothing occurs to prevent, understand — if nothing occurs to prevent — you will have an opportunity to sell the counterfeit package to Holmes tonight for a good round sum. And the money obtained from both these sources shall be divided between us as follows. You will take one hundred per cent and I — nothing.

(*Brief pause of astonishment*)

LARRABEE: Nothing!

MORIARTY: Nothing.

BASSICK: But we cannot negotiate those letters until we know who they incriminate. Mr Larrabee has not yet informed us.

MORIARTY: Mr Larrabee is wise in exercising caution. He values the keystone to his arch. But he will consent to let me know. (*Turns to* LARRABEE, *who, much disturbed, goes away. He glances at* PRINCE, *who is watching him. Then at* MADGE.)

MADGE: (*going to* MORIARTY) Professor Moriarty, that information we would like to give — only to you.

MORIARTY: (*Hands a card and pencil to* MADGE *from pocket.*) Write the name on that card. (LARRABEE *comes down near* MADGE, *uncertain whether to stop her. She writes a name and hands it to* MORIARTY. *He glances at it, then looks more closely. Looks up at* LARRABEE *and* MADGE *astonished.*) This is an absolute certainty?

LARRABEE: Absolute.

MORIARTY: It means that you have a fortune! (PRINCE *drinks in every word and look.*) Had I known this, you should hardly have had such terms.

LARRABEE: Oh, well — we don't object to —

MORIARTY: (*interrupting*) The arrangement is made, Mr Larrabee! I bid you good morning! (*Bows with dignity.* LARRABEE, PRINCE, MADGE *move toward door up center.* BASSICK *touches lever; ring of buzzer; bolts slide back on door.* BASSICK *motions* JOHN *who stands ready to conduct the party.*) Do not fail me on the counterfeit, madam!

MADGE: I shall not fail, sir! (*Goes up to door and exits.*)

MORIARTY: Wait in the office, Larrabee, and I will send you word about the letter you are to write!

LARRABEE: I'll wait for it, sir. (*Goes up to door.*)

MORIARTY: And meet me here at eleven to-night — unless you're notified to the contrary! (*Moves right.*)

LARRABEE: Eleven to-night, sir! (*He and* PRINCE *bow a little and exit at door up left center followed by* JOHN. *Door closes and bolts.*)

MORIARTY: (*Goes to door then turns sharply to* BASSICK.) Bassick, place your men, at nine to-night for Sherlock Holmes' house in Baker Street.

BASSICK: You will still go there *yourself*, sir!

MORIARTY: I will go there *myself*!

BASSICK: But this meeting tonight at twelve to trap Holmes in the Gas Chamber in Swandem Lane!

MORIARTY: Only in case I fail to kill him at his house at nine in Baker Street. In case of a slip we'll trap him at twelve in Swandem Lane! Either way I have him, Bassick! *I have him! I have him!*

CURTAIN

SECOND ACT

Second Scene

SHERLOCK HOLMES' *rooms in Baker Street, the large drawing room of his apartments. An open, cheerful room, not too much decorated. Rather plain. Walls and ceiling a plain tint. Furniture comfortable and good but not elegant. Easy chair, books, music, violins, tobacco pouches, pipes, tobacco in places about room, with some disorder but not slovenly. Various odd things hung about. Some very choice pictures hung on walls here and there. Etchings. Pictures do not have heavy gilt frames; all rather simple. Room more on the order of an artist's studio than a parlour. A number of lacquered tin boxes for documents on shelves. A wide door up right side to hall (and thus by stairway to street door). Door up left communicating with bedroom or dining room. A fireplace down or half down left side with cheerful grate fire burning and throwing a red glow into room. Mantel piece with pipes, tobacco and various knicknacks. Up left center a table with chemicals and various chemical apparatus. Shelves with phials above it. A big bay window up left center with window seats and cushions. Curtains drawn close. A blue spirit flame burning under a glass retort on chemical table up right center. A table down stage a little left of center. Cigars, cigarettes, matches on this table. Also bell to ring. Books, papers, writing materials on table. Two revolvers in drawer of this table. The lighting is so arranged that after the dark change, the first thing that becomes visible — even before the rest of the room — is the glow of fire, the blue flame of spirit lamp — and* SHERLOCK HOLMES *seated among cushions on the floor before the fire at left center. Light gradually on, but still leaving the effect of only firelight.*

SHERLOCK HOLMES *discovered on floor left center before fire. He is in dressing gown and slippers — has his pipe.* HOLMES *has pulled a lounge up back of him and leans against it. A violin is upon the lounge. Bow near or upon it, as if recently laid down. Other things scattered about him. He sits smoking awhile in deep thought.*

Enter BILLY, *the boy page, at door up right and comes down to back of table.*

VIII *Sherlock Holmes*, Act II, scene 2. Holmes confronts Moriarty

224

BILLY: Mrs 'Udson's compliments, sir, an' she wants to know if she can see you?

HOLMES: (*without moving, looking into fire thoughtfully*) Where is Mrs Hudson?

BILLY: Down stairs in the back kitchen, sir.

HOLMES: My compliments, and I don't think she can — from where she is.

BILLY: She'll be very sorry, sir.

HOLMES: Our regret will be mutual.

BILLY: It was most terrible important, sir, bein' as she wants to know what you'll 'ave for your breakfast in the mornin'.

HOLMES: Same.

BILLY: Same as wen, sir. (*Looks at* HOLMES.)

HOLMES: This morning.

BILLY: You didn't have *nothing*, sir — you wasn't 'ere!

HOLMES: Quite so — I won't be here tomorrow.

BILLY: Yes, sir. Was that all, sir?

HOLMES: Quite so.

BILLY: Thank you, sir. (*Exits at door up right. After long pause he re-enters.*) It's Dr Watson, sir . . . You told me as I could always show 'im up.

HOLMES: Well! I should think so. (*Rises and meets* WATSON.)

BILLY: Yes, sir. Thank you, sir . . . Dr Watson, sir!

       (*Enter* DR WATSON *at door up right.* BILLY *grins with pleasure as he comes in.* BILLY *exits up right.*)

HOLMES: (*extending left hand to* WATSON) Ah, Watson, my dear fellow!

WATSON: (*going to* HOLMES *and taking his hand*) How are you, Holmes?

HOLMES: I'm delighted to see you — perfectly delighted, upon my word — but — I'm sorry to observe that your wife has left you in this way!

WATSON: (*laughing*) Ha! Ha! She has gone on a little visit — (*Puts hat down.*) but how did you know?

HOLMES: (*Goes to chemical table and puts spirit lamp out, then turns up piano lamp.*) How do I know. Now, Watson, how absurd for you to ask me such a question as that. (WATSON *sits in easy chair, picking up cigarette from table.*) How do I know anything? (*Comes down a little way; gives a very little sniff an instant, smelling something.*) How do I know that you've opened an office and resumed the practice of medicine — without letting me hear a word of it? How do I know you've been getting yourself very wet lately? That you have an extremely careless servant girl — and that you've moved your dressing table to the other side of your room?

WATSON: (*First stops lighting cigarette and then turns and looks at* HOLMES *in astonishment.*) Holmes, if you'd lived a few centuries ago, they'd have burned you alive!

HOLMES: Such a conflagration would have saved me considerable trouble. (*Strolls left.*)

WATSON: Tell me now, how did you know all that?

HOLMES: (*Stands at table, pointing.*) Too simple to talk about. (*Points at* WATSON's *shoes.*) Scratches and clumsy cuts — on the side of shoe there just where the fire strikes it, somebody scraped away crusted mud — and did it badly — badly! There's your wet feet and your careless servant all in one. Face badly shaved on right side — used to be on left — light must come from other side — couldn't very well move your window — must have moved your dressing table.

WATSON: Yes, by Jove! but my medical practice — I don't see how you —

HOLMES: (*glancing up grieved*) Now, Watson! How perfectly absurd of you to come marching in here fairly reeking with the odor of iodiform, and with the black mark of nitrate of silver on the inner side of your right forefinger and ask me how I know —

WATSON: (*interrupting with a laugh*) Ha, ha! Of course! But how the deuce did you know my wife was away and —

HOLMES: (*breaking in*) Where the deuce is your second waistcoat button — and what the deuce is yesterday's boutonnière doing in today's lapel — and why the deuce do you wear the expression of a —

WATSON: (*toying with cigarette in chair at table*) Ha, ha, ha! Marvelous!

HOLMES: (*sneer*) Elementary! The child's play of deduction! (*He turns to mantel, takes a neat morocco case and a phial, which he brings to the table and lays carefully upon it. As WATSON sees HOLMES open case he rises and goes right restlessly and apparently annoyed at what HOLMES is about to do, throwing cigarette on table and sitting again soon. He opens the case and takes therefrom a hypodermic syringe. Carefully adjusts the delicate needle. Fills from phial, then rolls back left cuff of shirt a little. Pauses, looking at arm or wrist a moment. Inserts needle; presses piston home. WATSON has watched him with an expression of deep anxiety but with effort to restrain himself from speaking.*)

WATSON: (*As HOLMES puts needle in case again, he finally speaks.*) Which is it today? Cocaine or morphine, or —

HOLMES: Cocaine, my dear fellow, I'm back to my old love! A seven percent solution. (*Offers syringe and phial.*) Would you like to try some?

WATSON: (*Emphatically; rises.*) Certainly *not*!

HOLMES: (*as if surprised*) Oh! I'm sorry! (*Draws hypo and phial back and replaces them on mantel.*)

WATSON: *I* have no wish to break *my* system down before its time!

HOLMES: Quite right, my dear Watson — quite right — But you see, my time has come! (*Throws himself languidly into sofa, leaning back in luxurious enjoyment of the drug.*)

WATSON: (*Goes to table, resting hand on upper corner looking at HOLMES seriously.*) Holmes, for months I have seen you using these deadly drugs — in ever increasing doses. When they once lay hold of you, there is no end! It must go on, and on, and on — until the finish!

HOLMES: (*lying back, dreamily*) So must you go on and on eating your breakfast — until the finish.

WATSON: (*approaching HOLMES*) Breakfast is food! These drugs are poisons — slow but certain. They involve tissue changes of a most serious character.

HOLMES: Just what I want! I'm bored to death with my present tissues and am out after a brand new lot!

WATSON: (*going near HOLMES*) Ah, Holmes — I'm trying to save you! (*Puts hand on HOLMES' shoulder.*)

HOLMES: (*Earnest an instant; places right hand on WATSON's arm.*) You can't do it, old fellow — so don't waste your time. (*They look at one another an instant.* WATSON *sees cigarette on table, picks it up and sits in chair right center facing front.*) Watson — in the enthusiasm which has prompted you to chronicle, and — if you will excuse my saying so, to somewhat embellish — a few of my little — adventures, you have occasionally committed the error — or — indiscretion — of giving them a certain tinge of romance — which struck me as being just a trifle — out of place! Something like working an elopement into the fifth proposition of Euclid. I merely refer to this in case you should see fit at some future time — to chronicle the most important and far-reaching case in my entire career — one upon which I have labored for nearly fourteen months, and which is now rapidly approaching a singularly diverting climax; — the case of Professor Robert Moriarty.

WATSON: (*Hitches chair round and faces* HOLMES *interested.*) Moriarty! I don't remember ever having heard of the fellow!

HOLMES: The Napoleon of crime! Sitting motionless like an ugly venomous spider in the center of his web — but that web having a thousand radiations and the spider knowing every quiver of every one of them!

WATSON: Really! This is very interesting!

HOLMES: Ah — but the real interest will come when the Professor begins to realize his position — which he cannot fail to do shortly. By ten o'clock tomorrow night the time will be ripe for the arrests. Then the greatest criminal trial of the century! The clearing up of over forty mysteries . . . and the rope for every one!

WATSON: Good! What will he do when he sees that you have him?

HOLMES: Do? He will do me the honor, my dear Watson, of turning every resource of his wonderful organization of criminals to the one purpose of my destruction!

WATSON: Why, this is a dangerous thing, Holmes!

HOLMES: My dear Watson, it's perfectly delightful! It saves me any number of doses of those deadly drugs upon which you occasionally favor me with your medical views! My whole life is spent in a series of frantic endeavors to escape from the dreary commonplaces of existence! For a brief period I escape! Congratulate me!

WATSON: But you could escape them without such serious risks! Your other cases have not been so dangerous and they were even more interesting! Now the one you spoke of the last time I saw you, the recovery of those damaging letters and gifts from a young girl who — (HOLMES *suddenly rises, goes up left center and stands motionless.* WATSON *looks round at him, surprised. Brief pause.*) A most peculiar affair as I remember it. You were going to try the experiment of making her betray their hiding place by an alarm of fire in her own house — and after that —

HOLMES: Precisely — after that. (*Goes up stage and stands there a moment.*)

WATSON: (*Pauses.*) Didn't the plan succeed?

HOLMES: Yes, as far as I've gone.

WATSON: You got Forman into the house as butler?

HOLMES: (*Nods.*) Forman was in as butler.

WATSON: And upon your signal he overturned a lamp in the kitchen, scattered the smoke balls and gave an alarm of fire? (HOLMES *nods and mutters 'yes' under his breath.*) And the young lady — did she —

HOLMES: (*turning and interrupting*) Yes, she did, Watson. (*Goes down near him just above table as if he had recovered himself.*) It all transpired precisely as I planned. I took the packet of papers from its hiding place — and, as I told you I would, I handed it back to Miss Faulkner.

WATSON: But you never told me *why* you proposed to hand it back.

HOLMES: (*Stands just above table, hand on* WATSON's *shoulder.*) For a very simple reason, my dear Watson, that it would have been theft for me to take it. The contents of the packet was the absolute property of the young lady.

WATSON: What did you gain by this?

HOLMES: Her confidence, and so far as I was able to secure it, her regard. As it was impossible for me to take possession of the package without her consent, my only alternative is to obtain that consent — to induce her to give it me of her own free will. Its return to her after I had laid hands on it was the first move in this direction. The second will depend entirely upon what transpires today. I expect Forman here to report in half an hour.

> (*Light hurried step outside right. Short quick knock at door, and enter* TERESE *at door up right in great haste and excitement.* WATSON *rises, turns, and faces her near table.* HOLMES *turns to her on her entrance.*)

TERESE: I beg you to pardon me, sir, ze boy he say to come right up as soon as I come. Ah! I fear me zere eez trouble. Messieur — ze butlair — your assistant — ze one who sent me to you!

HOLMES: Forman?

TERESE: Heem! *Forman!* Zere eez somesing done to heem! I fear to go down to see.

HOLMES: Down where?

> (WATSON *goes over near fire and watches scene.*)

TERESE: Ze down! (*Gestures.*) Ze cellaire of zat house! Eet ees a dreadful place. He deed not come back. He went down — he deed not return.

HOLMES: (*Goes to table; rings bell and takes revolver from drawer and slides it into his hip pocket at same time unfastening dressing gown.*) Who sent him down?

TERESE: M'sieur of ze house! M'sieur Chetvood!

HOLMES: Larrabee.

TERESE: Yes.

HOLMES: Has he been down there long?

TERESE: No — for I soon suspect! Ze dreadful noise was heard — oh! (*Covers face.*)

HOLMES: What noise? (*Crosses to her; seizes her arm.*)

TERESE: Zee noise!

HOLMES: Try to be calm and answer me. What did it sound like?

TERESE: Ze dreadful cry of a man who eez struck down by some deadly seeng!

> (*Enter* BILLY *up right.*)

HOLMES: Billy! Coat — boots — and order a cab. Quick. (*Back again to table; takes a second revolver out.*)

BILLY: (*Darts off at door up left.*) Yes, sir.
HOLMES: (*to* TERESE) Did anyone follow him down?
(BILLY *is back in a second.*)
TERESE: I did not see.
HOLMES: Don't wait! The cab. (BILLY *shoots off at door up right, having
placed coat over sofa and boots on floor.*) Take that, Watson, and come
with me. (*Hands* WATSON *a revolver.* WATSON *advances a step to meet*
HOLMES.)
TERESE: I had not better go also?
HOLMES: No . . . Wait here.
(HOLMES, *ready to go, is about to take off dressing gown. Hurried
footsteps heard outside up right.*)
TERESE: (*seeing* FORMAN — *under her breath*) Ah! (*Backs away a little.*)
(*Enter* FORMAN *up right, coming rapidly on, covered with black
coal stains, and his clothing otherwise soiled. He has a bad bruise on
side of forehead. Not made up so that there is the slightest comedy
about his entrance.* HOLMES, *just above table, stops taking off
dressing-gown, slips it back on his shoulders again.*)
FORMAN: (*to* HOLMES, *who, as soon as he sees him, places revolver on table;
entirely matter of fact*) Nothing more last night, sir. After you left Prince
came in and they made a start for her room to get the package away, but I
gave the three knocks with an axe on the floor beams as you directed and
they didn't go any further. This morning, a little after nine —
HOLMES: One moment.
FORMAN: Yes, sir!
HOLMES: (*Quietly turns to* TERESE.) Mademoiselle — step into that room and
rest yourself. (*Indicates door down right.*)
TERESE: (*who has been deeply interested in* FORMAN's *report*) Ah! (*Shakes
head.*) I am not tired, monsieur.
HOLMES: Step in and walk about then. I'll let you know when you are required.
TERESE: (*After an instant's pause sees it.*) Oui, monsieur. (*Exits at door down
right.*)
HOLMES: (*Goes over and quietly closes the door after her. He then turns to*
WATSON, *but remains at the door with right ear alert to catch any sound
from within.*) Take a look at his head, Watson! (*Listens at door.* WATSON *at
once goes down to* FORMAN.)
FORMAN: It's nothing at all.
WATSON: An ugly bruise — but not dangerous. (*He goes quickly and sits on sofa,
facing around to* FORMAN.)
HOLMES: Very well. — At a little after nine you say — (*He has attention on door
at right where* TERESE *went off, while listening to* FORMAN, *but not in
such a marked way as to take the attention from what he says, and after a
few seconds, he sits nearby.*)
FORMAN: Yes, sir. This morning a little after nine Larrabee and his wife drove
away in a four wheeler. She returned about eleven without him — and a little
later old Leuftner came, and the two went to work at something in the
library. I got a sight of them from the outside, and found they were making

up a counterfeit of the package we're working for! You'll have to watch for some sharp trick, sir.

HOLMES: *They'll* have to watch for the trick, my dear Forman! And Larrabee — what of him?

FORMAN: He came back a little after three.

HOLMES: How did he seem?

FORMAN: Under great excitement, sir!

HOLMES: Any marked resentment toward you?

FORMAN: I think there was, sir — though he tried not to show it!

HOLMES: He has consulted someone outside. Was the Larrabee woman's behavior different also?

FORMAN: Now I think of it she gave me an ugly look as she came in.

HOLMES: Ah, an ugly look. She was present at the consultation. They were advised to get you out of the way. He sent you into the cellar on some pretext. You were attacked in the dark by two men — possibly three — and received a bad blow from a sand club. You managed to strike down one of your assailants with a stone or piece of timber and escaped from the others in the dark, crawling out through a coal grating.

FORMAN: That's what took place, sir.

HOLMES: They've taken in a partner. And a dangerous one at that! He not only directed this conspiracy against you, but he advised the making of the counterfeit package as well. Within a very short time I shall receive an offer from Larrabee to sell me the package of letters. He will indicate that Miss Faulkner has changed her mind, and has concluded to get what she can for them. He will desire to meet me on the subject — and will then endeavor to sell me his bogus package.

> (*Enter* BILLY *door up right with a letter. He comes down to* HOLMES.)

BILLY: Letter, sir! Most important, sir! (*After giving* HOLMES *the letter he stands waiting.*)

HOLMES: Unless I am greatly mistaken — the said communication is at hand. (*Lightly waves letter across in front of his face once as if getting the scent.*) It is. (WATSON *rises and goes up to lamp.*) Read it, Watson, there's a good fellow — my eyes — (*with a motion across eyes; half smile*) You know — cocaine

> (BILLY *goes with letter to* WATSON.)

WATSON: (*Opens letter and reads.*) 'Dear sir.'

> (*After* WATSON *is at lamp,* FORMAN *goes up stage and waits.*)

HOLMES: Who — thus — addresses me? (*Slides further onto seat, supporting head on pillows.*)

WATSON: (*Glances at signature.*) 'James Larrabee.'

HOLMES: (*whimsically*) What a surprise! And what has James to say this evening?

WATSON: 'Dear sir, I have the honor to inform you that Miss Faulkner has changed her mind regarding the letters, etc., which you wish to obtain, and has decided to dispose of them for a monetary consideration. She has placed them in my hands for this purpose, and if you are in a position to offer a good round sum, and to pay it down at once in cash, the entire lot is yours.

If you wish to negotiate, however, it must be to-night at the house of a friend
of mine in the city. At eleven o'clock you will be at the Guards Monument at
the foot of Waterloo Place. You will see a four wheeler with wooden shutters
to the windows. Enter it, and the driver will bring you to my friend's house.
If you have the cab followed or try any other underhand trick, you won't get
what you want. Let me know your decision. Respectfully, James Larrabee.'
>   (HOLMES, *during reading of letter, begins to write something in a*
>   *perfectly leisurely way. Light of fire upon him, on his left, as he*
>   *writes.*)

HOLMES: Billy.

BILLY: (*going to* HOLMES *at once*) Yes, sir.

HOLMES: (*reaching out letter to* BILLY *in back of him without looking*) Give this
    to the man — and —

BILLY: It was a woman, sir.

HOLMES: (*slight dead stop as he is handing letter*) Ah! — old or young? (*He does*
    not look round for these questions, but faces as he was, front, or nearly so.)

BILLY: Werry old, sir.

HOLMES: Hansom?

BILLY: Four wheeler, sir.

HOLMES: Seen the driver before?

BILLY: Yes, sir — but I can't think ware.

HOLMES: (*rising*) Give the old lady this — (*giving letter*) apologies for the delay —
    and look at the driver again.

BILLY: (*Takes letter.*) Yes, sir. (*Exits at door up right.*)

WATSON: My dear Holmes — you did not say you would go?

HOLMES: I certainly did. (*moving toward door at right*)

WATSON: But it is the counterfeit.

HOLMES: The counterfeit is just what I want.

WATSON: Why so?

HOLMES: (*Turns to* WATSON *an instant.*) Because with it, I shall obtain the
    original. (*Turns and speaks off at door right.*) Mademoiselle! (*Turns back.*)

WATSON: But this fellow means mischief!
>   (*Enter* TERESE *at door right.* WATSON *goes and stands with back*
>   *to fire.*)

HOLMES: (*Faces* WATSON, *touching himself lightly.*) This fellow means the same!
    (*to* TERESE) Be so good, mademoiselle, as to listen to every word. Tonight
    at twelve o'clock I meet Mr Larrabee and purchase from him the false bundle
    of letters to which you just now overheard us refer as you were listening at
    the keyhole of that door.

TERESE: (*slightly confused but staring blankly*) Oui, monsieur.

HOLMES: I wish Miss Faulkner to know this *at once*.

TERESE: I will tell her, monsieur.

HOLMES: That is my wish. But do not tell her that I know the packet and its con-
    tents to be counterfeit. She is to suppose that I think them genuine.

TERESE: Ah! Oui, monsieur! When you purchase you think you have the real!

HOLMES: Precisely. Say nothing whatever about it and she will naturally so con-
    clude. Otherwise why should I purchase?

TERESE: I shall say nothing, monsieur!

HOLMES: Quite so. (*Moves toward door with her.*) One thing more! Tomorrow evening I shall want you to accompany her to this place. Sir Edward Leighton and Count Von Stalburg will be here to receive the package from me, and I desire that she overhear the conversation which will then take place. You will receive further instructions as to this in the morning.

TERESE: Oui, monsieur. (*Turns and exits at once at door up right.*)

(FORMAN *goes to* HOLMES.)

HOLMES: Forman, change to your beggar disguise No. 14 and go through every place in the Riverside District. Don't stop till you get a clue to this new partner of the Larrabees. I must have it! (*Turns away toward* WATSON.)

FORMAN: Very well, sir. (*just about to go*)

(*Enter* BILLY *at door up right, just inside.*)

BILLY: If you please, sir, there's a man a-waitin' down at the street door — an' 'e says 'e must speak to Mr Forman, sir, as quick as 'e can.

HOLMES: (*Stops suddenly and stands motionless — eyes front. Pause.*) We'd better have a look at that man — Billy, show him up.

BILLY: 'E can't come up, sir — 'e's a-watchin' a man in the street. 'E says 'e's from Scotland Yard.

FORMAN: (*going toward door*) I'd better see what it is, sir.

HOLMES: No! (FORMAN *stops. Pause.* HOLMES *stands motionless a moment.*) Well — (*a motion indicating* FORMAN *to go*) Take a look at him first. *Be ready for anything.*

FORMAN: Trust me for that, sir! (*Exits at door up right.*)

HOLMES: Billy, see what he does.

BILLY: Yes, sir. (*Exit at door up right after* FORMAN.)

(HOLMES *stands an instant thinking.*)

WATSON: This is becoming interesting! (HOLMES *does not reply. He goes up to near door up right and listens, then moves to window and glances down the street, then turns and goes down to table.*) Look here, Holmes, you've been so kind as to give me a half-way look into this case —

HOLMES: (*looking up at him*) What case?

WATSON: This strange case of Miss Faulkner.

HOLMES: Quite so — one moment, my dear fellow. (*Rings bell. After slight wait enter* BILLY *at door up right.*) Mr Forman — is he there still?

BILLY: (*at door*) No, sir — 'e's gone. (*second's pause*)

HOLMES: That's all.

BILLY: Yes, sir. Thank you, sir. (*Exit at door up right.*)

HOLMES: As you were saying, Watson (*eyes front*), this strange case — (*Stops, but does not change position, as if listening or thinking.*)

WATSON: Of Miss Faulkner.

HOLMES: (*abandoning further anxiety, and giving attention to* WATSON) Precisely, of Miss Faulkner. (*eyes down an instant as he recalls it*)

WATSON: You've given me some idea of it — now don't you think it would be only fair to let me have the rest?

HOLMES: (*Looks at him.*) What shall I tell you?

WATSON: Tell me what you propose to do with that counterfeit package — which you are going to risk your life to obtain!

HOLMES: (*Looks at* WATSON *an instant before speaking.*) I intend, with the aid of the counterfeit, to make her willingly hand me the genuine. I shall accomplish this by a piece of trickery and deceit of which I am heartily ashamed — and which I would never have undertaken if I — if I had known her — as I do now. (*Looks front absently.*) — It's too bad. She's — she's rather a nice girl, Watson. (*Crosses to mantel and gets pipe.*)

WATSON: (*passing behind table, following* HOLMES *with his eyes*) Nice girl, is she? (HOLMES *nods with his back still to* WATSON. *Brief pause.* HOLMES *turns with pipe in hands and glances toward* WATSON, *then down.*) Then you think that possibly —

(*Enter* BILLY *quickly at door up right.*)

BILLY: I beg pardon, sir, Mr Forman's just sent over from the chemist's on the corner to say 'is 'ead is a-painin' 'im a bit, an' would Doctor Watson kinely step over an' git 'im somethin' to put on it.

WATSON: (*Moves at once toward door up right.*) Yes — certainly! I'll go at once! (*Picks up hat off sofa.*) That's singular! (*Stands puzzled.*) It didn't look like anything serious! (*at door up right*) I'll be back in a minute, Holmes! (*Exits.*)

(HOLMES *says nothing.* BILLY *is about to follow* WATSON *off.*)

HOLMES: Billy.

BILLY: Yes, sir!

HOLMES: Who brought that message from Forman?

BILLY: Boy from the chemist's, sir.

HOLMES: Yes, of course, but which boy?

BILLY: Must 'a bin' a new one, sir — I ain't never seen 'im before.

HOLMES: Quick, Billy, run down and look after the Doctor. If the boy's gone and there's a man with him it means mischief! Let me know quick! Don't stop to come up; ring the door bell! I'll hear it! Ring it loud!

BILLY: Yes, sir. (*Exit quickly at door up right.*)

(HOLMES *waits motionless at left a moment, listening. He moves quickly toward door up right. When half way to the door, he stops suddenly, listening, then begins to slide backward toward table. Stops and listens — eyes to front; turns toward door up right listening. Pipe in left hand — waits — sees pipe in hand, picks up match, lights pipe, listening, and suddenly there is a shout of warning from* BILLY. *Turns, at the same time picking up revolver from off table and putting it in pocket of dressing gown, with his hand still clasping it. He at once assumes easy attitude, but keeps eyes on door. Enter at door up right* PROFESSOR ROBERT MORIARTY. *He stands just within the door a moment looking at* HOLMES. *They stand regarding each other for a moment. Pause.*)

MORIARTY: It's a dangerous habit to finger loaded fire-arms in the pocket of one's dressing gown.

HOLMES: I'm pained to observe that you have your hands behind you. (MORIARTY *brings his hands from behind him.*) In that case the table will do just as well. (*Tosses revolver on table.*)

MORIARTY: You evidently don't know me.

HOLMES: (*Takes pipe out of mouth, holding it. With very slight motion toward revolver*) I think it quite evident that I do. Pray take a chair, Professor. (*Indicates chair right or right center.*) I can spare you five minutes — if you have anything to say.

MORIARTY: (*Bus. with watch; HOLMES bus. with revolver.*) All that I have to say has already crossed your mind.

HOLMES: My answer thereto has already crossed *yours*.

MORIARTY: It is your intention to pursue this case against me?

HOLMES: To the very end.

MORIARTY: I regret this — not on my own account, but on yours.

HOLMES: I share your regrets, Professor, but solely because of the rather uncomfortable position it will cause you to occupy.

> (*Slight pause. MORIARTY's eyes on HOLMES glitter with evil intent and suppressed anger. He takes a step or two.*)

MORIARTY: May I enquire to what position you are pleased to allude, Mr Holmes?

HOLMES: To the one occasionally assumed by a certain class of malefactor at the lower extremity of a rope, Professor Moriarty.

> (*Again the pause. MORIARTY eyes HOLMES like a beast of prey.*)

MORIARTY: (*Leans toward HOLMES.*) Have you the faintest idea that you would be permitted to live to see that day?

HOLMES: As to that, I do not particularly care, so that I bring you to see it!

MORIARTY: (*Springs at HOLMES.*) You will never bring me to see it! You will find — (*Suddenly recollects himself, changes to quieter tone.*) Ha! You are a bold man, Mr Holmes — to insinuate such a thing — to my face. (*Both sit; MORIARTY right center; HOLMES left center, pushing seat from under table with his foot.*) But it is the boldness born of ignorance. Do you think I would be here — if I had not made the street *quite safe in every respect*?

HOLMES: Oh! (*Shakes head.*) No! I could never so grossly overestimate your courage as that!

MORIARTY: Do you imagine that your friend and your man Forman will soon return?

HOLMES: Possibly not.

MORIARTY: But between us that is nothing. They will merely be detained — not harmed. Detained so that we can talk the matter over quietly, Mr Holmes, and not be disturbed. In the first place, I wish to call your attention to a few memoranda that I have (*putting hand toward pocket of coat*) jotted down — and —

HOLMES: (*Raises revolver with instant motion — but only a little above table. Hand that holds it rests on table.*) E — r — p! (*quick exclamation of warning as he lifts revolver*) Wait! wait! I wouldn't do that, Professor! We have to be a little careful, your honor, with a man of your great ability. There's a rumor extant that feeling for memorandum books is quite a little specialty of yours!

MORIARTY: (*Stops where he is.*) I was about to take out a small notebook — (*Again reaches toward pocket.*) which you will —

HOLMES: Ah! (*warning exclamation again*) Not yet! Don't take it out! (*Rings bell *on table with left hand.*) I always like to save my guests unnecessary trouble. (*short wait*)

MORIARTY: I observe that your boy does not answer the bell.

HOLMES: No. But I have an idea he will before long.

MORIARTY: (*significantly*) It will possibly be longer than you think, Mr Holmes.

HOLMES: Ah! — At least we'll try the bell once more, Professor! (*Rings bell. Short wait.*)

MORIARTY: Doesn't it occur to you that he may have been detained, Mr Holmes?

HOLMES: Quite so. But I also observe that you are in much the same predicament, Professor.

> (*Pause. HOLMES rings bell for the third time. Noise on stairway outside left. Enter BILLY up right with part of his coat and with sleeves of shirt and his waistcoat badly torn.*)

BILLY: (*up near door*) I beg pardon, sir — someone tried to 'old me, sir! (*panting for breath*)

HOLMES: It's quite evident, however, that he failed to do so.

BILLY: Yes, sir — 'e's got my coat, sir, but 'e ain't got *me*!

HOLMES: Billy!

BILLY: (*cheerfully*) Yes, sir! (*still out of breath*)

HOLMES: The gentleman I am pointing out to you with this six shooter desires to have us get something out of his left hand coat pocket, as he is not feeling quite himself to-day, and the exertion might prove injurious. Suppose you attend to it.

BILLY: Yes, sir. (*He quickly goes to MORIARTY, puts hand in his pocket and draws out a bull-dog revolver.*) Is this it, sir?

HOLMES: Quite so. Put it on the table. (MORIARTY *makes a grab for it.*) Not there, Billy! Look out! — Push it a little further this way. (BILLY *does so, placing it so that it is within easy reach of* HOLMES.) That's more like it.

BILLY: Shall I see if he's got another, sir?

HOLMES: Not at all necessary, Billy, he's just informed us that he hasn't.

BILLY: When, sir?

HOLMES: When he made a snatch for this one. Now that we have your little memorandum book, Professor, do you think of anything else you'd like before Billy goes? (MORIARTY *does not reply.*) Ah! I'm sorry, that's all, Billy.

> (*Pause. MORIARTY motionless; eyes on HOLMES. HOLMES puts his own revolver in his pocket quietly. MORIARTY remains motionless, his eyes on HOLMES, waiting for a chance.*)

BILLY: Thank you, sir. (*Exits at door up right.*)

> (HOLMES *carelessly picks up* MORIARTY's *weapon, turns it over in his hands a little below line of table for a moment, then tosses it back on table again — during which business* MORIARTY *looks after* BILLY *as he exits.*)

HOLMES: (*Taps revolver with pipe.*) Rather a rash project of yours, Moriarty — to make use of that — so early in the evening and in this part of the town.

MORIARTY: Listen to me. You crossed my path on the 4th of January. On the 23rd you incommoded me. And now, at the close of April, I find myself placed in such a position through your continual persecution that I am in positive danger of losing my liberty.

HOLMES: Have you any suggestion to make?

MORIARTY: (*head swaying from side to side*) No — I have no suggestion to make. I have a fact to state. If you do not drop it at once! your life is not worth that! (*snap of finger*)

HOLMES: I shall be pleased to drop it — at ten o'clock tomorrow night.

MORIARTY: Why then?

HOLMES: Because at that hour, Moriarty, your life will not be worth that! (*snap of finger*) You will be under arrest!

MORIARTY: At that hour, Sherlock Holmes, your eyes will be closed in death! (*Both look at one another motionless an instant.*)

HOLMES: (*rising as if rather bored*) I am afraid, Professor, that in the pleasure of this conversation I am neglecting more important business. (*Turns away to mantel at left and looks for match.*)

MORIARTY: (*Rises slowly, his eyes upon* HOLMES. *Suddenly catches sight of revolver on table. Pause. Nearing* HOLMES) I came here to see if peace could not be arranged between us!

HOLMES: Ah! yes (*smiling pleasantly and pressing tobacco in pipe*), I saw that, that's rather good!

MORIARTY: You have seen fit not only to reject my proposals, but to make insulting references coupled with threats of arrest!

HOLMES: Quite so! Quite so! (*Lights match and holds it to pipe.*)

MORIARTY: (*moving back a little so as to be clear of table*) Well, you have been warned of your danger — you do not heed that warning — Perhaps you will heed this!

> (*He makes a sudden plunge and seizes his revolver from table and at same instant aiming at* HOLMES' *head, he rapidly snaps the hammer in quick attempt to fire.* HOLMES *turns quietly toward him, still holding match to pipe so that the last snaps of the hammer are directly in his face. Very slight pause as* MORIARTY *is unable to fire.*)

HOLMES: Oh! Ha! — Here! (*as if recollecting something. Tosses away match and, feeling quickly in left pocket of dressing gown, brings out some cartridges and tosses them carelessly on table toward* MORIARTY.) I didn't suppose you'd want to use that thing again so I took all your cartridges out and put them in my pocket. You'll find them all there, Professor! (*Reaches over and rings bell on table with right hand. Enter* BILLY *door up right.*) Billy!

BILLY: Yes, sir!

HOLMES: Show this gentleman nicely to the door.

BILLY: Yes, sir! . . . This way, sir.

> (BILLY *stands within door up right.* PROFESSOR MORIARTY *looks at* HOLMES *a moment, clenches his face, turns boiling with rage, and exits quickly at door up right, muttering aloud as he goes.*)

HOLMES: (*after* MORIARTY'*s exit*) Billy! Come here!

BILLY: Yes, sir! (*He quickly comes down to right of easy chair.*)

HOLMES: Billy! — *You're a good boy*!
BILLY: Yes, sir! Thank you, sir! (*Stands grinning up at* HOLMES.)

CURTAIN

THIRD ACT

Scene. *The Gas Chamber at Stepney. A large, dark, grimy room on an upper floor of an old building backing on wharves, etc. Plaster cracking off. Masonry piers or chimneys showing. Grimy walls. Old boxes. Pile of discarded old chests. Uncanny and gruesome appearance as possible. Old bench with various odds and ends against wall, left. Heavy beams and timbers showing. Aspect of upper floor of an old warehouse. Wide door down left side opening off stage and up. Heavy plank door of much weight built solid and set in solid frame braced strong. Bolts on outside and bars to set with effect of noise of bolting and barring a heavy door. Door up left center to small cupboard, opening down stage and to left. The walls of cupboard can be seen when door opened. No bolt or lock on this door. Large window up right on oblique, closed. Grimy and dirty glass so nothing could be seen through it — but all panes in place — none broken. Appearance of window nailed with spike nails securely shut. Black backing — no light behind. Strong bars outside back of windows to show when window broken. These bars must not be seen through glass of window. An old plain table against wall up right center dark and soiled and grimy. It is quite long and rather narrow. Boxes on right side empty. One for use. A chair or two. Trash in one corner such as old broken trunks or chests. Heavy beams showing at corners and above, dark blue and smoke begrimed. Lights down or with blues on, as the only light in the place on rise of curtain is from a dim lantern carried on by* McTAGUE. *Very dark and subdued until lamp is brought in.*

CRAIGIN *and* LEARY *are discovered.* CRAIGIN *is sitting on a stool or box at right, glum and motionless, waiting.* LEARY *is sitting on table. Door at left arranged to swing slowly shut by itself when anyone opens it. Door at left opens and* McTAGUE *enters with safety lamp. He stops just within a moment, glancing around in the dimness. Soon he moves up near a masonry pier a little above the door and leans against it, waiting. All three are dressed in dark clothes and wear felt-soled shoes.*
LEARY: What's McTague doing 'ere?
McTAGUE: I was sent 'ere.
        (*All dialogue in this part of the Act is in low tones to give a weird effect echoing through the large grimy room among the deep shadows.*)
LEARY: I thought The Seraph was with us in this job?
CRAIGIN: 'E *ain't.*
LEARY: Who was the last you put the gas on?
        (*Pause*)
CRAIGIN: I didn't 'ear 'is name — (*pause*) — 'E'd been 'oldin' back money on a 'aul out some railway place.
        (*Pause*)

McTAGUE: What's this job he wants done? (*Sits on box, placing lamp on floor by his side. Pause.*)

CRAIGIN: I ain't been told.

   (*Pause*)

LEARY: As long as it's *'ere* we know what it's likely to be.

   (*Door left opens slowly and hesitatingly. Enter* SID PRINCE. *He stands just within door and looks about a little suspiciously, as if uncertain what to do. Pause. He notices that door is slowly closing behind him and quietly holds it back. He must in no way burlesque scene with funny business.* McTAGUE *holds lantern up to see who it is.*)

PRINCE: Does any one of you guys know whether this is the place where I meet Alf Bassick?

   (*Pause. None of the men notice* PRINCE. *After waiting a moment*)

PRINCE: From wot you say I take it you don't.

CRAIGIN: We ain't knowin' so much, young man. 'E may be 'ere an' 'e may not.

PRINCE: Oh. (*Comes a little further into room and lets the door close.*) I'm quite right then, thank you. (*Pause. No one speaks.*) Nice old place to find this 'ere is! (*No one answers him.*) An wen you *do* find it — (*Looks about.*) I — cawn't say as it's any too cheerful.

   (*He thereupon pulls out a cigarette case, puts a cigarette in his mouth, and feels in pocket for matches. Finds one; about to light it. He has moved up a few steps just as he concludes to smoke.*)

CRAIGIN: Here! . . . (PRINCE *stops.*) Don't light that! . . . *It ain't safe!*

   (PRINCE *stops motionless where above speech caught him for an instant. Pause.* PRINCE *begins to turn his head slowly and only a little way and glances carefully about, as if expecting to see tins of nitroglycerine. He sees nothing on either side and finally turns towards* CRAIGIN.)

PRINCE: *If* it ain't askin' too much, wot's the matter with the place? It looks all roight to *me!*

CRAIGIN: Well, don't light no matches and it'll stay lookin' the same.

   (*Pause. Door opens and* BASSICK *enters hurriedly at left. He looks quickly about.*)

BASSICK: Oh, Prince, you're here! I was looking for you outside.

PRINCE: (*going to* BASSICK*'s right*) You told me to be 'ere, sir. That was 'ow the last arrangement stood.

BASSICK: Very well. (*Glances about to see that the other men are present.*) You've got the rope, Craigin?

CRAIGIN: (*Points to bunch of loose rope on floor near him.*) It's 'ere.

   (PRINCE *remains listening and turning to men as they are spoken to.*)

BASSICK: That you, Leary?

LEARY: 'ere, sir!

   (PRINCE *looks up toward* LEARY.)

BASSICK: And McTague?

McTAGUE: 'ere, sir!

(PRINCE *turns toward* McTAGUE, *backing a little toward door left.*)

BASSICK: You want to be very careful with it tonight — you've got a tough one.

CRAIGIN: You ain't said who, as I've heard!

BASSICK: Sherlock Holmes.

    (CRAIGIN *rises and approaches* BASSICK, *and* LEARY *comes down on his left; upon which,* McTAGUE *draws nearer up center.* PRINCE *is standing near door or a little above it. Brief pause.*)

CRAIGIN: You mean that, sir!

BASSICK: Indeed I do!

CRAIGIN: We're goin' to count 'im out!

BASSICK: Well, if you *don't* and he gets away — I'm sorry for you — that's all!

CRAIGIN: I'll be cursed glad to put the gas on 'im — I tell you *that!*

LEARY: I says the same myself!

    (*Sound of* MORIARTY *and* LARRABEE *coming*)

BASSICK: Sh! Professor Moriarty's coming!

    (McTAGUE *places lamp on box at right.*)

LEARY: Not the guv'nor?

BASSICK: Yes. He wanted to see to this.

    (*The three men retire up at right and right center, waiting.* BASSICK *moves toward center.* PRINCE *moves up out of way on left. Door left opens. Enter* MORIARTY, *followed by* LARRABEE. *Door slowly closes behind them.* BASSICK *comes to* MORIARTY *as he enters.* LARRABEE *waits a moment near door left and then retires up near* PRINCE. *They watch the following scene. All voices low — quiet — in undertone — yet not light.*)

MORIARTY: Where's Craigin? (CRAIGIN *steps forward.* MORIARTY *crosses to him.*) Have you got your men?

CRAIGIN: All 'ere, sir.

MORIARTY: No mistakes tonight.

CRAIGIN: I'll be careful o' that!

MORIARTY: (*quick glance about*) That door, Bassick? (*Points up left center.*)

BASSICK: A small cupboard, sir! (*He goes quickly up and opens the door wide to show it.* LEARY *catches up lantern and swings it near the cupboard door.*)

MORIARTY: (*moving up center*) No outlet?

BASSICK: (*at cupboard*) None whatever, sir.

    (LEARY *swings lantern almost inside cupboard to let* MORIARTY *see.*)

MORIARTY: (*Turns and points up right.*) That window?

    (McTAGUE *quickly moves aside to right, near* CRAIGIN.)

BASSICK: (*moving out a little toward up center*) Spiked down, sir.

    (LEARY *turns to right and swings the lantern near window so* MORIARTY *can see.*)

MORIARTY: A man might break the glass?

BASSICK: If he did that he'd come against heavy iron bars outside.

CRAIGIN: We'll 'ave 'im tied down afore 'e could break any glass, sir!

MORIARTY: (*who has turned to* CRAIGIN) Ah! You've used it before. Of course you know it's air tight?

BASSICK: Every crevice is caulked, sir.

MORIARTY: (*Turns and points as if at something directly over the footlights.*) And that door?

> (LEARY *comes down right center and gives lantern a quick swing as if lighting place indicated.*)

BASSICK: The opening is planked up solid, sir, as you can see, and double thickness.

MORIARTY: Ah. (*Satisfied. Glances at door left through which he entered.*) When the men turn the gas on him they leave by that door?

BASSICK: Yes, sir.

MORIARTY: It can be made quite secure?

BASSICK: Heavy bolts on the outside, sir, and solid oak bars over all.

MORIARTY: Let me see how quick you can operate them.

BASSICK: They tie the man down, sir — there's no need to hurry.

MORIARTY: (*same voice*) Let me see how quick you can operate them.

BASSICK: (*quick order*) Leary! (*Motions him to door left, at same time coming two or three steps up and to left center.*)

LEARY: (*handing lamp to* CRAIGIN) Yes, sir! (*He jumps to door left and goes out, closing it at once, and immediately the sounds of sliding bolts and the dropping of bars is heard from outside left.*)

MORIARTY: That's all.

> (*Sounds of bolts withdrawn.* LEARY *enters at door left and waits.*)

MORIARTY: (*Goes to* CRAIGIN.) Craigin — you'll take your men outside that door and wait till Mr Larrabee has had a little business interview with the gentleman. Take them up the passage to the left so that Holmes does not see them as he comes in. Who's driving the cab tonight?

BASSICK: I sent O'Hagan. His orders are to drive him about for an hour so he doesn't know the distance or the direction he's going, and then stop at the small door on upper Swandem Lane. He's to get him out there and show him up to this door.

MORIARTY: The cab windows were covered, of course?

BASSICK: Wooden shutters, sir, bolted on secure. There isn't a place he can see through the size of a pin.

MORIARTY: (*satisfied*) Ah. — (*Looks about, going to center and half up.*) We must have a lamp here.

BASSICK: Better not, sir. There might be some gas left.

MORIARTY: (*well up center*) You've got a light there. (*Points to miner's safety lamp.*)

BASSICK: It's a safety lamp, sir.

MORIARTY: A safety lamp! You mustn't have that here! The moment he sees it he'll know what you're doing and make trouble! (*Sniffs.*) There's hardly any gas. Go and tell Lascar we must have a good lamp.

> (BASSICK *exits left.*)

MORIARTY: (*Looks about up right.*) Put that table over there. (*Points down right center.*)

> (CRAIGIN *and* McTAGUE *bring table from up center and place it down right center and oblique, not too far down.*)

MORIARTY: Now Craigin — and the rest of you — one thing remember. No shooting tonight! Not a single shot! It can be heard in the alley below. The first thing is to get his revolver away before he has a chance to use it. Two of you attract his attention in front — the other come up on him from behind and snatch it out of his pocket. Then you have him. Arrange that, Craigin.

CRAIGIN: I'll attend to it, sir.

> (*Enter* BASSICK *at door left with a large lamp, which gives good light, but burns a safety oil in a reservoir which will not break when the lamp is broken later in the scene.* BASSICK *crosses others to table and places lamp near left end of it, standing at lower side of table with back to front. Lights go on stronger when lamp is brought in.*)

BASSICK: (*to* McTAGUE) Put out that lamp.

> (McTAGUE *is about to pick up lamp.*)

CRAIGIN: Stop! We'll want it when the other's taken away.

> (McTAGUE *waits.*)

BASSICK: He mustn't see it, you understand.

MORIARTY: Don't put it out. Cover it with something.

CRAIGIN: Here! (*Goes up to right and takes lantern and, pulling out a large box from several others, places lantern within and pushes the open side against the wall so that no light from the lantern can be seen from front.* LEARY *follows* CRAIGIN *as if to assist in the business.*)

MORIARTY: That will do.

BASSICK: (*Approaches* MORIARTY.) You mustn't stay any longer, sir. O'Hagan might be a little early. (*Crosses to door down left and stands waiting.*)

MORIARTY: Larrabee — (*Moving a step or two forward.* LARRABEE *comes down on* MORIARTY's *left.*) You understand! *They wait for you.*

LARRABEE: I understand, sir.

MORIARTY: I give you this opportunity to get what you can for your trouble. But anything that is found on him after you have finished — is subject — (*Glances at* CRAIGIN *and others.*) — to the usual division.

LARRABEE: That's all I want.

MORIARTY: When you have quite finished and got your money, suppose you blow that little whistle which I observe hanging from your watch chain — and these gentlemen will take *their* turn.

> (BASSICK, *at door left holds door open for* MORIARTY.
> LARRABEE *moves up out of way as* MORIARTY *crosses.*)

MORIARTY: (*at door, turning to* CRAIGIN) And Craigin — at the proper moment present my compliments to Mr Sherlock Holmes, and say that I wished him a pleasant journey to the other side. (MORIARTY *exits at door left, followed by* BASSICK. CRAIGIN *and* LEARY *and* McTAGUE *remain up right and right center a moment after* MORIARTY's *exit.* LARRABEE, *near table, glances about critically.*)

LARRABEE: You'd better put that rope out of sight.

> (CRAIGIN *goes down right and picks up rope which he carries with him until his exit.* LEARY *and* McTAGUE *move across noiselessly at back to left.* CRAIGIN *stops an instant to examine window up*

right, looking at the caulking and shaking it to see that it is securely spiked. Others wait near door left. He finishes at window and crosses toward door.)

CRAIGIN: (*Joins* LEARY *and* McTAGUE *at door left. Speaks to* LARRABEE *from door.*) You understand we're on this floor just around the fur turn of the passage — so 'e won't see us as 'e's comin' up.

LARRABEE: I understand.

CRAIGIN: An' it's wen we 'ears that whistle, eh?

LARRABEE: When you hear this whistle. (*Stands by lamp right center.*)

(*Exit* CRAIGIN, LEARY *and* McTAGUE *noiselessly at door left. Pause. Door remains open.* PRINCE, *who has been very quietly up left center during foregoing scene, begins to move a little, nervously, and looks about. He looks at his watch and then glances about again. Goes over to window and examines it gingerly.* LARRABEE *is near lamp, looking at package of papers which he took from his pocket.*)

PRINCE: (*coming down in a grumpy manner; head down, not looking at* LARRABEE) Look 'ere, Jim, this thing ain't so much in my line!

LARRABEE: I suppose not.

PRINCE: (*Still glances about not looking at* LARRABEE.) Wen it comes to a shy at a safe of drillin' into bank vaults I feels perfectly at 'ome, but I don't so much care to see a man — (*Stops; hesitates.*) Well — it ain't my line!

LARRABEE: (*turning*) Here! (*Goes to him and urges him toward door left.*) All I want of you is to go down on the corner below and let me know when he comes!

PRINCE: (*Stops and turns to him.*) 'Ow will I let you know?

LARRABEE: Have you got a cab whistle?

PRINCE: (*Pulls one out.*) Cert'nly.

LARRABEE: Well, when you see O'Hagan driving up with him, come down the alley there and blow it twice (*urging* PRINCE *a little nearer door left*)

PRINCE: Yes. — (*Stops at door again.*) — but ain't it quite loikely to call a cab at the same time, you know?

LARRABEE: What more do you want? You can take the cab and go home.

PRINCE: Oh! Then you won't need me 'ere again?

LARRABEE: No.

PRINCE: (*Turns to go at door left.*) Oh! Very well — then I'll tear myself away. (*Exits.*)

(LARRABEE *crosses to table and fixes lamp. Gets two chairs and places them at table. As he places second chair, he stops dead as if having heard a noise outside, listens, and is satisfied all is well. Then walks about, thinking of the best way to conduct his negotiations with* HOLMES. *Takes out cigar and holds it a moment unlighted as he thinks, then takes out match and is about to light it. Enter* ALICE FAULKNER *at door left.* LARRABEE *starts up and looks at her. She stands looking at him.*)

LARRABEE: What do you want?

ALICE: It's true, then!

LARRABEE: How did you get to this place?

ALICE: I followed you — in a cab.

LARRABEE: What have you been doing since I came up here? Informing the
police, perhaps?

ALICE: No — I was afraid he'd come — so I waited.

LARRABEE: Oh — to warn him, very likely.

ALICE: Yes — (*pause*) — to warn him. (*Looks about room.*)

LARRABEE: Then it's just as well you came up!

ALICE: I came to make sure — (*Glances about.*)

LARRABEE: Of what?

ALICE: That something else — is not going to be done besides — what they told
me!

LARRABEE: Ah — somebody told you that something was going to be done?

ALICE: Yes.

LARRABEE: So! We've got *another* spy in the house!

ALICE: You are going to swindle and deceive him — I know that. *Is there anything
more*? (*Advances to him a little.*)

LARRABEE: What could you do if there was?

ALICE: I could buy you off! Such men as you are always open to sale!

LARRABEE: How much would you give?

ALICE: The genuine package — the real ones — all the proofs — everything!

LARRABEE: (*Advances above table. Quietly, but with quick interest*) Have you
got it here?

ALICE: I can get it in a few moments.

LARRABEE: Oh — (*Goes to table; slightly disappointed.*) So you'll do all that for
this man! You think he's your friend, I suppose!

ALICE: I haven't thought of it.

LARRABEE: Look what he's doing now! Coming *here* to buy those things of *me*!

ALICE: They're false! They're counterfeit!

LARRABEE: He thinks they're genuine, doesn't he? He'd hardly come here to buy
'em if he didn't —

ALICE: He *may* ask my permission still!

LARRABEE: Ha! (*Sneers; turns away.*) He won't get the chance!

ALICE: (*suspicious again*) There *is* something else!

LARRABEE: Something else! (*Turns to her.*) Why, you see me here by myself,
don't you? I'm going to talk to him on a little business. How could *I* do him
any harm?

ALICE: (*Advances.*) Where are those men who came up here?

LARRABEE: What men? (*Stands right of table.*)

ALICE: Three villainous looking men. I saw them go in at the street door.

LARRABEE: Oh — *those* men! They went up the other stairway. (*Points over
shoulder.*) You can see them in the next building if you look out of this
window.

> (LARRABEE *indicates window up right, which he is now standing
> near. ALICE at once goes rapidly toward window up right of table
> with her hand on it and makes a hesitating pause near table as she
> sees* LARRABEE *crossing to left near her, but moves on again
> quickly. At the same time,* LARRABEE *crosses toward left well up*

stage, keeping his eyes on ALICE *as she crosses to right below table. She comes to window up right and tries to look out, but, finding she cannot, she turns at once to* LARRABEE. *He is standing near door on the left. They stand looking at one another.* ALICE *begins to see that she has been trapped.*)

ALICE: (*Starts across toward door left above table.*) I'll look in the passageway, if you please!

LARRABEE: (*Takes one step down before door left quietly, and stands before door.*) Yes — but I don't please!

ALICE: (*Stops before him.*) You would not *dare* to keep me here!

LARRABEE: I might *dare* — but I won't. You'd be in the way!

ALICE: Where are those men?

LARRABEE: Stay just where you are and you'll see them very soon.

(LARRABEE *goes to door and blows whistle as quietly as possible. Stands a little to left center; short pause. No footsteps are heard as the men move noiselessly. Enter at door left* CRAIGIN, McTAGUE, *and* LEARY, *appearing suddenly. They stand looking in some astonishment at* ALICE.)

ALICE: I knew it! (*Moves back a step and leans hand on table. Senses that they are going to attack* HOLMES.) Ah! (*Under breath; after slight pause she turns and hurries to window, trying to look out or give an alarm. She then runs to cupboard door.* LARRABEE *stops her. She comes center, stops, and stands looking at them, at bay.* LARRABEE *waits, watching her movements.*)

ALICE: (*desperately*) You're going to do him some harm!

LARRABEE: Oh, no, it's only a little joke — at his expense.

ALICE: (*Moves toward him a little.*) You wanted the letters, the package I had in the safe! I'll get it for you! Let me go and I'll bring it here — or whatever you tell me — (LARRABEE *sneers meaningly.*) I'll give you my word not to say anything to anyone — not to him — not to the policemen — not to *anyone*!

LARRABEE: (*without moving*) You needn't take the trouble to get it — but you can tell me where it is — and you'll have to be quick about it, too!

ALICE: Yes, if you'll promise not to go on with this!

LARRABEE: Of course! That's understood.

ALICE: (*excitedly*) You promise!

LARRABEE: Certainly I promise! Now, where is it?

ALICE: Just outside my chamber window — just outside on the left fastening, between the shutter and the wall — you can easily find it!

LARRABEE: Yes — I can easily find it!

ALICE: Now tell them — tell them to go!

LARRABEE: (*Goes down to men.*) Tie her up so she can't make a noise. Keep her out there with you until we have Holmes in here, and then let O'Hagan keep her in his cab! She mustn't get back to the house — not till I've been there!

CRAIGIN: (*Speaks low.*) Go an' get a'hold Leary. Hand me a piece of that rope!

(McTAGUE *brings rope from under his coat. Rapidly gets it ready to gag and tie* ALICE. McTAGUE *takes handkerchief from his pocket to use as a gag.*)

LARRABEE: (*Takes a step or two down before* ALICE *so as to attract her attention front.*) Now then, my pretty bird —

ALICE: (*Moves back in alarm.*) You said — you said if I told you —

LARRABEE: Well, we haven't done him any harm yet, have we?

       (LEARY *is quietly stealing round behind her.* LARRABEE *is moving down before* ALICE *so that she backs away to up center.*)

ALICE: Then send them away! (*up center a little*)

LARRABEE: (*back to audience, looking left*) Certainly! Go away now, boys, there's no more work for you tonight!

ALICE: (*Looks at them terrified.*) They don't obey you! They are —

       (LEARY *seizes her. She screams and resists, but* CRAIGIN *and* McTAGUE *come at once up center so that she is quickly subdued and gagged with handkerchief and her hands tied. As struggle takes place, men work up center to near cupboard with* ALICE.
       LARRABEE *also eagerly watches them tie her up. Just as they finish a shrill whistle is heard in distance outside right at back, as if from street far below. All stop, listening. The prolonged shrill whistle is heard again.*)

CRAIGIN: Now out of the door with her!

       (*Whistle is heard.*)

LARRABEE: By God, he's *here*!

CRAIGIN: What!

LARRABEE: That's Sid Prince! I put him on the watch!

CRAIGIN: We won't have time to get her out!

LARRABEE: Shut her in there! (*Points to cupboard.*)

LEARY: Yes — that'll do.

CRAIGIN: In with her!

       (*Almost on the word, they have her in the cupboard with door shut and are standing before it.*)

LEARY: (*Still at cupboard door; others have turned so as to avoid suspicion if* HOLMES *comes in on them.*) There ain't no lock to this 'ere door!

       (McTAGUE *goes down to door left hurriedly.*)

LARRABEE: No lock!

LEARY: No.

LARRABEE: Drive something in!

CRAIGIN: Here, this knife! (*Hands* LEARY *a large clasp knife opened and ready.*)

LARRABEE: A knife won't do.

CRAIGIN: Yes, it will. Drive it in strong.

LEARY: (*Drives blade in door frame with all his force.*) 'E'll 'ave to find us 'ere!

CRAIGIN: Yes — and we won't wait, either! We'll go on and do 'im up! (*Goes to door down left.*)

LARRABEE: No, you won't! (*pause*) I'll see him first, if you please.

       (CRAIGIN *and* LARRABEE *face each other savagely an instant.*)

LEARY: Thems was orders, Craigin.

CRAIGIN: So it was!

McTAGUE: There might be time to get back into the passage! (*He listens at door left and cautiously looks off. Turns back into room.*) They ain't got up one flight yet!

LEARY: Quick, then!

> (LEARY *moves toward door left. Exit* LEARY, McTAGUE, *and* CRAIGIN *at door left. The door is not to close again until* HOLMES *is on.* LARRABEE *glances at cupboard door anxiously. Makes a quick dash to it and forces knife in with all his strength. Comes quickly down right of table, pulls off coat and hat, throws them on empty barrel, and sits quietly chewing on end of cigar. Enter* SHERLOCK HOLMES *at door left, walking easily as if on some ordinary business.*)

HOLMES: (*Seeing the apartment with a glance as he enters and pauses left center, disappointed. He laughs a little with no smile.*) How the devil is it that you blacklegs always hit on the same places for your scoundrelly business? Ha! (*chuckle of amusement*) Well! I certainly thought after all this driving about you'd show me something new!

LARRABEE: (*Looks up nonchalantly.*) Seen it before, have you?

HOLMES: (*Stands still at left center.*) W — ha! — well I should say so! (*Moves easily about, recalling dear old times.*) I nabbed a friend of yours in this place while he was trying to drop himself out of that window — Ed Colvin the safe breaker.

LARRABEE: Colvin! I never heard of him before!

HOLMES: No? Ha, ha! Well, you certainly never heard of him after! A brace of counterfeiters used these regal chambers in the spring of '89. One of them hid in that cupboard. We pulled him out by the heels.

LARRABEE: (*trying to get in on the nonchalance*) Ah? Did you? And the other?

HOLMES: The other? He was more fortunate.

LARRABEE: Ah, he got away, I suppose.

HOLMES: Yes — *he* got away — we took his remains out through that door to the street. (*Indicates door left.*)

LARRABEE: Quite interesting! (*Drawls a little; looks at end of his cigar.* HOLMES *is up left center a little looking about.*) Times have changed since then!

HOLMES: (*Darts a lightning glance at* LARRABEE. *Instantly easy again and glancing about as before. Drops down near* LARRABEE.) So they have, Mr Larrabee — so they have! (*a little confidentially*) Then it was only safe breakers, counterfeiters, pickpockets, and petty swindlers of various kinds! *Now* (*Pause; looks at* LARRABEE.)

LARRABEE: (*Turns and looks at* HOLMES.) Eh? What *now*?

HOLMES: Well — (*mysteriously*) — Between you and me, Mr Larrabee, we've heard not altogether agreeable rumors; rumors of some pretty shady work not far from here — a murder or two of a very peculiar kind — and I've always had a suspicion — (*Stops, sniffs very delicately; motionless pause. Nods ominously to* LARRABEE, *who is watching him.*) That's it! (*Moves up stage, and, as if casually looking about, gets over toward window. When within reach, he runs his hand lightly along the frame.*) My surmise was correct — *it is!*

LARRABEE: (*Turns to* HOLMES.) It is what?

HOLMES: Caulked.

LARRABEE: What does that signify to us?

HOLMES: Nothing to *us*, Mr Larrabee, nothing to us; but it might signify a good
deal to some poor devil who's been caught in this trap!

LARRABEE: Well, if it's nothing to us, suppose we leave it alone and get to
business. My time is limited.

HOLMES: Quite so, of course! (*Strolls down.*) I should have realized that these
reflections could not possibly appeal to you. (*Stands at table a little above*
LARRABEE.) But it so happens that I take a deep interest in anything that
pertains to what are known as the criminal classes, and this same interest
makes me rather curious to know (*Looks straight at* LARRABEE, *who looks
up at him.*) how you happened to select such a singularly gruesome place for
an ordinary business transaction.

LARRABEE: I selected this place, Mr Holmes, because I thought you might not be
disposed to take such liberties here as you practiced in my own house last
night.

HOLMES: Quite so, quite so. (*Looks innocently at* LARRABEE.) But why not?
(*They look at one another an instant.*)

LARRABEE: (*significantly*) You might not feel quite so much at home!

HOLMES: Oh – ha! (*a little laugh*) You've made a singular miscalculation there! I
feel perfectly at home, Mr Larrabee! (*He seats himself at table in a languid
and leisurely manner; takes cigar from pocket and lights it.*)

LARRABEE: Well, I'm very glad to hear it. (*He now takes out the counterfeit
package of papers and tosses it upon the table before them.*) Here is the little
packet which is the object of this meeting. (*He glances at* HOLMES *to see
effect.* HOLMES *looks at it calmly as he smokes.*) I haven't opened it yet, but
Miss Faulkner tells me everything is there.

HOLMES: Then there is no need of opening it, Mr Larrabee.

LARRABEE: Oh, well – I want to see you satisfied.

HOLMES: That is precisely the condition in which you now behold me. Miss
Faulkner is a truthful young lady. Her word is sufficient.

LARRABEE: Very well; now what shall we say, Mr Holmes? (*pause*) Of course, we
want a pretty large price for this. Miss Faulkner is giving up everything. She
would not be satisfied unless the result justified it.

HOLMES: (*pointedly*) Suppose, Mr Larrabee, that as Miss Faulkner knows nothing
whatever about this affair, we omit her name from the discussion. (*slight
pause*)

LARRABEE: Who told you she doesn't know?

HOLMES: You did. Every look, tone, gesture, – everything you have said and done
since I have been in this room has informed me that she has never consented
to this transaction. It is a little speculation of your own.

LARRABEE: Ha! (*sneer*) I suppose you think you can read me like a book!

HOLMES: No – like a Primer.

LARRABEE: Well, let that pass. How much'll you give?

HOLMES: A thousand pounds.

LARRABEE: I couldn't take it!

HOLMES: What do you ask?

LARRABEE: Five thousand.

HOLMES: (*Shakes head.*) I couldn't give it.

LARRABEE: Very well — (*Rises.*) — We've had all this trouble for nothing. (*as if about to pick up the packet*)

HOLMES: (*Leans back in chair and remonstrates.*) Oh — don't say that, Mr Larrabee! To me the occasion has been doubly interesting. I have not only had the pleasure of meeting you again, but I have also availed myself of the opportunity of making some observations regarding this place which may not come amiss.

LARRABEE: (*Rises and looks down at* HOLMES *contemptuously.*) Why, I've been offered for this little bunch of —

HOLMES: (*Stops him good naturedly.*) Yes — but you won't be again!

LARRABEE: Why not?

HOLMES: You're dealing with me.

LARRABEE: Will you give three thousand?

HOLMES: (*Rises.*) Mr Larrabee, strange as it may appear, *my* time is limited as well as yours. I have brought with me the sum of one thousand pounds, which was all that I wished to pay. If it is your desire to sell at this figure, kindly apprise me of the fact at once. If not, permit me to wish you a very good evening.

> (*Pause.* LARRABEE *looks at him, then glances nervously round up left once, fearing he heard something.*)

LARRABEE: Go on! (*Tosses packet on table.*) You can have them. It's too small a matter to haggle over!

> (HOLMES *reseats himself at once, back of table, and takes wallet from his pocket, from which he produces a bunch of bank notes.* LARRABEE *stands down right a little, watching him with glittering eye.* HOLMES *counts out ten one hundred pound notes and lays the remainder of the notes on the table at his right, with elbow on them, while he counts the first over again.*)

LARRABEE: (*sneeringly*) Oh! I thought you said you had brought just a thousand.

HOLMES: (*not looking up; counting the notes*) I did. This is it.

LARRABEE: You brought a trifle more, I see!

HOLMES: Quite so. I didn't say I hadn't brought any *more*.

LARRABEE: Ha! (*sneer*) You can do your little tricks when it comes to it, can't you?

HOLMES: It depends on who I'm dealing with.

> (HOLMES *hands* LARRABEE *one thousand pounds in notes.* LARRABEE *takes money and keeps a close watch at the same time on the remaining pile of notes lying at* HOLMES' *left.* HOLMES, *after handing the notes to* LARRABEE, *lays cigar he was smoking on the table, picks up the packet which he puts in his pocket with his right hand, and is, at almost the same time, reaching with his left for the notes he places upon the table when* LARRABEE *makes a sudden lunge and snatches the pile of bank notes, jumping back to right on the instant.* HOLMES *springs to his feet at the same time.*)

HOLMES: *Now* I've got you where I want you, Jim Larrabee! You've been so cunning and so cautious and so wise we couldn't find a thing to hold you for — but this little slip will get you in for *robbery*!

LARRABEE: (*at right*) Oh! You'll have me in, will you! (*short sneering laugh*) What are your views about being able to get away from here yourself?

HOLMES: I do not now anticipate any particular difficulty.

LARRABEE: (*significantly*) Perhaps you'll change your mind about that!

HOLMES: Whether I change my mind or not, I certainly shall leave this place — and your arrest will shortly follow!

LARRABEE: My arrest! Ha, ha! Robbery, eh! Why even if you got away from here you haven't got a witness! Not a witness to your name!

HOLMES: (*Slowly backs up center, keeping his eyes sharply on* LARRABEE.) I'm not so sure of that, Mr Larrabee! Do you usually fasten that door with a knife? (*Points toward door up left center with left arm and hand, but with eyes on* LARRABEE.)

> (*Very faint moan is heard from within cupboard up left center.* HOLMES *listens motionless an instant, then makes quick dash to door up left center and, seizing knife, wrenches it out and flings it on the floor.* LARRABEE, *seeing* HOLMES *start toward door of cupboard, springs up right center to head him off.*)

LARRABEE: Come away from that door!

HOLMES: (*Tears the door open and pulls* ALICE FAULKNER *out before* LARRABEE *gets near.*) Stand back! (*Turns on* LARRABEE, *supporting* ALICE *at same time.*) You contemptible scoundrel! What does this mean!

LARRABEE: (*up right center*) I'll show you what it means cursed quick. (*Takes step or two down left. Blows the little silver whistle attached to his watch chain and crosses to right below table.*)

HOLMES: (*Unties* ALICE *quickly.*) I'm afraid you're badly hurt, Miss Faulkner.

> (*Enter* CRAIGIN *at door left. He stands there a moment near door, watching* HOLMES. *He makes a signal with hand to others outside door and then moves noiselessly to left center.* McTAGUE *enters at door left noiselessly and remains a little behind* CRAIGIN, *below door left.*)

ALICE: (*Shakes her head quickly, thinking of what she sees and tries to call* HOLMES' *attention to* CRAIGIN *and* McTAGUE.) Mr Holmes! (*Points to* CRAIGIN *and* McTague.)

HOLMES: (*Glances around.*) Ah, Craigin — delighted to see you. And you, too, McTague. I infer from your presence here at this — particular juncture — that I am not dealing with Mr Larrabee alone.

LARRABEE: (*Stands at right, half down.*) Your inference is quite correct, Mr Holmes!

HOLMES: It is not difficult to imagine who is at the bottom of such a conspiracy as this. (CRAIGIN *begins to steal across to right noiselessly.* McTAGUE *remains before door left.* HOLMES *turns to* ALICE *again.*) I hope you're beginning to feel a little more yourself, Miss Faulkner — because we shall leave here very soon.

ALICE: (*who has been shrinking from the sight of* CRAIGIN *and* McTAGUE) Oh yes — *Do* let us go, Mr Holmes!

CRAIGIN: (*low deep voice, right center below table*) You'll 'ave to wait a little, Mr 'Olmes! We 'ave a matter o' business we'd like to talk hover!

(HOLMES *turns right center to* CRAIGIN. *Enter* LEARY *at door left and glides up left side in the shadow and begins to move toward* HOLMES *from up left. In approaching from corner up left, he glides behind door of cupboard up left center as it stands open, and from there down on* HOLMES.)

HOLMES: All right, Craigin — I'll see you tomorrow morning in your cell at Bow Street.

CRAIGIN: (*threateningly*) Werry sorry, sir, but I cawn't wait till morning. It's got to be settled tonight!

HOLMES: (*Looks at* CRAIGIN *an instant.*) All right, Craigin, we'll settle it tonight.

CRAIGIN: It's so werry himportant, Mr 'Olmes — so werry himportant indeed — that you'll 'ave to 'tend to it now.

(*At this instant* ALICE *sees* LEARY *approaching rapidly from behind and screams.* HOLMES *turns, but* LEARY *is upon him at the same time. There is a very short struggle and* HOLMES *throws* LEARY *violently off to left, but* LEARY *has got* HOLMES' *revolver. At struggle,* ALICE *steps back to side of room up stage. A short deadly pause.* LARRABEE *comes down right.* HOLMES *is motionless a little up center regarding the men.* ALICE *is up back against the wall.* CRAIGIN *faces* HOLMES *motionless from down stage right center. After the pause* LEARY *begins to revive and slowly gets up.*)

CRAIGIN: (*low voice to* LEARY) 'Ave ye got his revolver?

LEARY: (*Shows it.*) 'Ere it is!

HOLMES: (*Recognizes* LEARY *in the dim light.*) Ah, Leary! (*up center*) This is a pleasure indeed! It needed only your blithe personality to make the party complete! (*Sits and writes rapidly on pocket pad at the table right center, pushing lamp away a little and picking up cigar which he had left on the table and which he keeps in his mouth as he writes.*) There is only one other I could wish to welcome here, and that is the talented author of this midnight carnival. We shall have him, however, by tomorrow night!

CRAIGIN: (*right center*) Though 'e ain't 'ere, Mr 'Olmes, 'e gave me a message for yer. 'E presented 'is koindest compliments and wished yer a pleasant trip across.

HOLMES: (*writing; cigar in mouth*) Craigin, if you ever see the Professor again, tell him I hope (*Writes.*) the knot won't make a bad mark at the side of his head.

LARRABEE: (*sneeringly*) Ho, you're writing your will, I suppose?

HOLMES: (*writing, with quick glances up at the men*) No — (*Shakes head.*) — only a brief description of one or two of you gentlemen — for the police.

LEARY: And when will yer give it to 'em, Mr 'Olmes?

HOLMES: (*Writes.*) Nine — or nine and a half minutes, Mr Leary.

LARRABEE: Oh, you expect to leave here in nine minutes, eh?

HOLMES: No. (*Writes.*) In *one*. But it will take me about eight minutes to find an officer. This is a dangerous neighborhood.

LARRABEE: Well, when you're ready to start, let us know.

HOLMES: (*Rises and puts pad in pocket.*) I'm ready now!

(CRAIGIN, McTAGUE, *and* LEARY *suddenly brace themselves for*

action and stand ready to make a run for HOLMES. LARRABEE
also is ready to join in the struggle if necessary, down right.
HOLMES *moves backward from table a little to* ALICE. *She drops
down a step toward* HOLMES.)

CRAIGIN: Wait a bit! You'd better listen to me, Mr 'Olmes. We're goin' to tie ye
down nice and tight to the top o' that table.

HOLMES: Ha! Ha! Well, by Jove, I don't think you will! That's my idea, you
know!

CRAIGIN: An' you'll save yourself a great deal o' trouble if ye submit quiet and
easy like — because if ye don't ye might get knocked about some —

ALICE: (*under her breath*) Oh — Mr Holmes!

LARRABEE: (*to* ALICE) Come away from him! Come over here if you don't want
to get hurt!

HOLMES: (*to* ALICE *without looking round, but reaching her with left hand*) My
child, if you don't want to get hurt, don't you leave me for a second! (ALICE
moves closer to him.)

LARRABEE: Aren't you coming?

ALICE: (*breathlessly*) No!

CRAIGIN: You'd better look out, Miss — he might get killed!

ALICE: Then you can kill me too!

HOLMES: (*Makes a quick turn to her, with sudden exclamation under his breath.
For an instant only he looks in her face, then a quick turn back to* CRAIGIN
and men. Low voice, not taking eyes from men before him) I'm afraid you
don't mean that, Miss Faulkner!

ALICE: (*still above him on his left*) Yes, I *do*!

HOLMES: (*eyes on men; they shift about rapidly but never look toward* ALICE)
No — (*shaking head a trifle*) — You would not say it — at another time and
place!

ALICE: I would say it anywhere — *always*!

CRAIGIN: So you'll 'ave it out with us, eh?

HOLMES: Do you imagine for one minute that I *won't* have it out with you?

CRAIGIN: Well, then — I'll 'ave to give yer one — same as I did yer right 'and man
this afternoon!

HOLMES: (*to* ALICE *without turning; intense; rapid*) You heard him say that! As
he did my right hand man this afternoon!

ALICE: (*under breath*) Yes! Yes!

HOLMES: Don't forget that face! (*Points to* CRAIGIN.) In three days I shall ask
you to identify it in the prisoner's dock!

CRAIGIN: (*enraged*) Ha!

HOLMES: (*very sharp; rapid*) Yes — and the rest of you along with him! You
surprise me, gentlemen — thinking you're sure of anybody in this room, and
never once taking the trouble to have a look at that window! If you wanted
to make it perfectly safe you should have had those *missing bars put in*!
(CRAIGIN, LEARY, McTAGUE, LARRABEE *very slightly move
and 'Eh!' but instantly at tension again, and all motionless ready to
spring on* HOLMES. HOLMES *and* ALICE *motionless facing
them.*)

LARRABEE: Bars or no bars, you're not going to get out of here as easy as you expect.

HOLMES: (*Moves easily down near table right center.*) There are so many ways, I hardly know which to choose, Mr Larrabee!

CRAIGIN: (*louder; advancing*) Well, you'd better choose quick — I can tell you that.

HOLMES: (*suddenly; strong, sharp*) I'll choose at once, Mr Craigin — and my choice — (*quickly seizing chair*) — falls on this!

> (*On the word he brings the chair down upon the lamp with a frightful crash, extinguishing light instantly. All lights out. Only the glow of* HOLMES' *cigar remains visible where he stands at the table. He at once begins to move up right toward window, keeping cigar so that it will show to men and to front.*)

CRAIGIN: (*low sharp voice, to others*) Track 'im by the cigar! (*Moves at once toward window up right.*)

LARRABEE: (*remaining down right*) Look out! He's going for the window!

> (McTAGUE *and* LEARY *go quickly to window.* HOLMES *quickly fixes cigar in a crack or joint at side of window up right so that it is still seen. Smash of glass back of window.* HOLMES *instantly glides across left, well up stage and down left side to the door left, where he finds* ALICE. *On crash of window,* CRAIGIN, McTAGUE, LARRABEE, *and* LEARY *give a quick shout or exclamation.*)

LARRABEE: He'll get out! Jump on him! Quick, now!

> (*They spring up stage toward the light of cigar. Sound of quick scuffle and blows up right in darkness.*)

LARRABEE: Get that light!

CRAIGIN: The safety light! Where is it? (*very loudly*)

> (McTAGUE *kicks over the box which concealed the safety lamp. Lights come up.* HOLMES *and* ALICE *at door left.* ALICE *just going out at left.*)

HOLMES: (*turning at door left and pointing to window up right*) If you want that cigar you'll find it in a crevice by the window.

> (*All start toward* HOLMES *with exclamations and oaths.* HOLMES *quickly makes exit with* ALICE *at door left and slams it shut after him. Sounds of heavy bolts outside left sliding quickly into place, and bars dropping into position.* CRAIGIN, McTAGUE, *and* LEARY *rush against door and make violent effort to open it. After the first excited effort they turn quickly back to center.* LARRABEE, *who has stopped near center when he saw door closed, turns front with a look of hatred and rage on his face.*)

CURTAIN

FOURTH ACT

Scene. *Dr Watson's house in Kensington. The office or consulting room. Good sized room. Buff or yellowish tone to walls. Solid furniture. Easy chair. Wide double doors on right side opening to hall and street door. Door up left center and well to left on oblique communicating with the doctor's inner office or medicine room. A door in flat up center a little to right which opens to private hallway of house. The doctor's desk up left center covered with a litter of bottles, pamphlets, books, instruments, and the various things which would be found on a doctor's table. Cases of drawers with cabinets of bottles in rows to dress room. Books in cases. Two windows on left side which are supposed to open at side of house upon an area or lawn which faces the street. These windows have shades or blinds on rollers which can quickly be drawn down. At opening they are down so that no one could see into the room from the street. Large operating chair up right center with high back and cushions. DOCTOR WATSON is discovered at his desk center. MRS SMEEDLY, a seedy looking middle-aged woman, is seated right of desk with one phial in her hand.*

WATSON: Be careful to make no mistake about the medicine. You are not to give her this unless the cough becomes very much worse.

MRS SMEEDLY: I'll be sure to remember it, sir.

> (*The* DOCTOR *rises and* MRS SMEEDLY *rises also, looking round room an instant, then at once turns to him.*)

MRS SMEEDLY: I'm very much worried about her, doctor, very much worried! I couldn't begin to tell you how worried I am. It's really past belief!

WATSON: (*standing at desk*) Yes — well, if she's no better tomorrow I'll call. You will let me know, of course?

MRS SMEEDLY: Oh, yes, indeed, I will — (*again a quick glance about*) Good evening, sir.

WATSON: Good night, Mrs — (*Hesitates.*)

MRS SMEEDLY: Smeedly, sir.

WATSON: Ah, yes — Mrs Smeedly! I didn't quite catch the name. (*Writes on paper. She starts to go off at door up center.*) No — not that door! (*Walks to door right and opens it.* MRS SMEEDLY *stops in doorway up center and turns, but first gives a quick look about within doorway as* WATSON*'s back is turned.*) This way, if you please! (*Stands above door, holding it open.*)

MRS SMEEDLY: Oh! (*Goes to door right.*) I beg pardon, I'm sure.

> (*She exits at door right.* WATSON *eyes her sharply as she passes him. He is just turning away from door to return to his desk, when something outside door right where* MRS SMEEDLY *made her exit attracts his attention, and he stops and looks off in some surprise. Sound of door outside right closing. The* DOCTOR *turns and goes to his desk, sitting before it, and rings bell. Busies himself with paper. Enter* PARSONS, *a servant, at door right.*)

WATSON: Oh! Parsons! (PARSONS *turns to* WATSON. *Lower voice*) The woman who just left — do you know her?

PARSONS: (*trying to recollect*) No, sir! I can't say as I recollect 'avin' seen 'er before. Was there anything —

WATSON: Oh, no! Acted a little strange, that's all. I thought I saw her looking about the hall before she went out.

PARSONS: Yes, sir, she did give a look. I saw that myself, sir.

WATSON: (*after an instant's thought*) Oh, well — I dare say it was nothing. Is there anyone waiting, Parsons?

PARSONS: There's one person in the waiting room, sir, – a gentleman.

WATSON: (*Looks at his watch.*) I'll see him but I've only a short time left. If any more come you must send them over to Dr Anstruther. I spoke to him this afternoon about taking my cases on. I have an important appointment at nine.

PARSONS: Very well, sir; then you'll see this gentleman, sir?

WATSON: Yes.

> (PARSONS *exits at door right. Short pause.* WATSON *busy at desk.* PARSONS *opens door at right and remains outside. Enter* SID PRINCE *at right door. He comes in a little way and pauses.* PARSONS *closes door.* WATSON *looks up.*)

PRINCE: (*speaking in the most dreadful husky whisper*) Good evênin', sir.

WATSON: Good evening. (*Indicates chair right of desk.*) Pray be seated.

PRINCE: (*same voice all through*) Thanks. I don't moind if I do! (*Sits in chair up center near desk.*)

WATSON: (*Looks at him with professional interest.*) What seems to be the trouble?

PRINCE: Throat, sir. (*Indicates his throat to assist in making himself understood.*) Most dreadful sore throat!

WATSON: Sore throat, eh? (*Glances about for an instrument.*)

PRINCE: Well, I should think it is. It's the most 'arrowin' thing I ever 'ad! It pains me that much to swallow that I –

WATSON: Hurts you to swallow, does it? (*instrument where he can easily reach it*)

PRINCE: Indeed it does! Why, I can 'ardly get a bit of food down!

> (WATSON *rises and goes to cabinet up left center. Pushes gas burner out into position and lights it.*)

WATSON: Just step this way a moment, please! (PRINCE *rises and goes to* WATSON, *who adjusts reflector over eye, instrument in hand.*) Now mouth open – wide as possible! (PRINCE *opens mouth and* WATSON *places tongue holder on his tongue.*) That's it. (*Picks up dentist's mirror and warms it over gas burner.*)

PRINCE: (WATSON *is about to examine throat when he sees instrument and is alarmed a trifle.*) Eh!

WATSON: (*Puts in tongue holder and looks down* PRINCE's *throat. Looks carefully this way and that. He discontinues and takes instrument out of* PRINCE's *mouth.*) Say – ah!

PRINCE: Ah! (*Steps away and places handkerchief to mouth as if the attempt to say 'Ah!' had hurt him.*)

WATSON: (*a slight incredulity in his manner*) Where do you feel this pain?

PRINCE: (*Indicates with his finger.*) Just about there, doctor. Inside about there.

WATSON: That's singular. I don't find anything wrong. (*Pushes gas burner back to usual position.*)

PRINCE: You may not foind anything wrong, but I feel it wrong. If you would only give me something to take away this awful agony.

WATSON: Why, that's nothing! It'll pass away in a few hours! (*reflectively*) Singular thing it should have affected your voice in this way! Well, I'll give you a gargle – it may help you a little!

PRINCE: Yes – if you only would, doctor!

(WATSON *goes into surgery up left.* PRINCE *watches him like a cat.* WATSON *does not close the door of the room, but pushes it part way, so that it is open about a foot.* PRINCE *moves toward the door up left watching* WATSON *through it. Stops near door. Remains there a while. Seems to watch for his chance, for he suddenly turns and goes quickly down left side and runs up shades of both windows and is back watching* WATSON *through the door again. Seeing he still has time to spare, he goes to door up center and opens it, look-ing and listening off. Distant sound of piano when door up center is open and which stops when it is closed.* PRINCE *quickly turns back into room and looks over to door up left, again turns back and goes off a little way at door center, leaving it open so that he is seen peer-ing up above and listening. Turns to come back but just at the door he sees* WATSON *coming on at door up left. Stops.* WATSON *enters. Sees* PRINCE *in door up center and stops with a vial in his hand and looks at* PRINCE.)

WATSON: What are you doing in there? (*pause*) What were you doing in that hall?

PRINCE: Why, nothing at all, doctor! I felt such a draught on the back o' my neck, don't yer know, that I opened the door to see where it came from.

WATSON: (*Goes down and rings bell on his desk; pause. Enter* PARSONS *at door right.*) Parsons, show this gentleman the shortest way to the street door and close it after him.

PRINCE: But, doctor, ye don't understand!

WATSON: I understand quite enough! Good evening, sir!

PRINCE: Yer know a draught plays ob with my throat, sir — and seems to affect my —

WATSON: Good evening, sir — (*Sits and pays no further attention to* PRINCE.)

PARSONS: This way, sir, hiff you please.

PRINCE: I consider, sir, that you've treated me damned outrageous, that's wat I do, and ye won't 'ear the last of this very soon!

PARSONS: (*Approaches him.*) Come, none o' that, now! (*Takes* PRINCE *by the arm.*)

PRINCE: (*As he walks toward door with* PARSONS, *turns head back and speaks over his shoulder. Begins to shout out in his natural voice.*) Yer call yerself a doctor an' treat sick people as comes to see yer this 'ere way! (*Exits with* PARSONS *and continues talking till slam of door outside.*) You call yerself a doctor! A blooming foine doctor you are!

(PARSONS *has forced* PRINCE *out by the arm at door right. Sound of outside door closing follows shortly outside right.* WATSON, *after short pause, looks round room and, not observing that window shades are up, he rings bell. Enter* PARSONS *at door right.*)

WATSON: Parsons, go and ask Mrs Watson if she noticed anyone come up there — and take a look about to see if anything happens to be missing.

PARSONS: Missing, sir?

WATSON: Yes — I caught that fellow coming out of the door there, as I came in from my surgery.

PARSONS: I'll go and ask Mrs Watson, sir.

(PARSONS *exits at door up center. Piano heard.* WATSON *resumes work at desk, but soon looks up, thinking. Rises and goes to door up center again. Opens it and looks about. The piano stops shortly after he opens door, as if in midst of bar. He turns in the doorway and looks about from that position, trying to think what* PRINCE *could have been up to. Closes the door. Returns to his desk somewhat doubtfully, but finally sits and resumes work. Enter* PARSONS *at door up center.*)

PARSONS: Mrs Watson says she didn't notice anyone comin' up, sir — she was at the pianner.

WATSON: Oh, well — it's nothing, I dare say. (*Rises and gathers up a few things as if to go.*) I shall be at Mr Holmes' — in Baker Street. If there's anything special — Mrs Watson or anything, you'll know where to send for me. The appointment was for nine. (*Looks at watch.*) It's fifteen minutes past eight now — I'm going to walk over.

PARSONS: Very well, sir!

   (*Bell of outside door rings.* PARSONS *looks at* WATSON, *who shakes his head.*)

WATSON: No, I won't see any more to-night. They must go to Doctor Anstruther.

PARSONS: Yes, sir. (*Starts toward door right to answer bell.*)

WATSON: (*Looks and sees blinds up.*) Parsons! (PARSONS *turns.*) Why aren't those blinds down?

PARSONS: They were down a few moments ago, sir!

WATSON: That's strange! Well, you'd better pull them down now!

PARSONS: Yes, sir! (*Bell rings twice as* PARSONS *pulls blinds down. He exits right to answer bell, then returns at door right in a peculiar manner.*) If you please, sir — (WATSON *looks up at him.* PARSONS *goes nearer to* WATSON.) It ain't a patient at all, sir.

WATSON: Well, what is it?

PARSONS: A lady, sir — and she wants to see you — most particular, sir.

WATSON: What does she want to see me about?

PARSONS: She didn't say, sir. Only she said it was of the hutmost himportance to 'er if she could see you, sir.

WATSON: Is she there in the hall?

PARSONS: Yes, sir.

WATSON: Very well — I was going to walk for the exercise — but I can take a cab.

PARSONS: Yes, sir. Then I'll show 'er in?

WATSON: Yes.

   (*He goes on with his preparations.* PARSONS *exits at door right. Pause.* PARSONS *appears at door right, ushering in a lady, and exits when she has entered. Enter* MADGE LARRABEE *at door right. Her manner is entirely different from that in former scenes. She is the impetuous gushing society lady with trouble on her mind.*)

MADGE: (*as she enters*) Ah, doctor — how awfully good of you to see me! I know what a busy man you must be — but I'm in *such* trouble — oh, it's really too dreadful! — and they told me you might know, so I came here at once! You'll excuse my troubling you in this way, won't you?

WATSON: Don't speak of it, madam.

MADGE: Oh, thank you so much! For it did look frightful, my coming in like this
— but I'm not alone — Oh, no! — I left my maid in the cab — I'm Mrs H. De
Witte Seaton — (*trying to find cardcase*) Dear me — I didn't bring my cardcase — or if I did, I've lost it!

WATSON: Don't trouble about a card, Mrs Seaton. (*Indicates chair up center.*)

MADGE: Oh, thank you so much! (*Sits as she continues to talk.*) You don't *know*
what I've been through this evening — trying to find *someone* who could tell
me what to do! (WATSON *sits in chair at desk.*) It's something that has
happened, doctor — it has just simply happened — I know it wasn't his fault!
I know it!

WATSON: Yes, but whose fault!

MADGE: My brother's — my poor dear youngest brother — he couldn't have done
such a thing, he simply couldn't, and —

WATSON: Such a thing as what, Mrs Seaton?

MADGE: As to take the plans of our defenses at Gibraltar from the Admiralty
office — You see, he works there. He was the only one who knew about them
in the whole office — because they trusted him so! He was to make copies
and — oh, doctor — it's really too dreadful! (*Overcome, she takes out her
handkerchief and wipes her eyes. She is perfectly natural and not in the least
particular overdone.*)

WATSON: I'm very sorry indeed, Mrs Seaton —

MADGE: (*mixed up with sobs*) Oh, thank you so much! They said you were Mr
Holmes' friend — several people told me that, several — They advised me to
ask you where I could find him — and everything depends on it, doctor —
everything.

WATSON: Holmes, of course! He's just the one you want!

MADGE: That's it! He's just the one — and there's hardly any time left! They'll
take my poor brother away to prison tomorrow! (*Shows signs of breaking
down again.*)

WATSON: There, there, Mrs Seaton — pray control yourself.

MADGE: (*Choking down sobs.*) Oh, thank you so much! Now what would you
advise me to do?

WATSON: I'd go to him at once!

MADGE: But I've been! I've been and he wasn't there!

WATSON: You went to his house?

MADGE: Yes — in Baker Street. That's why I came to you! They said he might be
here!

WATSON: No — he isn't here.

MADGE: (*Looks deeply discouraged.*) But don't you expect him sometime this
evening!

WATSON: No. (*Shakes head.*) There's no possibility of his coming — so far as I
know.

MADGE: But couldn't you *get* him to come? It would be such a great favor to me
— I'm almost worn out with going about — and with this dreadful anxiety! If
you could get word to him to — (*Sees that* WATSON *is looking at her
strangely and sharply.*) — to come. (*brief pause*)

WATSON: (*rather hard voice*) I could *not* get him to come, madam. (*Rises.*) And I beg you to excuse me. I am going out myself. (*Looks at watch.*) On urgent business.

MADGE: (*Rises.*) Oh, certainly! Don't let me detain you! And you think I had better call at his house again?

WATSON: (*coldly*) That will be the wisest thing to do.

MADGE: Oh, thank you so much! (*Extends her hand, which* WATSON *takes.*) You don't *know* how you've encouraged me!

    (WATSON *withdraws his hand, as he still looks at her, and quietly rings bell on desk. Enter* PARSONS *at door right. He stands at door.*)

MADGE: Well — good night, doctor!

    (WATSON *simply bows coldly.* MADGE *turns to go to door right. Just as she turns there is a loud noise far in distance outside right as if in the street beyond the front door of house. The loud noise of hoofs, the crash of a capsizing vehicle, followed by excited shouts of men heard outside.* MADGE *stops suddenly on the crash and shouts;* WATSON *looks at* PARSONS.)

WATSON: What's that, Parsons?

PARSONS: I really cawn't say, sir, but it sounded to me like a haccident.

MADGE: (*Turns to* WATSON.) Oh dear! I do hope it isn't anything serious! It affects me terribly to know that anyone is hurt!

WATSON: Probably nothing more than a broken down hansom. See what it is, Parsons.

    (MADGE *turns and looks toward door again, anxiously.* PARSONS *turns to go. Sudden vigorous ringing of doorbell outside right followed by loud rapping on door.*)

PARSONS: There's the bell, sir! There's somebody 'urt, sir, an' they're a-wantin' you!

WATSON: Well, don't allow anybody to come in! (*Looks at watch.*) I have no more time! (*Hurriedly gathers up papers.*)

PARSONS: Very well, sir! (*Exit at door right, leaving door open.*)

MADGE: (*Turns from looking off at door and looks at* WATSON *anxiously. Looks back toward door again.*) But they're coming in, doctor! (*Retreats backward until a little above from* WATSON.)

WATSON: (*Moves toward door right.*) Parsons! Parsons!

    (MADGE *watches. Sound of voices outside right. Following speeches are jumbled together so that it is all over very quickly.*)

VOICE: (*outside*) We 'ad to bring 'im in, man!

VOICE: (*outside*) There's nowhere else to go!

PARSONS: (*outside*) The doctor can't see anybody!

VOICE: (*outside*) Well, let the old gent lay 'ere awhile, can't ye! It's common decency!

VOICE: (*outside*) Yes! yes! Let him stay!

    (*Enter* PARSONS *at door right.*)

PARSONS: They would come in with 'im, sir. It's an old gentleman as was 'urt a bit wen the 'ansom upset!

MADGE: Oh!

> (*Sounds of groans outside left, and the old gentleman whining out complaints and threats.*)

WATSON: Let them put him here. (*Indicates operating chair.*) And send at once for Dr Anstruther.

PARSONS: Yes, sir!

WATSON: Help him in, Parsons.

> (PARSONS *exits at door right.*)

MADGE: Oh, doctor! Isn't it frightful!

WATSON: (*Turns to door up center.*) Mrs Seaton, if you will be so good as to step this way you can reach the hall by taking the first door to your left.

MADGE: (*hesitating*) But I — I may be of some use, doctor!

WATSON: (*with a trifle of impatience*) None whatever! (*Holds door open.*)

MADGE: But, doctor — I must see the poor fellow — I haven't the power to go!

WATSON: (*Faces MADGE.*) Madam, I believe you have some ulterior motive in coming here! You will kindly —

> (*Enter at right door a white haired* OLD GENTLEMAN *in black clerical clothes, white tie, assisted by* PARSONS *and the* CAB DRIVER. *He limps as though his leg were hurt. His coat is soiled and torn on one shoulder. His hat is soiled. He is groaning and complaining as they assist him in and on to the chair.* MADGE *has retired up left above desk and watches* OLD GENT *closely from there without moving.* WATSON *turns toward the party as they come in.*)

OLD GENT: (*in quivering high voice*) Ah! (*Groans.*) Let me lie down! Oh! Why did the cabman allow such a thing to happen? Where is the doctor? (*to* CABMAN) I'll have you arrested for this! Oh! Oh! (*groans and exclamations of pain as he sits*)

PARSONS *and* CAB DRIVER: There now — we'll have ye comfortable in no time! There, sir! Don't worry, sir! The doctor 'e'll attend to ye, sir! (*They assist him to chair.*)

WATSON: (*low voice to* PARSONS) Have a cab ready for me. I must see if he's badly hurt. (*Starts to* OLD GENT.)

PARSONS: Yes, sir!

> (PARSONS *exits at door right; the* CABMAN *exits right after him.*)

WATSON: (*Steps quickly to door right, speaking off.*) Parsons — take that cabman's number. (*quickly, to* OLD GENT) Now, if you'll lie quiet for one moment, sir, I'll have a look at you.

> (WATSON *crosses to desk or cabinet as if to look for instrument. He turns just above upper window and stands looking at* MADGE. MADGE, *just as* DOCTOR *is at left, advances nearer to the* OLD GENTLEMAN *and looks at him closely. She suddenly seems to be satisfied of something, backs away, turning and reaching out as if to get to window up left and give signal, and comes face to face with* WATSON. *Smiles pleasantly at him and begins to glide downstage making a sweep around toward door on right side as if to get out.* MADGE *shows by her expression that she has recognized* HOLMES, *but is instantly herself again, thinking possibly that* HOLMES *is*

watching her, and she wishes to evade suspicion regarding her deter-
mination to get off at door right. Quick as a flash the OLD
GENTLEMAN *springs to the door down right and stands facing her.*
She stops suddenly on finding him before her, stands an instant,
then wheels quickly about and goes rapidly across toward window
down left.)

OLD GENT: (*quick at door right; sharply*) Don't let her pull up those shades.
    (WATSON, *who had moved up a little above windows on left,*
    instantly springs before them. MADGE *stops on being headed off in*
    that direction.)

WATSON: Is that you, Holmes?

HOLMES: Quite so. (*Moves wig.*)
    (MADGE *stands motionless.*)

WATSON: What do you want me to do?

HOLMES: (*easily*) That's all. You've done it.
    (MADGE *gives a sharp look at them, then goes very slowly for a few*
    steps and suddenly turns and makes a dash for door up center.)

WATSON: Look out! Holmes! She can get out that way!
    (MADGE *runs off at door up center.* HOLMES *is unmoved.*)

HOLMES: I don't think so. (*Saunters over to* WATSON'*s desk left of center. Picks*
    up a cigarette, takes wig off, and soon sits on desk. Finds matches and lights
    cigarette.) Have you ever observed, Watson, that those people are always
    making —
    (*Enter the* CABMAN *at door up center.*)

CABMAN: (*Speaks at once, so as to break in on* HOLMES.) I've got her, sir.
    (*Very brief pause*)

WATSON: Good heavens! Is that *Forman*?

HOLMES: (*Nods yes.*) Yes, that's Forman all right. Has Inspector Bradstreet come
    with his men?

FORMAN: Yes, sir. One of 'em's in the hall here holding her. The others are in
    the kitchen garden. They came in over the back wall from Mortimer
    Street.

HOLMES: One moment. (*Sits in thought.*) Watson, my dear fellow — (WATSON
    moves toward HOLMES *at desk.*) As you doubtless gather from the little
    episode that has just taken place, we are making the arrests. The scoundrels
    are hot on my track. To get me out of the way is the one chance left to them
    — and I'm taking advantage of their mad pursuit to draw them where we can
    quietly lay our hands on them — one by one. We've made a pretty good haul
    already — four last night in the gas chamber — seven this afternoon in various
    places and one more just now, but I regret to say that up to this time the
    Professor himself has so far not risen to the bait.

WATSON: Where do you think he is?

HOLMES: In the open streets — under some clever disguise — watching for a chance
    to get at me.

WATSON: And was this woman sent in here to —

HOLMES: Quite so. A spy — to let them know by some signal if she found me in
    the house. And it has just occurred to me that it might not be such a very bad

idea to try the Professor with that bait. Forman! (*Motions him to come down.*)

FORMAN: Yes, sir!

HOLMES: (*voice lower*) Bring that Larrabee woman back here for a moment, and when I light a fresh cigarette, let go your hold on her — carelessly — as if your attention was attracted to something else. Get hold of her again when I tell you.

FORMAN: Very well, sir! (*Exits quickly at door up center.*)

WATSON: Is there anything for me to —

HOLMES: No. Don't interfere just now.

> (*Enter* FORMAN *at door up center, bringing in* MADGE. *They stop down center.* MADGE *is calm, but looks venomous. Looks at* HOLMES *with the utmost hatred. Brief pause.*)

HOLMES: My dear Mrs Larrabee — (MADGE, *who has looked away, turns to him angrily.*) I took the liberty of having you brought in for a moment — (*Puffs; near end of cigarette.*) — in order to convey to you in a few fitting words — my sincere sympathy in your rather — unpleasant — predicament.

MADGE: (*Hisses it out angrily between her teeth.*) It's a lie! It's a lie! There's no predicament!

HOLMES: Ah — I'm charmed to gather — from your rather forcible — observation — that you do not regard it — as such. Quite right, too! Our prisons are so well conducted now! Many consider them quite as comfortable as most of the London hotels. Quieter and more orderly — and — I regret to say, not a general rendezvous for Cook's tourists.

MADGE: How the prisons may be conducted is no concern of mine! There is nothing they can hold me for — nothing!

HOLMES: Oh — to be sure! (*Puts fresh cigarette in mouth.*) There may be something in that! Still — it occurred to me that you might prefer to be near your unfortunate husband — eh? (*Rises from table and goes up center to gas burner. Slight good-natured chuckle.*) We hear a great deal about the heroic devotion of wives, and all that (*Lights cigarette at gas.*) — rubbish.

> (FORMAN *carelessly relinquishes his hold on* MADGE's *arm and seems to have his attention called to door at right. Stands as if listening to something outside.* MADGE *gives a quick glance about, and at* HOLMES.)

HOLMES: (*lighting cigarette at gas and apparently not noticing anything*) You know, Mrs Larrabee, it's sometimes difficult to foresee the turns that Fortune's wheel —

> (MADGE *makes a sudden dash for window down left, quickly snaps up shade and makes a rapid motion up and down before window with right hand; then turns quickly, facing* HOLMES *with triumphant defiance.* HOLMES *is still lighting cigarette.*)

HOLMES: Many thanks. (*to* FORMAN) That's all, Forman. Pick her up again.

> (FORMAN *at once goes to* MADGE *and turns her down left and waits in front of window.*)

HOLMES: Doctor, I don't care to be shot from the street. Would you kindly pull the shade down once more.

(WATSON *instantly pulls shade down.*)

MADGE: (*cruel triumph*) Ah! It's too late!

HOLMES: Too late, eh? (*Strolls a little.*)

MADGE: The signal is given! You will hear from him soon!

HOLMES: It wouldn't surprise me at all!

> (*Voices of* BILLY *and* PARSONS *outside right and door at right is at once opened and* BILLY *comes on a little way but is held back by* PARSONS *for an instant. He breaks away quickly from* PARSONS *and comes to right center. He is dressed as a street gamin and is carrying a bunch of evening papers to sell.* PARSONS *stays to right.*)

HOLMES: (*as* BILLY *comes over*) I think I shall hear from him *now*! Let him go, Parsons. Quick, Billy!

BILLY: He's just come, sir!

HOLMES: From where?

BILLY: The house across the street; he was in there a-watching these windows. He must 'ave seen something, for he's just come out. (*breathlessly*) There was a cab waitin' there in the street for the Doctor — and he's climbed up an' changed places with the driver!

HOLMES: (*slight motion of head toward* FORMAN) Ah — another cabman tonight!

BILLY: I got close an' 'eard 'em, sir! An' they're a-layin' to git you in that cab wen you come out, sir! But don't you do it, sir!

HOLMES: On the contrary, sir, I'll have that cabman in here, sir! Get out again, quick, Billy, and keep your eye on him!

BILLY: Yes, sir — thank you, sir! (*Exit at door right.*)

HOLMES: Watson, can you let me have a heavy portmanteau for a few moments?

> (MADGE *is now watching for another chance to get at the window on left.*)

WATSON: Parsons — my Gladstone — bring it here!

PARSONS: Yes, sir. (*Exits at door right.*)

WATSON: I'm afraid it's a pretty shabby looking —

> (MADGE *suddenly breaks loose from* FORMAN *and attempts to make a dash for window at left.* FORMAN *turns and instantly takes her again. Slight pause.*)

HOLMES: Many thanks, Mrs Larrabee, but your first signal was all that we required. By it, you informed your friend Moriarty that I was here in the house. You are now aware of the fact that he is personating a cab driver and that it is my intention to have him in here, and you wish to signal that there is danger. We don't care to have you do it. Take her out, Forman, and tell the Inspector to wait a few moments; I may send him another lot. You can't tell.

> (FORMAN *leads* MADGE *up to door up center as if to take her out. She pulls him to a step and gives* HOLMES *a look of the most violent hatred.*)

FORMAN: Come along now! (*Takes her off at door up center.*)

HOLMES: Fine woman.

> (*Enter* PARSONS *at door right, carrying a large portmanteau or Gladstone valise.*)

HOLMES: Put it down there. (*Points down before him at floor left of center.*) Thank you so much.

> (PARSONS *puts portmanteau down as indicated and returns to door right.*)

HOLMES: Parsons, you ordered a cab a short time ago. It has been waiting, I believe.

PARSONS: Yes, sir, I think it 'as.

HOLMES: Be so good as to tell the driver to come in and get a valise. When he comes, tell him that's the one.

PARSONS: Very good, sir. (*Exits at door right.*)

HOLMES: Watson, my dear fellow — (*Crosses to left center above desk.*) — in times like this you should tell your man never to take the first cab that comes on a call — (*Smokes.*) — nor yet the second. The third may be safe!

WATSON: But in this case —

HOLMES: I admit that in this case I have turned it to my advantage, but I speak for your future guidance.

WATSON: I shall try — (*Stops, hearing footsteps in the hall.*)

> (*Brief pause. Door at right opens.* PARSONS *enters, pointing out the portmanteau to someone who is following.*)

PARSONS: 'Ere it is — right in this way!

HOLMES: (*Goes to* WATSON *above desk. In rather loud voice to* WATSON) Well, good-bye, old fellow! (*Shakes hands with him warmly and brings him down left a little.*) I'll write to you from Paris — and I hope you'll keep me fully informed of the progress of events —

> (MORIARTY *enters at door right in the disguise of a cabman and goes at once to valise which* PARSONS *points out, trying to hurry it through and keeping face away from* HOLMES.)

HOLMES: (*Goes right on, apparently paying no attention to* MORIARTY.) As for those papers, I'll attend to them personally. Here, my man — (*to* MORIARTY, *who is right*) — just help me tighten up the straps a bit — (*He slides over to valise, and kneels, pulling at strap.* MORIARTY *bends over and does the same.*) There's a few little things in this bag that I wouldn't like to lose. And it's just as well to — eh? (*Looks round for an instant.*) Who's that at the window?

> (MORIARTY *quickly looks round without lifting hands from valise, and at the same instant the snap of handcuffs is heard, and he springs up with the irons on his wrists, making two or three violent efforts to break loose. He then stands motionless.* HOLMES *drops into chair at desk, cigarette in mouth.*)

HOLMES: (*very quiet tone*) Doctor — kindly strike the bell two or three times.

> (WATSON *steps to desk, gives several rapid strokes of the bell.*)

HOLMES: Thanks.

> (*Enter* FORMAN *at door up center. He goes to* MORIARTY *and fastens handcuff which he had on his own wrist to chain attached to that of* MORIARTY's.)

HOLMES: Got a man there with you?

FORMAN: Yes, sir, the Inspector came in himself.

HOLMES: Ah — the Inspector himself! We shall read graphic accounts in tomorrow's papers of a very difficult arrest he succeeded in making at Dr Watson's house in Kensington. Take him out, Forman, and introduce him to the Inspector. They'll be pleased to meet.

> (FORMAN *starts to force* MORIARTY *off, but he hangs back and endeavors to get at* HOLMES.)

HOLMES: Here! Wait! Let's see what he wants!

MORIARTY: (*Low voice; crosses to* HOLMES.) Do you imagine, Sherlock Holmes, that this is the end?

HOLMES: I ventured to dream that it might be.

MORIARTY: It is but a dream — I hear you are planning to go abroad tomorrow — to take a little trip on the continent.

HOLMES: And if I do?

MORIARTY: If you do, I shall meet you there! If not, I shall meet you here! It is quite the same! (*He looks at* HOLMES *an instant and then is taken out at door up center by* FORMAN.)

HOLMES: (*after a pause*) Parsons, I've quite finished with the valise, thank you. (PARSONS *picks up valise and exits right.*) Watson, my dear fellow — (*Smokes.*) — It's too bad. I suppose you imagine that now that this little episode in connection with Professor Moriarty is at an end, your office will no longer be required. Let me assure you — let me assure you — (*Voice trembles.*) — that the worst is yet to come.

WATSON: (*Stands in front of desk.*) The worst to — (*Suddenly thinks of something. Pulls out watch hurriedly.*) Why, good heavens, Holmes! We've barely five minutes!

HOLMES: (*In chair near desk; looks up at him innocently.*) For what?

WATSON: To get to Baker Street — your rooms! (HOLMES *still looks at him.*) Your appointment with Sir Edward and the Count! They were to receive that packet of letters from you.

HOLMES: (*Nods assent.*) They're coming here.

> (*Pause;* WATSON *looks at* HOLMES.)

WATSON: Here!

HOLMES: That is — if you'll be so good as to permit it.

WATSON: Certainly! But why not there?

HOLMES: The police wouldn't allow us inside the ropes.

WATSON: Police! Ropes!

HOLMES: Police — ropes — ladders — hose — crowds — fire engines —

WATSON: Why, you don't mean that —

HOLMES: (*Nods.*) Quite so. The scoundrels have burned me out.

WATSON: Good heavens! Burned you — (*Pause.* HOLMES *nods.*) Oh, that's too bad! What did you lose?

HOLMES: (*Rises and takes stage right center. An upward toss of both arms.*) Everything! Everything! I'm glad of it! *I've had enough!* This one thing — (*Strong gesture of emphasis with right hand. He stops in midst of sentence, a frown upon his face as he thinks. Then, in lower voice*) — ends it! This one thing — that I shall do — here — in a few moments — is the finish!

WATSON: You mean — Miss Faulkner? (*Goes to lower corner of desk.*)

HOLMES: (*Nods slightly in affirmative without turning to* WATSON. *Turns suddenly.*) Why, Watson — she trusted me! She — clung to me! There were four to one against me! They said '*Come here!*' I said '*Stay close to me!*' and she did! She clung to me — I could feel her heart beating against mine — and I was playing a game! A dangerous game! A dangerous game — but I was playing it! It will be the same to-night! She'll be there — I'll be here! She'll listen — she'll believe — she'll trust me — and I'll — be playing — a game — NO MORE! I've had enough! (*Wheels suddenly away and goes down right.*) It's my last case! (WATSON *has been watching him narrowly.*) Oh, well! What does it matter? Life is a small affair at the most! — A little while — a few sunrises and sunsets — the warm breath of a few summers — the cold chill of a few winters — (*Looks down at floor a little way before him in meditation.*) And then —

                (*Pause*)

WATSON: And then — ?

HOLMES: (*Glances up at him. Upward toss of hand before speaking.*) And then. (*Falling inflection; he turns on his heel and goes right.*)

WATSON: (*Moves near him.*) My dear Holmes — I'm afraid that plan of — gaining her confidence and regard went a little further than you intended — ?

HOLMES: (*Nods assent. Mutters.*) A trifle!

WATSON: For — her — or for you?

HOLMES: For her — (*Looks up at* WATSON *slowly.*) — and — for me.

WATSON: (*astonished; instant's pause*) But — if you both love each other —

HOLMES: (*Springs up and puts hand on* WATSON *to stop him.*) Sh — ! Don't say it! (*pause*) You mustn't — tempt me — with such a thought! That girl! Young — exquisite — just beginning her sweet life! — *I* — seared, drugged, poisoned — almost at the end! No! No! I must cure her! I must stop it — now — while there's time! (*pause*) She's coming here.

WATSON: Miss Faulkner?

HOLMES: (*Nods yes.*) Coming, Watson, out of the goodness of her heart, to me — She fears I'll involve myself in some trouble because the package of letters I am going to deliver is a counterfeit! Ha! Ha! She thinks I don't know that!

WATSON: She won't come alone?

HOLMES: No, Terese will be with her. It's through her, of course, that I let her know of the proposed delivery. A contemptible piece of business. I'd never go on with it, if I hadn't given my word! At least it will help to make her despise me — which she must do. (*He turns and goes to door up left, getting a book on the way, and placing it in the way of door closing. Turns to* WATSON.) When she comes let her wait in that room. You can manage that, I'm quite sure.

WATSON: Certainly. Did you intend to leave that book there?

HOLMES: (*Nods yes.*) To keep the door from closing; she is to overhear.

WATSON: I see.

HOLMES: (*at desk*) Sir Edward and the Count are quite likely to become excited. I shall endeavor to make them so. They may even use strong language. You must not be alarmed, old fellow.

(*Bell of outside door rings off right.* HOLMES *and* WATSON *look at one another.*)

HOLMES: (*going to door*) I'll go to your dressing-room if you'll allow me, and brush away some of this dust.

WATSON: By all means! (*Goes to door.*) Mrs Watson is in the drawing room. Do look in on her a moment — it will please her so much!

HOLMES: (*at door*) My dear fellow, it will more than please me! Mrs Watson! Home! Love! Life! Ah, Watson — (*Eyes glance about, thinking; he sighs a little absently, then suddenly turns and exits at door up center.*)

(WATSON *is at his desk, but not seated. Enter* PARSONS *at door right.*)

PARSONS: A lady, sir, wants to know if she can speak to you. If there's anyone 'ere she won't come in.

WATSON: Any name?

PARSONS: No, sir. I ast 'er an' she said it was unnecessary, as you wouldn't know 'er. She 'as 'er maid with 'er, sir.

WATSON: Show her in. (PARSONS *turns to go.*) And, Parsons — (PARSONS *stops and turns.* WATSON, *in a lower voice*) Two gentlemen, Count Von Stalburg and Sir Edward Leighton will come. Bring them here to the office at once, and then tell Mr Holmes. You'll find him in my dressing-room.

PARSONS: Yes, sir.

WATSON: Send everybody else away. I'll see that lady.

PARSONS: Yes, sir.

(PARSONS *exits at door right leaving it open. Brief pause.* PARSONS *appears outside door right showing some one to the room. Enter at door right* ALICE FAULKNER *followed by* TERESE. ALICE *glances apprehensively about, fearing she will see* HOLMES. *Seeing that* WATSON *is alone, she is much relieved and goes toward him.* TERESE *remains near the door right.* PARSONS *closes door right from outside.*)

ALICE: (*with some timidity*) Is this — is this Dr Watson's office?

WATSON: (*encouragingly, and advancing a step or two*) Yes, and I am Dr Watson.

ALICE: Is — would you mind telling me if Mr Holmes — Mr — Sherlock Holmes — is here?

WATSON: He will be here before long, Miss — e —

ALICE: My name is Faulkner.

WATSON: Miss Faulkner. He came a short time ago, but has gone upstairs for a few moments.

ALICE: Oh! (*with an apprehensive look*) And is he coming down — soon?

WATSON: Well, the fact is, Miss Faulkner, he has an appointment with two gentlemen here, and I was to let him know as soon as they arrive.

ALICE: Do you suppose I could wait — without troubling you too much — and see him — afterward?

WATSON: Why, certainly.

ALICE: Thank you. — And I — I don't want him to know — that — I — that I came.

WATSON: Of course, if you wish, there's no need of my telling him.

ALICE: It is — very important *indeed* that you *don't*, Dr Watson. I can explain it all to you afterward.

WATSON: No explanation is necessary, Miss Faulkner.

ALICE: Thank you. (*Glances about.*) I suppose there is a waiting room for — for patients?

WATSON: Yes, or you could sit in my inner office. (*Indicates door up left.*) You'll be less likely to be disturbed there.

ALICE: Yes — thank you. (*She glances toward door up left.*) I think I would rather be — where it's entirely quiet.

> (*Bell of front door outside right rings.*)

WATSON: (*Goes to door up left above desk.*) Then step this way. I think the gentlemen have arrived. (*Stands at door.*)

ALICE: (*to TERESE, as she goes toward door up left, turning at the door*) And when the business between the gentlemen is over would you please have someone tell me?

WATSON: I'll tell you myself, Miss Faulkner.

ALICE: Thank you. We'll wait in here, Terese. (*She exits at door up left.*)

> (WATSON *moves a little to right as* TERESE *passes toward door, so that when he speaks she turns on his left.*)

WATSON: (*to attract* TERESE's *attention*) Hm!

TERESE: (*as she was crossing she turns to* WATSON*: hardly more than movement of lips*) M'sieur.

WATSON: (*Speaks in a low voice so that* ALICE *could not by any possibility overhear.*) Have her sit where she can hear.

TERESE: (*low voice*) Oui, m'sieur. (*She quickly turns and exits up left, the whole being done so quickly that her detention could not be noticed by* ALICE.)

> (PARSONS *enters at door right.*)

PARSONS: Count Von Stalburg. Sir Edward Leighton.

> (*Enter* SIR EDWARD *and the* COUNT VON STALBURG *at door right. Exit* PARSONS *at door right, closing it after him.*)

WATSON: Count — Sir Edward. (*Bows and comes forward.*)

SIR EDWARD: Dr Watson! (*Bows.*) Good evening. (*Places his hat on pedestal.* VON STALBURG *bows slightly.*) Our appointment with Mr Holmes was changed to your house, I believe.

WATSON: Quite right, Sir Edward. Pray be seated, gentlemen.

> (SIR EDWARD *takes a chair and seats himself right center.* WATSON *sits near desk.*)

VON STALBURG: Mr Holmes is a trifle late. (*Sits near* SIR EDWARD.)

WATSON: He has already arrived, Count. I have sent for him.

VON STALBURG: Ugh!

> (*Slight pause*)

SIR EDWARD: It was quite a surprise to receive his message an hour ago changing the place of meeting. We should otherwise have gone to his house in Baker Street.

WATSON: You would have found it in ashes, Sir Edward.

SIR EDWARD: What! Really!

VON STALBURG: (*surprise*) Ugh!

(*Both look at* WATSON.)

SIR EDWARD: The — the house burnt!

WATSON: Burning now probably.

SIR EDWARD: I'm very sorry to hear this! It must be a severe blow to him.

WATSON: No, he minds it very little.

SIR EDWARD: (*surprised*) Really! I should hardly have thought it.

    (*Pause*)

VON STALBURG: Did I understand you to say, Doctor, that you had sent for Mr Holmes?

WATSON: Yes, Count — and he'll be here shortly. Indeed I think I hear him on the stairs now.

    (*Pause. Enter* HOLMES *at door up center. He is very pale. His clothing is rearranged and cleansed, though he still of course wears the clerical suit, white tie, etc. He stands near door a moment.* SIR EDWARD *and* COUNT *rise and turn to him.* WATSON *rises and goes to desk, where he soon seats himself.* SIR EDWARD *and the* COUNT *stand looking at* HOLMES. *Brief pause.*)

HOLMES: (*Comes forward. Speaks in low clear voice, entirely calm, but showing some suppressed feeling or anxiety back of it.*) Gentlemen, be seated again, I beg.

    (*Brief pause.* SIR EDWARD *and the* COUNT *reseat themselves.* HOLMES *remains standing near corner of desk, or near chair. He stands looking down before him for quite a while, the others looking at him. He finally begins to speak in a low voice without at first looking up.*)

HOLMES: Our business tonight can be quickly disposed of. I need not tell you, gentlemen — for I have already told you — that the part which I play in it is — more than painful to me. But business is business — and the sooner it is over the better. You were notified to come here this evening in order that I might — (*pause*) — deliver into your hands the packet which you engaged me — on behalf of your exalted client — to recover. Let me say, in justice to myself, that but for that agreement on my part, and the consequent steps which you took upon the basis of it, I would never have continued with the work. As it was, however, I felt bound to do so, and therefore pursued the matter — to the very end, — and I now have the honor to deliver it into your hands.

    (HOLMES *goes toward* SIR EDWARD *with the packet.* SIR EDWARD *rises and meets him.* HOLMES *places the packet in his hands.* COUNT VON STALBURG *rises and stands at his chair.*)

SIR EDWARD: (*formally*) Permit me to congratulate you, Mr Holmes, upon the marvelous skill you have displayed, and the promptness with which you have fulfilled your agreement.

    (HOLMES *bows slightly and turns away, moving near table.* SIR EDWARD *at once breaks the seals of the packet and looks at the contents. He begins to show some surprise as he glances at one or two letters or papers, and at once looks closer. He quickly motions to the* COUNT, *who goes to him at once. He whispers something to him, and they both look at two or three things together.*)

VON STALBURG: Oh! No! No!

SIR EDWARD: (*Stops examination and looks across to* HOLMES.) What does this mean? (HOLMES *turns to* SIR EDWARD *in apparent surprise.*) These letters! And these — other things! *Where did you get them*?

HOLMES: I purchased them — last night.

SIR EDWARD: Purchased them?

HOLMES: Quite so.

VON STALBURG: From whom, if I may ask?

HOLMES: From the parties interested — by consent of Miss Faulkner.

SIR EDWARD: You have been deceived.

HOLMES: What!

      (WATSON *rises and stands at his desk.*)

SIR EDWARD: (*excitedly*) This packet contains *nothing* — not a single letter or paper that we wanted. All clever imitations! The photographs are of another person! You have been duped! With all your supposed cleverness they have tricked you! Ha! Ha! Ha!

VON STALBURG: Most decidedly duped, Mr Holmes!

HOLMES: (*Steps quickly to* SIR EDWARD.) This is terrible! (*Goes back to* WATSON. *Stands looking in his face.* WATSON *takes his hand in sympathy.*)

SIR EDWARD: (*astonished*) Terrible! Surely, sir, you do not mean by that — that there is a possibility you may not be able to recover them!

      (*Enter* ALICE *at door up left and stands listening.*)

HOLMES: It is true.

SIR EDWARD: After your positive assurances! After the steps we have taken in the matter by your advice! Why — why, this is — (*Turns to* COUNT, *too indignant to speak.*)

VON STALBURG: (*indignantly*) Surely, sir, you do not mean there is no hope of it?

HOLMES: None whatever, Count. It is too late!

SIR EDWARD: Why, this is scandalous! It is criminal, sir! You had no right to mislead us in this way and you shall certainly suffer the consequences! I shall see that you are brought into court to answer for it, Mr Holmes. It will be such a blow to your reputation that you —

HOLMES: There is nothing to do, Sir Edward — I am ruined.

ALICE: (*coming forward*) He is not ruined, Sir Edward. (*Speaks in a quiet voice, perfectly calm and self-possessed. Draws the genuine packet from her dress.*) It is entirely owing to him and what he said to me that I now wish to give you the — (*Starts toward* SIR EDWARD *as if to hand him the packet.*)

      (HOLMES *steps forward and intercepts her with left hand extended. She stops, surprised.*)

HOLMES: One moment — (*pause*) — Allow me. (*He takes the package from her hand and tosses away the one he had.*)

      (WATSON *stands looking at the scene. Pause.* HOLMES *stands with the package in his hand, looking down for a moment. He raises his head as if he overcame weakness; glances at his watch, and turns to* SIR EDWARD *and the* COUNT. *He speaks quietly as if the climax of the tragedy were passed — the deed done.* ALICE's *questioning gaze he plainly avoids.*)

HOLMES: Gentlemen — (*Puts watch back in pocket.*) I notified you in my letter of this morning, that the package should be produced at a quarter past ten. It is barely fourteen past — and this is it. As you have already discovered, the one you have there is a counterfeit.

> (HOLMES *turns a little; sees* ALICE. *Stands looking at her.* ALICE *is looking at* HOLMES *frozen with astonishment and horror. She moves back left a little involuntarily.*)

SIR EDWARD *and* VON STALBURG: (*starting up with admiration and delight as they perceive the trick*) Ah! Excellent! Admirable, Mr Holmes! Ha! Ha! It is all clear now! Really marvelous! (*to one another*) Yes — upon my word!

> (*On* SIR EDWARD *and* COUNT *breaking into expressions of admiration,* WATSON *quickly moves toward them and stops them with a quick 'sh!' All stand motionless.* HOLMES *and* ALICE *look at one another.* HOLMES *goes quickly to* ALICE *and puts the package into her hands.*)

HOLMES: (*as he does this*) Take this, Miss Faulkner. Take it away from me quick! it is *yours*! Never give it up — use it only for what you wish!

SIR EDWARD: (*Springs forward with a wild exclamation.*) What! We are not to have it! (*Throws counterfeit package away.* VON STALBURG *gives an exclamation or look with the foregoing.*)

HOLMES: (*Turns from* ALICE, *but keeps left hand back upon her hands into which he put the package, as if to make her keep it. Strong — breathless; not loud; with emphatic shake of head*) No. You are not to have it!

SIR EDWARD: After all this!

HOLMES: After all this!

VON STALBURG: But, my dear sir —

SIR EDWARD: (*almost with the foregoing*) This is outrageous! Your agreement?

HOLMES: I break it! Do what you please — warrants — arrests — summons — will find me here! (*Turns and says under his breath to* WATSON.) Get them out! Get them away! (*Stands at right of* WATSON's *desk, back to audience.*)

> (*Brief pause;* WATSON *moves toward* SIR EDWARD *and the* COUNT *back of* HOLMES.)

WATSON: I'm sure, gentlemen, you will appreciate the fact —

ALICE: (*Steps forward, interrupting.*) Wait a moment, Doctor Watson! (*Crosses to* SIR EDWARD.) Here is the package, Sir Edward! (*Hands it to him at once.*)

> (WATSON *motions to* PARSONS *off right to come on.*)

HOLMES: (*Turns to* ALICE.) No! (*Comes down a little.*)

ALICE: (*to* HOLMES) Yes — (*Turns to* HOLMES: *pause.*) I much prefer that he should have them — since you came that night and asked me to give them to you, I have thought of what you said. You were right — it *was* revenge.

> (*She looks down a moment, then suddenly turns away to left.* HOLMES *stands motionless near corner of desk, his eyes down and looking a little to the right.* SIR EDWARD *places the parcel carefully in his inside breast pocket and buttons his coat.* PARSONS *enters at door right and stands waiting with* SIR EDWARD's *hat in his hand, which he took off the pedestal.*)

SIR EDWARD: We are certainly greatly indebted to you, Miss Faulkner — (*Looks at* VON STALBURG.)

VON STALBURG: To be sure!

SIR EDWARD: And to you, too, Mr Holmes — if this was a part of the game!

> (*There is a motionless pause all round.* SIR EDWARD *and* VON STALBURG *move toward door, buttoning coats.*)

SIR EDWARD: (*near door right*) Ha! Ha! It was certainly an extraordinary method of obtaining possession of valuable papers — but we won't quarrel with the method so long as it accomplished the desired result! Eh, Count?

VON STALBURG: Certainly not, Sir Edward!

SIR EDWARD: (*Turns at door right.*) You have only to notify me of the charges for your services, Mr Holmes, and you will receive a check. I have the honor to wish you — goodnight. (*Bows punctiliously.*) Dr Watson. (*Bows to* WATSON.) This way, Count!

> (WATSON *bows.* HOLMES *does not move.* COUNT VON STALBURG *bows to* HOLMES *and to* WATSON *and exits at door right, followed by* SIR EDWARD. PARSONS *exits, closing door after giving* SIR EDWARD *his hat.* WATSON *quietly exits at door up center.* HOLMES, *after a moment's pause, looks at* ALICE, *and then goes quickly to her.*)

HOLMES: (*Speaks hurriedly.*) Now that you think it over, Miss Faulkner, you are doubtless beginning to realize the series of tricks by which I have sought to deprive you of your property. I couldn't take it out of the house that first night like a straightforward thief — because it could have been recovered at law. And for that reason I resorted to a cruel and cowardly device which should induce you to relinquish it.

ALICE: (*not looking at him*) But you — you did not give it to them.

> (*Pause*)

HOLMES: (*in a forced, cynical, hard voice*) No — I preferred that you should do so, as you did.

> (ALICE *looks suddenly up at him in surprise and pain with a breathless 'what!' scarcely audible.*)

HOLMES: (*Meets her look without a tremor. Speaks slowly, distinctly.*) You see, Miss Faulkner, it was a trick — a deception — to the very — end. (ALICE *looks in his face a moment longer, and then down.*) Your maid is waiting — (*Indicates with a slight motion.*) — at the door.

ALICE: And was it — a trick — last night — when they tried to kill you?

HOLMES: I went there to purchase the counterfeit package — to use as you have seen.

ALICE: And — did you know I would come?

> (*Pause*)

HOLMES: No. (ALICE *gives a very subdued breath of relief.*) But it fell in with my plans notwithstanding. Now that you see me in my true light, Miss Faulkner, we have nothing left to say but good night — and good-bye — which you ought to be very glad to do. Believe me, I meant no harm to you — it was purely business — with me. For that you see I would sacrifice everything.

Even my supposed − friendship for you − was a pretense − a sham! Everything that you −

> (ALICE *stops him in the middle of a word. She had slowly turned away to front and a little left during his speech. She turns not too quickly and looks him in the face.*)

ALICE: (*quietly but distinctly*) I don't believe it.

> (*They look at one another.*)

HOLMES: (*after a while*) Why not?

ALICE: From the way you speak . . . From the way you − look . . . From all sorts of things! . . . (*with a very slight smile*) You are not the only one − who can tell things − from small details!

HOLMES: Your faculty of observation is − is somewhat remarkable, Miss Faulkner − and your deduction is quite correct! I suppose . . . indeed I *know* . . . that I love you. But I know as well what I am − and what you are − (ALICE *begins to draw nearer to him, gradually getting her head against his breast as he is speaking, but with her face turned away.*) I know that no such a person as I should ever dream of being a part of your sweet life! It would be a crime for me to think of such a thing! There is every reason why I should say goodbye and farewell! There is every reason − why −

> (*He suddenly stops. After an instant he begins slowly to look down to where her head rests against him. His left arm gradually steals about her. He presses her head close to him. Her head is against his breast and her face turned to front or near it, for the final spotlight which holds the two faces for a moment, then slowly fades out.*)

CURTAIN

FIRST PUBLICATIONS OF
WILLIAM GILLETTE'S PLAYS

Esmeralda. A comedy-drama founded on Mrs Frances Hodgson Burnett's story of the same name, by Frances Hodgson Burnett and Wm. H. Gillette. New York: [Madison Square Theatre], 1881.

All the Comforts of Home. A comedy in four acts, by William Gillette, as produced at the Boston Museum, for the first time, Monday, March 3rd, 1890. New York: H. Roorbach, *c.* 1897.

The Five-Act War Drama, Held by the Enemy, taking place in a Southern city which has been captured and occupied by Northern forces during the rebellion, written by William Gillette. New York: S[amuel] French [1898?]. (French's standard library edition)

An American Drama Arranged in Four Acts and Entitled Secret Service; a romance of the Southern Confederacy, written by William Gillette. New York: S. French, *c.* 1898. (French's standard library edition)

The Three-Act Farcical Comedy, Too Much Johnson, by William Gillette. New York: S. French, *c.* 1912.

Electricity; A Comedy in Three Acts. With introduction by Richard Burton. [Chicago: Drama League of American, 1913.] In: *The Drama, a quarterly review of dramatic literature*, no. 12, November 1913, pp. 5–123.

Secret Service. Revised edition. In: *Representative American Plays*, ed. with introduction and notes by Arthur Hobson Quinn. New York: The Century Co., 1917.

Sherlock Holmes; a drama in four acts, adapted by Arthur Conan Doyle and William Gillette from the story by Arthur Conan Doyle entitled 'The Strange Case of Miss Faulkner.' Rev. 1922 by Arthur Conan Doyle and William Gillette. London: S. French, Ltd; New York: S. French, *c.* 1922. (French's acting editions, no. 489)

Electricity; a comedy in three acts, by William Gillette. New York: S. French, *c.* 1924. (French's standard library edition)

The Red Owl; Tabloid Melodrama in One Act, [by] William Gillette. In: *One-Act Plays for Stage and Study.* London: [S. French], 1924, pp. [46]–80.

The Red Owl; Tabloid Melodrama in One Act, by William Gillette. New York: S. French, *c.* 1924.

Among Thieves. In: *One-Act Plays for Stage and Study.* 2d series. New York: S. French [1925], pp. [245]–67.

Sherlock Holmes; A Play, Wherein is Set Forth the Strange Case of Miss Alice Faulkner, by William Gillette. Based on Sir Arthur Conan Doyle's incomparable stories. With an introduction by Vincent Starrett, preface to this edition by William Gillette, reminiscent notes by Frederic Dorr Steele and line drawings by Frederic Dorr Steele. Garden City, New York: Doubleday, Doran & Company, 1935.

How Well George Does It! A Comedy in One Act. New York: S. French, 1936.
The Painful Predicament of Sherlock Holmes; A Fantasy in One Act. Chicago: B.
    Abramson, 1955.
Sherlock Holmes; A Comedy in Two Acts, by Arthur Conan Doyle and William
    Gillette. Rev. ed. New York: S. French [*c.* 1976].

SELECT BIBLIOGRAPHY

Beerbohm, Max. *Around Theatres*, 2 vols., New York: Alfred A. Knopf, 1930

Blackbeard, Bill. *Sherlock Holmes in America*, New York: Harry N. Abrams, 1981

Brady, Cyrus Townsend. *Secret Service*, Being the happenings of a night in Richmond in the spring of 1865 done into book form from the play by William Gillette. New York: Dodd, Mead and Co., 1912

Burton, Richard. 'William Gillette', *The Drama, a quarterly review of dramatic literature*, no. 12 (November 1913)

Carr, John Dickson. *The Life of Sir Arthur Conan Doyle*, New York: Harper and Brothers, *c.* 1949

Clapp, John Bouvé, and Edgett, Edwin Francis. *Plays of the Present*, New York: The Dunlap Society, 1902

Clark, Barrett H. *The British and American Drama of To-day*, New York: Henry Holt and Co., 1915

Cook, Doris. *Sherlock Holmes and Much More; or Some of the Facts About William Gillette*, [Hartford]: The Connecticut Historical Society, 1970

(preface). *The Curtain is Up on the William Gillette Exhibit. Honoring the Famous Actor—Playwright who was born at Nook Farm Hartford, Connecticut.* Sponsored by the Stowe—Day Foundation at Nook Farm Visitors' Center, Hartford, Connecticut. [Hartford, The Stowe—Day Foundation, 1970]

Dodge, Wendell Phillips. 'William Gillette', *The Strand Magazine*, 42 (October 1911)

Eaton, W. Prichard. 'Sherlock Holmes Returns', *New York Herald Tribune*, 17 November 1929

Frenz, Horst, and Campbell, Louise Wylie. 'William Gillette on the London Stage', *Queen's Quarterly*, LII (November 1943)

Gillette, William. *The Illusion of the First Time in Acting*, with an introduction by George Arliss, New York: Printed for the Dramatic Museum of Columbia University (Papers on Acting, I), 1915

Sherlock Holmes; A Play, Wherein is Set Forth the Strange Case of Miss Alice Faulkner, by William Gillette. Based on Sir Arthur Conan Doyle's Incomparable Stories. With an introduction by Vincent Starrett, preface by William Gillette, reminiscent notes by Frederic Dorr Steele and line drawings by Frederic Dorr Steele. Garden City, New York: Doubleday, Doran and Company, 1935

Sherlock Holmes; A Comedy in Two Acts by Arthur Conan Doyle and William Gillette, New York: Samuel French, *c.* 1976

Hamilton, Clayton. 'The Final Episode of Sherlock Holmes', *Theatre Magazine*, 1 (January 1930)

Hewitt, Barnard. *Theatre U.S.A. 1688 to 1957*, New York: McGraw-Hill, 1959

Keddie, James, Jr. 'About a William Gillette Collection', *The Baker Street Journal*, 12, no. 1 (1962)

Kerr, Walter. *Journey to the Center of the Theater*, New York: Alfred A. Knopf, 1979

Laborde, Charles B., Jr. 'Sherlock Holmes on the Stage after William Gillette', *The Baker Street Journal*, 24, no. 2 (1974)

MacFarlane, Peter Clark. 'The Magic of William Gillette', *Everybody's Magazine*, October 1911

Moses, Montrose J. 'William Gillette Says Farewell', *Theatre Guild Magazine*, no. 7 (January 1930)

Nichols, Harold J. 'William Gillette – Innovator in Melodrama', *Theatre Annual*, 31 (1975)

Quinn, Arthur Hobson. *A History of the American Drama from the Civil War to the Present Day*, New York: F.S. Crofts and Co., 1943

Schuttler, Georg William. 'William Gillette, Actor and Playwright', unpublished Ph.D. dissertation, University of Illinois at Urbana–Champaign, 1975

Shafer, Yvonne. 'A Sherlock Holmes of the Past: William Gillette's Later Years', *Players*, 46 (1971)

Shaw, George Bernard. *Plays and Players*, London: Oxford University Press [1952?]

Shepstone, Harold J. 'Mr William Gillette as Sherlock Holmes', *The Strand Magazine*, 22 (December 1901)

Sherk, H. Dennis. 'William Gillette: His Life and Works', unpublished Ph.D. dissertation, Pennsylvania State University, 1961

Stone, P.M. 'William Gillette as Sherlock Holmes', *The Baker Street Journal*, 10, no. 1 (January 1960)

'William Gillette's Stage Career', *The Baker Street Journal*, 12, no. 1 (1962)

Strang, Lewis. *Players and Plays of the Last Quarter Century. Vol. II. The Theatre of Today*, Boston: L.C. Page and Co., 1903